LIBYA:
A MODERN HISTORY

JOHN WRIGHT

THE JOHNS HOPKINS UNIVERSITY PRESS
BALTIMORE, MARYLAND

Published in the United States of America, 1982,
by The Johns Hopkins University Press,
Baltimore, Maryland 21218

Library of Congress Cataloging in Publication Data

Wright, John L.
    Libya, a modern history.

    Bibliography: p.282.
    Includes index.
    1. Libya—History. 2. Libya—Politics and
government—1969-   I. Title.
DT236.W74   961'.2   81-48183
ISBN 0-8018-2767-1   AACR2

Printed and bound in Great Britain

CONTENTS

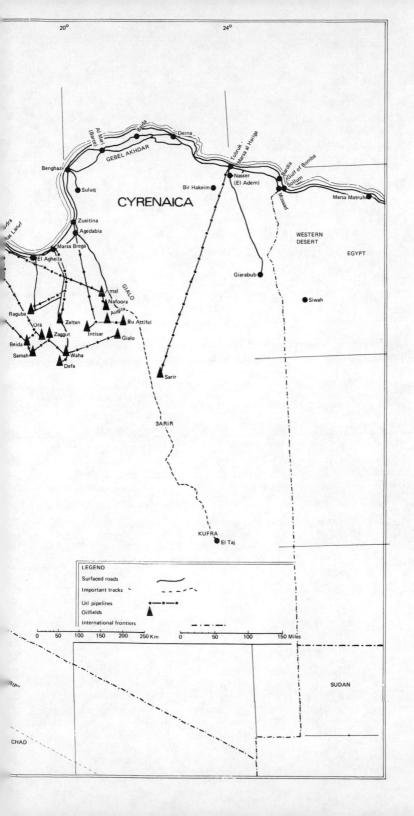

PREFACE

Ending my first book on Libya just before the 1969 revolution, I wrote that the kingdom was ready for more important things than in the days when, like Shakespeare's Bohemia, it was merely 'a desert country near the sea'. The remark seems to have been fully justified by the events of the past twelve years. Moammar Gadafi's Libyan Arab Republic, and latterly the unique political, economic and social experience of the Socialist People's Libyan Arab Jamahiriyah, together with the Libyan-initiated oil price and production revolution of the early 1970s, have made the country better known to a wider audience than any other events in its history, including even its role as the setting for the longest campaign of the Second World War.

In preparing the following chapters I have fairly freely drawn on my own written material on Libya in book, magazine-article and radio-script form, although many of my earlier conclusions have been modified by hindsight and changed circumstances. In my account of Libyan oil affairs I make no apology for having consulted many issues of the monthly *Petroleum Press Service*, or *Petroleum Economist* as it was renamed in 1974. For, having been a staff writer on the journal under both titles, I know that it has kept a uniquely succinct record of all important developments in the Libyan oil industry over the past 25 years.

JW
Richmond

1   A BUFFER STATE OF SAND

Libya has been under at least nominal foreign rule for most of its known history.[1] Time and again, the area of modern Libya has formed provinces of empires ruled from Asia, Europe or other parts of Africa. But such rule was usually limited to the coastlands of Tripolitania and Cyrenaica; in the interior, the long-established Berber tribes remained largely independent, recognising only the authority of their own leaders. Remarkably few effects of foreign rule have endured: this is a country rich in the ruins of alien and discarded cultures, whether Greek, Roman or Byzantine, Ottoman Turkish or Fascist Italian. 'In Libya you are made aware the whole time of the abandonment of things, the material leftovers of receding cultures.'[2]

The exception to this tradition of resistance to foreign domination and influence has been the slow but profound absorption of Muslim Arab invaders, as well as the Islamic religion and Arabic language they brought with them from Arabia in the seventh century AD, and again with greater effect in the eleventh. As a result of this assimilation, Libya is now wholly Islamised. Cyrenaica is probably the most thoroughly Arabised country outside the Arabian peninsula, while the Arabisation of the rest has been extensive, if not yet absolute.

In the eighteenth and early nineteenth centuries the partly native Karamanli dynasty ruled Tripoli, and nominally Libya as a whole, in practical independence of the nominal overlords, the Turkish Sultans at Constantinople.[3] But when in 1835 the Turks deposed the last of the Karamanli rulers and re-established the Sultan's direct rule, they broke the traditions of foreign domination by trying to assert their authority over the hitherto largely independent peoples of the interior. In doing so, they undertook the first of three foreign campaigns of conquest — two of them lasting over 20 years each — that Libya was to endure in the course of the following 100 years.

The Turks, already alarmed by Egypt's achievement of near-independence under Mohammad Ali, occupied Tripoli in 1835 largely to forestall further French expansion in North Africa after the seizure of nominally Turkish Algiers in 1830. Like the French in Algeria, the Turks in Tripoli chose a dynamic and interventionist policy, rather than a passive and defensive one. By the time the Turks had occupied

11

Misurata in 1836, their attempts to tax the peoples of the interior were already meeting unexpected resistance. The great Awlad Slaiman tribe, under its remarkable leader Abd-al-Jalil Saif-al-Nassir, had occupied Fezzan in the closing years of the Karamanli regime, and had then united lesser tribes of the Sirtica and south-east Tripolitania in opposition to Turkish penetration. At the same time, other tribesmen led by Shaikh Jumah bin Khalifa were preparing to defend the formidable northern escarpment of the Gebel Nefusah against Turkish assault.

The conquest of western Libya, more or less contemporary with the French conquest of northern Algeria, lasted 24 years. Both the Turks and the French soon realised the difficulties of subduing mountain and desert peoples who had probably known no government but their own since Roman times. In 1842 the Turks defeated and dispersed the Awlad Slaiman; Fezzan was occupied and Shaikh Abd-al-Jalil was killed; in the Gebel, meanwhile, Shaikh Jumah was captured and imprisoned; and in 1843 the important trading oasis of Ghadames was occupied. Turkish military successes in the 1840s owed much to the leadership of General Ahmad Pasha; like his Italian successor Rodolfo Graziani who 'pacified' the country 80 years later, he earned himself the nickname 'butcher' during his time in Libya.

The effects of the defeat of the Awlad Slaiman are felt to this day. After the death of Shaikh Abd-al-Jalil (whose exploits are still recalled in tribal poetry and song), the tribesmen moved southwards under the leadership of Abd-al-Jalil's son Mohammad to find new homes and livelihood beyond the control of the Turks. In 1854 the German explorer Heinrich Barth found members of the tribe in southern Fezzan and Kanem, north of Lake Chad.[4] They still live there, maintaining links with their kinsmen in Libya.

While the Turks were conquering Tripolitania and Fezzan, Cyrenaica was becoming the centre of a religious revivalist movement that was to be the making of modern, independent Libya, and was to establish Libyan influence in much of Saharan and Sahelian Africa. Its founder, Sayyid Mohammad bin Ali al-Sanussi, was born in Mostaghanem in Algeria in the late 1780s. After long religious study at Fez in Morocco he drew his first disciples round him and travelled through North Africa and as far as the Holy Cities of Mecca and Medina, preaching a return to pristine Islam and greater Islamic unity. In the Hijaz he became established as the Head of the new Order of the Sanussi, an orthodox organisation of Sufis, or mystics;

it was an ascetic fraternity, originally with a strong missionary purpose. At Mecca, Sidi Mohammad — or the Grand Sanussi as he was known to his followers — met his most powerful supporter, Amir Mohammad Sharif, who, as future Sultan of Wadai, was to be responsible for the spread of Sanussism into large parts of Black Africa.

About 1840, unable to return to Algeria because of the French conquest, the Grand Sanussi settled in Cyrenaica. About 1843 he established what was to become the Mother Lodge of the Sanussi Order, the *Zawia al-Baida*, the White Monastery, in the Gebel Akhdar. Cyrenaica at that time was a remote, forgotten country, almost without towns, thinly populated by a complex of semi-nomadic tribes of Arab bedouin. Although nominally Muslim, the people knew little of their religion, for when the Grand Sanussi arrived in Cyrenaica he is said to have found them fallen into heresies and to be in danger of rapid religious and moral degeneration.[5] He accordingly took upon himself the mission, as he expressed it, of 'reminding the negligent, teaching the ignorant, and guiding him who has gone astray'.[6]

The instruments of this policy were the brothers of the Order, the *Ikhwan*, whose missionary teaching carried the message of Sanussism across Saharan and Sahelian Africa, and the *zawius*, which were built at tribal centres, or at watering places on trade and pilgrim routes, and which served as monasteries, schools, hostels, sources of relief, advice and mediation and, in due course, as seats of administration. The Sanussi call for a return to pristine Islam was as acceptable to the bedouin of nineteenth-century Cyrenaica as the original message of Islam had been to those of seventh-century Arabia, and the initial proselytising role of Sanussism was inevitably political as well as religious. The Turks, who had neither the resources nor the will to govern the interior of the country adequately, interfered little in its affairs. They left the collection of taxes, the maintenance of law and order, the promotion of trade and the provision of rudimentary social services to the Sanussi, who thus became *de facto* rulers of the country under nominal Turkish sovereignty.

Sanussism had variable influence elsewhere. It became well established in Fezzan, but it never had the widespread following in Tripolitania that it had in Cyrenaica; in Wadai and other regions of what is now the Republic of Chad, as in the Western Desert of Egypt and other parts of Muslim Africa, it helped to foster a spirit of trust and respect that encouraged the development of trade and stability. But growing Sanussi influence inevitably aroused the suspicion of outside powers, and particularly of the French, who were slowly pushing into territories where the Order was active. The French blamed many of their set-backs in northern Africa on Sanussi hostility, and the Turks were glad to collaborate with an organisation which they saw as a useful agent against European expansion. Although Sanussism undoubtedly stiffened its followers' resistance to European domination in many parts of northern Africa, it was in Cyrenaica that the Order fostered in the many rival tribes a political coherence — almost, it might be said, a national consciousness — when they faced the supreme challenge of invasion by Italy at the beginning of the twentieth century.

From its original headquarters in the Gebel Akhbar, the Order moved in 1856 to the uninhabited oasis of Giarabub, nearly 300 kilometres south of Tobruk. Although Giarabub had few resources, it stood on important trade and pilgrim routes and was at the centre of the growing Sanussi sphere of influence in and beyond the Sahara; it was also politically neutral, being at the time well beyond the reach of the Turks or other foreign powers.[7] The Grand Sanussi was buried at Giarabub on his death in 1859. He was succeeded by his son, Mohammad al-Mahdi, under whose guidance the Order came to wield its widest influence.

In 1895 Al-Mahdi moved the seat of the Order to the Kufra group of oases which, despite their extreme remoteness, had well-established links with many parts of Saharan and sub-Saharan Africa. This shift of the central power southwards reflected the growing importance of Sanussism in the lands on the southern fringes of the desert. Yet even as Sanussism was reaching its greatest power, its very existence was being challenged by the French penetration of the African continent.

For centuries Europeans had been confined to small trading enclaves on the coasts of West Africa by tropical diseases, hostile natives and poor communications with the interior. It was not until the second half of the nineteenth century, following the development of the prophylactic use of quinine, breach-loading rifles and steam boats for the swift domination of the navigable reaches of the rivers flowing into the Atlantic, that European penetration, division and conquest of the continent got well underway. Earlier in the century the British had been the first to try opening up the African interior by the trans-Saharan route from Tripoli, the Mediterranean port nearest to the Great Desert. But British attention had later turned to the easier route to richer markets offered by the Nigerian river system, and the northern desert approach had been abandoned to the French or any other power that cared to make use of it. The French encroachment on lands under Sanussi influence built up over several decades from three directions: from the long-established French colony of Senegal, from southern Algeria, and up the Congo–Ubangui river system leading into the heart of the continent.

Throughout recorded history, North Africans had been pre-occupied with Black Africa and its trade. The exchange of goods between Negroland and the Maghrib enriched the sedentary and nomad Saharan peoples and North Africa's Mediterranean ports. According to the nineteenth-century French explorer Henri Duveyrier, the people of North Africa held that to become rich it was enough to travel to Sudan[8] to trade the manufactured goods of North Africa, West Asia and Europe for the raw produce of Black Africa — ivory, feathers, gold and, above all, slaves — all commodities which could withstand the high costs of trans-Saharan travel.

The first effects of the European penetration of Africa on the Sahara and Sudan were commercial, as the traditional trade between North Africa and the countries beyond the desert was diverted westwards and southwards along the new, secure railways and river steamer routes to the ports on the Atlantic coast. The result was the rapid decline of the traditional Saharan trade routes, some of them in use since pre-Roman times, as the commerce of the continent was drawn away from the interior lines of communication towards the ocean — a disruption that still defies attempts by the independent states of Africa to re-establish their traditional trade links.

Trans-Saharan commerce was further undermined by European prohibition and gradual abolition of one of its most profitable activities, the slave trade. But the Sanussi gained some temporary advantage by fostering trade on a previously little-used trans-Saharan route from Benghazi, which was opened up in the early nineteenth century to provide the expanding Sultanate of Wadai with a better road to the north. It passed through some of the worst stretches of the Sahara, controlled by notoriously predatory tribes. But under the Sanussi the route was made safe, wells were dug and its importance and prosperity increased, partially because of the security it offered in contrast to the chaotic conditions further east when

Egyptian Sudan was overrun by the followers of Mohammad Ahmad al-Mahdi in the 1880s and 1890s. The journey through Jalo, Kufra and Ennedi to the capital of Wadai at Abéché took some 70 days.[9] Textiles were the most important trade goods carried southwards by Tripoli and Benghazi merchants. Northwards came ostrich feathers, ivory and negro slaves. In the mid-nineteenth century slaves made up about half the value of all northbound trade across the Sahara, and it is estimated that of the 10,000 who survived the horrors of the desert crossing every year up to about 1860, half came through Turkish Libya.[10]

As a result of diplomatic pressure brought by Britain and other European powers from about 1840 onwards, the trans-Saharan slave trade was gradually suppressed. But the Wadai road, far beyond the reach of diplomatic and moral pressure by European powers penetrating West, East and Central Africa, remained well into the twentieth century a route for the supply of slaves to Benghazi for onward shipment to other provinces of the Ottoman Empire.[11]

For much of the nineteenth century Tripoli was one of the leading merchant towns of Africa; it was the Mediterranean port closest to the desert, and therefore to the large markets of Black Africa. Unlike Algiers and later Tunis, its traditional trade routes were not blighted by European invasion and conquest, although Turkish pacification did disrupt trade in the 1830s and 1840s. Three great and ancient trade routes led from Tripoli to Central Africa. The most direct went from Murzuk in Fezzan to Bornu, west of Lake Chad, in what is now northern Nigeria. The journey from Tripoli to the frontier of Bornu took 90 days.[12] Besides being fast, the route was also relatively safe up to about 1830, and it was the main desert crossing for slaves destined for sale in Fezzan and further north. But, unlike the Karamanlis before them, the Turks were unable to police this road effectively. The displaced Awlad Slaiman started attacking caravans; and trade was further disrupted by wars between Bornu and Wadai and by the plundering raids of the Tebu of the Tibesti Mountains and the Kel Owi Tuareg confederation of the Air massif.

As a result, traffic was by the mid-nineteenth century moving to the second route, more arduous but relatively safer, leading from Tripoli through Ghadames or Murzuk to Ghat, and thence to Air and Kano, the trading and textile capital of Hausaland. This was the richest trans-Saharan route for most of the nineteenth century, and its security was maintained by two great confederations of Tuareg tribes that were closely concerned with its prosperity — the Ajjer in the Ghadames–Ghat sector and the Kel Owi in the Air region.

A third important road led from Tripoli to the Niger Bend and to the once great trading city of Timbuctu, which still aroused in the romantic imagination of nineteenth-century Europe visions of material and intellectual splendours that had had little foundation in reality since the Middle Ages. As the French military and bureaucratic conquest of Algeria and the Algerian Sahara progressed, traders using this route tended to avoid the long-established outlets of Algeria and Tunis, preferring to use Ghadames and Tripoli instead.

It is not easy to assess the value of this largely unrecorded Saharan trade of the nineteenth century. The African Association in 1793 calculated the total value of trans-Saharan trade at £1 million annually, but Boahen estimates[13] the value of the two-way traffic in the nineteenth century at a yearly maximum of £125,000, particularly because the trade in gold was by then 'almost negligible'. He says: 'At the beginning of the nineteenth century, the mainstays of the Sudan export trade were Kano cloth, kola nuts and slaves.'[14] But Rossi says that in 1830 some 1,500 ounces of gold dust a year were still reaching Tripoli from across the Sahara, excluding tribute from Ghadames and Fezzan.[15] Schirmer estimated[16] at the end of the nineteenth century that at the absolute maximum the total two-way trade across the Sahara amounted to nine million French francs a year, the equivalent of the traffic of a port of the twentieth order.

Ironically, European interest in the supposed prosperity of the trans-Saharan trade was one factor in the European political intervention that eventually ruined the entire delicately balanced operation. The French in Algeria, and later the Italians in Libya, believed they could revive trans-Saharan trade once they had conquered and 'pacified' the desert; in fact, none of the foreign powers involved in the Sahara, not even the Turks, could sustain the political and economic conditions for prosperous trading.

Although the Turks had originally reoccupied Tripoli largely to forestall French expansion in North Africa, they reacted to, rather than anticipated, French penetration of the Sahara, first from Algeria and later from Senegal and the Congo basin. In 1850 the Sahara was still open to any outside power that cared to play for political or commercial influence there. The French presence was still barely felt beyond the fringes of the Algerian Sahara. Turkey laid vague claims to much territory in the hinterland of Tripoli, as did Morocco in the deserts beyond the Atlas Mountains. But if the tribes of the western Sahara offered Friday prayers for the well-being of the Sultan-Caliph of Morocco, as those of the central and eastern Sahara prayed for the Sultan-Caliph at Constantinople, this spiritual supremacy was about all the allegiance these two Commanders of the Faithful could exact from the Muslim tribesmen of the Great Desert.

When he came to power in 1848, Napoleon III initiated a policy of militant expansion in Africa with the aim of uniting Algeria with Senegal. In the 1850s a string of oases in southern Algeria accordingly became French outposts, and attempts were made to direct some of the desert's trade back to Algiers. But despite these clear signs of French expansion, the only representative the Turkish government kept in the leading trading oasis of Ghadames up to 1862 was a *mudir*, and it was only after the French had signed a commercial agreement with some minor local leaders of the Ajjer Tuareg confederation in November that year that the Turks took the trouble to build a fort at Ghadames and install a garrison of regular troops to protect the Sultan's political and commercial interests.[17]

A Turkish garrison was established at Ghat in 1875, and the practice of planting small garrisons at distant oases was to continue rather casually for the next 35 years in an effort to define the limits of Turkish sovereignty in North Africa. But since uninhabited desert offers few natural frontiers, and the extent of Turkish claims had never been properly settled, the Turks in Tripoli were clearly at a disadvantage when North Africa began to be taken over by European powers which insisted on drawing and maintaining rigid boundaries across territories which had never before known them. Because of their casual attitude to the whole question of frontiers and sovereignty, by the increasingly rigid standards of the nineteenth century, the Turks lost to neighbouring and more aggressive powers much of the territory that might have been considered to have belonged to the Sultan.

When the Egyptians under their autonomous ruler Mohammad Ali occupied Mersa Matruh and other settlements in the Western Desert as far west as the Gulf of Bomba, Constantinople felt no need to protest, since Mohammad Ali and his successors were indulgently considered to be Turkish subjects.[18] Similarly, the Turks felt no need to establish an exact frontier between Tripoli and Tunis so long as the *Beys* of Tunis ruled in nominal allegiance to the Sultan. But even after the French protectorate was established in 1881, the Turks did nothing to clarify the frontier between Tunis and Tripoli. As a result, the boundary which in the early nineteenth century had been shown running just to the east of Gabes, thus including the island of Gerba with Tripoli,[19] had by the 1880s moved east of Zarzis, and eventually reached Ras Agadir. By 1890, according to an Italian study, the French had incorporated 5,000 square kilometres of Tripolitania into Tunisia. When the frontier was finally agreed in 1910, Tunisia acquired further territory that might have been assumed to belong to Tripoli, while Ghadames was left just within Turkish territory, but so close to the new border that its value as a commercial centre was considered, by the Italians at least, to have been greatly reduced.

In the south, the extent of Turkish possessions was quite unknown. According to the explorer Gustav Nachtigal, Gatrun in southern Fezzan in the 1860s marked the limit of Turkish sovereignty. But an assertive foreign policy, backed by military demonstrations on the ground and by the pan-Islamic policy of the Sultan Abd-al-Hamid II, might have gained Turkey recognition of sovereignty as far west as Tuat (now in southern Algeria) and as far south as Borku (now in northern Chad). But Constantinople did nothing to press these claims, and it was too late to do anything by the time the Anglo-French convention of 1890 had defined British and Turkish spheres of influence in northern Africa.

By 1900 the Turks were sufficiently alarmed by the French advance on Borku from the south and west to consider the precautionary occupation of the Tibesti Mountains, inhabited by the ancient Saharan race, the Tebu. They were also considering the occupation of the important caravan oasis of Bilma to the south-west, but the French forestalled them by planting a garrison of Senegalese *tirailleurs* in the oasis in 1906. According to the traveller Hanns Vischer, who was there that year, the news of the occupation 'caused a general stir . . . for Bilma nominally belonged to Fezzan and to Turkey'.[20] But in 1906 the Turks did move into Tibesti, establishing their rule over the Rashadah Tebu from an administrative centre at Bardai. In the same year the oasis of Djanet, to the south-west of Ghat, was provisionally occupied, but two years later the French took it over. In 1909 the Turks extended their military occupation of Tibesti by installing garrisons of 35 men each at Bardai and Zouar. By August 1911 the Turkish flag was flying over the 'capital' of Borku, Ain Galakka (west of the modern Faya-Largeau), and there was a military detachment at nearby Yen.[21]

The French authorities in Chad, according to Rossi, recognised

Turkish sovereignty in Borku, while the Sanussi were hoping to enlist Turkish support against the French drive into Borku, Ennedi and Tibesti in 1910–11. Yet all these rather belated assertions of Turkish sovereignty came to nothing. In the autumn of 1911 there was to have been a conference in Tripoli to determine the southern frontiers of Turkish Africa. But it never took place because in the meantime the Italians had invaded Libya, and in 1912 Turkish garrisons were withdrawn from Borku and Tibesti, as from the rest of Libya, under the terms of the peace treaty with Italy. But the Italians, in an attempt to forestall the French advance, occupied Fezzan briefly in 1914, by which time both Borku and Tibesti had been taken by French troops, who moved in soon after the Turks withdrew.

During their last 30 years in Libya, the Turks had been hard pressed to protect the province from neighbouring expansionist powers — the Anglo-Egyptians to the east, the French to the west and south, and the 'pacific penetration' of the Italians to the north. Although the Turks, with the aid of the Sanussi in Cyrenaica, succeeded in keeping the central core of Libya intact, much marginal territory was lost. Despite some agreements on Libyan frontiers between the interested foreign powers in the early part of the twentieth century, there remained a legacy of disputed territorial claims.

By the critical European standards of the times, the Turkish administration in Libya in the nineteenth and early twentieth centuries may have been negligent and incompetent, but it was not needlessly harsh or overbearing; if it gave little to the country, it demanded little in return. Libya was certainly no worse governed than many other such places, and if the Libyans had no love for the Turks as rulers, the ties of religion were strong. This was a factor that was usually overlooked by nineteenth-century European visitors, who were inevitably critical of the signs of maladministration, economic decline and lack of social services they found in Turkish North Africa, but which did not necessarily upset the Libyans. The British traveller James Hamilton, writing of Cyrenaica in 1852, said: 'From what I have seen of the country, a spirit of discontent is universal — the Arabs regret their old independent pasha.'[22] Writing at the very end of Libya's Turkish period, the Italian Domenico Tumiati found that 'a real abyss separates the dominant from the subject race; the Turks are now as much foreigners to the Arabs as they were in the first years of their occupation. Few speak Turkish

. . . the Turkish troops live apart from the civil population.'[23]

Visitors were particularly critical of the primitive tax-farming and collecting methods. Edward Rae, reporting on Tripolitania in the 1870s, wrote: 'The government officials squeeze the poor Arabs cruelly. I have been told that the assessors will rate an Arab's crops at four times their value, and make him pay on that. Indeed, the Arab has sometimes to pay beyond the whole revenue of his crop.'[24] And Rossi, after noting some of the public works ordered by a few of the more enlightened of the country's nineteenth-century Turkish governors, says: 'This activity must not disguise the fact that practice compared badly with the good intentions; the country was basically badly governed and worse administered; its economic resources were exhausted by the rapacity of the officials; and there still operated a system of contracting out the collection of tribute to a few chiefs who exploited the population without mercy.'[25] But Turkish rule cannot have been all that burdensome, for in 1881 they were holding Cyrenaica with only 1,000 men, including 100 cavalry stationed at Barce (Marj) and a garrison of 300 at Benghazi; and at times during the late nineteenth century there were no more than 300 Turkish soldiers in all Cyrenaica.[26] Fifty years later the Italians, despite their modern arms and swift communications, could barely hold Cyrenaica with 20,000 men.

Nevertheless, the fact remains that the country became poorer in the later nineteenth century. The diversion of Saharan trade had created a temporary new prosperity in the middle of the century. But as more of Africa came under European rule, the difficult, dangerous, slow and therefore expensive Saharan trade routes were gradually abandoned for easier, safer, faster and therefore cheaper ones under European protection.[27] The abolition of the slave trade, although slow to take effect in the Sahara, eventually ruined the most lucrative of all the desert's commercial enterprises. At the same time, trade was harmed by political upheavals in the trading centres of Sudan on the other side of the desert, while many traditional Sudanese exports, notably gold and ivory, had not only become more scarce, but were facing competition from new and better sources: the development of South African ostrich farms to meet the apparently insatiable demands of European fashion practically ruined the Sudanese trade in ostrich feathers. The Jewish visitor Nahum Slouschz reported that in Tripoli at the beginning of this century, 'about one hundred families made a living by cleaning and dyeing ostrich feathers, but in 1907 I found nearly four hundred girls, who were in this trade, out of work'.[28] Slouschz also recorded that in 1906 there were only eight houses in Tripoli still trading with Sudan, and in 1909 there were even fewer. Hanns Vischer, writing in 1906 of his visit to the once great trading oasis of Murzuk in Fezzan, said: 'Murzuk has now lost its last source of income, and the Turkish administration of today is faced with the difficult problem of the confidence of the people in the value of their own country indepen-dent of the Arab trans-Saharan trade.'[29]

So the country fell back on its only other resources of agriculture and stockraising, both of them hostage to the notoriously fickle climate. In good years — about four seasons out of every ten — food surpluses were exported; in bad years — one or two each decade — only imports prevented mass starvation. In a good year such as 1850, according to the statistics of the French Consul,[30] Libya exported 212,700 hectolitres of cereals, 1,375 tons of olive oil, 11,787 head of cattle and over 400,000 kilos of Cyrenaican butter. Cattle — sometimes up to 40,000 a year — were exported on the hoof to Egypt, and to Malta for the victualling of the Royal Navy, while Cyrenaican wool was sold to Italy. But European visitors habitually criticised the low standards of farming and stockraising and the general neglect of the countryside. Most of them saw great potential for improvement, especially under European manage-ment.

In the 75 years of Turkish rule Tripoli declined from an indepen-dent, if bankrupt, state recognised by the leading powers of Europe, as well as the United States, to the underprivileged province of a disintegrating empire. Turkey's prime purpose in returning to the deserts between Egypt and Tunisia, and continuing to hold them until the eve of the First World War, was to deny any other power possession of this 'buffer state of sand', as the British traveller H.S. Cowper termed it in 1897. For most of the nineteenth century Turkish North Africa was hardly considered a prize worth taking by powers expanding into more rewarding parts of Africa and Asia. Yet when the European 'scramble' for African possessions began in the 1880s with the French seizure of Tunisia, Turkish fears for the vulnerability of Tripoli were renewed, and for the last 25 years of Turkish rule travel by Europeans in Libya was severely restricted.

Throughout the Turkish period Libya remained poor, neglected and sparsely populated. The country itself yielded insufficient revenues to finance its own development — not that the local admin-istration or the people would have necessarily favoured economic and social 'progress' on the European model. In the later nineteenth century European critics of Turkish rule expressed the view that the administration deliberately neglected development in order to make the country appear less attractive to foreign powers. Certainly the Turkish administration was unable, or unwilling, to provide economic alternatives when trans-Saharan trade began to decline.

The Turks, moreover, were not even successful in their self-appointed duty of preserving the integrity of their last African possession, as one of the 'Lands of Islam', from European Christian expansion. Although the extent of Turkish sovereignty had never been clearly defined, there is little doubt that through an aggressive, outward-going policy in accordance with the pan-Islamic ideals of the Sultan Abd-al-Hamid II, and allied with the Sanussi, Turkey in the 1870s and 1880s might have asserted her position in much of the country between Fezzan and Lake Chad. The large, if shadowy, hinterland of Tripoli, largely Islamised and extending far into Africa, might well have accepted the Sultan's rule. As it was, Turkey relinquished claims to these lands with remarkable lightness in the face of French expansion.

Turkey's legacy to Libya was largely negative. But Turkish rule did at least keep Tripolitania, Cyrenaica and Fezzan as a political group, and it maintained their unspoiled Islamic character well into the twentieth century. Because Turkish rule was incompetent — one critic described it as the negation of civil government — it enabled the Libyans to foster a practical self-reliance with which they were to meet the challenges of the twentieth century. And in recognising the quasi-independence of the Sanussi in Cyrenaica, the Turks left in Libya a unique source of regional and eventually national leadership.

Notes

1. For detailed accounts of Libyan history up to this century, see J. Wright, *Libya* (London and New York, 1969), and E. Rossi, *Storia di Tripoli e della Tripolitania dalla Conquista Araba al 1911* (Rome, 1968).

2. A. Thwaite, *The Deserts of Hesperides* (London, 1969), p. 162.

3. 'The present government of Tripoli is very mild; and even an aggrieved Jew has chance of obtaining justice, the offices of the state being often placed in the hands of the natives'. *The History of Africa* (London, 1830), p. 155.

4. H. Barth, *Travels and Discoveries in North and Central Africa* (London, 1857–8), vol. II, pp. 271–2. The Awlad Slaiman still live in Kanem, speaking Libyan Arabic; other fractions of the tribe fled into Chad under similar circumstances at the end of the Italian conquest of Libya in 1928–31. See A. Le Rouvreur, *Sahéliens et Sahariens du Tchad* (Paris, 1962), p. 297.

5. A.M. Hassanein Bey, *The Lost Oases* (London, 1925), p. 58.

6. Ibid., p. 60.

7. 'We marvelled at the Founder's choice of Jaghbub as an impregnable fortress surrounded entirely by deserts known in detail to members of the Sanussi and completely alien to their enemies.' P. Ward, *Touring Libya: The Eastern Provinces* (London, 1969), p. 71.

8. From the Arabic *Bilad al-Sudan*, 'Land of the Blacks'. In this context and elsewhere, unless more specifically defined, 'Sudan' refers to the broad belt of savannah country extending from the Senegal to the Nile, south of the Sahara and north of the tropical forests of West and Central Africa.

9. Actual days of travelling, not counting halts. For details of the route and length of stages in days, see F. Minutilli, *La Tripolitania* (Turin, 1912), p. 137.

10. A.A. Boahen, *Britain, the Sahara and the Western Sudan, 1788–1861* (London, 1964), p. 128.

11. At least until the First World War there was a steady traffic in slaves on the Wadai–Cyrenaica route and even in 1920–1, while on her extraordinary journey to Kufra, Rosita Forbes learned that caravans were carrying to Gialo oasis 'smuggled slave boys and girls of eight to ten years . . . solemn little beings, with chubby black faces peering out of the pointed hoods of minute camels'-hair burnuses'. R. Forbes, *The Secret of the Sahara: Kufara* (London, 1921), p. 109. The last slave caravan is said to have reached Fezzan in 1929.

12. Minutilli, *La Tripolitania*, pp. 138–9.

13. Boahen, *Britain, the Sahara*, p. 131.

14. Ibid., p. 126.

15. Rossi, *Storia di Tripoli*, p. 292.

16. H. Schirmer, *Le Sahara* (Paris, 1893), p. 366.

17. For further discussion of Turkish expansion in the Sahara in the nineteenth century, see Rossi, *Storia di Tripoli*, pp. 333–48: 'La penetrazione turca nell'interno della Libia e la questione dei suoi confini.'

18. Siwah is now well to the Egyptian side of the frontier, but 'the oasis of Auglia, as well perhaps as that of Siwah, likewise belongs to Turkish sovereignty'. M. Russell, *History and Present Condition of the Barbary States* (Edinburgh, 1835), p. 257.

19. Ibid., map.

20. H. Vischer, *Across the Sahara from Tripoli to Bornu* (London, 1910), pp. 168–9.

21. Rossi, *Storia di Tripoli*, pp. 346–7.

22. J. Hamilton, *Wanderings in North Africa* (London, 1856), p. 141.

23. D. Tumiati, *Nell'Africa Romana: Tripolitania* (Milan, 1911), p. 42.

24. E. Rae, *The Country of the Moors. A Journey from Tripoli in Barbary to the City of Kairwan* (London, 1877), pp. 95–6.

25. Rossi, *Storia di Tripoli*, p. 321.

26. G. Haimann, *Cirenaica (Tripolitania)* (Milan, 1886), p.190.

27. When the railway from Lagos reached Kano in northern Nigeria in 1905, one ton of goods could be sent by rail and sea Kano–Liverpool for half the cost of overland transport Kano–Tripoli.

28. N. Slouschz, *Travels in North Africa* (Philadelphia, 1927), p. 7.

29. Vischer, *Across the Sahara*, pp. 132–3.

30. Quoted by Rossi, *Storia di Tripoli*, pp. 314–15.

2 FOURTH SHORE[1]

By 1900 it seemed probable that Turkish Tripoli would be absorbed by the nearest European expansionist power, the kingdom of Italy. Tripoli was by then one of the few African territories not under European claim, mainly because it had only limited strategic importance, slight economic value, and because it was still part of a Turkish empire whose further dismantling threatened unpredictable international repercussions.

Italy was slowly forced into seizing Libya through the events of some 30 years. Tunisia is actually the point of North Africa nearest to Sicily, in more than purely geographical terms, but hopes of creating an Italian North African empire there were dashed by the recognition of the French protectorate in 1881. Although Italy was a newly united, newly independent nation, politically and economically undeveloped, she had aspirations to Great Power status, and in the late-nineteenth-century 'scramble' by European powers for African possessions she gained the rather unrewarding territories of Somalia and Eritrea; in 1896 she failed disastrously to annex Ethiopia, and so finally turned to as yet unclaimed Libya for strategic security in the Mediterranean and compensation for imperialist designs frustrated elsewhere.

The Mediterranean policy of successive Italian governments, particularly after the French occupation of Tunisia and the British occupation of Cyprus and Egypt, was conditioned by the possibility of a potentially hostile power seizing the ports of Turkish North Africa, from Tripoli to Tobruk, and using them as a base from which to threaten Italy itself and her increasingly important sea-borne trade. The possession of Tripoli, it was argued, would enable Italy to exclude other powers and to dominate both shores of the central Mediterranean, which had become a waterway of the first importance since the opening of the Suez Canal in 1869. Italian statesmen were particularly concerned about the expansion and future intentions in Africa of the French republic which, from the 1870s to the First World War, claimed, conquered and occupied a vast empire in North, West and Central Africa (arguably more impressive on the map than in reality) and which steadily absorbed

25

the hinterland of Turkish Tripoli, threatening ultimately to absorb Tripoli itself. But if France could seek compensations in Africa for the disasters of the Franco-Prussian war of 1870, so could newly united Italy assert her Great Power pretensions there. African colonies were, moreover, to provide outlets for Italian industrial goods, while supplying the mother country with valuable tropical produce. Such, at least, were some of the prospects opened before the public by an often persuasive imperialist lobby. But of all the claims made on behalf of African colonies, perhaps the most enticing, yet least realistic, was that they would provide an outlet for the nation's surplus population which, in the 20 years 1896–1915, emigrated at an average rate of half a million people a year[2] — a tragic outpouring of humanity whose labour and skills were almost totally lost to the mother country.

In reality, Italy's colonial ventures were to earn her more international opprobrium than prestige. Her poor and thinly populated African possessions were never an important outlet for Italian industrial goods, while their contribution to the national economy was always small.[3] Although just over 300,000 Italians were living in the empire[4] by 1939, they numbered less than the average annual increase in the population of metropolitan Italy in the years 1935–40.[5]

Italian diplomacy spent 30 years, on and off, preparing international opinion for the eventual occupation of Turkey's remaining North African possessions. The purpose was to ensure that once Italy moved there would be no unforeseen international repercussions, either in North Africa itself or elsewhere. It was an objective that became increasingly difficult to attain in the early-twentieth-century atmosphere of rising international tensions. The Italians were, as ever, concerned about French designs on Tripoli. Paris, in fact, seems to have had no desire to take Tripoli itself, but used the possibility of doing so as a bargaining point in relations with Italy. Germany and the United States were among other powers also 'interested' in Turkish North Africa, while in 1908 the Jewish Territorial Organisation seriously considered a plan for Jewish settlements in Cyrenaica.

Italy's method of building up her interests and influence in Turkish North Africa without provoking military complications was through a process of so-called 'peaceful penetration' of the economic and social life of the territory. From 1907 onwards 'peaceful penetration' was largely the work of the Banco di Roma which invested in local agriculture, light industry, mineral prospecting and shipping. Trade and communications with Italy expanded quickly, but were hampered by growing local hostility to all Italian activity.

Rome eventually used this hostility as a *casus belli*. In the summer of 1911 the Moroccan crisis, preparing the way for further French expansion in North Africa, compelled Italy to act to restore the balance of power in the Mediterranean. At the end of September an ultimatum was delivered to Constantinople, announcing Italy's intention of occupying Tripolitania and Cyrenaica. A massive sea-borne invasion was duly mounted in October and Tripoli, Benghazi, Derna, Tobruk and Homs were occupied. But hopes that Turkish North Africa would become Italian simply through diplomacy and a display of force proved illusory. There was no capitulation and the Libyans, far from hailing the invaders as liberators from Turkish oppression, did precisely the opposite by reinforcing the small Turkish garrison with thousands of their own volunteer warriors. Libyans fought alongside Turks as Muslim subjects of the Sultan, who had by then been rather belatedly recognised as Muslim North Africa's best defence against European Christian encroachment of a country which, in the words of a British Red Cross doctor who served on the Turkish side, 'does not give the impression that it is worth fighting for'.[6]

Although the Italians were using the newest weapons (aeroplanes and airships made their first battle trials in Libya in 1911–12),[7] there is evidence that the campaign was ill prepared and the troops poorly trained and unstable. As the great guns of their warships commanded the coastal strip, the invaders could not be driven from their heavily fortified coastal enclaves; but they took little offensive action, and by early 1912 the campaign had clearly reached stale-mate.

Falling on the fiftieth anniversary of Italian unity, the war was at first broadly popular in Italy, where it was seen as an assertion of national will after the defeats and humiliations of the past — it was 'the first truly autonomous act of Italian foreign policy'. The press grossly exaggerated the resources and agricultural potential of Libya, presenting it was a veritable *paese di bengodi* — a Land of Cockaigne — for future Italian migrants and settlers. The popular songwriters (*Tripoli, Bel Suol d'Amore*, etc.) and even the poets joined in the popular enthusiasm, Giovanni Pascoli with a vision of the great Italian proletariat bestirring itself for the Libyan adventure, and Gabriele d'Annunzio trumpeting the truly remarkable pioneering exploits of Italy's aviators over the African battle-fields. But the socialists and their allies were strongly opposed to the war, and they organised widespread strikes and other forms of protest.

> The socialist opposition at the beginning of the African war was derived from the fact that [the war] involved a break with the tradition of the *Risorgimento*; it seemed unrelated to the real problems of the country, and only an opportunity for the waste of useful capital instead of the promotion of 'internal colonialism'.[8]

On 5 November 1911 a Royal Decree had placed Tripolitania and Cyrenaica under the Italian Crown, although international law recognised no sovereignty over unconquered territory. But what had been decreed remained still largely undone a year later when secret negotiations between Turkey and Italy became suddenly public with the announcement that a peace treaty had been signed at Ouchy, near Lausanne, on 18 October. The ambiguously worded treaty left Italy in nominal control of Tripolitania and Cyrenaica, but residual Turkish rights included the supervision of Libyan religious affairs. Although the Italians do not seem to have realised it at the time, this arrangement not only ensured continuing Libyan recognition of the Turkish Sultan as spiritual leader, but also, in accordance with Muslim practice, as political leader.

Although the Italo-Turkish war was over, and the Great Powers recognised Libya as Italian, the Libyans still saw the Italians as Christian invaders of one of the 'Lands of Islam'; their popular resistance to this invasion was to continue for the next 20 years. It was a resistance that was to provide modern independent Libya with the invaluable credentials of battles, national heroes and 'martyrs', and the almost mystical prestige of a prolonged people's 'anti-colonialist struggle' waged against heavy odds.

By the end of 1912 the Italians had made little progress in conquering either the Libyans or their country. After a year of war, the invaders were, in effect, besieged in seven enclaves on the coasts of Tripolitania and Cyrenaica, and even the largest of these, at Tripoli, extended barely 15 kilometres from the town. In Cyrenaica some Turkish troops who should have left the country under the terms of the peace treaty were helping the Libyans, while the Sanussi Order was organising the united and effective resistance that Tripolitania was unable to offer. Late in 1912, the Head of the Order

Sayyid Ahmad al-Sharif, undertook to continue the war as the Sultan's representative and the Order, with its true political status in Cyrenaica tacitly recognised at last, thenceforth considered the rightful government of the territory it had undertaken to defend. But while the Order received moral support from Turkey and other Muslim lands, little material aid was forthcoming.

In the spring of 1913 the Italians attacked in Cyrenaica. They broke out of Benghazi and began the systematic occupation of the country between Benghazi and Derna. The Sanussi, unable to offer effective formal resistance, soon took to the type of guerrilla warfare suited both to the temperament of the Cyrenaican tribesmen and the broken, hilly country. By 1914 the Italians held the Cyrenaican coastlands and such towns and hamlets as there were in the northern arc of the territory, but much of the country in between was still under effective Sanussi control.

Tripolitania, by contrast, had been largely overrun because many Tripolitanian leaders lacked the will to continue the fight, there was no organisation like the Sanussi to lead a united resistance, and the country was less easily defended than the great broken uplands of Cyrenaica. The former deputy for Tripolitania in the Turkish parliament of 1908, Sulaiman Baruni, tried to rally the Berbers of the Gebel Nefusah to fight for their independence, but the attempt failed when the Italians, advancing at last from Tripoli, scaled the Gebel escarpment and defeated Baruni's followers at the Battle of Asabaa, between Garian and Yefren, in March 1913. Baruni escaped to Turkey. In July 1913 an Italian column occupied Mizda at the threshold of the Sahara.

In the meantime, military columns were extending French occupation into Borku and Tibesti where the Turks had garrisoned oases from about 1906 onwards in a belated attempt to assert their long-neglected sovereignty; the Turks had been obliged to withdraw garrisons from the south in 1912 to oppose the Italian invasion, thereby leaving a power vacuum which France readily filled. This French penetration of the hinterland of Tripoli was watched with growing anxiety in Rome, where by 1913 it appeared that only a swift Italian advance into Fezzan would deter French occupation of the southern oases.

Accordingly, the Italians invaded Fezzan in a great lumbering column in the summer of 1913, and by early 1914 the main oases had been occupied. But supply lines were dangerously long, and the tribes remained unconquered in the desert. In the late summer of

1914 they started attacking the supply caravans and the isolated garrisons in the oases. The need to participate in the fighting in Europe is commonly made the excuse for the Italian military collapse in Libya, but the fact is that the counter-offensive started in Fezzan a good nine months before Italy entered the First World War on the side of the Allies in May 1915, by which time the Libyan military situation was out of control.

At the end of 1914 the Italians had been driven out of Fezzan, and in April 1915 they suffered the worst defeat of the campaign when some of their supposed allies, Ramadan Suwayhili of Misurata and his followers, suddenly attacked and annihilated an Italian column near Sirte, capturing all its arms, ammunition and equipment. By the beginning of August 1915 the Italians held only four coastal towns in Tripolitania, while in Cyrenaica no garrison was more than 30 kilo-metres from the sea. The Italians were by no means the first of Libya's would-be conquerors who failed to hold the country beyond the coastal strip.

In Tripolitania the power vacuum left by the Italian withdrawal was filled by Ramadan Suwayhili and other local leaders who formed an independent republic with its capital at Misurata. But the republic's effectiveness was limited by its inability to find an undis-puted leader, by internal feuds, and by its inability to work with the Sanussi; Suwayhili, in particular, resented Sanussi influence in Tri-politania and drove their forces from the territory. This failure of the Tripolitanians and the Sanussi of Cyrenaica to work together in 1916 and in later years was to prove a fatal flaw in the Libyan resistance to Italian occupation; and even a generation later it was to jeopardise Libya's prospects of early independence.

The Misurata Republic was supported by Italy's First World War enemies, the Central Powers of Germany, Austria and Turkey. Their submarines ran the British Royal Navy's blockade of the Libyan coast to bring in money, arms and instructors. The Central Powers also gave support to the Sanussi in Cyrenaica, and at the end of 1915 they pressurised Sayyid Ahmad into attacking British forces in Egypt, already heavily engaged against the Turks in Sinai. Although the Sanussi achieved some early successes, they were even-tually driven back into Cyrenaica and, facing defeat and famine, the Order's will to resist was temporarily broken.[9]

Sayyid Ahmad then abdicated the leadership to his scholarly young cousin, Sayyid Idris, who had always disapproved of the cam-paign against the British, and who had tacit British support as leader and peacemaker; such was the beginning of an understanding between Sayyid Idris and Britain that was to last over 50 years. With Sayyid Ahmad's approval, Sayyid Idris opened negotiations with the British and the Italians in July 1916. By this stage of the war little consideration was given to residual Turkish interests in Cyrenaica. The Pact of London, signed in April 1915 on the eve of the Italian entry into the First World War, had promised Italy 'all the rights and privileges in Libya at present belonging to the Sultan of Turkey by virtue of the Treaty of Lausanne' which had ended the Italo-Turkish war in 1912.

But, with its newly recognised diplomatic status, it was now the Sanussi Order that spoke for the bedouin of Cyrenaica. The talks went slowly, but with the British in effect acting as mediators between Sayyid Idris and the Italians, peace terms were agreed in the spring of 1917. Britain was relieved of the Sanussi threat in the Western Desert; the Italians and the Sanussi were left confronting each other in a state of armed truce from their respective zones of occupation in Cyrenaica; and the autonomy of the Sanussi in the interior of the country was almost a recognised reality.

Italy emerged victorious from the First World War, but faced grave political, economic and social difficulties at home. Because the political will to use military force to restore the situation in Libya was lacking, genuine and in some ways far-sighted attempts were made to reach political compromises with the Sanussi in Cyrenaica and with the Tripolitanian Republic, which had been formally proclaimed at Misurata in 1918. Separate statutes for Tripolitania and Cyrenaica were issued in October 1919. In accordance with the current Wilsonian spirit of self-government, if not self-determination, each province was to have its own parliament and governing and local councils through which the Italians were to exercise a light-handed control; Libyans were to have the right to Italian citizenship and other benefits.

Little, in fact, came of these good intentions. Tripolitania beyond the Italian coastal enclaves was almost in a state of civil war as Ramadan Suwayhili, on behalf of the Tripolitanian Republic, tried to assert his authority over other tribal leaders, his personal rivals, until he was killed in battle in August 1920. The Italians were powerless to assert their authority, and no Libyan was able to lead the province. But by the end of 1920 the Tripolitanians, well aware of Italy's post-war political and military impotence, had rejected the very idea of Italian sovereignty, and their representatives in Italy were winning the support of opposition parties for official recognition of a fully independent Muslim state in Tripolitania.

In Cyrenaica the weakness of the Italian position and the unwillingness of local leaders to accept anything more than Italian economic influence led to a new agreement in October 1920 which recognised Sayyid Idris as the hereditary Amir of Cyrenaica and as head of an autonomous regime in the main inland oases. He in turn agreed to co-operate in putting the 1919 statute into effect. But the arrangements never worked satisfactorily, and by the end of 1921 Italo-Sanussi relations were strained once again.

Meanwhile in Tripolitania a new governor, Giuseppe Volpi, was showing an unexpectedly firm hand. As the Tripolitanians had no natural leader to follow, they turned to Cyrenaica and Sayyid Idris for support and leadership, swallowing their pride even to the point of proposing the extension of the Sanussi Amirate into Tripolitania. Representatives from Tripolitania formally offered Sayyid Idris the Amirate of all Libya in April 1922. By the time he accepted the offer in November it was no longer of much practical value because Governor Volpi had by then effectively forestalled this — for the Italians — potentially disastrous union of Tripolitania and Cyrenaica. He had done so simply by undertaking, practically on his own initiative, the military reconquest of the province, at the same time declaring martial law and rejecting all constitutional arrangements with the Libyans. By the time Benito Mussolini came to power in Rome in October 1922, the reconquest of northern Tripolitania was well under way, Volpi having in effect anticipated Fascist colonial policy by some ten months.

The crisis in Italo-Sanussi relations came to a head at the end of 1922 when Sayyid Idris saw that the peace he had negotiated was breaking down, that Italians and Sanussis could not share the country between them, and that there could be no compromise with the new Fascist government in Rome. He accordingly went into exile in Egypt, leaving the more martial members of his family to lead the people of Cyrenaica into the next inevitable battles. For Italians the advent of Fascism had ended the derided prevarications of previous Liberal governments and was opening a new phase in Italian colonial expansion. As Mussolini had said in 1921, 'We Fascists had the supreme unprejudiced courage to call ourselves imperialists.'

Tripolitania, Fezzan, and more particularly Cyrenaica, now entered on a new patriotic war against the invader that was to last nine years and cost many thousand lives (although not as many as th

Libyans now like to claim).[10] The war was to end in total Libyan defeat, but was nevertheless to provide an invaluable and undeniable basis for claims to an internationally recognised independence after the Second World War. The majority of Libyans were, of course, never involved in the fighting, which took the form of intermittent engagements and skirmishes between small numbers of nomads and Italian metropolitan and colonial troops over wide areas of mountain, steppe and desert. Like the Turks in Tripolitania before them, the French in Algeria for much of the nineteenth century, and the French and Spanish in contemporary Morocco, the Italian military found no easy way of matching the pugnacious guerrilla tactics of the North African nomad, either in the nothern mountains or in the open desert beyond. That it took Fascist Italy nine years to conquer all Libya is perhaps more a reflection of the heroic stubbornness and effectiveness of Libyan resistance than of Italian military shortcomings, given that other nations took as long, or longer, to achieve similar ends elsewhere in North Africa.

The most desirable parts of Tripolitania — the coastal plain and the northern uplands — were conquered relatively quickly and easily, for resistance was light. By the middle of 1924 the Italians held all the country north of the line Ghadames–Mizda–Beni Ulid and four-fifths of the estimated population of Tripolitania and Fezzan were within the Italian area. The military realised that those outside had eventually to be brought under control (for unconquered tribes were rebellious tribes) and that all Tripolitania and Fezzan had to be conquered and pacified to their furthest limits if the occupation was to be secure. But the mistake made in 1913–14 of marching straight into Fezzan with unconquered tribes still at large on the flanks was not to be repeated. The warlike tribes of the Ghibla, the broken pre-desert country south of Mizda, were seen as a tough obstacle to an eventual southward advance, and in the course of three years they were subjected to a slow process of political infiltration.

In Cyrenaica, meanwhile, the Italians had fairly swiftly occupied the northern lowlands in 1923–4; but when the fighting moved into the broken, wooded hills of the Gebel Akhdar they met popular guerrilla resistance, in ideal guerrilla country, involving most of the nomads of northern Cyrenaica. The leader of the Cyrenaican resistance was an elderly Sanussi shaikh and warrior, Omar Mukhtar, who, as official representative-general of the Sanussi, was commander-in-chief of all the tribal guerrilla bands, ranging in size from

100 to 300 men. The Cyrenaicans rarely had more than 1,000 armed men in the field at any time, yet such was their dash and mobility that for years on end they defied much larger, better-equipped yet cumbersome Italian forces. The Cyrenaican war was a convincing demonstration of the power of the guerrilla fighter, if properly motivated and led, and actively supported by the non-combatant population. Although the Italians called the Libyan fighters 'rebels' and the non-combatants *sottomessi* — those who had 'submitted' — there was no clear distinction between them, and the *sottomessi* were throughout the war the main source of supplies and recruits for the fighting bands; indeed, the Italians and the Sanussi Order were popularly known in Cyrenaica as the day and night governments respectively. Italian penetration and pacification of the Gebel was slow, and in 1926 the early centre of Sanussism at Giarabub, which had only recently been recognised to be in Libya rather than Egypt, was occupied in the false hope that its seizure would break the Sanussi will to resist elsewhere.

At the beginning of 1928 the Italians conquered the Sirtica desert separating Tripolitania from Cyrenaica. Making full use of aircraft and motor transport, and backed by good logistical organisation, they occupied 150,000 square kilometres of territory in five months, although 'rebel' tribes were swept aside rather than destroyed. But the two main areas of resistance in Tripolitania and Cyrenaica had at least been cut off from each other by the Italian advance. Later in 1928 the Ghibla was occupied and its tribes disarmed.

The importance the Fascist government attached to the conquest and development of Libya is clear from the high rank of the governors appointed in the 1920s and 1930s. In 1925 Count Volpi had been succeeded in Tripolitania by Emilio de Bono, a leader of the March on Rome that brought Mussolini to power in 1922, while Colonel Rodolfo Graziani made his name as the conqueror of Tripolitania. Then in 1929 the Marshal of Italy, Pietro Badoglio, was appointed governor of Tripolitania and Cyrenaica, which had been united for the better co-ordination of military operations. Under Badoglio's direction Graziani completed the conquest of Fezzan, which was more a matter of planning and logistics than a feat of arms, since no more than 1,500 weary warriors remained in the whole of western Libya to oppose the advance of the Italian war machine. At the end of March 1930 the Italian flag was raised over the wells of Tummo, Rome's most southerly claim in Fezzan.

Negotiations with Omar Mukhtar in Cyrenaica during the

summer of 1929 had broken down, and early the following year Badoglio, with Graziani as his deputy, was ready to complete the conquest of Libya. It was achieved by ruthless repression. Graziani adopted more aggressive military tactics, using large numbers of *ascari* from Italian Eritrea to dominate the rebellious areas by continual movement. There was little mercy for actual or suspected rebels, and according to the estimate of one foreign visitor about 12,000 Cyrenaicans were being executed yearly during Graziani's reign of terror in 1930–1.[11] Drastic steps were taken to control the *sottomessi*, who were still the rebellion's main source of recruits and supplies. In the summer of 1930 almost all the nomads of northern Cyrenaica were moved from the battle zone to huge concentration camps in the lowlands, where they survived on government welfare. To close the rebel supply-routes from Egypt, a 300-kilometre barbed-wire fence, patrolled by armoured cars and aircraft, was built along the frontier. The Sanussi Order, as the source and inspiration of resistance, was treated harshly; *zawias* were closed and their shaikhs arrested; mosques were closed and Sanussi practices forbidden; Sanussi estates were confiscated, and preparations were made for the occupation of Kufra Oasis in the far south-east as the last stronghold of the Sanussi in Libya and one of the few areas of the country not under Italian control. In a nice feat of logistics, Kufra was occupied in January 1931 and, in an exercise of the casual inhumanity that seems to have characterised the closing stages of the Cyrenaican war, refugees from Kufra were bombed and strafed by aircraft as they fled into the desert.[12]

Islamic patriotism and the struggle to live in their own land on their own terms were the forces uniting the usually quarrelsome Cyrenaican tribes against the Christian intruder. For the Libyans, the Italian aggression was particularly menacing because they saw it as a preliminary to their own dispossession and the mass settlement of immigrant peasants on the little good land there was.

By turning Cyrenaica almost into an armed camp, by arrests, deportations, confiscations and executions, and by the use of an overwhelming weight of modern military equipment, the Italians finally mastered the resistance and cornered the last, exhausted fighting bands in the fastnesses of the Gebel Akhdar. In September 1931 Omar Mukhtar, having defied Fascist Italy for nine years, was ambushed and captured; after a summary court martial, he was publicly hanged at Suluq. His death effectively ended the resistance, and in January 1932 Badoglio officially proclaimed the end of the

Cyrenaican war and the pacification of Libya. The vision expressed by Gabriele d'Annunzio 20 years before, *Splende la pace in Tripoli Latina*,[13] had at last been realised.

All Libya was now Italian, a land for Italians. For over 50 years foreign travellers had been remarking on the rich agricultural potential of Tripolitania and Cyrenaica, and on the suitability of the land and climate for Italian peasant settlement. As a British commentator wrote in 1912:

> It is plain that with wise and democratic control, under which the common people shall be given a fair chance, with the conjunction of all the latest scientific methods and machinery of production in industry and in agriculture, and with the unexampled pioneering ability and enthusiasm of the Italian emigrant, there will be built up one of the finest colonies in the world.[14]

Some Italians had visions of Cyrenaica raising ten million sheep and providing the finest wool, and 20 million olive trees — five times more than in the fertile *Région Sfaxienne* of Tunisia.[15]

Long before the invasion of Libya, a popular Italian vision was of Italy as a 'proletarian nation' — one whose greatest assets were the labour and manual skills of its large, still mainly rural population, since natural resources, investment capital and even a sizeable middle class were all lacking. It followed that Italy's quest for colonies was not motivated by the capitalist imperialism of other European powers, but by the urgent expansionist drive of a people with no resources but their own skills and energy who, if they had to emigrate, would be better off in Italian colonies rather than submerging their national identity in foreign lands. Thus Giovanni Pascoli, as one of the poetic voices of Italian expansionism, talked of the Libyan war of 1911 in terms of the great Italian proletariat having bestirred itself ('*La grande proletaria si è mossa . . .*'); his vision of the heartfelt necessity for Italian settler colonies later influenced official Fascist colonial policy.

So, although a leading industrial power, Italy between the World Wars sought solutions for her economic and social difficulties in agricultural regeneration, including colonial agriculture on the marginal and money-absorbing soils of Libya, rather than in industrial expansion. There were strategic and demographic arguments for this policy, at least so far as Libya was concerned; and there was a certain urgency to make the colony overwhelmingly Italian in character and population before rising Arab nationalism began to challenge the occupation of this particular portion of the Arab world; other arguments may be found in the nature and loyalties of Fascism. For Libya, the results of Fascist colonial policy were far-reaching: conquest at all costs, followed by the sudden arrival of large numbers of Italian settlers, and the rapid and intensive development of the colonial infrastructure.

Settlement colonisation started slowly in Libya, although between 1914 and 1929 nearly 180,000 hectares of agricultural land were acquired for Italian settlement. In the early 1920s the trend in Tripolitania was towards large estates, financed mainly with north Italian capital, and employing Italian or Libyan labour. Such methods did not accord with the Fascist policy of 'demographic colonisation' that evolved in 1928–9 as a system of state-sponsored and subsidised settlement of Italian peasant families on small individual farms that were eventually to become family property. The family, and not the individual, was the basic unit of settlement, since each farm was to be self-contained and run by its own labour.

Pioneer state settlements were started in 1933–4. But it was only in 1938 that Marshal Italo Balbo (who had become governor of the united colony of *Libia* four years earlier) supervised a spectacular scheme for the simultaneous settlement of 20,000 selected state-aided colonists on prepared family farms in Tripolitania and Cyrenaica. A further 12,000 colonists followed in 1939. They came from most parts of Italy; they were landless, poor, but enthusiastic to meet the backbreaking and often heartbreaking challenges of a new life in Africa where, aided by state subsidies, they had a good chance of becoming outright owners of their farms within about 20 years.

Financially, demographic colonisation was hugely costly, as a British witness of the 1938 settlement noted:

It will be several decades before any of these immigrants begin to contribute their quota as taxpayers . . . everything depends on the state continuing to pour money into Libya for many years to come . . . there is no foreseeable revenue that could balance the cost of garrisoning the coast and policing the desert.[16]

But colonists were needed to make Libya an 'Italian country', to counterbalance the native population', to consolidate Italian strategic control of the central Mediterranean basin, and to provide the mother country with corn, olive oil and other produce. According to the government's plans, there were to have been 100,000 colonists in the country by 1942, and the settlement of half a million by the early 1960s was envisaged.

By the end of the 1930s Libya's future prosperity depended on large and continuing subsidies that Italy could ill afford. It has been estimated that the Italian state invested a total of 1,830 million lire in Libya during the Italian occupation,[17] as well as many hundreds of millions of lire in indirect investments; private investments are estimated to have matched those of the state at 1,840 million lire. Up to 1936 most public investment went into roads, railways, ports and other public works; but in the final six years of Italian administration most money was spent on land reclamation and agricultural projects. In 1940 Italy's plans for creating a 'fourth shore' in Libya came nearest to realisation. Since 1936 the Italian population of the colony had doubled to over 110,000 (70,000 in Tripolitania), or nearly 12 per cent of the total population.[18] About 4,000 Italian families were settled on the land in Tripolitania and more than 2,000 in Cyrenaica; about 225,000 hectares were being developed by settlers in the two provinces.

'Before the advent of Fascism, Libya was in a state of disorder', wrote an Italian commentator in 1935. 'Now, after a few years, order, peace and confidence — the law of Italy — have been everywhere restored. The foundations of the country's renasence . . . have been firmly laid. The great Latin emblem of the Lictors' *fasces* has given the land a new baptism of life, consecrating it afresh for European civilisation . . .'[19] Mussolini had declared in 1934: 'Civilisation, in fact, is what Italy is creating on the fourth shore of our sea; western civilisation in general and Fascist civilisation in particular.'[20] By the outbreak of the Second World War Libya had reached an impressive level of material development, particularly in comparison with the primitive conditions the Italians had found in 1911. 'The building, town planning and sanitary activities of the Italians have been remarkable', wrote a British observer in 1942.

> Whatever else may be said of their rule, the spick-and-span and even imposing appearance of every place they have taken over from Rhodes to Benghazi, must be admitted . . . irrigation, colonisation and hard work have wrought marvels. Everywhere you see plantations forced out of the sandy, wretched soil . . . it is all a triumph over adverse conditions.[21]

And another British observer wrote in 1939, 'I had never seen the white man, without native labour, down on his hands and knees, squeezing the grain out of the soil.'[22]

The Italians had given the country a basic modern infrastructure, with the *Litoranea*, the great Egypt – Tunisia coastal highway completed in 1937, providing a communications backbone, and also a potential invasion route to the Suez Canal or into French North Africa. The *Litoranea* was described in 1938 as 'nothing but a military highway thinly camouflaged as a road to encourage the motoring tourist'.[23] As another commentator wrote in 1938, 'Libya can no longer be counted out, as a sort of no-man's land of small significance; its resources are limited, but they are being exploited to the utmost, while its strategic value has become very great.'[24] By that time there were 40,000 Italian troops in Libya, as well as 20,000 'native levies' and 'cadres capable of bringing the establishment up to 100,000'.[25]

Libya in the 1930s was primarily a settlement colony for Italians and the country was run largely for their benefit.

> Here the Arab is lost . . . in the manner of his kind he quietly effaces himself before the multiplying signs of Fascist triumph . . . the Arab is not unhappy; and now that Graziani is gone he is not bullied; he is just paralysed by the speed of things that make no effort to explain themselves or carry him along with them.[26]

In January 1939 the four provinces of Tripoli, Misurata, Benghazi and Derna became an integral part, and the nineteenth region, of metropolitan Italy. One of the official reasons given for this change of status was 'the continual manifestation of loyalty on the part of the Muslim population'.

Although Libya was the homeland of up to three-quarters of a million Libyans, they were inferior citizens (as were most natives in African colonies at the time) and the granting of *Cittadinanza Italiana Speciale* and other petty benefits to selected individuals from 1939 onwards could not disguise the fact. The structure of Libyan society had been undermined by the years of fighting, by the flight of refugees (particularly to Egypt), by internal migration in response to new economic pressures, and as a result of the deliberate Fascist policy of destroying the power of the Sanussi Order, abolishing the traditional tribal assemblies, and weakening the authority of the shaikhs and other established leaders. As a result, Libyans could only look for leadership and guidance to the domineering and authoritarian Fascist regime that imposed its will throughout Italy and the Empire; Libyans could hardly expect freedoms the Italians themselves no longer enjoyed. In Cyrenaica, in particular, the bedouin remained passively hostile to the Italians and all their works, embittered by memories of the long war and the concentration camps, and by Italian settler colonisation which, just as they had long foreseen and feared, was now depriving them of their best pasture land.

The Italians, for their part, recognised the value of the Libyans as a reserve of menial manpower for the colony's ambitious development schemes (and as soldiers in the Abyssinian campaign), and large numbers of them, particularly in Tripolitania, abandoned their old ways to become wage-earners in the modern cash economy. An observer wrote in 1939:

> The Arab population in Libya today is less poor than it has ever been in the past. There is no unemployment. The very colonial development that has turned some of the Cyrenaican natives off the soil has filled the pockets of the remainder, who can scarcely be expected to sympathise. Everywhere that one travels, from the Tunisian frontier to the Egyptian, they are at work. At seven lire a day, on the roads, the houses, the aerodromes, the aqueducts, clearing the bush and erecting the civic centre and new military barracks and military stores that are springing up from one end of Libya to the other.[27]

Nevertheless, no clear programme for the Libyans' future had emerged by 1940. The Fascist government was aware of growing nationalist pressures elsewhere in the Arab and Islamic worlds (indeed, it did much to encourage them), but expected to counter them in Libya by the reality of the overwhelming Italian settler presence. And in the face of continuing Libyan and wider Arab hostility towards the Italian record during the Cyrenaican war, Mussolini at a ceremony in Tripoli in 1937 took upon himself the role of Protector of Islam, a move which was judged at the time to be 'no empty theatrical gesture, but a serious bid for the patronage of the Muslim World'.[28]

A reading of Fascist colonial policy, as it seemed to be evolving on the eve of the Second World War, suggests that the Italian settler colony would have consolidated itself alongside and in parallel with an Italianised Libyan Muslim society of manual labourers, petty officials and newly settled peasant farmers whose Italian-directed basic education would have instilled them with 'respect and devotion' for the mother country. The Libyans were to be 'economic collaborators' and 'co-participants' in the development of the colony.[29] As an Italian commentator wrote in 1941:

> Fascist native racial policy is separatist, but also associative–collaborative; it is a just middle way between the excess of domination and the excess of assimilation; it fulfils social, ethical and juridical criteria; it is based on racial differentiations that the natives themselves would not want narrowed, while human justice necessitates that they are not widened.[30]

Such an evolution might have been possible in some parts of Tripolitania, although even there it is doubtful whether the Libyans would ever have had the necessary motivation and faith in government intentions to fit neatly and passively into the Italian scheme of things; and certainly the less co-operative bedouin of Cyrenaica seemed destined for a largely forgotten and poverty-stricken existence on the pre-desert steppes too barren for Italian settlement. But Marshal Balbo seemed to be forecasting something of an ideal future for Libya when he declared: 'There will not be rulers and ruled in Libya; instead we shall have Catholic Italians and Muslim Italians, united in the common fold as constructive elements in a great and mighty organisation, the Fascist Empire.'

In the event, Italian intentions for the Libyans' political and economic future had not passed much beyond basic arrangements before disastrous involvement in the Second World War put an end to the Italian African Empire.

Notes

1. Gabriele d'Annunzio wrote of the Libyan campaign of 1911–12: 'Essa fa dell'Italia dei tre mari/La grande patria delle quattro sponde' (*Canzoni d'Oltremare*).

2. Miège, *L'Imperialismo Coloniale Italiano dal 1870 ai Giorni Nostri* (Milan, 1976), p. 84.

3. See ibid., ch. XI and XII.

4. Libya, the Dodecanese and Italian East Africa (Eritrea, Somalia, Ethiopia).

5. Ibid., p. 262.

6. E.H. Griffin, *Adventures in Tripoli* (London, 1924), p. 44.

7. For further details, see J. Wright, 'Aeroplanes and Airships in Libya, 1911–1912', *Maghreb Review*, vol. 3, no. 10 (November–December 1978); and *Primi Voli di Guerra nel Mondo, Libia MCMXI* (Rome, 1961).

8. M. Degl'Innocenti, *Il Socialismo Italiano e la Guerra di Libia* (Rome, 1976), p. 61.

9. For the harsh conditions prevailing in Cyrenaica in 1915–16, see R.S. Gwatkin-Williams, *Prisoners of the Red Desert* (London, 1919).

10. In a speech in September 1979, Colonel Gadafi claimed that 750,000 Libyans had died in the struggle against the Italians (Jamahiriyah News Agency, Bulletin no. 490, 6 September 79, p. 3) and Major Abd-al-Salam Jallud, in a speech in May 1973, claimed the loss of 'no less than 750,000 fighters' (BBC, *Summary of World Broadcasts*, ME/4299/A/3). These claims, and other frequent assertions that 'half' the Libyan nation died during the years of Italian occupation — either as a direct result of the fighting, or by execution, or as a result of disease and deprivation — are not borne out by the available statistics. Many 'losses' were in fact exiles.

In 1911 a Turkish census gave the population of Tripolitania and Fezzan as 576,000, while Cyrenaica had an estimated 250,000 — a total of 826,000. During the Italian occupation, the population of all Libya was variously given as 795,000 in 1929 (*Touring Club Italiano*), 700,000 in 1934 (Miège, *L'Imperialismo Coloniale Italiano* p. 191), 888,400 in 1938 (RIIA, *The Italian Colonial Empire* (London, 1940), and 751,000 in 1939 (League of Nations). Assuming the 1911 figure of 826,000 to have been approximately correct, the population could have dropped by some 125,000 by 1934 on the basis of Miège's figure; on the other hand, it could have risen by some 60,000 on the basis of the RIIA figure. Whatever the case, allowance must also be made for mass Italian immigration in the later 1930s, the Italian community totalling some 110,000 by 1940 (C.G. Segrè, *Fourth Shore* (Chicago, 1974), p. 161).

In 1947 the British Military Administration put the population of all Libya at 803,915 (*Handbook on Tripolitania* (Tripoli, 1947), Appendix I, p. 77). In 1954 a census held in Libya under United Nations auspices gave a total population of 1,088,000 (M. Murabet, *Some Facts about Libya* (Malta, 1961), p. 70). This was a considerable increase over any figure for the Italian period, and an increase of 262,000 over the 1911 figure. The 1954 census reflected the loss through repatriation of some 80,000 Italians during the Second World War, as well as the exodus of some 30,000 Tripolitanian Jews in 1948–51. But it equally shaved the return of uncounted thousands of Libyan exiles from Egypt, the Maghrib and other parts of the Islamic world since the Second World War.

Without belittling the undoubted sufferings of the Libyan people, it seems only fair to note that available figures — approximate though they are — show no evidence of the enormous population losses in the period 1911–32 claimed by the Libyans. A fall of some 125,000 in the population between 1911 and 1934 is a possibility, and to this figure should be added Italian immigration of some 50,000 up to that date. Thus a net fall of some 175,000 in the native population up to 1934 seems possible.

The United Nations Commissioner in Libya in 1950–51, Dr Adrian Pelt, believed the assertion that half the Libyan nation died in the 'struggle for freedom' 'must be an over-statement'. His researches suggested that the total death roll from all causes except natural death between 1912 and 1943 was in the region of 250,000 to 300,000 (Pelt, *Libyan Independence and the United Nations* (New Haven, 1970), p. 500, n. 89). Pelt based his assumption on a population of 'just over one million' during the Italian occupation. It is perhaps only fair to add that while many Libyans died in the fighting against the Italians, many Libyan lives were saved by the enormous improvements in the public health services that followed the Italian conquest (see Quadrone, *Sahara: Genti e Paesi* (Milan, 1938), pp. 159–239).

11. K. Holmboe, *Desert Encounter* (London, 1936), p. 203.

12. For a heartless account of this episode, see D.M. Tuninetti, *Il Mistero di Cufra* (Benghazi, 1931), pp. 159–60.

13. Peace shines out in Latin Tripoli.

14. C. Lapworth, *Tripoli and Young Italy* (London, 1912), p. 140.

15. M. Dei Gaslini and L.F. De Magistris, *L'Oltremare d'Italia in Terra d'Africa:*

Visioni e Sintesi (Bergamo, 1930–1), pp. 102, 104.

16. M. Moore, *Fourth Shore, Italy's Mass Colonisation of Libya* (London, 1940), pp. 216–17, 221.

17. *Amministrazione Fiduciaria dell'Italia in Africa* (Florence, 1948), p. 173. *The Economic Development of Libya* (Baltimore, 1960), p. 27, estimates this sum as equivalent to $150 million in pre-Second World War dollars, at pre-war exchange rates.

18. Proportionately, Libya had in 1940 rather more resident Europeans than even Algeria had in the peak year of 1954 (Segrè, *Fourth Shore*, p. 161 and n. 2).

19. A. Piccioli, *The Magic Gate of the Sahara* (London, 1935), p. 86.

20. A. Piccioli, *La Nuova Italia d'Oltremare. L'Opera del Fascismo nelle Colonie Italiane* (Milan, 1934), introduction.

21. A.H. Brodrick, *North Africa* (London, 1943), p. 27.

22. G.L. Steer, *A Date in the Desert* (London, 1939), p. 162.

23. H.H. Macartney and P. Cremona, *Italy's Foreign and Colonial Policy, 1914–1937* (London, 1938), p. 4.

24. J. Soames, *The Coast of Barbary* (London, 1938), p. 277.

25. Ibid., p. 278.

26. Steer, *Date in the Desert*, p. 132.

27. Ibid., p. 164.

28. Macartney and Cremona, *Italy's Foreign and Colonial Policy*, p. 187.

29. P. Di Camerota, *La Colonizzazione Africana nel Sistema Fascista*: *I Problemi della Colonizzazione nell'Africa Italiana* (Milan, 1941), pp. 67, 82–3.

30. Ibid., p. 83.

3   A CHILD OF THE UNITED NATIONS

For Libyans who found themselves under the authoritarian rule of Italian Fascism[1] after the final defeat of the Cyrenaican resistance, or in exile in Egypt or other parts of the Islamic world, there seemed no prospects of national autonomy and freedom. Yet the First World War, by pitting the great European powers against each other, had already revealed a weakness in their system of world domination, and had raised some hopes of independence from European rule for colonial subjects. In Libya, the Turks and their European allies had even supported the cause of Tripolitanian and Cyrenaican independence as part of the common war effort against Italy. Although Libyan national aspirations were dashed after the First World War, the outbreak of the Second World War some 20 years later gave the Libyans, among other colonial peoples, an opportunity this time to support the war effort of combatant powers which were not only victorious, but were willing and able to put their wartime promises into effect. Thus when Italy joined the Second World War in June 1940 as the ally of an apparently victorious Nazi Germany, Libyan exiles in Egypt found Great Britain a more reliable ultimate guarantor of their national aspirations than Ottoman Turkey or Imperial Germany and Austria had proved to be 25 years earlier.

The immediate objectives of the large Italian forces in Libya in the summer of 1940 were the British positions in the Western Desert of Egypt, and ultimately the Suez Canal. But the invasion of Egypt that General Graziani might have successfully completed by bold action in 1940 turned into the longest campaign of the war when the British counter-attacked in the winter of 1940–1, thereby bringing German reinforcements to the aid of their Italian allies. Cyrenaica, occupied and then evacuated twice by the British before its third and final conquest following the battle of El Alamein in late 1942, suffered heavily in the fighting. The infrastructure built up at such cost by the Italians was largely destroyed (Benghazi alone had over a thousand air raids); by the end of 1942 all Italian colonists had been evacuated from the province for their own safety. Without any prompting, the

Cyrenaican bedouin had simply returned to claim their own; their flocks and herds grazed undisturbed in the colonists' neglected fields and found shelter in the abandoned farmhouses. 'The fight to maintain civilisation here was too unequal, too disappointing, too hard', wrote the war correspondent Alan Moorehead. 'Under our eyes the land was returning to its old sterility.'[2] Tripolitania, by contrast, saw little of the fighting and was relatively undamaged by the war.

Tripoli fell to the British Eighth Army on 23 January 1943 and the Allied conquest of Libya was completed by February. While the Eighth Army was advancing on Tripoli, the main oases of Fezzan had been overrun by a Free French brigade under General Leclerc; its supply lines stretched precariously back through Chad and other pro-Gaullist territories of French Equatorial Africa to the Atlantic.

In 1939 there were an estimated 14,000 Libyan exiles in Egypt alone. 'Destitute and nearly without cattle, they had settled on the fringe of the Western Desert', wrote a British army officer who came to know them well. 'They were semi-nomadic and very miserable; some of them had completey foresaken the traditional life of the desert and had joined the cosmopolitan riff-raff that made a shady living round Alexandria harbour.'[3] In the autumn of 1939, many of these exiles saw Italy's expected involvement in the war as an opportunity to free their country from Italian rule. Some 51 Tripolitanian and Cyrenaican exiles' leaders met in Alexandria to bridge their regional differences and to discuss a common course of action under the leadership of Sayyid Idris. When Italy entered the war the following June, many Tripolitanian exiles were frankly afraid to oppose and antagonise one of the apparent victors. But the Cyrenaicans, and particularly Sayyid Idris, believed that in supporting the British war effort, Libyan exiles stood to gain the liberation of Cyrenaica if Britain was victorious; if not, they had nothing to lose, for Libya would remain Italian if the Axis won the war.

British military authorities in Egypt had for some time been considering the possibility of enlisting the support of Libyan exiles and, after the Italian declaration of war, Sayyid Idris was invited to raise a Sanussi force from Libyans in exile in Egypt and neighbouring countries.

At a second meeting of exiles in Cairo in August 1940, various resolutions were passed calling for participation in the war alongside the British army and under the banner of the Sanussi Amirate. At the same meeting, a Sanussi Amirate in Cyrenaica and Tripolitania was proclaimed. It was also agreed that representatives of both provinces were to form the Amir's advisory council, and that a provisional Sanussi government was to be set up; the Amir was empowered to make political, military and financial agreements with the British government to further the cause of Libyan independence; Britain was also expected to finance the Sanussi war effort and administration.

A recruiting office was opened in Egypt and five infantry battalions of volunteers were eventually mustered as the Libyan Arab Force. These troops made a marginal contribution to the Allied war effort in North Africa. Some were present during the fighting in the Derna–Tobruk sector in early 1942,[4] but the Libyan Arab Force as a whole was, in effect, only a gendarmerie, fulfilling police and guard duties as 'base troops' well behind the lines, and thereby relieving front-line units of these routine but very necessary tasks. A British intelligence officer who came to know the Libyans well, particularly behind the lines of Cyrenaica, wrote:

> Their services to us were not spectacular. They did not rise in arms against our enemies — in the first months of the war they had no arms to rise with — and in any case we never wanted them to do this . . . but it was the Arabs inside Cyrenaica . . . who served us so well and who, above all, never lost hope. And they had good reason to lose it . . . there was not much to give the Arabs confidence that Britain would be victorious.[5]

Some Tripolitanian notables shared that view. They also resented Sanussi pretensions to leadership in their province, and they criticised the decision of Sayyid Idris to collaborate with the British before he had been given sound guarantees of independence for all Libya. In fact, during 1940 and 1941 Sayyid Idris kept pressing the question of independence with the British authorities in Egypt. Although they shared his views on the desirability of a self-governing amirate, administered with the help of British advisers, they were not prepared to make definite promises until the war was over. But if Sayyid Idris was apparently satisfied with private verbal assurances, his followers, and particularly the Tripolitanians, were not; their pressure on him was such that he even had to threaten to withdraw from active collaboration with Britain. It was to give the Sayyid and his followers an official public assurance about Britain's intentions that the British Foreign Secretary, Anthony Eden, made a statement in the House of Commons on 8 January 1942. After briefly outlining the development and scope of Sanussi collaboration and paying tribute to this contribution to the British war effort, he said: 'His Majesty's government is determined that at the end of the war the Sanussi of Cyrenaica will in no circumstances again fall under Italian domination.'[6]

The Eden statement did not even promise independence for Cyrenaica, and it failed to mention Tripolitania — an omission that seemed to the Tripolitanians to imply prior British recognition of Sanussi leadership over all Libya. The statement, which even Sayyid Idris considered negative, might indeed have been read as a forewarning of domination by Britain or another power. Nevertheless, after the British rejection of his outright demand for a guarantee of Libyan independence, made in February 1942, Sayyid Idris declared himself satisfied with the oral promises he had been given, at least so far as Cyrenaica was concerned. He realised that the British were not prepared to give him written pledges on Libyan independence that they might not have been able to honour after the war (as was the case with British pledges on the Middle East given during the First World War), but preferred to give all possible support to their allies' aspirations when the war had been won.[7]

Following the third and final British occupation of Cyrenaica, the commander of the British Eighth Army, General Bernard Montgomery, announced in a message to the people on 11 November 1942 that the province was to be administered by the British military government until the end of the Second World War and not, he was careful to stress, merely until the end of the fighting in North Africa. He added: 'The military government will not enter into questions relating to political affairs of the future, but will endeavour to rule with firmness, justice and consideration for the people of the country.'[8] By early 1943 Tripolitania was also under British military administration, while Fezzan and parts of central Libya, following their conquest by the Free French, were administered by the French military.

The British Military Administration (BMA) in Tripolitania and Cyrenaica, and the French administration in Fezzan, ruled in accordance with the terms of the 1907 Hague Convention on the conduct of war. Libya was Occupied Enemy Territory and, as laid down by international law, its government was on a 'care and maintenance' basis. Laws and institutions in force at the time of occupation remained in effect, but purged of their obviously Fascist provisions.

The administrations in all three provinces did, in practice, go well beyond the strict terms of their original mandates by fostering development of the social services, and particularly Arab education; in Fezzan, the French made many basic improvements to the lives of the largely destitute communities they found there. The administrations' greatest handicap was the prolonged uncertainty about their future. As the BMA in Tripolitania said about itself after some four years of existence:

> The principal defect has been the temporary nature of the Administration and, being temporary, its prolonged existence. Long term policies have been ruled out, with a consequent discontent among two groups, those with the political aspirations of their country at heart, and the merchants.[9]

By the end of the Second World War, Libya was in a sorry state. The people were politically retarded, under-educated (illiteracy was estimated at 94 per cent), untrained and impoverished: annual income *per capita* was barely £15; infant mortality was a horrifying 40 per cent; there was little trade and much unemployment; banks had been closed since 1943 and Italian development funds had dried up. In Cyrenaica, much of the infrastructure had been destroyed and most Italians had fled. Tripolitania had been less damaged and still had an economically and socially vital community of some 40,000 Italians; about one-third of them still lived on the colonial farms, many of which were just becoming commercially productive. But the outlook was poor and the BMA noted: 'The unpleasant fact must be faced that Tripolitania is a country without natural resources of wealth other than agriculture.'[10] Libya's main difficulty was that until its future status had been decided and its stop-gap military administrations replaced by more permanent forms of government, there could be little post-war recovery or development.

It was against this background of political, economic and social destitution that Libya's prospects were considered by the four Great Powers — Britain, France, the United States and the Soviet Union — which, at a long series of meetings, sought mutually acceptable solutions to the many outstanding international issues left over from the war.

While Fascist Italy had seen Libya's future largely in terms of the socio-economic experiment of 'demographic colonisation', the country's sole interest to outside powers after the Second World War was strategic. By 1943 Britain, France and the United States had armed forces stationed there, and Libya was to each an asset of unique value, according to their differing strategic priorities. Britain found Cyrenaica and Tripolitania useful additions to the Mediterranean strong points dominating the still vital sea route from the Atlantic to Singapore, while the airfields at El Adem near Tobruk and at Castel Benito (later Idris) outside Tripoli became staging posts on the air routes to East Africa, the Indian Ocean and the Far East.

The United States Air Force had taken over the airfield at Mellaha, just east of Tripoli, in 1943, and by the end of the war had reportedly spent $100 million[11] on its development. This first permanent United States air base in Africa marked the extension of American military activity into an area long dominated by Europe. The strategic value of Wheelus Field (renamed after an American officer killed in Iran) increased as the Cold War intensified, and it eventually became one of a series of US bases in southern Europe, Turkey and North Africa countering Soviet expansion into the Mediterranean.

Fezzan, bordering on Tunisia and Algeria, and also on French West and Equatorial Africa, was of prime concern to Paris as a buffer territory protecting the exposed flank of the enormous French African empire from potentially disruptive outside infiltrations and influences.[12] The French administration in Fezzan followed southern Algerian practice: Foreign Legion and *Spahi* units were based in the former Italian forts dominating the larger oases, and officers were responsible for political affairs and administration. The territory was governed with the collaboration of a prominent family, the Saif-al-Nassir, who had been leaders of the Fezzanese resistance to the Italians; although considerable, the family's prestige was not comparable to that of the Sanussi in Cyrenaica. Ahmad Bey Saif-al-Nassir had gone into exile in Chad after the Italian occupation of Fezzan, and he and his followers had returned with the victorious Free French forces in 1943.

The French did much to integrate Fezzan administratively and financially with Algeria, thus isolating it from the rest of Libya. Progressive French policy in economic and social affairs was accompanied by a distinctly repressive view of political activities. These carrot and stick methods gave many Fezzanese an equivocal attitude towards the French administration, but in the long run they did little to consolidate a French position or even a lasting influence in Fezzan comparable to that enjoyed by the British in Cyrenaica.

The military interests of the three main Western powers in Libya — and particularly the French interests in Fezzan — were to be complicating factors in the long post-war debate on the future of a territory still nominally Italian and whose inhabitants, politially, economically and socially, were judged wholly unfit for independence by the relatively critical standards of the time, when self-government in India or elsewhere was still assumed to be 'conditional upon minimal competence'.

While the Second World War lasted, the Libyans, and particularly the Cyrenaicans, had accepted deferment of international decisions on their future. But when the fighting was over, they found the necessary decisions depended on unanimous agreement between the Council of Foreign Ministers of the 'Big Four' (whose meetings came increasingly to reflect the growing rifts between the Soviet Union and the three Western wartime victors), leading eventually to the conclusion of a peace treaty with Italy.

Tripolitania, and to a lesser extent Cyrenaica, in the meantime became cauldrons of rich political activity as diverse groups, influenced by new Arab and foreign ideologies brought home by returning exiles, tried to form their own notions of the country's future. Tripolitania, particularly, has never known such freedom and diversity of politics and press as were allowed under the British Military Administration once the war was over.[13]

Cyrenaica emerged from the war politically stronger than Tripolitania. Sayyid Idris was a convincing leader, genuinely supported by most Cyrenaicans, and respected and recognised by the British authorities. In 1946 the political aspirations of the tribes and the townspeople were given a forum in the Sanussi-dominated National Congress. After the visit of a War Office working party in 1946, the province began to move towards internal self-government. But while the older Cyrenaicans were still thinking in terms of independence for their province alone, the younger generation, with its wider outlook, saw Cyrenaica as part of an independent and united country and a portion of the Arab world. These views found a forum in the Omar Mukhtar Club, whose more moderate Benghazi branch, later renamed the National Association of Cyrenaica, 'came more and more to play the part of a progressive but nevertheless loyal opposition in Cyrenaican politics'.[14]

With its republican experience of 1918–22 Tripolitania was, by contrast, still largely republican in outlook; it was also more bourgeois and progressive than traditionalist, tribal and pro-Sanussi Cyrenaica. But the Tripolitanians were again in danger of becoming, as after the First World War, the leaderless victims of their own factious politics. The province, with a relatively large and distinctly vocal Italian community[15] having rights and aspirations of its own, had no guarantee such as Cyrenaica had been given by the British government that it would not again come under Italian rule — indeed, there were signs of growing international support for the return of some former African possessions to post-Fascist republican Italy.

In the face of the very real possibility of renewed Italian administration, the Tripolitanians were politically weak and leaderless; they were also divided, not only by traditional rifts between families, tribes and communities, country and town, nomad and farmer, but also by conflicting views on the fundamental political issue of Sanussi leadership. There were those who, looking back to the early 1920s, believed that only by accepting Sanussi leadership throughout Libya could Italy be held off and the country united. But to many others, the Sanussi were still anathema, to be opposed at any cost.

By 1947 Tripolitania had at least half a dozen political parties. All advocated Libyan independence, union of the three provinces and membership of the newly formed League of Arab States; the main difference between them was the Sanussi leadership issue. The outstanding political figure was Bashir Bey Sadawi. Libyan-born, he had been associated with the Tripolitanian Republic after the First World War and had later gone into exile, becoming royal adviser in Saudi Arabia. In March 1947 he had established the National Council for the Liberation of Libya in Cairo with Arab League support to promote greater political unity in Tripolitania and closer co-operation between Tripolitania and Cyrenaica. Sadawi was a sincere supporter of Sayyid Idris as the one leader who could unite Libya, and despite many prevarications on other issues, he never abandoned this view.

Another advocate of Sanussi rule over a united Libya was the United National Front, founded in 1946 to oppose an Italian return to Tripolitania. The front's plans were presented to Sayyid Idris in the summer of 1946, but early in 1947 contacts were broken off because the Cyrenaicans were not prepared to jeopardise their chances of independence should the Tripolitanians fail to have their own case for independence recognised, as seemed likely at the time.

The Nationalist Party stood for the complete independence of a united Libya; the Free National Bloc was opposed to Sanussi leadership and was mildly republican in outlook. Financed by Egyptian royalists, the Egyptian–Tripolitania union emerged as a splinter of the Free National Bloc, advocating a union of Egypt and Libya under the Egyptian Crown. Both the Libyan Labour Party and the Liberal Party wanted Sanussi leadership over a united country. In 1948 the Independence (*Istiqlal*) Party was formed as a breakaway from the United National Front. The *Istiqlal* is said to have been financed by Italian interests trying to convince Tripolitania notables of the advantages of the restoration of some form of Italian administration over Tripolitania, thereby also indirectly serving the interests of France in Fezzan; the British authorities eventually put a stop to this activity.[16] Divisions within the Italian community were reflected, on the one hand, by the neo-Fascist Italian Representative Committee which advocated Italian trusteeship for Tripolitania and, on the other, by the left-wing Association for the Progress of Libya, led by the Marxist Dr Enrico Cibelli with a programme of Libyan independence. Complete independence was also the goal of the Popular Democratic Front, supported mainly by Italian labourers and artisans. Although some parties claimed thousands of members, or even the support of the majority of Tripolitanians, membership of most groups in reality amounted to hundreds, if not dozens, and most Tripolitanians neither understood the issues nor cared much about them, and never became involved in party politics.

But while there was discord within Libya, there was more in the world outside; and, paradoxically, the country was put on the road to independence because the many foreign powers with an interest in its future were unable to agree what that future was to be: thus, after many years of wrangling, it remained to a supra-national body, the UN, to take the necessary decisions.

At the end of the war, Italy still held legal sovereignty over Libya, Somalia and Eritrea.[17] Their future had been considered at the Potsdam Conference in 1945 and at the meeting of the Council of Foreign Ministers of Britain, France, the United States and the Soviet Union in London in September that year. Because of disagreement, a settlement was postponed until the council's next session in Paris in the summer of 1946, when it was agreed that a decision would be taken within one year of the peace treaty with Italy coming into effect on 15 September 1947. Under this treaty (signed on 15 February 1947), Italy renounced her rights and claims to Libya

Eritrea and Somalia. But the territories were to remain in their existing state until their future had been decided, a decision that provoked outbreaks of anger and political activity among Libyans and Italians in Libya, who up to then had been the least consulted of all the interested parties.

When the peace treaty with Italy was signed, the Council of Foreign Ministers agreed to send missions 'to ascertain the views of the local populations' in the Italian colonies before a final decision on their future was taken. A Four-Power Commission accordingly arrived in Libya early in 1948. Despite the prevailing political disharmony, it found a surprisingly unanimous desire in Tripolitania for national unity, independence and Arab League membership. In Cyrenaica, all organised political activity had been channelled since the beginning of the year through a single political party, the National Congress, which was able to impress on the commission the apparently unanimous desire for independence and Sanussi government. The Cyrenaican view of union with Tripolitania, as expressed to the commission, was that it would be acceptable only under Sanussi rule. In Fezzan, 44 per cent of those interviewed were in favour of continued French administration — a reflection, perhaps, of progressive French economic and social policies. The commission's report, which was considered at the Four-Power conference of deputy Foreign Ministers in London in the summer of 1948, put on record the almost unanimous Libyan desire for full independence, but considered that the country was politically, economically and socially unprepared for it.

The international debate on Libya's future, spread over several years, threw up differing proposals for independence and trusteeship by combinations of various potential administering powers; proposals in due course tended to be modified in response to the shifting patterns of post-war international tensions and alliances. Britain's attitude was consistently governed by the wartime pledge that Cyrenaica would never again come under Italian rule, and by the need to keep bases in Cyrenaica, at least, to consolidate the British position in the Mediterranean and the Near East. Both the United States and the Soviet Union took an apparently disinterested stand (apart from the occasion when the Soviet Union proposed Soviet trusteeship for Tripolitania), but their various proposals for Libya's future were inevitably influenced by the development of the Cold War, the breakdown of East–West co-operation, and the need for both Moscow and Washington to gain the goodwill of post-war

Italy, a potential member of the Western alliance yet one having the largest Communist Party in Western Europe.

France was probably the least disinterested of all the 'interested' powers. The French were most reluctant to withdraw garrisons from Fezzan, and were concerned about the example an independent Libya would set to the more 'advanced' French possessions in North Africa, where there had been recent outbreaks of strong nationalist activity. A French-occupied Fezzan, besides providing necessary staging posts in those days of short-haul aircraft on the air routes to Chad and other French African territories, shielded Algeria and Tunisia, as well as parts of French West and Equatorial Africa, from the most direct Egyptian and Asian nationalist influences. Thus French trusteeship over Fezzan was, to Paris, a highly desirable goal.

After the war, Italy made a strong case for the return of African colonies acquired before the advent of Fascism. Although Italian sovereignty over these territories was renounced under the 1947 peace treaty, this did not exclude the possibility of Italian trusteeship in any of them, and a considerable body of international opinion, particularly in Latin America, favoured this solution.

But since, in three years of debate, no single proposal had gained the necessary unanimous approval of the Big Four Foreign Ministers, and there was clearly a stalemate, the matter was referred to the General Assembly of the United Nations in September 1948 in accordance with one of the more far-sighted provisions of the Italian peace treaty. The chances of finding a solution appeared better in the larger UN forum, which needed only a two-thirds majority decision rather than unanimity, where voting was on the basis of equality, and where no member had a veto; there was also more opportunity for compromise, lobbying and the public airing of views.

Before the General Assembly debate got under way, Britain and Italy tried once more to settle Libya's future between them. The plan drawn up by the British Foreign Secretary, Ernest Bevin, and the Italian Foreign Minister, Count Carlo Sforza, and published on 10 May 1949, proposed the granting of trusteeships to Britain in Cyrenaica, to Italy in Tripolitania and to France in Fezzan; Libya was to become independent after ten years, if the United Nations General Assembly approved. The so-called Bevin–Sforza plan actually infringed the Italian peace treaty terms, which had already consigned the issue to the General Assembly for settlement.[18] It was intended to satisfy British, Italian and French interests in particular, and American and Western interests in general. Although opposed by the Soviet and Arab blocs, the plan nevertheless had wide support, particularly among the Latin American states which at that time represented about one-third of the total UN membership of 58 nations. It seemed the only arrangement likely to win the two-thirds majority necessary for adoption in the General Assembly, and a resolution based on the plan just gained a majority vote in the First Committee (Political).

But meanwhile, strikes and demonstrations in Tripoli and elsewhere, which generated wide public sympathy for the Libyan case, notably in the Arab world, left no doubt as to popular opposition to the plan, and above all to the Italian trusteeship proposal. It was in organising these protests that several Tripolitanian political groups merged as the Tripolitanian National Congress Party under the leadership of Bashir Bey Sadawi. While the Bevin–Sforza plan could be interpreted as a foreign device to keep Libya divided, it also reflected the failure of the Tripolitanians and the Cyrenaicans to agree on unity, as they had failed to do after the First World War and were still failing to do in 1948–9 after ten more years of debate. Italy's departure had left a power vacuum that Britain and France had naturally filled for want of any Libyan or foreign alternative.

A resolution based on the Bevin–Sforza plan was expected to scrape through the third session of the General Assembly in the spring of 1949 on the slimmest of majorities. Members of the Libyan and other Arab delegations did much lobbying and the Libyans persuaded the delegate of Haiti, Emile Saint Lot, that the plan would delay, and might even prevent, Libyan independence. When the General Assembly voted on the plan on 18 May 1949 Haiti, having abstained at the committee stage, voted against the clause recommending Italian trusteeship over Tripolitania, which was thus one vote short of the necessary majority for adoption. With the failure of the Italian trusteeship vote, the Latin Americans had no further reason to support the remainder of the resolution, and they actually voted against it, causing its heavy defeat. Further consideration of the question was then postponed to the General Assembly's fourth session in the autumn.

In the second half of 1949, British, American and other Western thinking on the Libyan question moved rapidly from trusteeship to independence. Within two weeks of the vote, Britain released plans for Cyrenaican self-government under Amir Idris. The announcement followed consultations with various Western and Commonwealth governments, but not with the United Nations. On

16 September the Cyrenaican government duly became responsible for most internal affairs; foreign affairs, defence and military bases remained under British control.

Although the British government announced that 'in taking these steps . . . nothing will be done to prejudice the eventual future of Libya as a whole', the fact remained that much had already been done. For in transferring internal power to Amir Idris in the summer of 1949 while the future of Libya was still before the United Nations, Britain, in effect, unilaterally decreed that if there was to be an independent Libyan state at all — and later that year the General Assembly decided that there was — it would take only the form that Idris, Britain and Britain's Western allies wanted: a federal monarchy under the Sanussi crown. And since Cyrenaica had already achieved self-rule, the case for similar autonomous but nationally divisive arrangements for Tripolitania and Fezzan became that much stronger.

Thus in February 1950, barely three months after the United Nations vote for Libyan independence, the French set up a transitional regime in Fezzan with an elected Representative Assembly of 58 members who in turn elected Ahmad Bey Saif-al-Nassir as *Chef du Territoire*. As chief executive, he gave three councillors responsibility for internal affairs. The French Military Governor continued to look after foreign affairs, defence, air traffic control (Fezzan was an important staging post) and minerals prospecting (the search for oil in the neighbouring Algerian Sahara had started in 1947). Although the French moves did not go so far as the British arrangements in Cyrenaica, they also served to pre-determine the form of the Libyan state well before the Libyans themselves were able to make their views publicly and officially known.

Various motives suggest themselves for the swift change in Western attitudes to Libya's future after the rejection of the Bevin-Sforza plan. The British, the United States and the Italian governments had plainly concluded that their interests would be served better by an independent state rather than by one administered under United Nations trusteeship. It is not clear what part the future security of military bases played in this change of view, but had the country passed under any form of UN trusteeship, the administering powers would have been unable to establish new bases and would have had to give up existing ones. But 'as an independent entity, Libya could freely enter into treaties or agreements with the Western powers looking toward the defense of the Mediterranean and North

Africa. This is exactly what the Soviet Union feared and Libya did.'[19] The British government may well have concluded that trusteeships on the Bevin–Sforza model would mainly benefit France and offer little advantage to Britain (especially if Britain's position could be secured in an independent Cyrenaica) because they would have opened the way for a Franco-Italian alliance in western Libya with the prime purpose of protecting French interests elsewhere in North Africa. It has even been suggested that popular demonstrations in Tripoli against the Bevin–Sforza plan were organised by the British; certainly the British administration did not ban them, and the National Congress Party and Sadawi himself received encouragement and material backing from the British administration up to mid-1950.[20] Italy also refused to help the French: the government in Rome was persuaded of the advantages of complete Libyan independence; Count Sforza adopted a generous policy in support of this view; and, perhaps by way of compensation for her co-operation, Italy gained a ten-year trusteeship over Somalia.

France was truly disappointed by the defeat of the Bevin–Sforza plan and was, as ever, dismayed by the prospect of Libyan independence, which by late 1949 was gaining wide international favour. But other Western powers believed that support for Libyan independence would be an act of goodwill towards emerging Asian, African and Latin American nationalism in general, and Arab nationalism in particular, for trusteeship inevitably smacked of colonialism. It has even been suggested[21] that Western, and notably American, support for Libyan independence was a means of allaying some of the Arab hostility generated by the Western attitude to the Zionist cause in Palestine.

When the fourth session of the General Assembly opened in September 1949, independence was generally considered to be the only solution for Libya likely to gain the two-thirds majority vote necessary for adoption. In drafting the appropriate resolution, the main issues to be settled by the First Committee were the means and timing of Libyan unity and independence, and here there were wide divergences of opinion. The Soviet Union, abandoning its previous notions of collective trusteeship for all Libya, proposed the country's immediate independence, the withdrawal of all foreign forces and liquidation of all foreign bases within three months. Britain, anxious to be relieved of the costly and thankless tasks of administering Tripolitania and Cyrenaica, favoured immediate independence, but the United States and Pakistan wanted it

postponed for three years, with continuation of the existing adminis
trations. Italy, although not a UN member, took part in the discus
sions, and representatives of the Cyrenaican National Congress, the
Tripolitanian National Congress Party and the *Istiqlal* Party, as wel
as the Tripolitanian Jewish community, were also heard.

In October a subcommittee started compiling a resolution reflect
ing drafts and suggestions made by the delegations of Iraq, Pakis
tan, India and the United States; Britain and France had made i
clear during committee debates that they did not intend to promote a
united Libya. 'Their aim apparently was to encourage the creation o
three separate states (Tripolitania, Cyrenaica and Fezzan) which
might subsequently, if they could, form a union among themselves'
wrote the future UN commissioner in Libya.[22] Although British
amendments which would have had the effect of dividing the
country into three zones of influence were dropped, the draft resolu
tion that was adopted by the First Committee on 12 November 1949
made only passing reference to Libyan unity. Its main provision
were:[23]

1. That Libya, comprising Tripolitania, Cyrenaica and the
    Fezzan, shall be constituted an independent and sovereign
    state;
2. That this independence shall become effective as soon a
    possible, and in any case not later than 1 January 1952;
3. That a constitution for Libya, including the form of the
    government, shall be determined by representatives of the
    inhabitants of Cyrenaica, Tripolitania and the Fezzan meet
    ing and consulting together in a National Assembly;
4. That, for the purpose of assisting the people of Libya in the
    formulation of the constitution and the establishment of ar
    independent Government, there shall be a United Nation
    Commissioner in Libya appointed by the General Assembly
    and a Council to aid and advise him.

Seven further paragraphs covered the future duties and respon
sibilities of the administering powers in the three territories, the
procedure to be followed in implementing the General Assembly
resolution, and membership of the Commissioner's council. It wa
finally recommended that upon establishment as an independen
state, Libya was to be admitted to the United Nations.

It was on 21 November 1949 that the General Assembly, with a vote of 48 to one (Ethiopia) and nine abstentions (including France and five Soviet bloc countries) adopted the resolution on Libyan independence. Two weeks later the General Assembly appointed the UN Assistant Secretary-General, Dr Adrian Pelt of the Netherlands, as UN Commissioner in Libya — but not before he had put aside his own 'serious misgivings' about his suitability for the job.

Notes

1. The Libyans, in common with the Ethiopians, the Eritreans and some of the Somalis, are the only ex-colonial peoples who were actually ruled by a Fascist colonial regime that so many other ex-colonial subjects claim to have experienced.

2. A. Moorehead, *African Trilogy* (London, 1944), p. 242.

3. V. Peniakoff, *Popski's Private Army* (London, 1950), p. 26.

4. *Ibid.*, pp. 32–43.

5. W.B. Kennedy Shaw, *Long Range Desert Group. The Story of its Work in Libya, 1940–1943* (London, 1945), p. 150.

6. House of Commons Official Report, Parliamentary Debates (*Hansard*) (London), vol. 377, cols. 77–8 (8 January 1942).

7. M. Khadduri, *Modern Libya. A Study in Political Development* (Baltimore, 1963), pp. 36–7.

8. Quoted in Lord Rennell of Rodd, *British Military Administration of Occupied Territories during the Years 1941–47* (London, 1948), p. 249.

9. British Military Administration, *Handbook on Tripolitania* (Tripoli, 1947), p. 44.

10. *Ibid.*, p. 33.

11. *New York Times*, 13 February 1945.

12. A. Pelt, *Libyan Independence and the United Nations* (New Haven, 1970), pp. 56–7; N.A. Arsharuni, *Inostranniy Kapital v Livii (1911–1967)* (Moscow, 1970), pp. 40–1.

13. C. Souriau-Hoebrechts, *La Presse Maghrébine* (Paris, 1969), pp. 48–9; CRESM, *La Formation des Élites Politiques Maghrébines* (Paris, 1973), p. 128.

14. Pelt, *Libyan Independence*, p. 44.

15. The Italian community in Tripolitania totalled 40,536 in 1946, or some 5 per cent of the total Libyan population of 803,915. BMA *Handbook on Tripolitania*, Appendix I, p. 77.

16. G. Assan, *La Libia e il Mondo Arabo* (Rome, 1959), p. 17. As he points out, a party with such a policy was strangely named.

17. Ethiopia, occupied by Italy during 1936–41, had again been internationally recognised as an independent sovereign state.

18. Pelt, *Libyan Independence*, p. 79.

19. H.S. Villard, *Libya. The New Arab Kingdom of North Africa* (Ithaca, 1956), p. 33–4.

20. Pelt, *Libyan Independence*, p. 438, n. 9.

21. Assan, *La Libia*, p. 18.

22. Pelt, *Libyan Independence*, p. 100.

23. Resolution 289 (IV); *Question of the Disposal of Former Italian Colonies.*

4 TOWARDS INDEPENDENCE

When the United Nations Commissioner arrived in Tripoli in January 1950 for a three-week exploratory visit, he tried to make it clear that his task was to 'assist the people of Libya in the formulation of their constitution and in the establishment of an independent government'. In a not wholly successful attempt to correct a popular misconception, he stressed, 'It is not my function to govern your territory; that remains within the competence of the administering powers until you assume it yourselves.'

One of Commissioner Pelt's first tasks was to complete the membership of the ten-member Council for Libya, envisaged in the General Assembly resolution, that was to 'aid and advise' him. The representatives of Egypt, France, Italy, Pakistan, the United Kingdom and the United States to this popularly named 'Council of Ten' had already been appointed by their respective governments. Pelt asked for one agreed candidate for each of the three Libyan provincial seats, and the one seat of the combined Italian, Jewish, Maltese and Greek communities of Tripolitania.[1]

Fezzan named one candidate, Haj Ahmad al-Sanussi Sofu, the *Qaid* of Murzuk. Amir Idris proposed eight possible Cyrenaican representatives, from which Pelt chose the Cyrenaican Minister of Public Works and Communications, Ali Assad al-Jirbi. The Tripolitanian political parties had proposed seven different names. But among them Mustafa Mizran, one of the vice-presidents of the National Congress Party, 'enjoyed so much support' that Pelt found it fairly easy to choose him. Giacomo Marchino, the Italian vice-president of the Savings Bank of Libya, was appointed to represent the Tripolitanian minorities.

As established on 5 April 1950, the Council for Libya thus had a distinctly 'Western' bias. It had one representative of each of the three main Western powers (Britain, France and the United States) as well as two Italian representatives (one of the Italian government and one of the Tripolitanian minorities), while two of the Libyan members, the representatives of Cyrenaica and Fezzan, were 'acceptable' to the respective administering powers. Only the representatives of Tripolitania, Mustafa Mizran, although originally th preferred candidate of the British administration, once appointed 'turned out to be anything but a mouthpiece for British views'.[2] As Pelt also remarks, 'Although he kept his feelings within politically acceptable bounds, his suspicion of British and French policy was profound.' With the representatives of Egypt and Pakistan, Mizran came to form a minority anti-Western group on the council.[3]

It was now that the awful practical difficulties of bringing three disparate provinces into an independent state began to emerge from the day-to-day realities of constitution-making. Cyrenaica had the supreme advantage of the acknowledged leadership of Sayyid Idris, a fair degree of regional autonomy, and broadly unanimous, if somewhat coerced, public opinion. But it was also politically, economically and socially underdeveloped, much damaged by war, and it had less than one-third of the total population.

The 50,000 Fezzanese carried little weight, but because they feared a repetition of the Tripolitanian domination they had suffered under the republic at the end of the First World War, they were prepared to support the Cyrenaicans on most issues. Foremost was the establishment of a kingdom under the Sanussi crown, with the provinces joined in equal status in a federation; such, indeed, was the only form of state Amir Idris was prepared to rule. For the Cyrenaicans and the Fezzanese, as well as the two administering powers, feared that in a unitary state the traditional and close-knit interests of the two provinces would be overwhelmed by the more numerous Tripolitanians with their more 'advanced' and disruptive political outlook and their generally republican, pan-Libyan and pan-Arab politics. It was felt that federation, by contrast, would safeguard the integrity and individuality of both Cyrenaica and Fezzan and, so long as the Cyrenaicans approved of them, guarantee Britain's right to maintain bases in that province; similarly, a federal system seemed to offer France a better chance of keeping bases and influence in Fezzan.

Tripolitania, with two-thirds of the population, was richer and more developed than the other provinces but suffered, as always, from lack of leadership and political cohesion. Unlike Cyrenaica and Fezzan, Tripolitania also had relatively large and active foreign and religious minorities with rights and aspirations of their own. The majority of Tripolitanians seemed to favour a unitary state. Moderates criticised federation for its added administrative complications and expense; others denounced it as a plot by Britain and France to maintain their influence in Cyrenaica and Fezzan.

Despite their larger population, the Tripolitanians still found themselves in a minority on the Preparatory Committee of 21 members set up in July 1950 to recommend the election, and the composition, of the Libyan National Assembly, and to draft the Constitution. Commissioner Pelt had originally suggested an entirely Libyan committee, with members from each of the three provinces chosen by local assemblies elected in Tripolitania and Cyrenaica at mid-year; the Fezzanese representatives were to have been named by the *jemaa*, the assembly modelled on the traditional gathering of notables or their representatives, which had been set up by the French at the beginning of 1950.

Although the Cyrenaican elections took place in June, those planned for Tripolitania were never held — apparently because of opposition to participation by the Italian and other minorities (although they could all claim to be 'inhabitants' of Tripolitania mentioned in the General Assembly resolution) and because of concern about possible interference in the voting by the British administration. But the British had not tried to influence the June elections in Cyrenaica, although the Cyrenaican administration itself took steps to ensure that opposition groups active mainly in Benghazi and Derna were excluded from the provincial assembly; the Omar Mukhtar Club was dissolved and some of its members imprisoned.[4] Commissioner Pelt expressed the belief that

> the Tripolitanian parties, especially the National Congress Party feared that the elections might well deteriorate into an embarrassing demonstration of the political disunity and personal rivalries that unfortunately played such a large part on the Tripolitanian scene. There was also a risk that the elections would show up the gross exaggerations in which the members of all parties without exception had indulged to bolster their prestige and make propaganda for their cause.[5]

Thus by the middle of June a formula for selection rather than election of a preparatory committee of 21 members was accepted by a majority of the advisory council. The Amir was asked to propose the names of seven Cyrenaican representatives, while the *Chef du Territoire* of Fezzan was to name seven Fezzanese. After consultations with Tripolitanian political leaders, Pelt was to propose the names of seven 'outstanding personalities' to represent Tripolitania. But before the committee could be formed, Cyrenaica and Fezzanese opposition to the representation of the Tripolitanian minorities had to be met with a promise that settlement of the legal status of the Italians after independence would not be prejudiced by their representation on the committee. There was no difficulty in accepting the named representatives of Cyrenaica and Fezzan, but for Tripolitania, twelve parties and organisations submitted a total of 65 candidates, and 50 names were in addition proposed by leading personalities and notables. After lengthy consultations, Pelt's choice of seven Tripolitanian representatives — six of them members of the National Congress Party or its affiliates — was approved by a majority of the advisory council.

The Preparatory Committee (or 'Committee of Twenty One'), the first all-Libyan institution in the country's modern history, met on 27 July 1950 under the chairmanship of the Mufti of Tripoli, with the Tripolitanian minorities represented by an Italian. Within ten days it had adopted a Cyrenaican proposal for a National Assembly of 60 deputies, 20 from each of the three provinces, although the Tripolitanians had insisted that a truly democratic body would be based on proportional representation. This first decision effectively predetermined the form of the future Libyan state.[6] The issue of the election or selection of the National Assembly took longer to resolve, largely because the committee's Fezzanese members were being subjected to the delaying tactics of the French, who were becoming increasingly concerned about the example Libyan independence might have in all French Africa north of the Equator. Thus, while the Fezzanese representatives stood out in favour of election, the Tripolitanians and Cyrenaicans wanted nomination; they argued that elections would need too much preparation and might be 'influenced' by the administering powers. It was not until October that the Fezzanese, after the intervention of the Amir and an unexplained change of attitude in Paris, were persuaded to agree to nomination 'on condition that the chief political parties of Tripolitania, as also that section of the population which did not belong to any political party, were represented in the Assembly'.[7] At the same meeting, it was agreed that non-Libyan minorities would not take part, nor be represented, in the National Assembly. But the committee also put on record that: 'There is genuine intention and general feeling that all civil, religious and social rights of all minorities and foreigners should be fully safeguarded in the future constitution of Libya.'[8] Intentions and feelings were, however, to change profoundly in the years to come.

The committee then decided that Amir Idris was to select the Cyrenaican representatives on the National Assembly, and the Fezzanese *Chef du Territoire* those of Fezzan; these nominees were in due course accepted without comment. As for Tripolitania, it was agreed that the chairman of the committee, the Mufti of Tripoli, was to name 20 representatives after holding 'the necessary conversations and consultations'.

Nominations duly presented to the committee by the Mufti at the end of October comprised nine members of the National Congress Party of Tripolitania, or its affiliated parties, five members of the *Istiqlal* Party, and six independents. Although the committee approved the list as it stood by 16 votes, one Tripolitanian member voted against it, one abstained, another Tripolitanian member and the representative of the Tripolitanian minorities were absent, as was one Cyrenaican member. The Mufti's nominees thus had been approved by only three of the committee's seven Tripolitanian members, and when the fact became known, it aroused public protests and demonstrations. Although the committee completed its work at the end of November in an atmosphere of mutual congratulation, the selection of the Tripolitanians became a matter of sharp but ineffectual debate among members of the advisory council some months later. The Egyptian representative, Kamil Salim, asserted that Tripolitanians representing two-thirds of the national population had, in effect, been selected by the other third. Khalidi believes that 'the decision of the committee represented a series of compromises on the part of all concerned . . . But the committee's decision was a significant defeat for the advocates of a unitary state and it paved the way for the setting up of a federal form of government.' This was precisely why the committee's work aroused such hostile criticism within Libya and abroad.

Externally, the main forum of criticism was the United Nations General Assembly and the *ad hoc* political committee which in October 1950 had before them Commissioner Pelt's *First Annual Report* on Libya's constitutional progress. The most hostile critics were the Arab and other Asian delegates, and notably those of Egypt and Pakistan who applied to the proposed arrangements for Libya those already greatly overworked terms 'undemocratic' and 'unconstitutional'; they also criticised the trend towards the establishment of a federal state. Invited to address the General Assembly Commissioner Pelt said the National Assembly had been appointed and not elected very much against his own advice; the equality of representation between the provinces had been a matter of 'unavoidable political expediency'; he also expressed 'grave doubts' as to whether an appointed rather than an elected National Assembly 'would have the necessary moral and political authority to elaborate a final and definitive constitution for Libya'. But when the Egyptian delegate urged that the National Assembly be made an elected body, Pelt pointed out that there was no time for elections if Libya was to become independent by the end of 1951. One of Pelt's constant difficulties during his mission was to reconcile the demands of the tight timetable of the 1949 UN resolution on independence and the need to follow sound democratic principles in the constitution-making process. But there is no doubt that if the Egyptian proposal had been adopted, nearly a year of constitutional work would have been undone.

On 17 November 1950 the UN General Assembly adopted a resolution reaffirming the 1949 resolution on independence and calling on the authorities concerned to take all the necessary steps to ensure the early, full and effective implementation of that resolution 'and particularly the realisation of Libyan unity'. The new resolution recommended the National Assembly to set up a provisional government by 1 April 1951, while the administering powers were to transfer powers progressively to the provisional government before 1 January 1952. The resolution, in effect, set the United Nations seal of approval on the constitutional progress made to date by Pelt, his advisory council and the Committee of Twenty One; it recognised the National Assembly as a lawful body and it quietened international criticism of the Committee of Twenty One and its actions.

But it did not quieten Tripolitanian critics and their Egyptian sympathisers. First among the critics was Bashir Bey Sadawi, whom Commissioner Pelt acknowledges to have been 'a well-intentioned man with much political acumen and the vision, though not always the strength of character, of a statesman'.[10] As a fervent and long-standing advocate of a united Libya, and of proportional representation in an elected National Assembly, he was supported by the League of Arab States and its first Secretary General, Abd-al-Rahman Azzam, who 30 years before had been political adviser to the Tripolitanian Republic. Sadawi also had the support of the Egyptian representative on the advisory council, while the Pakistani member had formed 'a close personal friendship' with him.[11] Although Sadawi apparently had wide support in Tripoli and along the Tripolitanian coastal strip, where his views carried considerable weight, a contemporary observer of the Tripolitanian political scene has suggested that 'besides his Egyptian legal adviser, who follows him like a (substantial) shadow wherever he goes, Bashir Bey has too many other connections with Egypt, where he spends most of his time, and is inclined to be too autocratic for his popularity to be enduring, even with his own people'.[12]

Yet, paradoxically, Sadawi recognised Amir Idris as the future head of state, knowing full well that the Amir was committed to a federal policy. Sadawi's failure to reach a proper understanding with the Amir on such basic issues in 1950 was to lead to his downfall, the disappearance of his party, and the absence of a recognised and effective opposition in independent Libya.

Empowered to decide the structure and constitution of the new state, the National Assembly held its first meeting in Tripoli on 25 November 1950. As Khalidi says: 'To some this represented the first concrete step towards federalism; moreover, it dealt a serious blow to the hopes and aspirations of the advocates of a unitary state in Libya.'[13] Nevertheless, it now seems reasonable to assume that even if the National Assembly had been elected, it would have been unable to choose any other form of state than the one that emerged, for that decision had already been taken by Idris and his Western supporters.

Before starting its main task of drafting the Constitution, the Assembly agreed unanimously on 2 December (but only after some Tripolitanian objections) that Libya was to be established as a democratic, federal and sovereign state, the form of government being a constitutional monarchy with Amir Idris king-designate of the United Kingdom of Libya.

News of the Assembly's decision on federation generated strong protests in Tripoli, organised by the National Congress and possibly backed by malcontents who had not yet found a seat in the National Assembly. Commissioner Pelt, on his return from the UN General Assembly in New York, found his desk in Tripoli 'piled high' with petitions of protest, most of them from Tripolitanian coastal towns. On 19 December National Congress supporters demonstrated in front of the Islamic Arts and Crafts School in the centre of Tripoli where the National Assembly was meeting. Although the demonstrators shouted their loyalty to the king-designate, they denounced federalism as a colonialist 'divide-and-rule' plot. The demonstrators were dispersed by British military police and the Tripoli newspaper *Al-Mirsad*, which had criticised federation, was suppressed.[14]

Opposition to the National Assembly was much discredited by the publication in January 1951 of a document in which Bashir Bey Sadawi's special adviser had endorsed the National Assembly decision of 2 December on the establishment of Libya as a federal state under the rule of King Idris. According to Khalidi, 'It called upon the king-designate to assume all constitutional powers and to establish three separate local administrations in Libya, on the understanding that the leader of the majority in Tripolitania (presumably Bashir Bey) would be called on to form the Tripolitanian government.'[15] Pelt says that an explanation current at the time of the 'self-contradictory fluctuations' in Sadawi's tactics was that

> having been convinced for a long time of the need for reaching a basic agreement with the Cyrenaicans and their leaders, he had followed their federal ideas hook, line and sinker, confident that once firmly in the saddle as Prime Minister of Tripolitania, he would be able to impose a more highly centralised form of state.[16]

The National Assembly had also been criticised by the Secretary-General of the Arab League who, in an interview with *Il Tempo* of Rome on 5 January 1951, described the creation of the Assembly and its decisions as illegal and contrary to the wishes of the Libyan people and the United Nations resolution. To counter this and other adverse comment in the Arab press and on the radio, the National Assembly sent a mission to Cairo in late January to reassure the Arab League of the Assembly's competence and of the need for a federal system of government. The Council of the Arab League finally decided to leave the matter to Egypt, since it was a member of Pelt's advisory council, and the Egyptian representative accordingly continued to attack the National Assembly as illegal, as well as the federal principle, and he even tried to withdraw from the council on the grounds that 'imperialist powers were now in control of it'.

In the meantime, the National Assembly had set up a six-member Working Group to draft each section of the Constitution, as well as an eighteen-member Committee on the Constitution to appraise, analyse and approve each draft before submitting chapters to the Assembly for adoption after three readings. The Working Group made full use of the constitutions of other federal and unitary states, as well as the Universal Declaration of Human Rigths, in arriving at a workable compromise between the decentralisation implicit in a federal form of government and the centralisation necessary to enable the federal government to exercise such powers as foreign policy and defence.

Few changes were made as the completed chapters were passed up to the Committee on the Constitution, and the entire draft was presented to the National Assembly in September 1951. At the end of the month the Assembly went to Benghazi, 'far removed from the foreign interferences and pressures that were inevitable in Tripoli'.

The deepest of several disagreements between the deputies was the choice of national capital. The Tripolitanians and Fezzanese jointly proposed Tripoli, while the Cyrenaicans would only accept Benghazi. Tripoli was the obvious choice, for Benghazi was so isolated and war-damaged (it had suffered over a thousand air raids) that it was considered quite unsuitable to house a government. But the Cyrenaicans feared that unless their city was named as capital and seat of government it would never be rebuilt. Agreement was finally reached on a compromise proposal by the king-designate, naming Tripoli and Benghazi as joint capitals, with the seat of government alternating year by year (later every two years); it was an arrangement that was to cause much inconvenience, expense and government inefficiency in the years to come. But once the capital had been chosen, other outstanding issues were quickly resolved.

At the very end of the constitutional debate, the king let it be known that he had waived his exclusive right to declare war and conclude peace and to enter into treaties, preferring to entrust these powers to parliament. The amendment was enthusiastically received, not only as a sign of the king's apparent democratic outlook, but because it also meant that the future status of foreign military bases would not be determined by the king alone, but by the collective decision of parliament. The king's initiative, says Pelt 'was an act of the highest political foresight and wisdom'.[17] This move, according to Khalidi, 'annulled the Cyrenaicans' efforts to make the royal personage a powerful monarch and proved to his opponents that the king was in fact a democrat and an astute politician, as well as a parliamentarian'.[18]

The full Constitution of 213 articles was approved by the National Assembly on 7 October. Drawn up before Libya existed as an independent state, the Constitution was a set of rules and ideals for the government to follow rather than the reflection of any existing practice. Although based on American and other models, the Constitution had in practice to be adopted to the everyday workings of what was still very largely a traditional tribal society and one, moreover, with no experience of self-government.

The Constitution declared the United Kingdom of Libya (*Al-Mamlakah al-Libiyyah al-Mutahhidah*) a hereditary monarchy; its form was federal and its system of government representative. Tripolitania, Cyrenaica and Fezzan were 'provinces' of the kingdom, the word 'province' being chosen in preference to 'state' to emphasise national unity. The parliament, consisting of a House of Representatives and a Senate, could initiate legislation, as could the king. The Senate had 24 members, eight from each province, half appointed by the king and half elected by the provincial Legislative Councils. Members of the House of Representatives were elected by adult male suffrage at a ratio of one deputy to every 20,000 inhabitants. This gave Tripolitania 35 and Cyrenaica 15 deputies; the 60,000 Fezzanese were allowed five. The king had the power to veto legislation and to dissolve the elected parliament at his own discretion. A federal government of ministers was selected from the parliament; the federal government was answerable to parliament, and its exclusive responsibilities included foreign affairs, defence and currency matters.

The king appointed the Prime Minister and the provincial governors. Three-quarters of the members of the Tripolitanian and Cyrenaican Legislative Councils were elected by the people and the rest appointed by the respective provincial governors; all members of the Fezzanese council were elected. Each province had an elected council of eight *Nazirs* holding Agriculture, Communications, Education, Finance, Health, Internal Affairs, Justice and Public Works portfolios. A Supreme Court was set up to settle disputes between the federal and provincial administrations, or between provinces, and to act as the highest appeal court; its judges were appointed by the king. The Constitution also provided guarantees for foreign minorities, as well as a wide range of theoretical civil liberties, based on Western codes, and some fairly progressive clauses concerned marriage, labour, standards of living, freedom of language and free compulsory education; practice in the first impoverished years of independence was inevitably to fall far short of the constitutional ideal.

At the beginning of November the National Assembly debated and approved the draft Electoral Law. The Assembly remained in session until independence, but did no further business.

Planning the transfer of powers from the British and French administrations to the future Libyan federal and provincial governments started early in 1951. On 8 February a Co-ordination Committee met in Tripoli under the supervision of Commissioner Pelt to consider the transfer initially of administrative and financial powers.

Cyrenaica had exercised internal autonomy since the middle of 1949, and in June 1951 local Assembly elections were held; steps had already been taken to ensure exclusion of opposition groups from election. In February 1951 the National Assembly passed a resolution establishing local governments in Tripolitania and Fezzan to receive powers transferred by the administering authorities. And in March a provisional federal government was set up by the National Assembly to receive relevant transferred powers. The transfer of powers to the federal and provincial governments started in October, and by mid-December nearly all had been handed over, except those relating to foreign affairs and defence. Final powers giving Libya 'the attributes of sovereignty' were not transferred until Independence Day. The Prime Minister of the provisional federal government was Mahmud Muntasser, a member of a distinguished Tripolitanian family, Italian-educated and a protégé of the British.

By early 1951 it had become clear to Commissioner Pelt that both Britain and France were eager to grant increasing powers to local government in the territories under their administration. For both powers, says Pelt, 'the ultimate purpose was plainly to weaken the future federation by strengthening the position of the provinces'.[19] He accordingly lodged official complaints with the British authorities in Tripoli and with the French in Sebha. The National Congress Party in Tripolitania felt even more strongly about these developments and it had, unwisely, been given no representation either in the provincial government or in the Tripolitanian administration. The party made its views known in street demonstrations, and by early 1951 the political climate in Tripolitania was threatening.

The storm broke during the first official visit of the king-designate to Tripoli in May 1951. On the eve of the visit, members of the Congress Party were 'taken out of circulation' — exiled into the interior, placed under house arrest or imprisoned. According to the opposition, over 800 people were detained; according to the Tripolitanian administration, the total was 105. These measures did not prevent angry demonstrations during the formal entry of the king designate into Tripoli, when crowds protested against the Tripolitanian administration and called for a united Libya. Five hand grenades were thrown; only two of them exploded, one of them i

front of the royal car as it drove, escorted by a cavalcade of tribesmen, through the centre of Tripoli. Policemen and some of the
crowd were slightly injured. There were a few arrests, but no charges
of bomb-throwing. The Congress Party denied responsibility, and
the incident was seen 'more as a show of disaffection than as a
serious attempt at assassination'. Although the attack marred the
formal entry of the king-designate into his premier city, it also seems
to have turned general apathy into considerable popularity for Idris
himself. But during the summer of 1951, the Congress Party continued to charge the National Assembly with incompetence, and
Sadawi went so far as to state that the whole question of Libyan independence should be reconsidered by the United Nations General
Assembly so that there could be a fresh decision reflecting the wishes
of the people.

Throughout his mission, Pelt was very much aware of the country's
economic and social difficulties. He believed that the United Nations
had a special duty to help the Libyans 'in establishing sound
administrative services fitted to the needs and resources of the country, and in promoting a viable economy that the state might endure'.

Libya, Pelt noted in his *First Annual Report*, was 'an underdeveloped area with a marginal agricultural economy, basically handi-
capped by inadequate rainfall and poor soil'. Irrigation, dry farming
and animal husbandry offered prospects for a viable agricultural
economy, and there were possibilities for developing the fishing
industry. The Commissioner had learned that the combined average
annual grants-in-aid of the British and French administrations had
in recent years approached $4 million — excluding occupation costs
— a revelation that came as a salutary shock to some of the administrations' Libyan critics.

'The Arab population of Libya', wrote Pelt, 'stands in need of as
much financial and technical assistance as the United Nations can
supply . . . it is obvious that the country requires very substantial
outside assistance to maintain even its present standards, and yet
more for development in the economic and social fields.'[20] Failure to
improve farming techniques and to inject capital, he warned, could
result in economic regression into nomadism 'with inevitable social
and political consequences which may jeopardise the very existence
of the new state'.

Pelt also found the school system inadequate, but the staff and
money for improvements were lacking. The British and French

administrations had done much to train staff for administrative posts. In 1950, says Pelt, there was some argument whether there were 16 or 18 Libyan university graduates in all; there was practically no secondary schooling for Arabs, and illiteracy was estimated at 90 per cent.

As Pelt saw them, the country's most pressing needs in 1950 were training of civil servants; establishment of budget and fiscal services; development of agriculture, animal husbandry and soil, water and forestry services; expansion of education; and improved public health services, although much ill-health was largely due to malnutrition. There were in 1950 three French doctors in all Fezzan, 18 doctors in Cyrenaica and 80 Italian doctors in Tripolitania; there was no saying how they were to be kept on after independence, and no Libyan doctors were even in training.

The Secretary-General of the United Nations, various UN specialised agencies, the International Bank for Reconstruction and Development and the International Monetary Fund all promised to help. But it was plain that until the machinery of international bureaucracy had been suitably primed with detailed technical studies, little technical aid would be forthcoming.

Accordingly, three United Nations technical assistance teams made study-tours of Libya in 1950–1. One of them, headed by the economist Benjamin Higgins, prepared a six-year social and economic development plan which was adopted by the government soon after independence. The plan recognised that the country had one great untapped source of wealth in the latent skills of its people, and it thus laid great emphasis on education and training and 'teaching the Libyans to do better what they are already doing'.

Harsh truths emerged when serious discussions of the finances of the future independent state started in 1951. Annual income was estimated at $35 *per capita*. The balance of payments was in 'chronic and heavy deficit' covered only by foreign aid. In 1950, income from exports ($6.35 million) covered less than half the cost of imports ($14.19 million). The deficit was made good by military expenditure of $6.74 million and grants-in-aid of $3.74 million, such was the extent of Libyan reliance on foreign military spending and aid. The three separate currencies introduced by the British and French forces in 1942–3 were still in circulation.[21] Britain put forward a case for Libya's admission to the Sterling Area. Although there were French and other objections, the British suggestion was accepted, mainly because Britain was the only country to have made any fairly firm proposals for post-independence financial aid. Libya was to join the Sterling Area with a federal unit of currency, the Libyan Pound, on a par with Sterling.

Commissioner Pelt had already called on the governments of Britain, Egypt, France, Italy and the United States to discuss future economic aid with him, and a firm offer to cover the ordinary budget and balance of payments deficits came from Britain. Pelt, still suspicious of British motives, pointed out that 'control of the budget meant virtual control of the state'.[22] It was also decided to channel some foreign aid through a Libyan Public Development and Stabilisation Agency (LPDSA) that was to finance the type of development that would normally have been included in the government's capital or extraordinary budget; no repayments of capital or interest were envisaged. A Libyan Finance Corporation (LFC) was also set up, mainly to provide credit for Italian farmers in Tripolitania who were one of the mainstays of the economy.

Under a temporary aid agreement signed with the provisional government in December 1951, Britian undertook to provide the LPDSA and the LFC with up to £500,000 in 1952, fully backed the first Libyan currency issue and promised financial help for the first three months of independence to the Cyrenaican and Tripolitanian administrations, which were in turn to finance the federal government. Britain also undertook to make good the federal, Tripolitanian and Cyrenaican budget deficits for the 1952–3 financial year, and France made similar provisions for Fezzan. Libya thus had guaranteed financial support for the first fifteen months of independence. But the Libyans were apparently disappointed that such aid had come from Britain and France rather than the United Nations and its specialised agencies.

Libyan independence was proclaimed on 24 December 1951, one week before the deadline set by the United Nations. Early in the morning, the last powers held by the British and French Residents were transferred to the provisional government. The foreign administrations were brought to an end and the National Assembly was dissolved. The provisional government was fully in control, the Constitution was ready to go into effect, and the way was open for the normal declaration of independence, which the king made at a ceremony at the Manar Palace, Graziani's former residence in Benghazi. The king then sent for the Prime Minister of the provisional government, Mahmud Muntasser, whose resignation was tendered and accepted. The king thereupon asked him to form the first national government; the king also appointed the first provincial governors, and Libya applied for membership of the United Nations and its agencies.

The Libyans never chose to name any of their streets after British or French soldiers who had 'liberated' their country from the Italians during the Second World War. But from independence to the overthrow of monarchy in 1969, the great *lungomare* in Tripoli and Benghazi was named after Adrian Pelt. Throughout his mission, he had 'no other source of influence and no other strength than that provided to him by the moral authority of the United Nations'. His task had been completed in haste — he believed that two years were too short to do all that was needed. During his time in Libya, he had no executive powers; he was an adviser, a conciliator, a co-ordinator supplying, as he put it, 'the necessary motive power and guidance to ensure that Libya followed the right path to independence in the set time limit'.

Libya's attainment of independence under United Nations supervision was a credit to the organisation. As Pelt noted in his final *Supplementary Report*, the original General Assembly resolution on Libyan independence had been welcomed as ' . . . a test of the ability of the United Nations to arrive at solutions of difficult international problems which had previously escaped settlement and as the inauguration of a new method for the peaceful and orderly transfer of a colony into an independent state'. The United Nations passed the test and Libya became one of the five independent states of Africa and, after Egypt, the continent's second independent Arab state.

Yet 'it would be an exaggeration to pretend that all Libyans were happy on independence day', Pelt wrote.[23]

> Two groups were not, the protagonists of unitarianism in Tripoli and the extreme federalists in Benghazi. The first criticized the new state because it was insufficiently centralized and too much dominated by the country's traditionalist forces. The second deplored with nostalgia the loss of the large measure of autonomy they had hoped to maintain in a loose federation, hating to see their way of life disturbed by the modernists from the western province.

Of the two groups, it was the 'protagonists of unitarianism' who were to cause the young state the more trouble.

Notes

1. The Italian community totalled 40,536 in 1946 (BMA *Handbook on Tripolitania*, (Tripoli, 1947), Appendix I, p. 77). Jews numbered 28,031 in 1946 and 'others' (presumably mainly Maltese and Greeks) totalled 2,757 (ibid.). But 'In 1950, shortly after the arrival of the United Nations Mission, the British Authorities estimated that the number [of Jews] had gone down to just over 20,000. In May 1950, the same authorities stated that this figure had further declined to approximately 16,000' (A. Pelt, *Libyan Independence and the United Nations* (New Haven, 1970), p. 544). By 1964, the Jewish population of Libya totalled merely 6,300, 90 per cent living in Tripoli. Most Jews in Libya 'considered themselves — and were considered by the Moslem Libyans — citizens of the country' (ibid., p. 342).

The very ancient Jewish community had probably been established in the Gebel Nefusah of Tripolitania since pre-Roman times and had been augmented by conversions of Berbers and by the influx of Iberian Jews at the end of the Middle Ages. Jews were forced out of Libya as a result of events leading up to and following the foundation of the State of Israel in May 1948. The exodus was started in 1945 by attacks on the Jewish quarters in Tripoli and other towns which Professor Bernard Lewis (*Daily Telegraph Magazine*, no. 326, 22 January 1971) described as a 'massacre'; 130 Jewish dead were officially counted by a British administration that should have protected them, and property damage was estimated at £500,000. After the first Arab-Israeli war of 1948–9, the Jewish communities of Tripolitania abandoned their homes and made their way to the coast where small Italian boats were waiting to take them to Israel. In Cyrenaica, a Jewish population of 4,500 in 1948 had fallen to 200 by 1950 (N.A. Arsharuni, *Inostranniy Kapital v Livii (1911–1967)* (Moscow, 1970), p. 46). A total of 30,656 Jews (more than the total Jewish population in 1946, according to the BMA figures) is said to have left Libya between the foundation of Israel in May 1948 and the end of 1951; almost half left in 1949 alone (Vernant, *The Refugee in the Post-War World* (London, 1953), Table 5, p. 448). The remnant of the community regrouped in Tripoli and prospered there until the 1967 Middle East war when anti-Jewish demonstrations drove the majority to Italy or Israel. The very few remaining Jews were finally expelled and their property expropriated by the revolutionary regime in 1970.

2. Pelt, *Libyan Independence*, p. 183.

3. Ibid., p. 208.

4. Martin, 'La Libye de 1912 à 1969' in CRESM, *La Libye Nouvelle, Rupture et Continuité* (Paris, 1975), p. 42.

5. *Libyan Independence*, p. 243.

6. I.R. Khalidi, *Constitutional Development in Libya* (Beirut, 1956), p. 31; Pelt, *Libyan Independence*, p. 290.

7. Khalidi, *Constitutional Development in Libya*, p. 33.

8. Ibid., p. 33.

9. Ibid., p. 35.

10. *Libyan Independence*, p. 256.

11. N. Epton, *Oasis Kingdom* (London, 1952), p. 129.

12. *Ibid.*, p. 135.

13. *Constitutional Development in Libya*, p. 40.

14. G. Assan, *La Libia e il Mondo Arabo* (Rome, 1959), p. 21.

15. *Constitutional Development in Libya*, p. 43.

16. *Libyan Independence*, p. 492.

17. Ibid., p. 643.

18. *Constitutional Development in Libya*, p. 64.

19. *Libyan Independence*, p. 737.

20. *First Annual Report of the United Nations Commissioner in Libya*,

paras. 180−2.

21. The Egyptian Pound (the standard currency of the British Eighth Army) in Cyrenaica, where the Libyans refused to accept any form of Italian currency; the MAL (Military Authority Lira) at 480 to the Pound Sterling in Tripolitania; and the Algerian and Tunisian Francs in Fezzan.

22. *Libyan Independence*, p. 703.

23. Ibid., pp. 841−2.

5   THE KINGDOM OF LIBYA

The kingdom of Libya, an apparently fragile product of bargains and compromises between internal and external interests, lasted nearly 18 years, bringing a certain precarious stability to the central Mediterranean. During those years the kingdom showed an unexpected resilience in surviving a succession of crises. The first, coming within two months of independence, established a tradition of intolerance towards any serious domestic opposition.

In reverse of normal procedure, the Constitution had been drafted and independence proclaimed before national elections had been held; these were scheduled for 19 February. Convinced that it had wide popular support in northern Tripolitania, the National Congress Party put up candidates in all 35 Tripolitanian constituencies. Sadawi urged voters to support candidates who would be 'true and honest' representatives. The party, which was pressing for United Nations supervision of the vote, complained to the king of government interference in the election campaign. The king promised a party delegation that the elections would be held in an atmosphere of freedom and justice. Thus reassured, the National Congress on 4 February announced its candidates and its policies, which included the achievement of Libyan unity and the 'realisation of the country's true independence'. Since Tripolitania was to have nearly two-thirds of the seats in the new elected parliament (35 out of 55), it seemed that if the National Congress could carry the province, it would be able to dominate the house, amend the Constitution, and abolish the federal system, thereby undoing all the constitutional work of recent years that had been specifically intended to prevent the domination of the independent kingdom by Tripolitanian republicans. And while the party made loyalty to the king its priority, it was rumoured that once in power, it intended to abolish the monarchy.

Voting went off smoothly, with secret ballots in the ten urban constituencies. Suffrage was not universal; only about 140,000 sane and solvent adult males (about one-seventh of the total population) were eligible to vote. The results, announced on 20 February, gave the National Congress Party convincing majorities in seven constituencies in and near Tripoli, but they also recorded heavy defeats by pro-government candidates in the tribal hinterland. The nationwide results gave the government 44 out of 55 seats in the house. Amazed and angered by its failure to win any Tripolitanian rural seats, the party accused government officials of manipulating the voting. Party demonstrations in Tripoli on 20 and 21 February got out of hand when groups of armed men entered the city, public property was damaged, and it seemed that more was intended than a mere display of protest. The police acted promptly and in force, but order was only restored after a dozen deaths and many injuries. The first United States Ambassador to Libya, Henry Villard, pointed out:

> If there was violence, it was quelled not by foreign troops but by the Libyan police themselves, with tear gas and gunfire. In a remarkable exhibition of discipline, they had routed an insurrection of armed mobs of their own countrymen, whose party leaders, beaten at the polls, attempted to seize power by force . . . Libya had offered an encouraging demonstration of a capacity to handle her internal affairs.[1]

Leaders of the National Congress were arrested and Sadawi was swiftly deported on the convenient excuse that he had not renewed his Libyan citizenship following his earlier political service in Saudi Arabia.[2]

When both houses of the first all-Libyan parliament in history were ceremonially opened by the king in Benghazi on 25 March, elected National Congress members were allowed to take their seats, but the party was dissolved. It had basically been an urban middle-class organisation; although not particularly radical, it had attracted Communist[3] and trade union supporters, as well as xenophobic and pan-Arab elements that were bound to be viewed with suspicion by the king and other pro-Western conservatives who were consolidating their control over the country.

Nevertheless, the party had signally failed to realise that its relatively advanced national political programme was far beyond the understanding and aspirations of most voters in the interior of Tripolitania. Issues the party raised were of little concern to those who preferred to vote for known and trusted tribal candidates and who, moreover, were practically obliged to do so by the oral ballot system. The same false assumptions about the political consciousness of the tribes had been made by the handful of idealistic young politicians in the Tripolitanian Republic some 30 years earlier; for the fact remains that the 'popular masses' of rural Libya are not readily moved by abstract political notions outside their experience or concern.

The 1952 electoral crisis was largely contained by the police, but the real cost was the disappearance of a recognised and effective opposition just as the country's supposedly democratic parliamentary system was coming into being. The monarchy had rid itself of the most dangerous source of opposition in the province where royalist support was weakest, but the party system never re-emerged. In its future relations with the provinces, the federal government was to be deprived of the support for central authority that the National Congress Party, with its policy of national unity, might have provided; as it was, the Cabinet alone was left to cope with the overbearing powers of the provincial governments.

Far from reorganising and consolidating itself after independence, the Libyan nationalist movement largely withered away. In future years, all nationalist opposition groups were to be small, frightened, semi-clandestine and ineffectual. Libyan politics under the monarchy were parochial and immature, while most Libyans remained politically apathetic;[4] during the first years of independence, overt political activity was confined to the tiny trade union movement.

Fundamental rivalry between Tripolitania and Cyrenaica and their inability to subordinate provincial interests to those of the federal government were the prime symptoms of the nation's continuing disunity in the early years of independence. Poor communications between Tripoli and Benghazi, the physical and social contrasts of the two cities, and even the continuing need for visas for travel between the two provinces[5] helped to sustain the impression that Tripolitania and Cyrenaica — let alone remote Fezzan — were almost separate countries.

Shortly after independence, differences arose over the respective powers, on the one hand, of the federal government and the Prime Minister and, on the other, of the provincial governors appointed by the king, who were tending to act almost as heads of independent states; the carefully-devised Constitution, with its theoretical balance between federalism and unitarianism, offered no solution. The controversy led to the resignation in February 1954 of Prime Minister Muntasser after the failure of an attempt to trim the powers of the king in order to strengthen those of the federal government and the Prime Minister. Muntasser's resignation was seen as a victory for the supporters of provincial authority; he was succeeded by the former governor of Cyrenaica and head of the royal *Diwan*, Mohammad al-Sakisli. His appointment was not apparently intended to be a long one, and his ministry in fact lasted only two months. In January 1954 the king had dissolved the Tripolitanian legislative council, constituted nine months earlier, for alleged failure to co-operate with the federal government. Then, in April, the newly established Supreme Court ruled that the order of dissolution was unconstitutional, and the ruling was made to appear as a deliberate attempt to oppose the king's authority. Sakisli resigned and was succeeded by his Minister of Communications, Mustafa bin Halim, a 33-year-old Cyrenaican who had spent most of his life in Egypt. As a British visitor to Libya noted, Bin Halim 'seemed so totally undismayed by the vast problems lying ahead of his country'.[6]

By the mid-1950s it was becoming clear that the king, and not the federal government, was the linchpin of national unity and independence. In theory, the king was a constitutional monarch, albeit an inviolate one with such remarkably broad powers that the system of government was effectively one of rule by the crown's nominees. In practice, the king emerged as the supreme arbiter of national affairs, so that neither Prime Minister nor Supreme Court could successfully challenge his ultimate authority. As Ambassador Villard wrote at the time, 'such a concept was probably not that of the foreign sponsors of Libya's constitution, but the undisputed word and firm rule of a disinterested sovereign may be the one practical means of holding the country together'.[7]

Although his main supporters were still the tribes of Cyrenaica (many of his personal staff and guards were Tebu from the former Sanussi centre at Kufra), the king derived additional authority from his undeniable personal prestige. It was the prestige, enhanced by a certain popular awe, of an elderly, ascetic scholar and spiritual leader who, through some 40 years of negotiation and diplomacy, had brought the Libyan people to some sort of nationhood and independence. Yet his exercise of power was rarely obvious. He never made an important policy statement, and he expressed little opinion in public on affairs of state. Despite his almost wily understanding of the ways and weaknesses of Libyans, he remained apparently remote from the workings of government, deploying instead a discreet system of palace power and patronage that served to dissociate the monarchy from any direct decision-making.

When he came to the throne, the king was aged 61 and seemingly still in the uncertain health that had proved a diplomatic asset more than once in the past.[8] Since 1933 he had been married to a cousin, Fatima, daughter of Sayyid Ahmad al-Sharif, who had been head of the Sanussi Order from 1902 to 1916. The royal couple had no children, and the question of the succession led to another potentially disastrous internal crisis in October 1954.

Since 1916 the king's loyal and eventually very close personal adviser had been the enigmatic Ibrahim al-Shalhi, latterly controller of the Royal Household. The king's trust in Shalhi 'aroused the curiosity of many foreign observers as well as the suspicion of many a Libyan'.[9] But it seems to have been a relationship of a type common in Arab society between a notable and his personal servant or secretary, who was traditionally a slave.[10] Through his closeness to the king, Shalhi quietly wielded a degree of influence at court that was heartily resented by many members of the large royal family, and particularly by the 32 male descendants of Sayyid Ahmad al-Sharif. It was Shalhi who had tried to stop them using their privileged position to promote their business and financial interests in a country where 'to live like a Sanussi' was a common expression for the good life. They believed that he had come between them and the king, even to the extent of excluding them from the Sanussi succession, which they claimed for their branch of the family. But to Idris the monarchy and the leadership of the Sanussi Order were two distinct and separate institutions, the monarchy having, in effect, been established by himself. It was his view that while any eligible male relative could become the next Head of the Order, the successor to the throne had to be a member of his branch of the family — his colourless but loyal younger brother, Mohammad al-Rida, in fact.

Among the princes who held Shalhi responsible for the king's restrictive view was a grandson of Sayyid Ahmad, 19-year-old Al-Sharif bin al-Sayyid Muhi-al-Din al-Sanussi; there is no doubt that he had been much influenced by the air of family intrigue in which he had been brought up. After the family had failed in a final attempt to undermine Shalhi's standing with the king, Sharif shot and killed Shalhi in a Benghazi street on 5 October 1954 and was immediately arrested. As soon as the king realised that other members of the royal family were implicated and that there could be much wider repercussions, and even armed conflict between family factions and their numerous clients, he proclaimed a state of siege and had all the Sanussi family placed under house arrest. Two weeks later it was announced that seven younger princes were to be exiled to the oasis of Hon and that all the family, except those in direct line of succession, were to lose their titles and their right to hold government posts. On 20 October the line of succession was restricted by royal decree to the king's branch of the royal family.

Sharif may have hoped that the assassination would be popular; in the event, it was seen as a family quarrel of no particular significance. Sharif had presumably relied on the protection of his powerful family; he was nevertheless tried for murder, found guilty and hanged after an unsuccessful appeal.[11] The close influence of the Shalhi family on the king continued. Ibrahim's eldest son, Busairi, succeeded his father and wielded almost as much power up to his death in a motor accident in 1964. Five years later Busairi's younger brother, Omar, became the royal adviser.

After Ibrahim Shalhi's assassination, the king moved his home from Benghazi to Tobruk, where there was a British garrison, and where he was reported to have found the climate more agreeable. The events of 1954, and the king's swift and decisive deployment of his authority, had undoubtedly ended family rivalries. In June 1955 the king married Alia Abd-al-Kadr Lamlun, the daughter of an Egyptian businessman, but the marriage was childless and was dissolved in 1958. The king's brother and heir apparent, Mohammad al-Rida, died suddenly in 1955, and in 1956 Mohammad's second son, Hassan al-Rida, was named as heir. The Crown Prince tried to strengthen the royal family's links with Tripolitania by marrying the daughter of a Tripolitanian notable and by making his home in the province. But he was not a leader to inspire a popular following, being known as 'the man without a shadow'.

In the early 1950s, Libyan governments were too poor, weak and inexperienced to have much choice of foreign policy. They therefore took an unassuming stand between the Western powers on whose support the economy and ultimately the stability of the state depended, and the growing claims of Arab nationalism. The Egyptian free officers' revolution of July 1952, and particularly the ascendancy of Colonel Gamal Abd-al-Nasser after 1954, gave weak, royalist and pro-Western Libya a tempestuous, domineering and often subversive neighbour during the early years of independence.[12]

The first open foreign-policy move came early in 1953 when, with no explanations for the long delay in applying for membership, the kingdom was warmly welcomed as the eighth member of the Arab League. After this very necessary gesture to Arab solidarity, Libya turned to the West and in July signed a 20-year Treaty of Friendship and Alliance with Britain. The outcome of some 18 months of quiet negotiations, the treaty provided for 'peace and friendship' between the two countries and mutual aid in the event of war or armed conflict.[13] In return for military facilities in the kingdom, including overflying rights, Britain promised a yearly £1 million grant for economic development, and an annual £2.75 million in budgetary aid for the years 1953–8; British arms supplies were also promised.[14] The treaty, which aroused wide Libyan and Arab opposition, particularly in Tripolitania, gave Britain an alternative, if less satisfactory, Middle East base when evacuation of the Suez Canal Zone started in 1954. It also provided staging posts (more necessary in that pre-jet era of relatively short-range air transport) at Idris airport near Tripoli and at El Adem outside Tobruk on the strategic air corridors to places of continuing British interest in Africa, the Indian Ocean and the Far East; it also provided unique desert training grounds where the battles of 1940–2 could be studied on the spot.

Negotiation of a similar agreement with the United States took rather longer, partly because it aroused more Libyan and general Arab hostility. The agreement was not signed until September 1954, following a visit to Washington by Prime Minister Bin Halim. The United States was entitled to retain the air base at Wheelus Field, just outside Tripoli, and certain other areas up to the end of 1970. In return, the United States undertook to pay $42 million in various forms of aid during the period covered by the agreement, and to deliver $3 million-worth of grain for immediate drought relief. Described by the Americans as 'an important contribution to the defense of the free world', the agreement formalised the role of Wheelus Field as a link in the chain of US bases built up round the Sino-Soviet bloc in the early years of the Cold War.[15] Wheelus also acted as a Military Air Transport Service staging post, while in conjunction with the Al-Watiyah bombing range in western Tripolitania, it served as a fine-weather training centre for US aircrews based in Western Europe. When Moroccan independence in 1956 raised doubts about the future security for foreign bases there, the headquarters of the US Seventeenth Air Force was transferred from Morocco to Wheelus. The agreement was not approved by parliament until considerable opposition had been overcome and the king had dismissed the president of the Senate, Omar Mansur Kikhia, who had publicly criticised its terms. The agreement was approved by parliament on 30 October only after Bin Halim had put forward a persuasive case for the economic advantages to be gained: Wheelus was, in fact, the country's largest single source of regular income and the largest single employer of Libyan labour — apart from farming — before the oil boom.

In the early 1950s Libya's strategic position was the one asset for which the Western powers were prepared to give substantial budgetary and development aid. While it is easy to criticise the early post-independence governments for allowing the country to 'live off its geography' and become 'a base for imperialism', it is hard to see what alternatives there were at the time, given the kingdom's desperate and inevitable reliance on foreign financial support and its clear inability to defend itself. What is certain is that equivalent aid sums, local employment opportunities and other benefits brought by the British and American agreements would not in actual practice have been forthcoming from Nasser's Egypt or other 'sympathisers' had the Libyans heeded Cairo's constant broadcast advice to rid themselves of foreign bases.

The kingdom was wary of revolutionary Egypt, and official relations remained cool throughout the 1950s. But Egyptian influences were inevitably strong, for the administrative, judicial and education systems were largely based on Egyptian models; judges, teachers and bureaucrats were recruited in Cairo; the Egyptian press was in general circulation; and Cairo Radio was heard throughout the land.

Just as the French had long feared and foreseen, independent Libya became involved in the mounting nationalist crisis in the French Maghrib. In November 1954, Bin Halim agreed to the shipment of supplies through Libya from Egypt to nationalists in Algeria, where the revolutionary war of independence had just started, while parliament began to put pressure on the government to force the evacuation of French garrisons, totalling some 400 men, still stationed at the Fezzanese oases of Sebha, Ghat and Ghadames under a temporary arrangement reached at independence. These men were invaluable because they could intercept the flow of arms, agents and supplies from Egypt far more effectively than larger forces patrolling the sketchy 1,000-kilometre Libyan–Algerian frontier.

Paris had hoped for a base-leasing agreement such as Britain and the United States had gained, but in the light of the growing crisis in the Maghrib, the Libyan government was wary of French influence in Fezzan and was willing to negotiate only on the basis of total evacuation. In August 1955 a treaty of 'friendship and good neigh-bourliness' stipulated the withdrawal of French troops from Fezzan by late 1956; France was guaranteed certain air and surface transit rights, as well as frontier rectifications in favour of French African territories; in return, about $1 million of development aid was pro-mised. By the end of 1956, French fears were fulfilled when Fezzan became a main supply route for the Algerian revolution. Libya's diplomatic success in forcing evacuation from Fezzan set an example that newly independent Tunisia and Morocco were to follow.

Other sources of Franco-Libyan hostility included the occasional hospitality Tripoli gave to Algerian exiles and the Algerian provi-sional government, and the series of French atomic-bomb tests in the Algerian Sahara. Relations became particularly strained after French and Algerian forces fought an engagement on the Libyan frontier, if not in Libya itself, in October 1957; as a result of similar incidents in 1958, a Franco-Libyan commission was set up to investi-gate further violations.[16] Franco-Libyan relations did not begin to improve until after Algerian independence in 1962.

Outstanding issues with Italy were settled in October 1956 by an agreement that brought $7.7 million in aid, confirmed the transfer six years before of most Italian public property to Libya, and recog-nised certain Italian commercial rights. The agreement also allowed the Italian government to spend an estimated $3.7 million on com-pleting Tripolitanian colonisation schemes by 1960. As had been intended in 1938, colonists were to become outright owners of their land, regardless of how it had been acquired. But those who had already returned to Italy, or planned to do so, could sell out to Libyans and freely transfer the capital. By February 1960 settlement of 1,272 families (5,100 persons) had been completed. But by the end of October 1961, nearly three-quarters of the farms in the settlement projects had been sold to Libyans. By 1964, only about 120 colonist families remained in Tripolitania, and their decision to stay was to prove an act of misplaced faith in the country's future.

Establishment of diplomatic relations with the Soviet Union in 1955 was seen at the time as an assertion of some independence in foreign policy. But offers of Soviet economic aid were rejected, and Bin Halim told the first Soviet ambassador that he had no intention of opening Libya to Communist influence.[17] Bin Halim's main pur-pose in flirting with Moscow seems to have been to win Soviet support for Libya's admission to the United Nations, long delayed by Soviet opposition. He was not successful, and Libya and 15 other states were only admitted in December 1955 as part of a compromise arrangement between the Soviet Union and the West.

It was above all the Suez crisis of 1956 that highlighted the kingdom's essential dilemma of economic and military dependence on the West, on the one hand, and the demands of national sovereignty and obligations to the Arab world, on the other. Libya fully supported Egypt's nationalisation of the Suez Canal in July 1956, and at the end of October sought and obtained a British guarantee that bases and troops in Cyrenaica and Tripolitania would not be used against Egypt. There was wholehearted sympathy for Egypt when Britain and France joined Israel in attacking the Canal Zone. A state of siege was proclaimed, but Bin Halim's position became almost impossible as relations with both Egypt and Britain were simultaneously put to the test of loyalty. Although the Prime Minister, with the advice of the king, managed to bring the country through the relatively brief crisis with both Western and Arab ties intact, his personal standing with Egypt was undermined and was to be a factor in his resignation in May 1957. Attempts by the Egyptian military attaché supervising the transhipment of arms to Algeria to incite armed opposition during the crisis led to his expulsion, brought a personal note of apology from President Nasser to King Idris, and reinforced official suspicions of long-term Egyptian intentions. Although there was some pressure on the government to revise the Anglo-Libyan treaty, relations with Britain and France were maintained. But the British government was led to question the value of bases that had been effectively neutralised by diplomatic action at the very moment when they might have been of the greatest use, and in 1957 Britain began to reduce her forces in Libya.

Meanwhile, Tunisian independence had given Libya a chance of new links with the Arab Maghrib. In January 1957 Bin Halim and President Habib Bourguiba signed a 20-year treaty of friendship and co-operation marking the practical start of the drive for greater Maghrib unity, a policy seen by President Bourguiba, in particular, as a potential counterweight to Egyptian influence in North Africa. Seeking further contacts outside the Egyptian sphere of influence, Bin Halim in January 1957 welcomed the Turkish Prime Minister on an official visit that was attacked by Cairo Radio. One outcome of the visit was a $5.5 million Turkish arms shipment to Libya in November 1957 that was forwarded to Algeria after the delay of some months necessary to convince French observers that it had been delivered to the Libyan army.[18] In March 1957 Bin Halim accepted the terms of the recently announced 'Eisenhower Doctrine', the American economic and military aid programme intended to counter what at the time was seen as rising Communist influence in the Middle East and North Africa. The outcome was an annual increase of $7 million in American economic aid and the promise of American arms. Bin Halim met domestic criticism by pointing out that the country was receiving more aid without any corresponding increase in active commitments to the West.

Bin Halim's foreign policy, conducted at a time when East-West Cold War rivalries were spilling over into North Africa and the Middle East, was neither wholly subservient nor manifestly hostile to any other power. It was a compromise policy, colourless perhaps, but well-suited nevertheless to Libya's contemporary needs, commitments and limited capabilities. In refusing to ally the kingdom too strongly with any one camp in the Arab world, in particular, Bin Halim was inevitably criticised at home and abroad. But the fact that Libya had no quarrels, never indulged in the common Arab habit of breaking off diplomatic relations, maintained a certain political independence, and demonstrated a remarkable capacity for attracting foreign aid, said something for the success of a modest policy of all-round passive co-operation.

Abd-al-Majid Kubar, who succeeded Bin Halim in May 1957, showed similar skill in attracting foreign financial support while in no way increasing overt Libyan commitments. In April 1958 he negotiated £3.25 million a year in British aid up to 1963 under the terms of the Anglo-Libyan treaty, as well as supplies of British arms and free military training, without any further conditions on Libya's part. He also announced that Britain's annual contribution of £1 million to the Libyan Public Development and Stabilisation Agency would end, but that the United States would pay $5.5 million to the agency over the next five years instead. In 1960, American assistance was raised to $10 million.

By 1959 a commentator could write: 'Financially, few countries can be more fortunate than Libya. She has a balanced budget, no public debt and no overseas debt and the outlook for the immediate future is rosy.'[19] The greatly improved financial position was partly due to increased foreign-aid receipts, but from the mid-1950s onwards local spending by international companies searching for oil opened up a new source of income. By the 1957/8 financial year, total foreign aid amounted to $38.32 million;[20] in 1957 spending by foreign oil companies amounted to $43.4 million.[21]

Total annual foreign aid to Libya increased nearly fourfold during the 1950s, from $10.5 million in 1952/3 to $41.7 million in 1959/60. There was a remarkably big increase, from $25.9 million in 1956/7 to $38.3 million in 1957/58, largely due to a doubling in United States aid. A Soviet commentator[22] points out that western aid to Libya, and particularly American aid, increased substantially after the start of large-scale oil prospecting in 1955. The implication is that the kingdom had become a property of potential economic value to the West and that its leaders thus needed to be 'sweetened' with extra foreign aid until oil revenues made such charity unnecessary.

According to *The Economic Development of Libya*, foreign aid from all sources over the period 1952/3 to 1955/6 was $64.4 million.[2] The total for the period 1956/7 to 1959/60 was $112.7 million. This near-doubling in aid in the later 1950s can be clearly attributed to increases in United States aid as a result of the Eisenhower Doctrine and other policies intended to support pro-Western regimes in general, rather than to any specific concern about the security of oil prospects in Libya. In the decade when the independent kingdom weaned on Western aid and the spending of Western armed force and oil prospectors, progressed from near-destitution to a more hopeful state of poverty, the Soviet Union gave nothing, although it is only fair to record that Soviet offers to aid were rejected after diplomatic relations had been opened in 1955.

Like Bin Halim, premier Kubar was adept at allaying Arab suspicions of Libya's close ties with Britain and other Western powers. Soon after the revolution and overthrow of the monarchy in Iraq on 14 July 1958, British troop reinforcements were sent to Cyrenaica while the king and the government only recognised the new regime of Brigadier Abd-al-Karim Kassem on 4 August after considerable Arab pressure. Ten days later, the government sent an appeasing note to Cairo, affirming for the first time that Libya was 'an integral part of the Arab nation' (a statement to that effect was not to be written into the Constitution until 1963) and that the kingdom would continue to oppose foreign armed intervention in the Middle East. Once again, the right gestures had been made, and in Cairo the note was described by the semi-official *Al-Ahram* as Libya's most positive action since independence. While ties with the West remained unimpaired, it was nevertheless by then clear that Libya was not a base from which Britain could hope to influence events in the Middle East and the eastern Mediterranean, and that the country's main military value was as an air staging post and training ground.

By the beginning of the 1960s, Libya's place in the world was rapidly changing: there was already an assured future income from oil revenues and the continued spending of the international oil companies, while the use of longer-range transport aircraft and the general slackening of international tensions meant that foreign powers no longer found their Libyan bases as valuable as they had seemed to be in the early 1950s. With the quickening of economic life and the fuller integration of the country into the Western economic system following the discovery of oil, the opportunities for nepotism, bribery and corruption spread and multiplied until they were to permeate public and private affairs and practically every level of society to such a degree that they were to be cited amongst the main justifications for the overthrow of the regime in 1969. The Crown Prince was to tell the 'People's Court' that tried him in 1971: 'I saw corruption in all fields, especially in financial and political circles.' He added that he used to tell the king what he saw and heard, but the king had done nothing.[24] But in 1960 the king and parliament were still able to take a moral stand against practices that had not yet got out of hand. In July the king had written to members of the federal and provincial governments, denouncing bribery and nepotism in official circles. And in October parliament showed an unexpected sense of unity and responsibility when deputies from the three provinces took the government to task over the cost of a road-building contract that had inexplicably tripled in the time taken to complete one-third of the work. The government only escaped a vote of no confidence through the resignation of the Prime Minister.

His successor was a Fezzanese, Mohammad bin Othman, whose main policies were announced to be the restoration of public confidence in government and greater popular understanding of government policy. Yet the Libyan people as a whole had small reason for confidence in their post-independence governments, and little opportunity for understanding their policies. For despite careful United Nations supervision of its independence and its nicely composed constitutional arrangements, the Libyan kingdom was from the outset little more than a benign despotism administered by an oligarchy of leading families and tribal and commercial interests. Political activity within the oligarchy took the form of clandestine competition between individuals and representatives of various interests for promotion and position, alliance and support. King Idris himself had settled the basic character of his new regime after the 1952 elections when he made it plain, by the exile of Bashir Bey

Sadawi and the dissolution of the Tripolitanian National Congress Party, that he would tolerate no organised opposition.

Overt political activity in the 1950s was limited to the trade unions, while parliamentary opposition was confined to individual members who were rarely able to look beyond their own local interests and obligations to wider provincial or national issues. For, although general elections were held every four years, successful candidates were usually those with the requisite family and tribal support in their own constituencies, since the old loyalties remained strong, not only in the countryside and in the oases, but also to a surprising degree in the towns. Once elected, a representative was expected primarily to serve the personal interests of his own tribal electors and kinsmen according to the traditional patronage system. Political issues played little part in election campaigns: all the candidates broadly supported the government, and only the personalities and standing of the candidates generated any sense of electoral contest, while the 1956 elections, for instance, saw two-thirds of the candidates returned unopposed. Electoral results were easily manipulated. Constituencies were small, and only about 5,000 adult males in each were eligible to vote (women were given the vote in 1963). But, because of ignorance and apathy, the average turn-out was only about 2,500, while the oral voting system used in rural constituencies up to 1960 discouraged opposition. The social structure and geography of the country made it nearly impossible for an individual or a group to gain a provincial or national political following. Political parties and clubs were officially banned and there was no political activity in the four-year intervals between general elections; there were no opportunities for public meetings or for the publication of messages and manifestos; and the press and information services were tightly controlled. There were, moreover, no burning national or even provincial issues that a demagogue or a determined opposition group were able to seize upon to rouse a generally apathetic public primarily concerned with the difficulties of daily existence; indeed, even in the prosperous 1970s, general political apathy was to prove one of the main obstacles to thoroughgoing political revolution. As a commentator wrote at the beginning of the 1960s:

> The only programme for which there might be sufficient popular enthusiasm to create a party — the abolition of the treaties giving the British and the Americans the right to establish military bases in the country and the pursuit of a more dynamic, more pro-Arab

foreign policy — is one which neither the king nor successive Libyan governments have shown themselves prepared to tolerate.[25]

Yet if, despite all the well-intentioned provisions of foreigners, Western-style democracy failed to take root in the 1950s, the Libyans themselves seem hardly to blame, given their bewildering experience of government over the half-century up to 1951 — Ottoman imperialism, moderated after 1908 by the Young Turks; Italian liberalism alternating with tribal anarchy and Sanussi paternalism; then Italian Fascism; and finally British and French military administrations. All these forms of rule, no matter how well-intentioned some undoubtedly were, were basically authoritarian, and not one of them allowed the Libyans full freedom of political expression or prepared them for the responsible exercise of modern parliamentary democracy. Even under the military administrations, wide powers were concentrated in the hands of the Chief Administrators and the burgeoning Libyan bureaucracy. But when the king and his ministers took over the system, they had none of the restraints or guidance from London and Paris such as had regulated the British and French administrations.

No post-independence administration lasted long, and governments became more unstable as members of the ruling oligarchy competed more strongly for certain ministerial portfolios and associated privileges. In the years 1951–63, there were five federal governments and ten government reshuffles: portfolios were later swopped more often as the 'rewards' of certain offices became greater — between 1963 and 1969 there were seven governments and fifteen reshuffles. During the life of the kingdom, governments became progressively larger: there were, on average, eight federal ministers in the 1950s; by the late 1960s there were over twenty.[26]

The trade union movement, although as undeveloped as the economy in the 1950s, might have become the focus for political activity, in effect taking the place of banned political parties. As a commentator wrote in the mid-1960s, 'More than a few of the political leaders of the nation are destined to emerge from the Libyan labour movement.'[27] But in 1961 the movement was temporarily subdued after a trial of strength with the Tripolitanian provincial government. In September that year, against a background of rapidly rising living costs, wages of public employees were increased, and a labour-management advisory committee recommended higher minimum wages for private-sector workers. The Tripolitanian government ignored the recommendation, except for the very lowest paid, and as a result some 4,000 members of the Libyan General Federation of Trade Unions (LGFTU), headed by a former National Congress Party member, Salim Shita, went on strike. At that time the Tripolitanian government was led by one of Shita's political rivals, Ali Dhili, and the government took strong action against the strike in what may well have been a deliberate attempt to suppress the trade union movement entirely.[28] Shita and other union leaders were arrested and held without trial; police occupied the LGFTU offices and strike-breakers were called in. The International Confederation of Free Trade Unions, of which the LGFTU was a member, tried unsuccessfully to intervene.

At the end of September the federal government amended the labour law, severely restricting union membership and the right to strike; about one-third of LGFTU membership was thereby effectively barred from union activities. When brought to trial in November, Shita and 19 other union leaders were acquitted and discharged, but some of September's strikers lost their jobs, giving rise to fears among some observers that Libya was to be the scene of a fierce social struggle just as the new oil wealth was opening up encouraging prospects for economic and social advancement. But with the trade union movement effectively cowed, it was left to the students to take up the cause of opposition after 1961.

A clandestine 'opposition' in the late 1950s and early 1960s was essentially republican in outlook, although the king himself was generally respected. The opposition tended to see the foreign bases as the regime's first line of defence against insurrection or other internal troubles (although, in fact, when the army did move against the monarchy in 1969, the remaining foreign bases were conspicuously inactive). But as a result of this reasoning, the prime targets of opposition criticism were the regime's continuing close links with the two powers, Britain and the United States, that were still seen as its main protectors. Although internally muted and semiclandestine, this criticism gained in strength and credibility through being publicly re-echoed by so many external critics of Libya's foreign policy in general and base-leasing agreements in particular.

Slowly mounting domestic pressure against foreign bases had an unexpected ally in Busairi Shalhi who had inherited his murdered father's position as court chamberlain and who had almost the same influential relationship with the king. But, unlike his father, Busair was not an anglophile, and it has been suggested[29] that he was in touch with some of the regime's clandestine opposition, and that every gradual shift of the regime towards Arab nationalism was the result of his influence.

Organised opposition groups within the kingdom remained shadowy, small and ineffective. They were disunited, although their ideas of 'national liberation', republicanism and Arab unity were nearly identical. They were, almost naturally, largely composed of the younger, educated and urbanised members of moneyed families. But Libya, at least in the first decade of independence, had none of the large institutions in and around which an organised regional or national opposition could coalesce: the first university, when opened in Benghazi in 1956, had only 31 students; the army was small (no more than 5,000 men in the 1950s), widely dispersed and largely uneducated; workshops and industries in general were too few and too small to harbour nascent political movements.

The regime was more narrowly paternalistic than oppressive: its only martyrs were those killed when street demonstrations got out of hand; it kept few political prisoners, for rather than punish its opponents it preferred to buy their acquiescence with bursaries, jobs, sinecures and even seats in parliament. It nevertheless guarded against trouble by keeping all potential sources of domestic opposition under close watch, and a supposedly ubiquitous 'secret police' was assumed to have a close interest in every café conversation.

Throughout the years of the monarchy, the regional police forces were always larger than the army; they were also better organised, at least as well equipped, and in theory more loyal. After the Second World War, many Cyrenaicans who had served in the Libyan Arab Force joined a new British-organised constabulary called the Cyrenaica Defence Force (Cydef); it was always assumed that its tribal recruits owed strong personal loyalty to Idris, both as Amir and later as king. The force eventually numbered some 6,500 men and included para-military units equipped with artillery, machine guns and armoured cars — the army had no heavier equipment until the late 1960s. It was always assumed that the main purpose of this force was to protect the monarchy from armed insurrection, or even an attempted *coup* by the army itself. With the development of the Cyrenaican oilfields, Cydef undertook the policing of vulnerable oil installations, and thereby also acquired light aircraft and an extensive radio communications network.

The Tripolitanian police force of some 4,200 men, also originally

British-organised, had less of the character of a heavily armed Prae-
torian Guard. The police in Fezzan numbered about 600, bringing
total national police strength to well over 11,000 men. Police forces
were organised on a regional basis until 1963, but even when combined into a single National Security Force under the Interior
Ministry, they kept strong regional identities.

Despite these precautions, the main threat to the monarchy more
usually appeared to be foreign rather than domestic. In the 1950s
and for most of the 1960s, political ideologies were foreign to
Libyans. But the country could not be shut off from the outside
world; the Arab and foreign press circulated fairly freely and the
powerful medium of Cairo Radio's 'Voice of the Arabs', as well as
the BBC and other foreign stations, had a large and impressionable
audience which included the young Moammar Gadafi, and which
became both larger and younger with the arrival of the cheap transistor radio in the 1960s. The large number of Egyptian teachers in
Libyan schools (825 in 1964), the training of young Libyans in
Egypt, and wide Egyptian cultural influence were other channels by
which Nasserite, pan-Arab, anti-Western, ideas influenced those
who cared about such things. Gamal Abd-al-Nasser was the most
admired 'foreign' statesman, and his portrait was almost as widely
displayed as the king's. While many Libyans could respond to the
basic appeal of Nasserism, Egyptians were on the whole not liked
— nor indeed were most other Arabs and foreigners — and there
was widespread suspicion of Egyptian intentions; that was hardly
surprising, perhaps, in view of the regular Egyptian use of pro
paganda, diplomatic pressure and plain subversion against its West
ern neighbour.

After Nasserism, Baathism[30] was the rival ideology of socialism
and Arab nationalism that generated a following, particularly among
the small intellectual class, during the years of the monarchy. But
under the onslaught of Nasserite propaganda, Baathism lost much
ground after the break-up of the Egyptian–Syrian union after only
three years in 1961.

Communism aroused little response, being seen as a dangerou
challenge both to Arab nationalism and to Islamic tradition. Th
fundamentalist Egyptian-based Muslim Brotherhood had a wide
appeal, especially among those who saw Arab nationalism largely in
terms of Islam. Despite official statements affirming it, the kingdon
of Libya was never much of a supporter of pan-Arab causes: it wa
not until the 1963 amendment of the Constitution that the kingdon

even formally acknowledged itself to be 'a part of the Arab home-land'.[31] From the official Libyan point of view, the most attractive and realistic movement towards closer Arab association was to be found among neighbours in the Arab Maghrib.[32] Although Maghrib unity was seen as a potential counter-weight to the influence of the Arab Mashriq in general and Egypt in particular, the kingdom was only represented by an observer at the 1958 Conference for the Unification of the Arab Maghrib at Tangier, and thus played no part in the conference decision that federation was best suited 'to the realities of the participating countries'. In practice, even elementary economic and social co-operation was slow to develop, but during the decade after the Tangier conference, Libyan government minis-ters increasingly affirmed their faith in Maghrib unity. At the end of 1964, Libya played a full part in another meeting in Tangier, this time under the auspices of the United Nations Economic Commis-sion for Africa, that agreed to the establishment of three permanent institutions to plan and implement regional economic development and integration; and in 1967 a permanent consultative committee for the Maghrib was set up in Tripoli to draft plans for economic co-operation and the regional division of labour.

As a 'portion of the African continent', the kingdom also offi-cially supported the cause of African unity, and in 1961 was repre-sented at the Casablanca conference of so-called African neutralists, attended by Morocco, Egypt, Ghana, Guinea, Mali and the Algerian provisional government. But the spirit of positive pan-Africanism of the 'Casablanca Group' was too strong for current Libyan thinking, and it was at the conference of moderate African states held at Monrovia, Liberia, the same year that aims closer to Libya's own were expressed. Growing awareness of the community of newly independent African states was shown by sending a delegation to the founding meeting of the Organisation of African Unity at Addis Ababa in May 1963, representation at later OAU meetings, and join-ing other states in condemning and boycotting the white regimes of southern Africa. Nevertheless, the first attempts to form links merely on the basis of African solidarity were not very rewarding, and ties with Africa south of the Sahara remained scant; although Ghana appointed a resident ambassador to Tripoli soon after gain-ing independence in 1957, there was little apparent justification for doing so.

Libya was not even a very good neutralist. Although the govern-ment supported the principles of the 1955 Bandung conference of non-aligned states (and even named a Tripoli street after the venue), the kingdom was for many years too closely associated militarily and economically with the main Western powers to be a convincing member of the non-aligned movement and, together with Jordan, was the only Arab league member not to attend the conference of so-called 'neutrals' organised by Presidents Nasser and Tito in Belgrade in September 1961; Libya was not, in fact, able to face such meetings until the Cairo non-aligned gathering of October 1964.

Following the king's own ideas, Libya refused to become involved in Arab polemics. 'Do not enter into disputes lest you fail and lose all your power' was a cautionary adage from the Koran that could well have been the kingdom's foreign-policy guide for at least the first fifteen years of independence. But, as a result, the Libyan role in Arab councils was usually dull, cautious and largely uninfluential, and thus occasionally a source of annoyance to Arab critics. There was always official sympathy, and at least token support, for Arab causes, but before the arrival of large oil revenues, limited national resources and energies were applied to economic and social development at home rather than squandered on foreign adventures. But such a policy did not protect Libya from interference by other Arab states. In 1962 the government purged the army's small officer corps of Nasserist influences. Two years later, groups of Baathists were rounded up for trial and were given light prison sentences. Nevertheless, continuing Nasserist propaganda and other forms of pressure began to bear results in the early 1960s, to the extent that by 1965 a commentator could write: 'Libya is the only one of the North African states over which Egypt has any direct political influence.'[33]

The reason for this continuing Egyptian interest was oil: exports started in 1961, and thereafter the almost frantic development of oil resources brought in a swiftly rising tide of revenues: they increased from a mere $3 million in 1961 to $40 million in 1962, $211 million in 1964 and to just over $1,000 million in 1968.[34] Besides opening prospects for economic and social development on an unprecedented scale, this new wealth enabled, and even obliged, the state to remodel its own internal structure and to modify foreign policies that had proved adequate only in the first, impoverished decade of independence. For the fact was that by the early 1960s Libya had become property of immense financial value.

At the tenth anniversary of independence, on 24 December 1961, King Idris acknowledged 'the wealth God has given us from our soil', but he warned that 'the struggle ahead will not be less strenuous than during the past ten years . . . prosperity has its own problems'. One such problem was that most of the commercial oilfields found up to 1961 were in Cyrenaica — despite the fact that the boundary between the Tripolitanian and Cyrenaican oil-concession zones had been shifted half a degree (some 50 kilometres) eastwards of the political boundary towards the main oil-bearing basin of the Sirtica to give Tripolitania more oil of its own. But later oil discoveries only confirmed the fact that Cyrenaica, and not Tripolitania, was the kingdom's main oil-bearing region. The abolition of the federal system and the creation of a unitary state — the very issues that had so taxed the nation and its sponsors at the time of independence — were achieved swiftly and smoothly in 1962–3, without the Cyrenaicans ever making a public issue of the fact that it was largely Cyrenaican oil that was bringing about the economic and social transformation of the whole country. The state was far too brittle to withstand implications of one province declining to commit its new oil wealth to the benefit of all; and unity, by amalgamating the hitherto competing development claims of one central and three provincial governments, undoubtedly promoted fairer distribution of the new wealth throughout the nation.

First, in December 1962, the provincial administrations became subordinate to the federal government. Then, in April 1963, further constitutional amendments approved by parliament abolished the provincial administrations and the federal government altogether, and combined their powers into one central government. The three provinces were replaced by ten administrative districts,[35] and the country was renamed The Kingdom of Libya.

For twelve years, one and a half million people had been ruled by four governments sitting in two national and three provincial capitals. In this bureaucrats' paradise, there had been fifteen federal ministries and an average of eight in each of the provinces; Tripolitania and Cyrenaica had each employed more civil servants than the federal government. Liaison between the provincial and federal administrations had been poor and the provinces, often acting independently, had followed their own policies and had duplicated the central government's work. But in 1963 the provincial bureaucrats naturally found themselves new posts in a central administration that was being greatly expanded to cope with responsibilities taken over from the provinces and with new areas of administration opened up by the arrival of oil revenues: five new ministries were formed in 1963 alone. Some of the civil servants recruited at that time were apolitical, recently qualified young technologists with some grasp of the opportunities and difficulties of a traditional society suddenly endowed with large and unearned oil wealth; but it remained broadly true that selection and promotion in government service depended on background and connections.

While oil provided the means of achieving national unity, it also generated social and foreign relations complications that surfaced violently for the first time in 1964. In January, students went onto the streets of Benghazi to demonstrate support for a Cairo meeting of Arab states discussing action against Israel's proposed diversion of the River Jordan waters. Undisclosed numbers of students were killed and injured when the Cyrenaica Defence Force was called out to clear the streets. Typically, there was no official statement, and rumour did its worst; the *Cyrenaica Weekly News* could only report that 'several' youths had been killed. In Tripoli, demonstrators marched to the Prime Minister's office, where a tearful premier Muhi-al-Din al-Fikini, expressed deep sorrow and regrets for the Benghazi incidents, and then promptly resigned. This would-be liberal and reforming Prime Minister had reportedly been to see the king (who was in residence at Suani ben Adem, near Tripoli) to demand the resignation of Mahmud Bukuwaytin who, as commander of the Cyrenaica Defence Force, was technically responsible for the police action in Benghazi, although he had been out of the city at the time.[36] Bukuwaytin was the son-in-law of the king' murdered chamberlain, Ibrahim al-Shalhi, and the king preferred to ask for Fikini's resignation rather than Bukuwaytin's. With the country in a volatile mood and loyalties in question, a man of Bukuwaytin's calibre, and a close member of the royal inner circle was less dispensable than any Prime Minister. Mahmud Muntasse was brought back for a second term as premier, and significantly he also took over responsibility for internal security.

Although calm was restored, President Nasser was determined to make an issue of the fact that, after three years as an oil exporter an earner of oil revenues, Libya was still harbouring foreign bases. In speech broadcast through the Arab world by Cairo Radio on 2 February, he demanded assurances that these bases would not be used against the Arab states in the event of war with Israel. Taking its cue from Nasser, the Libyan press called for liquidation of the bases and in March the Prime Minister, under pressure from both houses of parliament, told Britain and the United States that the government was not prepared to renew or extend the base agreements. (France, with Algeria at last independent and with reduced commitments elsewhere in Africa, had stopped operating military flights through Ghat, Ghadames and Sebha in 1963.)

These developments were very much taken to heart by the king to whom, according to premier Fikini, the bases represented a personal obligation that could not be abandoned.[37] On 21 March, after a stormy meeting with the Cabinet, it was made known that the king had decided to abdicate on the grounds of ill-health, and had shut himself up in his palace at Tobruk. It seems that abdication was the final gesture of disapproval of the proposal to break the long-standing British link that had sustained Sanussi interests for nearly 50 years. But not all Libyans shared the king's view that, since the country had become a most coveted prize following the discovery of oil, responsibility for its defence was more than the Libyan armed forces could undertake alone.

On 23 March the government's position was clarified when the Minister of State, Omar Baruni, said that despite the desire to have the bases closed, Libya wished to maintain economic and trade relations with Britain and the United States, and to continue the British training of the army and navy and the American training of the air force. And later, after an apparently spontaneous demonstration outside the palace by ministers, senators, deputies and Cyrenaican tribesmen, the king was dissuaded from abdicating, for it was plain that the Crown Prince was not an acceptable successor, at least so long as the king lived.

Britain and the United States opened talks on the future of their bases later in 1964, and in August the Prime Minister announced that evacuation had been agreed in principle. Britain, whose bases in Tripolitania were no longer of much strategic or political value, evacuated them by early 1966, but small British garrisons remained in Cyrenaica — at Benghazi, Tobruk and at the El Adem airfield on the plateau overlooking Tobruk. In October 1964, two Libyan–American commissions started discussing the evacuation of Wheelus Field, but there seemed to be no urgency to the negotiations.

The disturbances of 1964 gave very clear warning that all was not well in the kingdom of Libya. In less than a decade, the structures of a traditional society had started to disintegrate under the pressure of the new economic and social opportunities generated first by the oil exploration boom, and then by the country's rapid emergence as an oil exporter and earner of oil revenues of the first order. Probably the most startling feature of social disruption was internal migration. The abandonment of the countryside had started in the 1930s under the Italians who, for all their vaunted totalitarianism, had been unable to control it. But the movement had intensified after independence when nomads and cultivators alike, simultaneously driven by the drought of 1955–9, and drawn by the demand for labour in the new oil industry (and particularly in its many satellite service industries), uprooted themselves from traditional ranges and homelands to move to the towns in expectation of immediate and rewarding participation in the national economic transformation. Between 1954 and 1964 the population of Tripoli grew by 64 per cent, from 130,000 to 213,000, while Benghazi's doubled, from 70,000 to 137,000, with most of the newcomers housed in festering suburban shanties that were breeding grounds for every type of social ill and discontent.[38] After 1959 the movement from the land became a mass exodus, with few migrants returning home when rainfall and farming prospects improved.

These migrants left a simple life of plain diet, limited needs, strong family and tribal ties, and ignorance of modern technology. In the towns, 'they earn better money and buy more goods, but they do not necessarily eat better, and housing conditions are frequently worse than in the country'[39] — and their traditional social links were in disarray. They saw the burgeoning and often conspicuous wealth of Tripoli and Benghazi around them and the rise of a new class of merchants and entrepreneurs, politicians and senior civil servants. This juxtaposition of a materially advanced and newly prosperous society with what was 'still predominantly a primitive rural community' was the source of new, if ill-defined, resentments not harboured in the past against traditional leaders. Resentments fed the popular suspicion that, despite all the declarations of good intent by the state, oil wealth was not being fairly distributed but, with official collusion, was rapidly accumulating in the hands of a minority of enterprising Libyans and their resident foreign associates.

Income figures *per capita* can be misleading, and although according to the statistics, average income had increased roughly tenfold between 1950 and 1963, the majority of people still fared badly. The average income of $370 *per capita* in 1963 'only indicates a potential that may eventually trickle down to the lower social strata. This, however, has not yet [1967] taken place and, as a result the levels of nutrition are still what they have been for centuries

— very low . . . many people are found to subsist largely on bread and tea.'[40]

At the same time, the kingdom was gaining an urban class of bureaucrats, civil servants, teachers and businessmen which had far less cause for complaint than the rural migrants, but was far more vocal in expressing imagined or half-digested grievances. This was particularly true of the younger members of this class, who were going in ever-increasing numbers to the new secondary schools and colleges, where they came under the Nasserist guidance of their many Egyptian teachers. Like other and less well-educated Libyans, they were also absorbing the more strident but more effective message of Cairo Radio's 'Voice of the Arabs' which the cheap battery-powered transistor radio had made almost universally accessible: indeed, since the early 1960s the transistor has clearly had a profound if unquantifiable influence on Libya and the whole Arab world.

Two almost contradictory forces seemed to be at work in Libya in the 1960s. On the one hand was the popular desire to share in the tangible benefits of the oil boom, and on the other an undefined yearning for intangibles, either political or spiritual, beyond mere foreign-induced material progress. In the event the regime, perhaps because it was essentially more paternal than totalitarian, was not able to provide swift satisfaction for the aspirations of modern Libyan society, nor to calm its fears about its own transformation as it sped into an uncertain future.

Yet it is debatable whether any regime at the time, no matter how well-intentioned, could have distributed the benefits of oil wealth fast and fairly enough to satisfy unbounded popular expectations without at the same time undermining the country's profoundly Islamic character. For in assuming the traditional responsibilities of the tribe and the extended family, the state was obliged to invest in relatively slow-yielding social projects, many of which began to produce their full results only after the 1969 revolution. Nevertheless, the royalist regime must be criticised for failing to curb the too conspicuous corruption, wealth-getting and consumption of many of its leading figures, and it was this failure that was to contribute to its eventual downfall. Even the building of the entirely new administrative capital at Baida, high up in the Gebel Akhdar some four hours' drive from Benghazi, was an extraordinarily corrupt, costly and inconvenient folly. The site, in the heart of Sanussi country, was that of the first Sanussi *zawia* in Libya, and was said to have been chosen by the king as a means of keeping government officials and politicians away from the corruptions and temptations of Tripoli and Benghazi. Be that as it may, the purchase of land, at suitably inflated prices, by the state for building at Baida greatly enriched the local and politically dominant Barassa tribe whose leader, Hussain Mazigh, was *wali* of Cyrenaica in the 1950s and Prime Minister from 1965 to 1967.

While the regime may have had some cause for ignoring the events of 1964, taking refuge in the belief that the nation would soon adjust to the impact of oil revenues, the far more vicious outbursts of June 1967 gave most explicit warning that the kingdom faced a severe crisis of confidence. For nearly three years in the mid-1960s, the country seemed to bask in growing and tranquil prosperity under the benign premiership of Hussain Mazigh, who neatly combined financial, political and social opportunism. Parliamentary elections held in October 1964 and then repeated in May 1965 to return a house composed entirely of pro-government members seemed to have little relevance to the nation's growing political poverty. The kingdom was little concerned with the troubles of the outside world — it continued to make all the appropriate noises and gestures in public — although the actions and intentions of Nasserite Egypt were still a source of worry as, apparently and not altogether reasonably, were those of newly independent and aggressively socialist Algeria. But the supposed Algerian 'threat' detected at the height of the *rapprochement* between Presidents Nasser and Ahmed Ben Bella faded away after the overthrow of Ben Bella by Colonel Houari Boumedienne in mid-1965.

The troubles of 1967 were particularly vicious because they were not really characteristic of the country, and because the scale of violence was wholly unexpected. When, after weeks of mounting tension, Israel went to war against the Arab states on the morning of 5 June 1967, Libya had no force capable of fighting alongside the Egyptians in Sinai, despite a government statement stressing Libyan pride in its Arab nationhood, willingness to face the challenge of Zionism, and determination to fight for the liberation of Palestine. Troops had been moved up to the Egyptian frontier on 1 June to await further orders, and recruiting offices had been opened.

On 5 June mobs, apparently instigated by Cairo Radio and at least partly organised, took to the streets of Tripoli, killing Jews and firing their property. Following false claims by President Nasser and King Hussain of Jordan of British and American participation in the war on Israel's side, there were attacks on British and American property in Tripoli and Benghazi.[41] By 7 June the government had, in effect, ceased to exist, and oil-industry workers refused to load waiting tankers in accordance with an Arab oil-producers' embargo agreed at a Baghdad meeting a week earlier. Continuing demonstrations, meanwhile, had plainly become less of an expression of frustration at inability to strike back at Israel than a means of protesting against the regime and its pro-Western policies. National morale was further depressed by the news that members of the government had fled abroad, and the internal situation remained tense for many weeks.

Oil workers, led by an American-educated oil-industry lawyer and future post-revolutionary Prime Minister, Dr Sulaiman al-Maghrabi, ignored government appeals to reopen to ships of 'friendly nations' oil terminals that had been closed on 7 June. The oil companies had meanwhile ordered their tankers out of territorial waters, and on 14 June one of the major oil companies issued a confidential internal report, repeated daily for the next week, warning that Libya was 'on the verge of revolt' and that workers had been called on to destroy British and American installations. The oil company report was a fair assessment of the mood in the country at the time, but there was no individual or group ready and able to exploit the popular call for the weapons to finish the job. As it was, national bewilderment and frustration were expressed by means of a total oil embargo (costing an estimated $1.5 million/day in lost revenue) that remained in force until early July, when it was continued only against Britain, West Germany and the United States because of their supposed 'collusion' with Israel.

The government of Hussain Mazigh resigned on 1 July. The king, in a final demonstration of confidence-restoring decisiveness, appointed a new administration bringing together various essential talents under the premiership of Abd-al-Kadr Badri. Although the Badri government lasted only three months, it was sufficiently sure of itself by August to put on trial and imprison seven leaders of the defiant oil workers (including Sulaiman Maghrabi) on charges of incitement to strike and demonstration. In many ways the events of 1967 provided a clear warning that the days of the monarchy were ending and that the death of King Idris, with the general expectation of a disputed succession, might yet be anticipated by a *coup*.

At the Arab summit in Khartoum at the end of August Libya at last found an Arab role as an aid-donor. By then the third-richest

Arab oil state after Saudi Arabia and Kuwait in terms of annual revenues, if not yet in reserves, Libya joined the other two in pledging funds to help Egypt and Jordan recover from the effects of the war with a contribution set at $84 million/year 'until the traces of Israeli aggression are removed'.[42] It was money that was probably better spent than the contribution of $42 million to the 'useless' United Arab Military Command that had been squeezed from a reluctant kingdom by Egyptian pressure in 1965. The decision, also taken at the Khartoum summit, to end all Arab oil-export embargoes still in force allowed the new commitments to Egypt and Jordan to be met without financial embarrassment.

Libyan standing in the Arab world had been further enhanced by the demand made on 15 June, certainly as a result of Egyptian prompting, for the closing of the British and American bases and the evacuation of all foreign troops. On 3 August it was announced that the 1,000-strong British infantry garrison would be withdrawn from Benghazi within six months. But no mention was made of the British garrison at Tobruk (close to both the king's usual residence and the British Petroleum oil terminal at Marsa al-Hariga that had been opened only six months earlier). Nor was there any announcement about the Royal Air Force staging post at El Adem, some 30 kilometres south of Tobruk, which was manned by 800 men and which, after the closure of the Benghazi staging facilities, provided less conspicuous means of access for troops flown in for desert training. And there still seemed no prospect of the Americans withdrawing from Wheelus Field until their agreement expired in 1970. Indeed, *The Times*[43] thought that negotiations over the bases were 'presumably designed to elucidate whether, after reflection, Libya really wants to be abandoned naked to her friends, or whether some western presence should be preserved'.

Restoration of confidence after the shocks of the summer was apparently completed by the appointment of a new government at the end of October. The new Prime Minister was a Cairo-educated lawyer and former Minister of Justice, Abd-al-Hamid Bakkush. Aged only 35 on his appointment, Bakkush was said to have been the world's youngest premier in office at the time, and he brought into his Cabinet some of his contemporaries who had already shown ministerial abilities. Two such men were Ali Attiga, who became Planning Minister, and Omar Jauda, who took over the health portfolio. Bakkush was young enough, and had the ideals and background, to understand and sympathise with the post-independence

generation of young Libyans. He and his self-confident younger colleagues seemed at last the men able to give the country a new sense of
purpose and a stronger personality of its own. Bakkush set up a
ministerial committee, on which representatives of the universities
also served, to encourage national consciousness. Ministers went on
the radio to explain government policy and the Prime Minister, in a
speech to the Senate, announced his intention of encouraging
citizens, as he put it, 'to take part in general services, instead of letting the government do everything'.

Showing a degree of confidence in his own authority rare in
Libyan leaders, Bakkush at the beginning of 1968 brought to trial
106 people (94 of them Libyan and the rest of various Arab nationalities) on charges of plotting subversive and terrorist activities over a
period of seven years, inciting demonstrations and organising strikes,
including the oil-industry strike of 1967. The accused were mostly
young and included (*in absentia*) the future Secretary-General of the
Popular Front for the Liberation of Palestine, George Habbash.
They were alleged to have received their orders from the Beirut-
based Arab Nationalist Movement set up by Habbash in the 1950s,
and which by 1967 had become a Marxist–Leninist revolutionary
group. Sentences, announced in February, were typically moderate
— fines, short prison terms and, for the foreigners, deportation as
well.

The Prime Minister's announcement of a five-year defence plan in
October 1967, including an increase in army strength from 7,000
to 10,000 men, was characteristic of the new process of 'Libyanisation'. Both the British-trained and equipped navy and the
American-trained and equipped air force were still in their early formative stages. Manpower and training, rather than money, were the
main factors limiting the size of the armed forces.

Up to the mid-1960s, a passive foreign policy and base-leasing
agreements seemed the best defence for a nation unable to provide
adequate forces of its own. But with the evacuation of the British
military all but complete and the Americans due to leave at the end of
1970, the country was by 1968 obliged to start looking to its own
security to safeguard its independence and its oil wealth. Since cost
was no longer a prime limitation, the government had towards the
end of 1966 begun to consider buying the most advanced missiles
available and training the relatively few specialists needed for their
operation, instead of entrusting the defence of the kingdom to scarce
manpower enrolled in conventional armed forces of unpredictable

loyalties. After long negotiations, a contract with an initial value of at least \$280 million, but rising eventually to as much as \$1,400 million, was signed in April 1968 with the British Aircraft Corporation, which was to supply *Thunderbird* high- and medium-level anti-aircraft missiles and *Rapier* low-level missiles to intercept of aircraft attacking below radar cover. The contract included radar detection and control equipment and the training of Libyan operators in Britain. The entire system was to be mobile for additional protection, and in obedience to the laws of desert warfare that abhor static defences. The system was designed to give formidable striking power against air assault, and particularly against low-level attacks on airfields; critics who questioned both its cost and the identity of the expected aggressor said nothing in public at the time about how the contract had been won. But it has been suggested that the second Five-Year Plan was postponed to help meet the cost of the contract, and that the system would in practice be operated by seconded British technicians; the contract, in short, was allegedly a way of maintaining a British military presence; and 'the British are less likely to panic in a crisis than the Libyans'.[44] The contract was also criticised as inappropriate for Libyan defence needs, involving as it did the employment of highly trained personnel badly needed in other fields.

Although it was always tacitly assumed that the kingdom was defending itself primarily against Nasserist Egypt, the fact remained that since the 1967 war, defeated Egypt had ceased to appear a menacing neighbour and had instead become a grateful recipient of Libyan financial aid. President Nasser, agreeably surprised at Libya's practical demonstration of solidarity with the Arab cause after the war, at last seemed well disposed towards the kingdom. The Libyans themselves were becoming increasingly aware that the presence of foreign bases belied any pretence to a truly independent foreign policy, while the Arab world generally saw the missiles contract as part of Libya's growing need to prove its independence as a non-aligned state.[45]

This new standing was fostered by Bakkush in a series of foreign visits in 1968. His visit to France in April, the first by a Libyan premier, was in part seen as a reflection of his determination to give his country a wider international role and to demonstrate to the Arab world in particular that it intended to be unfettered; it was a demonstration that would hardly have been convincing had he gone to London or Washington first. In the event, his planned visits to

Britain and the United States were overtaken by his unexpected resignation in September 1968.

Although the reason for the resignation was reported to have been disagreement with the king over government appointments, it was suggested that Bakkush had been eased from office by conservative rivals critical both of his youthful, progressive zeal and the cost and purpose of the missiles contract with Britain. Nevertheless, for nearly a year he had seemed to epitomise the spirit of more indepen-dent, self-confident and vigorous Libya.

Bakkush was succeeded by an altogether more cautious figure, his former Foreign Minister, Wannis Gadafi, some ten years his senior. It was under Gadafi's administration that another arms agreement with Britain was finalised in April 1969. In providing for the supply of Britain's advanced heavy tank, the *Chieftain*, together with anti-aircraft guns and artillery, the agreement seemed to contradict the notion behind the earlier missiles contract of building up armed forces better equipped to repel foreign aggressors than to mount a *coup d'état*. The agreement actually raised more public debate in Britain than in Libya, and in the House of Commons questions were asked as to why Libya suddenly needed all these costly British wea-pons under 'unconditional' terms, when similar arms had been refused to Israel.[46]

Despite inevitable but often harshly unfair criticism of all the king-dom's works and deeds by the post-1969 regime, the fact remains that Libya made remarkable economic and social progress between 1951 and 1969, even though the available means, before the full exploitation of oil, were often extremely meagre. In later years it was easily forgotten, or not known, just how destitute the kingdom had been in 1951, particularly in comparison with the easy and spreading affluence of 1969. Up to the late 1950s, Libyan nomads had been quite willing to risk death every day in the wartime minefields to earn a living by salvaging abandoned military equipment: in certain years after 1945, scrap metal from this source contributed up to 13 per cent of total exports by value.[47]

At independence, Libya was one of the poorest countries in the world, with annual income estimated at $35 *per capita*. Contem-porary official reports were sombre, perhaps unduly so: 'Income per head would appear slightly higher than in India, but markedly lower than in Turkey and most other Middle Eastern areas.'[48] 'The whole of the Libyan economy operates at a deficit; the country does not produce enough to maintain even its present low standard of living.'[49]

> The standard of housing is extremely low; a large part of the population lives in primitive huts, tents or caves, lacking furniture and the simplest conveniences. Clothing is home-made out of home-grown wool. The poor are clad in rags and walk barefoot even during the fairly cold winters.
>
> . . . there seems to be little doubt that the standard of living in general is dangerously close to the minimum of existence; it is precariously balanced and at each recurring drought it tends to fall below that minimum; in such periods it is authoritatively reported that the already high death rates, particularly of children and old people, further increase.[50]

Benjamin Higgins, the economist appointed by the United Nations to plan the country's economic and social development, wrote:

> Some observers have contended that Libya is an *over*developed country in the sense of being exhausted; the present problems of drought, soil erosion and drifting sands are the product of past errors of over cutting, over grazing, over irrigation and over tilling, followed by abandonment. If this view is correct, the problem in Libya is one of arresting decay and replacing it with progress, rather than one of launching economic development where no development has taken place in the past.[51]

National poverty was reflected by social ills — high birth and death rates (and a particularly horrifying infant mortality rate); much sickness from malnutrition in a generally healthy climate; widespread illiteracy and ignorance; and shortages of education and training in the skills necessary for economic and social advancement and self-government. Yet the country's main untapped resources were plainly the latent skills of the people, and the emphasis in the Higgins development study of 1953 was accordingly on 'teaching the Libyans to do better what they are already doing'.[52] But the 'special education problems' were seen by Higgins to include the attitude of 'most Libyans' towards work, which was

> conditioned by centuries of foreign rule, the vagaries of climate recurrent drought, malnutrition, and an emphasis on contentmen

rather than an emphasis on material accumulation. Ordinary income incentives do not seem to be completely effective in persuading Libyans to work harder, longer or better. Yet if Libyan productivity is to rise significantly, some incentives must be found to increase the quantity and quality of effort expended. The same may be said of willingness to assume the risks of enterprise. Here is another educational problem.[53]

According to the International Bank for Reconstruction and Development in 1960, economic progress was delayed by

the prevailing attitude towards appointments to government jobs, which are frequently made on the basis of personal friendship or family connections rather than merit . . . manual labour is commonly regarded in Libya as undignified, and most boys who go to secondary school or university consider it beneath them to work with their hands.[54]

Acknowledging that 'true economic and political independence cannot be achieved in a country that relies heavily on foreign financial aid for its very livelihood', foreign expert opinion of the early 1950s considered the only hope for raising national income and the standard of living lay in farming, eked out by fishing, tourism, handicrafts and simple industries for the processing of farm produce. But the outlook for agriculture, with the perennial drawbacks of low rainfall and poor soil, was still as daunting as the Italians had found it, and perhaps more so since there was no prospect of development funds or expertise on the relatively lavish scale Italy had provided in the 1930s.

Commissioner Pelt in 1950 judged the Italian-owned farms of Tripolitania to be the territory's 'greatest economic asset'.[55] But it was also pointed out that 'while the Arab system [of farming] is primitive, yielding a low agricultural surplus, it is essentially in equilibrium. The Italian system, on the other hand, is technically more advanced and more efficient, but it has so far been unable to exist without outside aid and is correspondingly vulnerable.'[56]

Yet despite official recognition of its importance and the need to increase its attractions and rewards, farming developed slowly in the 1950s and 1960s. Besides the environmental handicaps, farm improvement was hampered by lack of skills and capital; by migration of labour; by salinisation of land and the fall in groundwater levels in farming districts as a result of modern irrigation; and by traditional land and water ownership rights, evolved for nomadic animal grazing and shifting cultivation, that gave the settled farmer neither the security nor the incentive to improve his land and raise its output. As a result, 'land which had been developed before 1940 was being farmed at a lower level of efficiency than twenty years before'.[57] While, according to Italian statistics, there were 2.6 million hectares under all types of cultivation in Tripolitania in 1925, the 1960 agricultural census recorded only 1.7 million hectares in arable and permanent crops, including fallow land.[58] Produce that might have been exported was generally of low quality but surprisingly high price.

Agricultural decline was plainly reflected in the country's failure to feed itself. Under the British administrations, Tripolitania and Cyrenaica in some years earned a surplus on their trade in food and livestock, but by the 1950s there was a constant food deficit. In 1956 the total value of imported food and food products reached about $14 million; imports rose to $21.3 million in 1962 and to $77.3 million in 1968. Farm export earnings fell from $3.4 million in 1956 to $1.7 million in 1961 and to only $90,000 in 1968.[59] The slaughterhouses had to turn to Sudan for cattle, to the Balkans for sheep, and American corn oil was sold in a land where the Italians had planted three million olive trees.

The rise in national income from an estimated $42 million in 1950 to $157 million in 1959 was less the result of higher domestic productivity than of increased foreign activity — notably in oil exploration, foreign aid and military spending. But the injection of these funds stimulated the traditionally enterprising traders and merchants to undertake new commercial and building activities, and to invest in a wide range of new service industries (although, in common with their class in other developing countries, they were most reluctant to invest in manufacturing enterprises). Nevertheless, experts of the 1950s who were so pessimistic about the country's economic future seemed to have overlooked the inherent capacity for business enterprise of a nation that for hundreds of years had maintained profitable trade with distant parts of Africa beyond the Sahara.[60]

Starting in the mid-1950s, the search for oil by free-spending international companies gave an immediate stimulus to the general economy, but proved disastrous for agriculture by drawing off the most active and enterprising workers, thereby helping to ensure that those who remained were few, expensive to hire and generally the less skilled. The numbers of Libyans working at any one time in the oil-exploration camps or in the subsidiary services of the oil industry were never particularly large, but

> the impact of oil employment in Libyan society cannot be measured simply in terms of the number of workers involved. Because of the nature of operations and the high rate of labour turnover, probably twice the number presently [1961] employed have at some time worked in petroleum exploration. The experience has had an unsettling effect on the individuals directly involved as well as on the local communities from which they come.[61]

If the economy and the structure of society were being distorted by outside forces before the discovery and exploitation of oil, the full impact of large-scale revenues was even more unsettling.[62] Oil revenues started in 1961, and over the next eight years government revenues grew as shown in Table 5.1.

Table 5.1:   Government Oil Revenues 1961–9

Year	Revenue ($ million)
1961	3
1962	40
1963	108
1964	211
1965	351
1966	523
1967	625
1968	1,002
1969	1,175
Total	4,038

Source: *Petroleum Economist, OPEC Oil Report* (1979).

As early as 1958 the government had decreed that 70 per cent of oil revenues was to be spent on economic and social developments as a means of spreading the new wealth quickly through all levels of society. In 1960 the government set up a development council to co-ordinate the work of agencies handling foreign aid and domestic planning, and the International Bank for Reconstruction and Development (the World Bank) was asked to survey the nation's economic prospects. But cautious plans were overtaken by the unexpected and unprecedented speed with which oil was exploited and the revenues increased. It was not until 1963 that the government in effect caught up with the implications of burgeoning oil wealth and set out its development priorities in a loosely co-ordinated Five-Year Economic and Social Development Plan (1963–8).

As stated by the Prime Minister, the main object of this first Five-Year Plan was 'to ensure the early improvement of the standard of living of the people, particularly those of limited income who did not benefit from the economic prosperity'.[63] Of total planned spending of $473.5 million,[64] agriculture and forestry were to receive $81.9 million and public works ($108.3 million) was the only sector to be given more. The reason, as explained by the Prime Minister, was that farming was 'deemed to represent the backbone of our national economy, not only because it is a main source of work and income for the majority of our people, but because it is a contributory factor to the settlement of inhabitants and strengthens the social and economic interrelationships among the various sectors'.[65]

Among the main components of agricultural development plans were credits, price support and subsidised equipment and fertilisers, as well as irrigation, land reclamation and settlement projects. In practice, some measures seemed to fall not far short of bribery to induce those still on the land to stay there, and as the habits of consumer spending became more widespread, loans and grants were frequently misused by small farmers corrupted by such easy access to the new wealth. Although the plan proposed 'to improve the economic condition of the farmers', its generalised promises had, in effect, to compete against the more real and immediate economic and social attractions of the northern towns, now that Libyans were freer to choose where and how they made their livings. Nevertheless, farming output did increase by an average annual rate of around 4.5 per cent during the plan period, although its overall share of gross domestic product continued to decline as the contributions of the oil, construction and service industries increased.

Under the first Five-Year Plan, most money and effort were concentrated on the modernisation of the national infrastructure. Although the plan proposed to raise the level of industrial output 'in quantity, kind and quality' to promote domestic consumption and the export of industrial products, and to achieve a higher level of industrial employment, only $19 million was allocated to this sector while private capital continued to seek larger and easier profits in trade, real estate, building and the service industries.

The plan ran into difficulties largely because there was far more money to spend than had been foreseen, such was the unexpected and unprecedented growth in oil revenues. Such ambitious schemes as the reconstruction of the entire main coastal highway and the proposed solution of the housing shortage by the building of 100,000 new homes in five years (the Idris Housing Scheme) so distorted spending when added to the plan, that it eventually lost its coherence and perspectives. Total spending doubled from the original allocation of $473.5 million to $943.3 million. The start of the second Five-Year Plan, envisaging a total outlay of $3,218.6 million, was accordingly postponed for a year, to 1969, to allow for the completion of projects unfinished under the first Plan and to give more time for the preparation of the second.

According to Dr Ali Attiga, the dynamic young Planning Minister appointed by premier Bakkush, the second Plan was intended to promote the diversification of the economy and to increase productivity in agriculture and manufacturing. It was proposed 'to gradually shift the emphasis from investment in the basic physical infrastructure to the development of productive enterprises in agriculture and industry, including petrochemical and energy-based industries to the extent that the market opportunities can be developed'.[66]

A very real economic transformation took place in the decade 1959–69, despite all the economic and social constraints, excesses and imbalances — not least among them inflation, high costs, shortages of skills and labour, and an overmanned, largely incompetent and venal bureaucracy. It was a decade in which governments' well-intentioned, if at times ill-judged, attempts to make provision for the future began to provide a basic economic and social infrastructure which, imperfect though it was, the new regime was able to adapt and develop to its own ends after 1969.

The welfare system built up in the 1960s as a means of alleviating at least the worst effects of poverty in the midst of new-found affluence was on a scale well beyond the means of any developing country without exportable oil reserves. By the 1969/70 academic year, nearly one Libyan in five was receiving a full-time free education: enrolment from primary level to university totalled 365,000 — eleven times greater than in 1950/1, when few children received more than primary schooling, and when there was no university and little vocational training. By 1968 it was estimated that 85 per cent of those eligible to attend school actually did so, compared with 10 per cent in 1951, and the government could fairly claim that 'the policy of education for the many and not for the few is leading to universal secondary education'. Yet despite general education and an assault on adult illiteracy, the number of university graduates and specialists of all kinds remained low. The Libyans themselves were under no particular pressure to excel, since the goods, services and manpower[67] that they were unwilling or unable to provide themselves could all be imported. Thus shortages of physicians and other medical staff were one of the main constraints on the expansion of the health services, despite the availability of funds for buildings, equipment and training. Nevertheless, through the expansion of the National Social Insurance Institute (INAS — *Istituto Nazionale Assicurazione Sociale*), first set up on a limited scale in 1957, Libya by 1969 was well on the way to becoming a model welfare state providing lifelong social security.

Although the kingdom had made some remarkable advances and the future appeared promising, the apparently satisfied face of society in 1969 masked discontents unvoiced since 1967 that had seemingly been silenced by the 1968 trials of 'conspirators'. The king, old but by no means as tired and sick as he had claimed to be on many suitable occasions over the past 50 years, was thought to be losing his control over the affairs of state. It was generally assumed that on the king's death or abdication the Crown Prince was unlikely to inherit the rich prize that Libya had become, at least not without a struggle. The prince had not been allowed to perform political duties, but the king had refused his requests to be relieved of his post.[68] The 'easy calm' that some observers reported to have noted since the 1968 trials in reality hid various preparations for a seizure of power anticipating the death or abdication of the king.

Power already seemed to be flowing into the hands of the Shalhis. There was no member of the family at the king's side from the death of Busairi Shalhi in 1964 until April 1969 when the younger of his two brothers, Omar, was persuaded to take on the role of royal counsellor, a post of even greater power, influence and rewards than it had been in the days of Ibrahim or even Busairi Shalhi. Omar quickly consolidated his political and social position by marrying the daughter of the former Prime Minister and leading Cyrenaican Hussain Mazigh, in an ostentatious ceremony that only served to confirm popular ideas about the easily acquired wealth of the country's leaders. In the meantime the second brother, Colonel Abd-al-Aziz Shalhi, had become Chief of Staff.

Quite possibly anticipating untoward developments, the king made a dignified exit from his country in June 1969 when he went on what was planned as a long health cure in Greece, accompanied by Queen Fatima and Omar Shalhi; they moved to Turkey in August. The king was never to see Libya again.

Notes

1. H.S. Villard, *Libya. The New Arab Kingdom of North Africa*, (Ithaca, 1956), pp. 8–9.
2. He returned to the service of the Saudi monarchy and died in exile in 1957.
3. Its main Communist supporter was Dr Enrico Cibelli, who had been deported from Libya at the end of 1951.
4. 'In Tripoli, the barnlike ex-Italian structure that served the Parliament stood in the centre of town, accessible to all, but after the initial wave of curiosity had passed, public attendance dropped to a minimum. It raised a question in the minds of outside observers whether there was, in fact, much public interest in or understanding of the obligations which independence entails.' Villard, *Libya*, p. 34.
5. Ostensibly to stop Italians returning to Cyrenaica.
6. R. Carrington, *East from Tunis* (London, 1957), pp. 131–2.
7. Villard, *Libya*, p. 58.
8. The fact that the king lived into his tenth decade suggests that he had never been as frail as had been generally assumed. A British journalist, attending the royal opening of the Marsa al-Hariga oil terminal in February 1967 (when the king was nearly 77), had seemed to speak the disrespectful truth when he confided to colleagues, 'I'm glad to see His Majesty continuing to look healthily decrepit.' The king outlived the journalist.
9. M. Khadduri, *Modern Libya* (Baltimore, 1963), p. 249.
10. Writing of slaves in Libya in the early 1920s, the Egyptian traveller A.M. Hassanein Bey said: 'They [male slaves] have more power and are taken more into the confidence of their masters than free men. They are very well treated and become members of the family . . . The favourite slave of Sayed Idris, Ali Kaja, is not only the most trusted man of Sayed Idris, but he has more power and authority among the Beduins themselves than many a free man. Such a slave is treated as a confidant' (*The Lost Oases* (London, 1925), p. 180). Shalhi, although not a slave, seemed to fill a very similar role.
11. The body is said to have been exposed in public for 20 minutes at the exact spot where Shalhi had been killed 'as a ghastly object lesson to a wondering crowd of spectators' (Carrington, *East from Tunis*, p. 129). Salim al-Atrash, the lawyer who defended Sharif, complained to the 'People's Court' in 1971 that he had been harassed as a result. 'He had faced many difficulties and had constantly been watched and deprived of his sense of security. . .' (BBC, *Summary of World Broadcasts*, ME/3831/A/4).
12. Personal relations between King Idris and President Nasser seem nevertheless to have been cordial; Nasser was the best man at the king's wedding to an Egyptian in 1955.
13. For discussion of the 'Radford Plan', see p. 122.
14. Budgetary aid was increased in 1958 to £3.25 million/year, but the development contribution ceased.
15. Although the Americans insisted that Wheelus had no aggressive purpose, Ambassador Villard, writing in the mid-1950s, pointed out that its 'phenomenally

long runways' were 'capable of taking the largest bomber yet built' (*Libya*, p. 139).

16. The situation was not helped by the occasional shifting of the rare frontier marker-barrels by the French army, apparently more as a sport than out of any desire to extend French territory.

17. The establishment of relations was described by US Ambassador Villard as 'a sudden intrusion of the Soviet camel's nose into the Libyan tent' (*Libya*, p. 24). Although the Soviet Embassy in Tripoli was opened in 1956, the first Libyan Embassy in Moscow was not set up until 1962 and Libyan policy towards the USSR was seen by the Russians as 'somewhat contradictory' (V.L. Bodyanski and V.E. Shagal, *Sovremyennaya Liviya (Spravochnik)* (Moscow, 1965), p. 225).

18. Humbaraci, *Algeria. A Revolution that Failed* (London, 1966), p. 20.

19. 'Libya: Seven Years of Independence', *World Today* (February 1959). And on 13 December 1959 the *New York Times* reported: 'Since the United Kingdom of Libya was established . . . in 1951, the United States has poured more than $100 million of aid into Libya. Libya has received more United States aid *per capita* than any other country.'

20. *The Economic Development of Libya* (Baltimore, 1960), Table 1, p. 41 (converted at $2.80 to £L1).

21. 'Libya: Seven Years of Independence'.

22. N.A. Arsharuni, *Inostranniy Kapital v Livii (1911–1967)* (Moscow, 1970), pp. 73–5.

23. Table 1, p. 41. Figures quoted by Arsharuni (*Inostranniy Kapital*, Table on p. 74) are calculated on a rather different basis, which makes pre-1955 aid appear less and post-1955 aid more than Table 1 of *The Economic Development of Libya* suggests.

24. BBC, *Summary of World Broadcasts*, ME/3822/A/1–2.

25. R. Segal, *Political Africa. A Who's Who of Personalities and Parties* (London, 1961), p. 355.

26. CRESM. *La Formation des Élites Politiques Maghrébines* (Paris, 1973), pp. 123–33.

27. J. Norman, *Labor and Politics in Libya and Arab Africa* (New York, 1965), p. 54; see also pp. 43–5. Dues-paying membership of trade unions rose from 2,000 in 1951 to 37,000 in 1965 (W.I. Zartman (ed.), *Man, State and Society in the Contemporary Maghrib* (London, 1973), Table 21, p. 503).

28. W. Ananaba, *The Trade Union Movement in Africa: Promise and Performance* (London, 1979), p. 79.

29. G. Assan, *La Libia e il Mondo Arabo* (Rome, 1959), p. 231.

30. Originating in the complex political, social and confessional milieu of Syria under the slogan of 'unity, freedom and socialism', the *Baath* — translated as 'resurrection' or 'renaissance' — is an anti-Marxist socialist-party organisation that sees economic development as the means of social change; in practice, it relies on the army to hold power.

31. *Constitution of the Kingdom of Libya. As Modified by Law No. 1 of 1963*, article 3.

32. From the Arabic for 'sunset', '*Maghrib*' is specifically the name for Morocco. But the notion of *Jazirat al-Maghrib*, the Island of the Maghrib, includes also Algeria, Tunisia and Tripolitania and, more recently, the Western (ex-Spanish) Sahara and the Islamic Republic of Mauritania as well. The Sirte Desert is commonly considered the eastern boundary of the Maghrib, from which Cyrenaica is thus at least theoretically excluded. The *Mashriq* is the Arab world in Asia.

33. P. Mansfield, *Nasser's Egypt* (Harmondsworth, 1965), p. 83.

34. 'OPEC Oil Report', *Petroleum Economist* (London, 1977), Table V, p. 38.

35. Benghazi, Derna and Gebel Akhdar in Cyrenaica; Gebel Garbi, Homs, Misurata, Tripoli and Zawia in Tripolitania; Sebha and Ubari in Fezzan.

36. Testifying before the 'People's Court' in 1971, Fikini confirmed that he had

asked the king to dismiss Bukuwaytin and to bring him to trial. He had also asked for the dismissal and trial of the senior officers of Cydef, the mobile forces and the police in Benghazi and Tripoli. He had requested the disbandment of Cydef and the mobile forces, the reorganisation of the police and the arming of the army, and the granting to it of 'the power to carry out its true role' (BBC, *Summary of World Broadcasts*, ME/3831/A/4–5).

37. Ibid. Fikini said that while on a visit to Washington, he had personally discussed the removal of foreign bases with President John F. Kennedy and had found him 'completely understanding'.

38. The shanty-town population of Tripoli was at the very least 25,000 in 1954, and by 1964 it was probably very much larger than the estimate of 40,000; 'the general appearance of bidonvilles indicates a terrible poverty' (R.S. Harrison, 'Migrants in the City of Tripoli, Libya', *Geographical Review*, vol. LVII (1967). The long-established Benghazi shanty town of Sabri housed at least one-quarter of the city's total population (H.M. Bulugma, *Benghazi through the Ages* (1972), p. 69). Bulugma writes: 'The shanty town of Sabri . . . gives a clear picture of a primitive and miserable society living on the lowest margins of human subsistence. In winter, the people suffer from dirt, mud and rain. Summer conditions are better than those of winter, but millions of flies live on the dirt and sewage found all over the place. In brief, it is undoubtedly the poorest living area in the whole of Libya. Neither modern dwellings nor medical services, sanitation, hygiene, piped water or electricity are yet known, despite the fact that the eastern part of the area lies along the main northern entrance to the city . . . since the [Second World] war the shanty town, because of its extreme poverty and high population density, has become a moral problem, especially since the official prohibition of alcoholic liquor and licensed brothels immediately after independence [in Cyrenaica]' (pp. 88–90).

39. International Bank for Reconstruction and Development, *The Economic Development of Libya* (Washington, DC, 1960), p. 71.

40. J.M. May, *The Ecology of Malnutrition in Northern Africa* (New York, 1967), p. 24.

41. It was actually after the war that the Raccah and Luzon families of Tripoli, 13 people in all, were massacred outside the city by an army officer. In Cyrenaica, the number of deaths was put at 23 at least (*Corriere della Sera*, 24 June 1967) and in Tripoli at 20 (*Daily Telegraph*, 22 August 1967). For a graphic account of events in Benghazi, see A. Thwaite, *The Deserts of Hesperides* (London, 1969), pp. 163ff. The noise and sight of American transport aircraft taking off from Wheelus Field with evacuated American families during the week of the war fed popular rumour that Wheelus was being used as a base for attacks on the Arab belligerent states by the United States Air Force, if not by the Israelis themselves.

42. According to Anthony Nutting, the Libyan representatives at Khartoum were reluctant to offer anything, claiming that they had no authority to do so. 'But when [the Sudanese Prime Minister Mohammad] Mahgoub told them that the conference could wait while they telephoned to Tripoli for instructions, the necessary authority was speedily obtained' (*Nasser* (London, 1972), p. 435).

43. 8 August 1967.

44. Smith, 'North African Arms Race', *Atlantic Magazine* (January 1969). In 1974 Abd-al-Aziz Shalhi was questioned by the 'People's Court' about his membership of the military committee set up to study the missiles contract, and he indicated that the decision to order the system had been a political rather than a military one and that the British Ambassador had interfered with the committee's work. The court also heard how bribery had been used to persuade the military committee to accept the British Aircraft Corporation's proposals (BBC, *Summary of World Broadcasts*, ME/4574/A/1–2).

45. 'Libyan Missiles — Defence against Whom?', *Middle East Economic Digest* 10 May 1968).

46. *The Times* (18 June 1969) said that the basis for complaints about the deal was first that Libya might transfer the tanks to Egypt for use against Israel, but 'apart from the fact that the Libyans require their Chieftain tanks more for the defence of their country against Egypt than for Egypt's possible offence against Israel, this criticism overlooks the point that Egypt's ability to dislodge Israel from her present military position does not arise from a shortage of tanks'.

47. See F. Tondeur, *Libye, Royaume des Sables* (Paris, 1969), pp. 116–19. This French photographer says that when he first crossed Libya in 1953, the collecting of battle scrap was still in full swing and the stock was far from exhausted. Scrap dealers in Tripoli, Benghazi and above all in Derna and Tobruk, built up solid bank accounts within a few years, 'while at the same time hundreds of nomads blew themselves up. The work sites were unhealthy; in certain parts, the earth was sown with mines so numerous that, nearly thirty years later, many thousands are still intact, treacherously concealed beneath the sands.' Italian divers worked for years breaking up the sunken wrecks off Bardia, Tobruk and Derna for scrap.

48. Lindberg, *A General Economic Appraisal of Libya* (New York, 1952), p. 32.

49. Higgins, *The Economic and Social Development of Libya* (New York, 1953).

50. Lindberg, *General Economic Appraisal of Libya*, p. 32.

51. Higgins, *Economic and Social Development of Libya*, p. 6.

52. Ibid., p. 47.

53. Higgins, 'Education and the Economic and Social Development of Libya', introduction to *Educational Missions: Report of the Mission to Libya* (Paris, 1952), p. 14.

54. IBRD, *Economic Development of Libya* p. 7.

55. A. Pelt, *First Annual Report* (New York, 1950), p. 19.

56. Lindberg, *General Economic Appraisal of Libya*, p. 10.

57. Penrose, Allan and McLachlan, *Agriculture and the Economic Development of Libya* (London, 1970), p. 54.

58. C.G. Segrè, *Fourth Shore* (Chicago, 1974), p. 54.

59. Penrose, Allan and McLachlan, *Agriculture and Economic Development*, p. 11; conversion at $2.80 to £L1.

60. See R. Farley, *Planning for Development in Libya. The Exceptional Economy in the Developing World* (New York, 1971), pp. 110–11; 178–9.

61. F.C. Thomas, 'The Libyan Oil Worker', *Middle East Journal*, vol. 15. (Summer 1961).

62. For a full account of the development of the Libyan oil industry, see Chapter 11.

63. Kingdom of Libya, Ministry of Planning and Development, *Five-Year Economic and Social Development Plan, 1963–1968* (Tripoli, n.d.), p. 10.

64. Conversion at $2.80 to £L1.

65. *Five-Year Plan*, p. 14.

66. Attiga, 'The Second Plan. Shift from Investment to Regular Production', *Financial Times* survey 'Libya' (6 March 1969).

67. It was estimated that the country would need 100,000 skilled workers to complete the second Five-Year Plan satisfactorily (*Middle East Economic Digest*, 4 April 1969).

68. BBC, *Summary of World Broadcasts*, ME/3822/A/1–2.

6   AT A SINGLE BLOW

It may be argued that the Libyan monarchy was doomed from the outset. Western notions of kingship are alien to the Arabs, and kingdoms have been among the prime targets of Arab nationalism. While Idris might have remained the beloved old Amir of an oil-less and British-protected Cyrenaica until his death, as king of Libya with no convincing successor, he was both an inadequate custodian of the coveted prize that his kingdom had become, and a source of potential turmoil on his death or abdication. In the event, a small group of junior army officers who were prepared to break their oaths of loyalty to the king and briefly risk their lives, seized the prize and settled the succession issue in one swift and decisive *coup*, for few kingdoms can have fallen as easily and as ripely as Libya's did.

The actual military seizure of power on the night of 31 August/1 September 1969 was accomplished within four hours.[1] It was the work of small motorised groups comprising members of an organisation of Free Unionist Officers, and troops acting under their orders. They occupied the radio stations, airports and other key installations in Tripoli, Benghazi and Baida, neutralised other armed forces and the police, sealed off the country and arrested some members of the royal family, senior officers, members of the government and state officials; many more were to be rounded up in the following days. There was little bloodshed, but more than has ever been officially acknowledged — there were gun battles with loyalists at Idris Airport outside Tripoli, at a police station in Benghazi, at the main Cydef camp at Garnada, not far from Baida, and possibly elsewhere.[2]

By 6.30 a.m. the author and leader of the night's operations, Captain Moammar Gadafi, was at the radio station in Benghazi, drafting the announcement of his successful *coup d'état*. He broadcast it himself, but anonymously, at 7.30 a.m.

> People of Libya! In response to your own will, fulfilling your most heartfelt wishes, answering your incessant demands for change and regeneration and your longing to strive towards these ends; listening to your incitement to rebel, your armed forces have

undertaken the overthrow of the reactionary and corrupt regime, the stench of which has sickened and horrified us all. At a single blow your gallant army has toppled these idols and has destroyed their images. By a single stroke it has lightened the long dark night in which the Turkish domination was followed first by Italian rule, then by this reactionary and decadent regime, which was no more than a hotbed of extortion, faction, treachery and treason.[3]

He went on to announce the formation of the Libyan Arab Republic, promising freedom, unity, equality and social justice. And, almost as an afterthought, he reassured the foreign communities about the intentions of the revolution, stressing that it was not directed against any state, international agreements or international law, but was a purely internal affair. Later in the day it was announced that all constitutional institutions of the former regime had been abolished and that all power in the Libyan Arab Republic was vested in a Revolution Command Council. (Gadafi himself was to remain anonymous for another week, while the council's eleven other members were to remain unknown for four more months.)

Libyans, and the world as a whole, were taken by surprise, not least because the *coup* had succeeded so easily and, as the events of the following days were to show, was to face no serious domestic or foreign opposition. Although it was carried out with the semi-comical incompetence and good luck characteristic of such successful ventures, it had succeeded for several sound reasons.

The timing, because accidental, was brilliant; it had, in effect, been forced on the plotters by the knowledge that if they failed to act by 1 September, they would have been dispersed by suspicious authorities. The timing was also right because the king was out of the country and was thus unable to act as a figure-head to rally counter revolutionary forces in Cyrenaica, in particular. Many members of the government were also away, it being the hottest time of the year when, traditionally, those who could do so went abroad on holiday or business. And there was much rumour of *coups* at large in the country (anti-monarchist leaflets had been distributed for the first time that summer), so that all potential *coup*-makers were perhaps under equal suspicion.

But the *coup* also succeeded because it was no opportunist grab for power, but the result of sustained ideological and practical preparations for the overthrow of the Sanussi monarchy that had been started at least ten years before. Finally, it succeeded because it was not effectively opposed — not by the army, the police or Cydef or the Cyrenaican tribes, not even by the ousted political leadership; indeed, almost as remarkable as the *coup* itself was the complete moral collapse of members of the old regime, from the king and the Crown Prince down, in the face of this first really serious challenge to their authority.

When the king, still on holiday at the Turkish resort of Bursa, was told of the *coup* on 1 September, he was reported to have dismissed it as an event 'of no importance' and to have declared that he intended to return home in due course, as arranged. He was apparently hoping that the *coup* was benign or, if not, that it would not succeed.

But the anti-royalist nature of the *coup* became clear later the same day when the Crown Prince broadcast an announcement that he had willingly abandoned all his constitutional and legal rights to the throne and that he was asking all the people to support the new regime 'because I support it'. On 2 September the king and his entourage sailed (he never travelled by air) for Greece, with the king still insisting that he would return home in due course. At the same time his adviser, Omar Shalhi, flew to London, where he asked to see the Foreign Secretary, Michael Stewart, apparently to solicit British military support. A Foreign Office spokesman said that Stewart 'had done most of the listening' during the twenty-minute meeting; but it was soon clear that there was to be no British military action and no move from the British or American bases to interfere in the *coup*. The British and American governments had doubtless already agreed that any attempt to intervene and restore the monarchy would be counter-productive; it was necessary to consider relations with a new regime that had already been recognised by several Arab states; British and American investments in the country were large (the American stake in the oil industry alone was estimated at $1,500 million); Libya had become the largest single supplier of crude oil to Britain (where North Sea oil was as yet undiscovered); the 1953 Anglo-Libyan treaty provided for British intervention only in the case of an external threat which the *coup* clearly was not; and particularly since the withdrawal of garrisons from Tripoli in 1966 and Benghazi in 1968, British forces that remained in the country, while still capable of safeguarding the king personally, were plainly insufficient to maintain or restore his regime.

Shalhi's flying visit to London had aroused anger in Libya, where possible British intervention was still feared as the biggest threat to the new regime. Broadcasts by Libyan radio began to take on an anti-British tone, and the radio claimed that Britain had only been dissuaded from military intervention by the Soviet naval presence in the Mediterranean. Shalhi later flew to New York, but was reportedly dissuaded from going on to Washington to see State Department officials. London and Washington had quickly appreciated the likely reaction to their policy of relying on the pro-Western bias of a ruler and regime that had been violently overthrown.

On 5 September the editor of the semi-official Cairo newspaper *Al-Ahram*, Mohammad Hassanain Haykal, devoted the greater part of his usual Friday article to the full text of what he described as a secret protocol to the 1953 Anglo-Libyan treaty, providing for British military intervention in Libya, possibly with United States help, and specifically aimed against 'Egyptian intervention'. According to Haykal, the plan, code-named 'Radford', had been obtained through an archivist in the British Defence Ministry and had been in Arab hands since 1965. Haykal claimed that the plan had been prepared to deal with a situation such as had just arisen, or with something similar, but 'the lightning success of the revolution' had given no chance for the plan to be put into operation. This would seem to be a reasonable assessment, for the plan had allowed for a four-day alert, and its highly elaborate provisions, according to the *Al-Ahram* text, provided for the movement of land, naval and air forces from Britain and British bases in Germany, Malta and Cyprus, with some of them due to arrive in Libya only three full weeks after the start of the operation. In London, a Foreign Office spokesman denied the existence of secret British plans to protect the regime of King Idris, and said that Britain had no intention of intervening in Libyan internal affairs. Although there may have been no specific obligation to protect the regime of King Idris as such there could well have been an obligation to protect the king in person, and there was 'adequate circumstantial evidence' that the text published by *Al-Ahram* was a genuine contingency plan for British intervention at Libya's request in the event of external aggression.[4]

By this time Haykal had already returned from Libya, where he had been the first official guest of the new regime. The Egyptians had been as surprised as anyone by the *coup*, and it was only when the new regime proclaimed its aims to be 'freedom, socialism and unity' in that order that it was recognised as Nasserist in affiliation rather than Baathist, in which case its slogan would have been 'unity socialism and freedom'; the order of words was important because it symbolised the ideological split between the Baath and Nasser.[5]

On 1 September the new leaders sent a message to Cairo through the Egyptian consulate in Benghazi, asking to see somebody from Egypt. Asked whom they wanted, the only name that came immediately to mind, apart from Nasser himself, was Haykal. He was accordingly sent to find out what was happening. During a 36-hour visit he met, and was subjected to the 'rib-crushing embraces' of the young leaders of the *coup* including, finally, the still anonymous Moammar Gadafi himself. Writing some years after the event, Haykal said:

> It was quite a shock to see how young he was and I began to think that perhaps I had been tricked and that this man could not be the leader of a successful revolution. But once he started to talk I revised my views. He spoke eloquently on many subjects, and then suddenly said that he and his brother officers wanted union with Egypt . . . 'Tell President Nasser we made this revolution for him. He can take everything of ours and add it to the rest of the Arab World's resources to be used for the battle.'[6]

Writing in *Al-Ahram* after his return to Cairo, Haykal described the new leaders as 'living examples of the most magnificent and beautiful things Arab nationalism can offer'. He judged this new revolution to be 'many times more important than the Iraqi revolution of 1958' because 'Libya is one of the most important foreign bases on Arab territory'.

In the meantime, the king had accepted the revolution as a fact. In an interview with the London *Daily Express* on 5 September, he disowned Shalhi's mission to Britain and the United States and made it clear that he did not intend to return home. He said the people had chosen him to be king — 'it was not a situation I very much enjoyed. All my life I think I was tired of being king.' He revealed that he had tried to abdicate on 4 August, but had been persuaded to postpone a decision until his return from holiday in the autumn. Whether the Crown Prince would have taken the throne 'would have depended upon him and the Libyan people'.

Through the mediation of President Nasser, the new regime agreed to release Idris's adopted daughter, Sulayma, and the former king and his immediate family in due course accepted Nasser's invitation to settle permanently in Egypt. They moved into a modest government villa in the Cairo suburb of Dokki where Idris, despite his supposed frailty and ill-health, lived on into his tenth decade.

In the first days after the *coup* the most prominent officer — the one assumed by the outside world to be the new leader — was 36-year-old Colonel Saad-al-Din Bushwairib. But on 8 September it became clear that he had merely been used as a figure-head for younger and more junior officers who wished to remain anonymous for their own safety. The name of Captain Moammar Gadafi[7] was made known publicly for the first time with the announcement of his promotion to the rank of colonel and his appointment as Commander-in-Chief of the Armed Forces in recognition of his services to the successful take-over of power in Benghazi; he was thereafter correctly assumed to be the head of the Revolution Command Council whose other members still remained strictly anonymous.

There was still no reason why anyone outside his own family, student and army circles should have known anything about this very junior officer of signals.[8] He was born in June 1942, just as the war in North Africa was rolling to a climax at El Alamein, where a decisive victory was to give Britain a dominance over Libyan affairs that was to last until Gadafi himself was able to seize power a generation later.

His birthplace was the low tent of his father, a semi-nomad pitched somewhere south of Sirte in the open desert that formed the family's traditional range-lands. The Sirtica, although administratively part of Tripolitania in the west and part of Cyrenaica in the east, has always been an extended frontier district, a historically ungovernable no man's land between the main centres of population round Tripoli, Benghazi and the southern oases. In being born there Moammar Gadafi acquired the politically invaluable credential of being neither a true Tripolitanian, nor a Cyrenaican, nor even a Fezzanese, but a *bedu* of the open desert that is common to all Libya and from which many Libyans like to think they themselves once came.[9]

This only son so clearly needed to learn and receive a formal education that at great family sacrifice he was sent at the age of 10 to school in Sirte, where his schoolfellows looked down on him as a poor desert *bedu*; at night he slept in the mosque and at holidays he trudged back to the family encampment. When he was 14 he went with his family to Fezzan, and at Sebha Preparatory School he m and befriended Abd-al-Salam Jallud, who was to become his right-hand man. Gadafi arrived in Sebha in 1956, the year that mounting tension between Arab nationalism and the West came to a head over Suez. He started to feed his new-found interest in current affairs by listening to the radio, tuning mostly to the Nasserist, anti-western 'Voice of the Arabs' beamed across the Arab world from Cairo, and by absorbing forbidden political books and pamphlets from Egypt, including a much-read copy of Nasser's *Philosophy of the Revolution*. It was then that he came to recognise Nasser as the only leader offering the younger generation, in particular, hope for the future of Libya and the Arab world. He thus began to influence and harangue his fellow pupils and to organise them in demonstrations — 'they demonstrated over Lumumba's death, over the explosion of the French atomic bomb in the Sahara, over the Algerian revolution: any occasion would do'.[10] Gadafi became known in Sebha as a militant; the police intervened; he was expelled from school and he and his family had to leave Fezzan. But it was at Sebha that the revolution started, ten years before it came to power, with the formation of a Central Committee and the holding of secret meetings among the town's secondary-school boys. But, as Gadafi said many years later, 'Although our objectives appeared much like dreams, we had faith at the time that they would materialise one day.'

By the time he left Sebha, he had shaped his own basic political thinking and he had already adopted (with the intense conviction necessary to hold and lead others) many of the views that were to give such distinctive colours to the Libyan revolution. From his upbringing in a traditional desert nomad society of close family and clan ties, and from his schooling (largely by Egyptian teachers) he had acquired a strong Islamic faith and moral code and an austere, egalitarian and simplistic outlook on life.

Despite his expulsion from Sebha, Gadafi managed to continue his education up to university entrance level at the secondary school in Misurata, the second town of Tripolitania, where he already had some connections and influence. By the time he went to Misurata in 1961, he was convinced that the army's support was essential for a successful revolution. He had already ruled out civilian politics as a means of change: he had found opposition groups inside Libya weak, disorganised and without ideas; and he had decided against joining forces with outside organisations such as the Baath or George Habbash's Arab Nationalist Movement (still in its pre-Marxist stage) because of the time and effort they wasted in divisive argument.

Yet he and his schoolfellows were clearly incapable of influencing the army from outside, not least because the officers came from a narrow social class and were still largely apolitical. But he saw that the officer corps could be infiltrated from below by the better-educated and more classless generation that had grown up since independence. In 1963 the first general meeting of Gadafi's movement, bringing together followers from Sebha, Misurata and Tripoli, decided that Gadafi and two others would enrol at the Military Academy in Benghazi specifically to form a nucleus of Free Unionist Officers whose long-term purpose was to make a *coup* possible by gaining sufficient support for it within the army.

Thus, when Gadafi joined the Military Academy in 1964, his organisation became a military one. A separate civilian wing that was to have worked alongside the military organisation to arouse 'popular consciousness' seems to have played no significant role after 1964. A central committee of Free Unionist Officers within the Military Academy recruited members from every new officer-cadet intake Omar al-Mihaishi, whom Gadafi ordered to join the Military Academy at the same time as himself, later explained how, 'when we entered the army . . . we had to change our methods completely Ideology was not going to help us, for the officers were not ready intellectually to follow us in that field. So it was on nationalism tha we had to depend, a sentiment deeply felt in the army, and on personal relationship, or friendship.'[11]

Young Libyans like Gadafi and his associates presented the old regime with one of its most acute dilemmas. In making full use of the wider educational and career opportunities and the greater social mobility of post-independence Libya, they were quietly acquiring the means of challenging the regime itself. Indeed, it seems strange that the young Gadafi, with his record of public political agitation had even been considered eligible for a commission in the army: possibly the authorities were hoping to curb his political enthusiasm with the status, discipline and material rewards of a young officer, as other would-be trouble-makers had been tamed before him — although if such was their intention, they had badly misjudged their man. Nevertheless, it is unlikely that Gadafi's known politica record would have been treated as lightly by many regimes, and certainly not by his own.

The Military Academy had a reputation for turning out your

officers 'poised, smart and arrogant'; Gadafi seems to have been none of these. He and the nucleus of the Free Officer movement graduated from the academy in 1965 and, after a signals course in Britain in 1966 (which apparently he did not enjoy and which, as his only experience of foreign education, seems only to have reinforced his Islamic nationalism), he was commissioned in the army signals corps. He was posted to the army headquarters at Gar Yunis barracks just outside Benghazi — a not inconvenient centre from which to contact and control his widening network of conspirators.

With the Arab defeat in the war of 1967 providing an additional goad to action,[12] the central committee of the Free Unionist Officers used to meet regularly on holidays and, because all members had to attend all meetings, much clandestine travelling was involved. Members were also bound by a strong code of ethics and were obliged to pray and study regularly; many of them were taking part-time courses at Benghazi University, and for three years after leaving the Military Academy, Gadafi read for, but never took, a degree in history.

By 1969, when other preparations for a *coup* were well under way, the Free Unionist officers started sounding out some of their more senior colleagues. Up to then, all recruiting had been among officers no more senior than themselves, or among officer-cadets and NCOs. But the only senior recruits to the movement were two colonels, Musa Ahmad and Adam al-Hawwaz.

At the beginning of 1969, Captain Gadafi estimated that the Free Officer movement could mobilise enough men, armour and ammunition to neutralise all other armed forces at a given signal. Accordingly, 12 March was chosen as the date for the *coup*, only to be followed by six months of postponements, mounting tension and increasing risk of discovery.

The Free Unionist officers had already decided that three conditions were essential for success:[13] all senior Libyan commanders of the armed forces had to be in the country; the king had to be away from his centres of support in Cyrenaica; and all members of the government had to be in one place. The *coup* attempt timed for 12 March was postponed because the greatest of Egyptian singers, Um Kalthum, gave a public performance in Tripoli late that night; many of the senior officers due for arrest were among the audience of seven thousand, and the occasion was considered inappropriate, not only because the performance was televised, but because it was in aid of *Al-Fatah*. Action timed for 24 March was put off when it became clear that military intelligence was suspicious and the king, presumably alerted, unexpectedly left Tripoli for his British-protected 'fortress' at Tobruk. Another opportunity on 13 August had to be ignored.

In the meantime, other events of 1969 had provided the young officers with fresh stimulus for action. In August a deranged Australian set fire to and damaged the Al-Aqsa Mosque in Israeli-occupied East Jerusalem. This desecration of its third-holiest shrine shocked all Islam, and for the Arabs, in particular, was yet another reminder of the urgent need to rid Jerusalem of an occupier unable or even unwilling to protect the holy places. To the Free Unionist officers their *coup* was Libya's first necessary move in the liberation of Jerusalem, and there was a reference to the Al-Aqsa fire in the very first broadcast to the nation after the *coup*: '. . . prepare to face the enemies of Islam, the enemies of humanity, those who have burned our sanctuaries . . .'.

Meanwhile, the Shalhi brothers were visibly tightening their grip on the country. Abd-al-Aziz was already Chief of Staff of the army, while Omar had become the king's counsellor in April. Omar's wedding (reported to have cost £L2 million) to the daughter of Hussain Mazigh, the former premier and chief of the powerful Barassa tribe of Cyrenaica, appeared to puritanical junior officers not only vulgar show of corruptly acquired wealth, but also confirmation of the Shalhis' ambitions for even greater political power. It is generally accepted that by 1969 the Shalhis 'had long since perfected their plans, not so much for a *coup d'état* as for the "preservation" of their own highly privileged status'.[14] The king had again been expressing a wish to abdicate and had apparently been persuaded only to postpone his decision to do so. It has been suggested[15] that Libya's Western allies and President Nasser knew about the Shalhi plans before the king went on holiday in June and had agreed not to interfere so long as the West's oil and strategic interests were unaffected and the cash subsidies to Egypt continued; Britain would have kept close control over the armed forces through the missile and *Chieftain* tanks supply contracts.

It has also been suggested that senior army officers were also preparing their own *coup*, while prominent businessman and technocrats were also said to have plans for the future of the country under the at least nominal leadership of one or another member of the royal family. In short, the Free Unionist officers may have been by no means the only group planning a *coup* in 1969, although Gad himself has denied that another movement could have succeeded, even partially, in taking over. 'The Free Officers had infiltrated the entire army . . . nobody but we ourselves could have got the army moving.'[16] The Free Officers nevertheless had the good fortune to strike first, after the date of their *coup* had been forced upon them. This was because they were already under suspicion, and about 40 of them were being posted at short notice on technical courses in Britain for which they were due to leave on 2 September; they therefore had to strike before they were dispersed.

Many observers believed that violent change had become inevitable in Libya by the late 1960s. What was expected, at least according to the defence dispositions, was invasion by Egypt, and/or possibly by Algeria, followed by Western counter-intervention. In the event, when the *coup* did come, it was mounted by officers acting entirely on their own initiative, and so junior as to have been largely discounted as a serious threat to the monarchy.

Gadafi and his associates believed that they had many sound reasons for making their *coup*. The first of their targets was the monarchy itself, an alien institution, apparently established and still maintained by foreign decree to serve foreign interests; from Gadafi's viewpoint, the Sanussi family were primarily landed aristocrats rather than religious ascetics like himself. After the monarchy, the Shalhis were only the most obvious offenders among those who had bound the administration of the country into webs of corruption and nepotism, squandering the national wealth on such follies as the building of Baida and the missiles contract with Britain; foreigners (and especially the resident Italian community)[17] were seen to enjoy a privileged status while Libyan Arab social traditions and culture were eroded by the worst forms of 'cultural imperialism'. Like many other Libyans who cared about such things, Gadafi saw the foreign bases not only as a continuing affront to Libyan independence, but also as a potential springboard for the Western assault on neighbouring revolutionary Arab states. It was a source of special resentment that while the kingdom was so subservient to the West as to allow the continued existence of the bases, Libya showed scant official enthusiasm for vital Arab issues in general and the Palestine cause in particular. Even the economic policies of the kingdom were an affront to many Libyans besides Gadafi and his immediate followers who considered that the international oil companies were taking easy profits from underpriced Libyan oil, while the people were denied their just share of national wealth that should have been spent on economic development and social welfare. Or, as Radio Moscow put it on 2 September in its first comment on the *coup*, 'ending the plundering by the Western monopolies, mainly the oil monopolies, is in the fundamental interests of the Libyan people'.

In taking it upon themselves to right these not uncommon wrongs — as they perceived them — Captain Gadafi and his associates found themselves in the early morning of 1 September 1969 the anonymous and as yet unacknowledged arbiters of the future of over two million people and the fourth most extensive country in Africa, masters of a strategically sensitive Mediterranean coastline of some two thousand kilometres, and recipients of a daily oil revenue of over $3 million. They had undoubtedly snatched a great prize: as yet unknown was whether they could keep it, and the use they would make of it.

Notes

1. For a full account of events that night, see M. Bianco, *Gadafi: Voice from th Desert* (London, 1975), pp. 46–64.
2. In Benghazi, there was almost continuous small-arms fire for 28 hours — a extremely extended *feu de joie*, if such it was.
3. Bianco, *Gadafi*, p. 65.
4. *Arab Report and Record*, issue 17 (1–15 September 1969), p. 364.
5. M. Heikal, *The Road to Ramadan* (London, 1975), p. 69. Iraq, where th Baath had returned to power the previous year, was the first country to recognise th new regime; Egypt was the second.
6. Ibid., p. 70.
7. *Guardian* (22 May 1973) carried a leading article that discussed the many wa of transliterating 'Gadafi' from Arabic into Roman script, and came to the concl sion that there were 432 possible permutations. Actually there are more — at lea 648, and that does not include the exotic 'Kazafuy' (*New Middle East*, July 197 p. 29). 'Gadafi' is used here and throughout for the sake of brevity, if not accurac
8. For a full — and fulsome — biography of Gadafi, see Bianco, *Gadafi*.
9. Gadafi's family was of the small Gadadfa tribe. Berber in origin, but lo Arabised, the Gadadfa was one of the tribal groups known as *Arab al-Gharb*, t Arabs of the West, which in a series of wars in the nineteenth century had been forc out of Cyrenaica and into the harsher surroundings of the Sirtica by an alliance stronger tribes, including the Barassa and the Magharba (E. De Agostini, *Popolazioni della Cirenaica* (Benghazi, 1922–3), pp. 26–7). With his sense history, young Gadafi may have fed his resentments with the knowledge that his o people had once been driven off their land and into the wilderness by two of the v same tribes that had become predominant in the Libyan kingdom. In the mid-ni teeth century, the Gadadfa came under Sanussi influence. With tribal lands extend south and west of Sirte, and with commercial connections with the oasis of Hon, t also came under the political domination of the Saif-al-Nassir family, leaders of Awlad Slaiman of Fezzan, who fought both the Turkish and Italian conquests Libya. The Gadadfa had historical links with Chad. They were among the many tri

that supported the Awlad Slaiman in their wars against the Kel Owi Tuareg in Kanem in the mid-nineteenth century (Barth, *Travels and Discoveries in North and Central Africa* (London, 1857–8), vol. II, p. 274). And after the Italian conquest of the central desert around 1930, two to three hundred Gadadfa tribesmen were among the many Libyans from the Sirtica who sought refuge in Chad ('Muammar El Kadhafi', *Maghreb*, no. 48 (1971)).

10. Bianco, *Gadafi*, p. 15.

11. Ibid., p. 32.

12. In a Palestine Day speech in 1970, Gadafi said that the 1969 revolutions in Libya and Sudan were 'no better proof of the Arab nation's firm determination following the 1967 defeat' (BBC, *Summary of World Broadcasts*, ME/3381/A/4).

13. Legum and Drysdale, *Africa Contemporary Record, 1969* (Exeter, 1970), pp. 13, 19.

14. P. Seale and M. McConville, *The Hilton Assignment* (London, 1973), p. 42.

15. H. Breton, 'La Libye Républicaine', *Annuaire de l'Afrique du Nord,* vol. VIII (1969).

16. Bianco, *Gadafi*, p. 84.

17. As recently as 1966 the centre of Tripoli was closed to traffic for an afternoon to enable the annual *Corpus Christi* procession to follow its customary route from the Cathedral of *Sacro Cuore* through streets decorated according to proper Italian custom with carpets and bright stuffs draped from balconies.

7   A YEAR OF REVOLUTION

Junior army officers are poorly qualified to lead a modern state, even one with bureaucratic, economic and social structures as simple as Libya's. Colonel Gadafi and his revolutionaries had come to power with a luminous faith in their own prejudices and provisional ideology but, as they were soon to learn, the routines of government demand more than faith and ideology, and the first months of revolutionary rule were accordingly characterised by paralysing indecisiveness on all but a few broad issues and the prime necessity of safeguarding the revolution. While the revolutionary leaders knew what they wanted to abolish — foreign bases, Western domination and influence, as well as a political, economic and social climate in which those like the Shalhis could flourish — it was soon clear that they had few constructive ideas of their own about shaping the new Libya.

One of the first acts of the Revolution Command Council (RCC) was to announce adherence to existing international obligations, treaties, contracts and pan-Arab policies, as well as continuation of crude oil exports. A week after the *coup*, the RCC named a nine-man Cabinet under the premiership of Dr Sulaiman al-Maghrabi, the Palestine-born leader of the 1967 oil workers' strike who had been released into exile from the resultant prison sentence only a few weeks before the September *coup*. The new Foreign Minister was Salih Busair, a former journalist and member of the National Assembly who had gone into exile in Egypt in 1955 to avoid arrest for his outspoken criticism of the regime.[1]

Colonel Musa Ahmad (Interior) and Colonel Adam al-Hawwaz (Defence) were the only soldiers in the Cabinet and, as the only senior officers with an active part in the *coup*, they were sympathisers with the Free Officers rather than committed members of the group. The formation of the Cabinet showed that the RCC intended to govern indirectly through vigorous civilian technocrats offering acceptable revolutionary credentials and charged with the task of implementing the general policy of the state as drawn up by the RCC.

It was Gadafi, as leader of the RCC, who at popular rallies a

132

Benghazi, Sebha and Tripoli[2] in the first weeks of the revolution out-lined the provisional ideology of the new regime (which clearly owed much to President Nasser's version of Arab nationalism) and defined what he understood by the three catchwords of his revolu-tion — freedom, socialism and unity. His stated views on freedom, including the belief that it was 'the natural right of every individual' politically, economically and socially, seemed to owe much to the French eighteenth-century notion of man as naturally good, but the victim of an unjust social system; and later in his career Gadafi was to enjoy comparison with Rousseau. Gadafi saw Libya as the victim of injustice; as he told the people of Sebha: 'God has not created this people poor, nor has He imposed poverty on it, nor created it a slave . . . they were the vicious and the charlatans who made a slave of this people which was born free'. In the months following his seizure of power, Gadafi's actions reflected his belief that Libya's ills would be cured when true independence was achieved, following evacuation of the foreign military bases and the end of the foreign economic and cultural domination. But it also became clear that 'freedom' in the Libyan Arab Republic would not include the right to form political parties (they were considered a bar to Arab unity), nor the right to a parliament ('not necessary in a just and true society', according to Gadafi), nor freedom of expression (except, possibly, at supervised public seminars). The army, which in the 'Constitutional Proclama-tion' of 11 December 1969[3] claimed to be acting 'in the name of the popular will', remained the sole source of power. Asked why there were no civilians in the RCC, Gadafi said that officers truly had the conscience to represent better than anyone else the demands of the Libyan people. 'This is because of our origins, which are mostly very humble . . .'[4] While Dr Maghrabi and his Cabinet colleagues were to find it impossible to work effectively so long as their every decision had to be approved by the RCC, Gadafi continued to insist that the armed forces had acted in response to the people's orders and had accordingly brought about not a mere military *coup d'état*, but a tumultuous popular revolution' that would become a 'deep and comprehensive' one.

Gadafi's socialism was 'sincere collective work to reach a society of justice and sufficiency' and 'a distribution of prosperity among the people'. Echoing Mussolini, Gadafi asserted that work was 'the sacred duty of every individual', and he insisted that socialism would be built and social justice realised through the 'sacred alliance of the people's working forces', which he defined as 'workers, peasants, unexploiting capitalists, intellectuals and soldiers'. From this emerged one of his basic propositions — that his socialism was the 'socialism of Islam', derived from the people's 'heritage, beliefs and great history'. He suggested that Islam itself was a *socialist* creed, although he soon added qualifications: 'it can be said that the spirit and basic principles of Islam are not incompatible with socialism, even if they are not clear like the socialism of today'.[5]

There was to be much talk of 'Islamic socialism' in revolutionary Libya, but it never became clear how far the country's particular political, economic and social systems were supposed to reflect either authentic Islamic models or Gadafi's reinterpretation of them for the sake of modern practice; for, as Maxime Rodinson points out, 'Le Coran, parole de Dieu, autorité principale et irréfragable, n'est pas un traité d'économie politique'.[6]

Unity, the third catchword of the revolution, had 'existed among the Arabs for thousands of years', and was 'an inevitable necessity'. Its realisation was hindered 'only by artificial borders established on the Arab people by imperialism'. Palestine would be liberated 'when the Arab land had become one solid front'. Although the prime purpose of Arab unity was to wage successful war against Israel, Gadafi also saw it as a means of ensuring the partnership of the Libyan people in the coming Arab political, economic and technological revolution that was to make the united Arab nation a leading world power. Unhappily, the realisation of Arab unity did not depend on Libya alone, and Gadafi was to find that Arab leaders — including Gamal Abd-al-Nasser — reciprocated his enthusiasm for unity as a panacea for Arab troubles up to the point of agreement, but not so far as implementation.

The Arabic for revolution, *thawra*, derives from a root meaning stirring up, arousal and, by extension, revolt and rebellion. Arab revolution thus implies rejection and violent change of the *status quo*.[7] But Gadafi and his associates, certainly in their early months in power, were not even particularly dynamic (they lost too much sleep arguing over administrative details that should never have concerned them) and they were certainly not violent. They were young, paralysingly unsure of themselves, and their very title of 'free officers' implied that they were allied to no political party or doctrine. They had to devise their own political ideology, and this inevitably took time, although it was soundly based on Arab nationalism and took Nasserism as its model. Gadafi was meanwhile presented as a charismatic leader, and he indeed very quickly became a dominating figure whose obvious piety aroused strong emotional responses among a still intensely religious people.[8]

The new leadership nevertheless had to act to satisfy some of the popular expectations aroused by the overthrow of the monarchy. But in its first months in power, it could only fall back on its three catchwords of 'freedom, socialism and unity' and appeal to the majority of politically unschooled Libyans through an overworked and outdated ideology in which 'colonialism', 'imperialism' and the former regime were blamed for all the nation's ills, while revolutionary 'achievements' were largely confined to foreign affairs.

The regime had initially secured its position and had neutralised the most obvious sources of potential internal opposition by arresting members of the royal family, all politicians and prominent officials, and more than 300 high-ranking police officers and over 250 army officers with the rank of major or above. Many underwent televised trials before a new 'People's Court', but sentences were light. Immediately after the *coup*, the army had disarmed the police (which had always been considered one of the main props of the monarchy) and had confiscated their vehicles and heavy equipment. Early in 1970, some police units were integrated into the regular army, which quickly expanded to an estimated 20 thousand men; other police units were disbanded, and the rest were placed under the direct control of the Interior Ministry, which from 1970 onwards was headed by a member of the RCC. And soon after the *coup*, Egyptian security men were drafted into the armed forces and the police to guard against both counter-revolution and extremism; quite possibly, these Egyptian 'reinforcements' prevented the Libyan revolution from drifting into extremism in its early formative stages.

Most of those arrested in the immediate aftermath of the *coup* were released before the end of 1969 because their skills and experience were too valuable to be wasted. The regime was obliged to re-employ many senior men and trust to their loyalty, while the acquiescence of potential opponents was bought with generous pensions. Nevertheless, the RCC found itself increasingly reliant on the civil service for essential advice, as well as for routine administrative ability.

The regime further consolidated its position by banning all party political activity and by clamping down on possible sources of opposition. Thus in May 1970 a new labour law dissolved all existing trade unions and federations (which had defied the former regime in 1961 and 1967) and placed 'considerable restraints' on new unions.[9]

The process of eliminating the private press started soon after the *coup* when subsidies given under the monarchy were sharply reduced. Then in January 1970 it was announced that only the regime's new official newspaper *Al-Thawra* (*The Revolution*) would be given the 'lucrative advertisements placed by government ministries'.[10] At the same time, radio and the newly established television service were skilfully used to promote the causes of the revolution.

That Cyrenaican tribal loyalty to the Sanussi throne had effectively been exposed as a myth was another source of strength to the new regime. The army that had overthrown the monarchy had itself been partly composed of Cyrenaican tribesmen, while the fact that the king had been abroad at the time of the *coup* had deprived any would-be supporters of his symbolic leadership; Tobruk had been alone in waiting three or four days before accepting the overthrow of the monarchy. Nevertheless, Cyrenaica's reaction to the *coup* and many of its effects was surprisingly docile. Cyrenaica had in a way been the senior partner in the kingdom, but after 1969 it lost a primacy derived largely from the Sanussi heritage and Sanussi leadership of the long Cyrenaican resistance to the Italians. After the *coup* there was a tendency to play down the specifically Cyrenaican resistance, and there was a new official emphasis on the exploits of such Tripolitanian resistance leaders as Ramadan Suwayhili (who, significantly, had ended his career as a dedicated enemy of the Sanussi). The Cyrenaicans remained passive and uncomplaining when the centres of power were openly transferred from Benghazi and Baida to Tripoli, the Cyrenaica Defence Force was brought under the control of the army,[11] the Sanussi Islamic University at Baida was closed (in November 1970), and eventually the ex-king and former Amir of Cyrenaica was tried and sentenced to death *in absentia*. If there were complaints in the east that Libya's new-found prosperity and rising significance in international affairs were largely due to the exploitation of Cyrenaican oil, they were not loud enough to be heard abroad.

In effect, the new regime overthrew the hard decisions of 1950–1 that had made Cyrenaica the equal of Tripolitania in the Libyan federation; instead, the process that had started with the creation of the unified kingdom in 1963–4 was speeded up and Tripolitania, with its larger population and higher social development, quickly achieved its naturally dominating position in the Libyan republic.

Inevitable disillusion with the revolution had set in by the end of 1969, particularly among the urban moneyed classes who found public and private life not markedly freer or better than under the monarchy, and who were worst hit by the post-revolutionary economic recession. But the poorer classes everywhere, concerned less with political freedoms than with economic rewards, felt generally better off as a result of the raising of the minimum wage, lower rents and better work terms.

The new leaders, most of them from poor backgrounds, were young, enthusiastic and patently sincere Islamic fundamentalists and Arab nationlists. Such qualities earned them genuine popularity, at least among the uncritical majority unable to foresee how this leadership could become like any other Third World military dictatorship. Popularity was also seasoned by Gadafi's own special gift of understanding and appealing directly to the common people. For in the early stages of the revolution, these lean young officers appeared as an assurance that Libyan affairs would thenceforth be ruled by sympathetic representatives of those who, in the midst of the country's swelling prosperity, had been among the deprived and the disregarded.

Nevertheless, with all expressions of contrary opinion at least as effectively silenced as ever they had been under the monarchy, critics and opponents of the new regime were driven to plotting and subversion, as Gadafi and his associates had been while in opposition. Again, the army was the one organisation large enough yet sufficiently close-knit to provide the conditions for disaffection to mature. The first internal plot against the regime was publicly revealed 100 days after 1 September, on 10 December 1969, before it had become dangerous; it had apparently been uncovered by Egyptian security men attached to the armed forces. The ringleaders were the only senior officers in Gadafi's group, the Defence Minister, Adam al-Hawwaz and the Interior Minister, Colonel Musa Ahmad. An attempt to overthrow Gadafi and set up a new government under the presidency of Colonel Hawwaz, with Colonel Ahmad as his deputy, had been planned for 7 December, but seems to have been ineptly prepared. Although Gadafi dismissed the *coup* attempt as 'a matter of grudge by some senior officers against the unitary and free officers who are mainly junior officers',[12] he acted swiftly to reinforce the position of the RCC.

The plot was the outcome of more than mere rivalry within the small circle of still largely anonymous leaders. Publication in the Tripoli and Beirut press of the revolutionary notions of Colonel Hawwaz had already led to conflict between him and his younger

colleagues.[13] According to Libyan Radio, the *coup* plot was the work
of a 'misled group' who believed 'it would turn back the wheel of
history out of a belief that 1 September was the beginning of a series
of military *coups*'.[14] The *coup* attempt had been timed to coincide
with the opening of the Anglo-Libyan talks on the military bases,
and Gadafi claimed in an interview of 10 December that 'the plotters
wanted imperialism to stay on in Libya. They wanted the bases to
stay in Libya. They wanted to obstruct the negotiations. They
enjoyed support from the bases.'[15] Possibly no other allegation
could have as effectively ensured genuine popular condemnation of
those who, in the words of Libyan Radio, 'tried to steal the revolution' — but it was an allegation that was never proved.

Together with some 30 other officers, Hawwaz and Ahmad were
tried by a military court in March 1970 on charges of plotting to
overthrow the regime. Sentences of life imprisonment for Hawwaz
and Ahmad were finally announced on 8 August, while 23 other
officers were sentenced to prison terms ranging from one to thirteen
years. News of the sentences was greeted with demonstrations
against their leniency in Tripoli and elsewhere. After a retrial, new
sentences announced in October included death for Hawwaz and
Ahmad and three other ringleaders; others had their terms of
imprisonment increased. Popular demand for harsher treatment had
followed the discovery of another plot in July and Gadafi's subsequent comment that the new plotters had probably been encouraged by the leniency shown to the Hawwaz group; nevertheless, the
death sentences were not carried out.

One immediate outcome of the Hawwaz plot was the issue by the
RCC on 11 December 'in the name of the Arab people of Libya' of a
constitutional proclamation, pending preparation of a permanent
constitution.[16] The proclamation named the RCC as the 'highest
authority' in the republic: 'it exercises the functions of supreme
sovereignty and legislation and draws up the general policy of the
state on behalf of the people' (Article 18). It appointed, and could
dismiss, the Cabinet (Article 19); the armed forces were declared to
'belong to the people', but 'shall be under the full control of the
RCC' (Article 26). The proclamation also stated the RCC's intention
'to liberate the national economy from dependence upon and influ
ence by the outside world' (Article 7).

At the same time, the RCC moved to neutralise future opposition
by issuing a 'Decision on the Protection of the Revolution'.[17] I
warned: 'Anyone who takes up arms against the republican regime

of the Revolution of 1 September or takes part in an armed band for this purpose shall be sentenced to death.' Anyone committing 'an act of aggression' against the regime was to be imprisoned.[18]

By January 1970 the RCC felt secure enough to reveal the names of all its members for the first time.[19] This was possibly done on the advice of President Nasser, who had warned of the dangers of usurpers 'stealing' the revolution from its unknown leaders. A week later the RCC consolidated its control over the administration when the largely civilian Maghrabi Cabinet resigned, apparently because of friction over RCC insistence on ratifying every Cabinet decision. The new Cabinet announced on 16 January had been expanded from nine to thirteen posts. Gadafi became Prime Minister and Minister of Defence, with Abd-al-Salam Jallud as deputy premier and Minister of the Interior and Local Government (giving him effective control of the police). RCC members Major Bashir Hawadi, Captain Omar Mihaishi and Captain Mohammad Mugaryif were given three other key domestic portfolios. Salih Busair kept the Foreign Affairs portfolio, but there was a new Oil Minister, Dr Izz-al-Din Mabruk, previously a government lawyer specialising in oil affairs. Together with the new Cabinet, a National Defence Council was formed under Gadafi's chairmanship to reorganise the armed forces and to study closer inter-Arab military co-operation.

In July 1970 another *coup* attempt was revealed with the news that a large cache of arms and ammunition had been found at Sebha in May. Speaking at a Tripoli rally on 23 July, Colonel Gadafi said that those responsible were 'reactionary retired police officers and contractors who had profited from the defunct regime'.[20] The attempt, which seems to have lacked ideological motivation or popular support, had apparently been led from abroad by a cousin of the ex-king, Abdallah bin Abid al-Sanussi, and was also said to have involved a number of leading figures of the former regime living in exile, including the former premiers Hussain Mazigh and Abd-al-Hamid Bakkush. It was planned to use five thousand foreign mercenaries, supported by some American Central Intelligence Agency men, flown in from Chad; after seizing Sebha, the mercenaries were to have marched on Tripoli and Benghazi. The broadcasting station and the headquarters of the RCC in Tripoli were to have been seized; RCC members were to have been shot, and the first broadcast by the new regime was to have included an announcement of the abolition of socialism.[21] Twenty men were later tried for their part in the plot (four of them *in absentia*) and were given long prison terms.

There were to be further attempts on Gadafi and his regime in the early 1970s.[22] Perhaps the most spectacular plot involved the abortive assault planned on behalf of Omar Shalhi on the main prison in Tripoli. The idea was that European mercenaries landed by sea would free and arm the 150 political prisoners held there, most of them leading figures of the old regime. It was intended that the assault would act as 'an explosive charge to trigger off a chain reaction of revolt and bring Gadafi down'.[23] Almost as bizarre was the reported charging of Gadafi's motorcade at night by a lorry on the narrow Tripoli airport road in 1971; the lorry driver and some of Gadafi's motor-cycle escort were killed. But it has never been publicly established whether this incident was really an assassination attempt, or merely a more than usually spectacular example of bad driving.

These events show that Gadafi's future as the youngest Arab leader was constantly in doubt and that, after the uncovering of the senior officers' plot, the main active opposition to his rule seemed, at least in the early 1970s, to come from leading figures of the former regime. Such opposition was inevitably based abroad, and thus fed suspicions of foreign subversion.

Among the achievements of the revolution in its first year were the erasing of the more obvious and intrusive symbols of subservience to 'colonialism and imperialism'. This meant the end of the foreign bases and the Italian and Jewish communities, the nationalisation of foreign banks, the beginning of the far-reaching confrontation with the international oil companies, and the elimination of such symbols of foreign influence as cathedrals,[24] churches and night-clubs, street and other public signs in Latin script, and the production and sale of alcohol.

By 1969 Libya was conspicuous among Arab states in still 'living on its geography' by leasing military bases to foreign powers when there was no longer even the excuse of economic necessity for doing so. To Gadafi and his associates, the bases were reminders of Libya's lack of 'true independence'. Their evacuation had been one of the main themes of public speakers since the start of the revolution. At a popular rally in Tripoli in mid-October 1969, Gadafi declared that evacuation had become a basic condition of Libyan freedom, and he threatened that the whole country would become a battlefield if British and American forces did not leave 'by reasonable means'. The first formal move came on 29 October with a note asking Britain to evacuate her bases as soon as possible.

Britain's best course seemed to be to leave promptly, and to use the fact of having done so as a means of establishing fresh relations with a new regime that had already expressed a desire for continuing friendship. Among Britain's bargaining counters was the contract made with the former regime to supply two hundred *Chieftain* tanks — advanced equipment that no armed forces outside Britain then possessed, and which the new regime particularly coveted because it had been denied to Israel. It was also a fact that the two remaining bases were no longer as important to Britain as the Libyans believed they were. British commitments in the world had greatly contracted since the signing of the Anglo-Libyan treaty in 1953 and this, together with the development of longer-range and more versatile transport aircraft, meant that Britain had less need of air staging posts than in the 1950s. The loss of desert training grounds in Cyrenaica could not be made good,[25] but, as the British Defence Minister, Denis Healey, estimated later in the House of Commons, 'the effect of the loss of our other facilities in Libya on our military capability is negligible'.[26]

The Libyans had their own bargaining counters, including a threat to withdraw Sterling balances, which had stood at £384 million in August 1969,[27] revision of arms sales contracts, nationalisation of British oil and other interests and, as a last resort, open armed attack. A British junior minister told the House of Commons on the day the talks opened that

> It is our object . . . to establish a totally new relationship with the new government in Libya. The original agreement was intended primarily for the defence of Libya at Libya's request. If Libya no longer wishes that defence, then it is not for us to impose such a relationship on the country.[28]

In the event, agreement over the bases was reached remarkably quickly in two negotiating sessions totalling only six hours. By the time the talks opened on 8 December, withdrawal of British forces and dependants had already started.[29] At the first session the British Ambassador, Donald Maitland (who had the advantages of having presented his credentials *after* the revolution, and of fluent Arabic), conceded the principle of total withdrawal, and at the second a week later (held in a much friendlier atmosphere) he announced a withdrawal deadline of 31 March 1970. He then concentrated on gaining acceptance for a joint communiqué stressing the importance of future Anglo-Libyan co-operation. For Britain, the outcome of the talks offered greater potential than actual benefits, but the atmosphere was thought to have been cleared for further negotiations on the whole future of Anglo-Libyan relations.

The last British troops left Tobruk on 28 March. Departure three days before the promised deadline was arranged to avoid 'incidents' as the Libyans started withdrawal celebrations. As his last act before embarking, the British commandant drove down from El Adem[30] to the British war cemetery near Tobruk to sign the visitor's book as a simple but pointed reminder of how and why British forces had first arrived in Italian Libya nearly 30 years before.

Meanwhile, the Americans had agreed to evacuate Wheelus Field by 30 June 1970, although not without some Congressional criticism of the government for handing over the base, together with its radar, electronics equipment, ammunition dumps and other facilities to what one Congressman termed 'a radical, leftist Arab revolutionary government'. The full evacuation of Wheelus[31] was completed on 11 June. Ten days earlier, Gadafi had roundly denied rumours that bases would be handed over to 'other foreign forces' by repeating his assertion that Libya was determined to keep itself free of foreign bases. 'Revolutionary Libya will never substitute a foreigner for another foreigner or an intruder for another intruder, but wants her territory free for ever.'[32] The surprisingly speedy evacuation of the bases was held up to the country and the world as not only 'victories over imperialism', but also practical demonstration of the ability of the new leadership to achieve the results that had eluded the monarchy.

Despite prompt British acquiescence over the bases issue, relations between London and Tripoli did not improve, largely because of prolonged disagreement over arms supplies. In November 1969 it was reported that the RCC had decided to cancel the British Aircraft Corporation missiles contract negotiated by the former regime for the defence of the kingdom from air attack; in 1969, the revolutionary regime had no reason to fear an assault such as Egypt was to launch eight years later. After Gadafi came to power, the British government began to question the wisdom of supplying such plainly aggressive weapons as *Chieftain* tanks to a regime that was becoming one of the most militant — in word, if not yet in deed — in the Arab world. Although not geographically one of the 'front-line' Arab states in the continuing conflict with Israel, Libya had already made it clear that any weapons supplied would be used on the Egyptian front against Israel. Eventually the whole question of British arms supplies degenerated into a wrangle over reimbursement of 'down-payments' on *Chieftain* tanks that Britain would not supply and missiles that Libya did not want; it was a wrangle that was to upset Anglo-Libyan relations for a long time to come.

But France under General de Gaulle's successor, President Georges Pompidou, put aside misgivings about supplying to revolutionary Libya the same formidable assault weapons that had recently been denied to Israel. What was so intriguing about the agreement by France to supply Libya with the equipment for what amounted to a complete and highly advanced air force, was the extreme reluctance of those involved in the transaction first to admit to its existence, and then to its size. President de Gaulle had embargoed sales of French arms to all states actively involved in the 1967 Middle East War. Although the embargo did not apply to Libya, the fact that Tripoli was by December 1969 clearly moving towards some form of union with Egypt raised serious doubts about the even-handedness of a French policy that had already denied to Israel 50 *Mirage V* war-planes and spares that had been ordered and paid for before the 1967 war; the 72 *Mirage III* already in service with Israel had played a leading role in the 1967 battles.

On 19 November 1969, the Paris correspondent of the *Jerusalem Post* reported that the Libyan government was dropping hints that it was willing to buy some of Israel's embargoed aircraft. Then a report in the *New York Times* on 19 December that France was to sell arms worth $400 million to Libya (including 50 *Mirage* aircraft and 200 tanks) was roundly denied by the Libyan government, while the French Defence Ministry would only admit that 'trade talks' were being held.[33] Further press reports followed, but at the Arab summit conference at Rabat on 22 December the Foreign Minister, Salih Busair, said there was no arms agreement with France.

Nevertheless, persistent rumours that France was selling up to 15 *Mirages* to Libya — a country traditionally armed by Britain and America — aroused the disquiet of the United States government, in particular, and provoked sharp criticism in the British and American press.[34] On 9 January 1970 it was announced that the French government had approved a contract between the Libyan government and Avions Marcel Dassault[35] not for 15, but for 50 *Mirage V* aircraft, the first 15 to be delivered in 1971 and the rest over a longer period. The sales agreement[36] placed fairly specific restrictions on the deployment and use of the aircraft — they had to be 'based' in Libya and maintained and repaired there. While there was no actual restriction on their going outside Libya, their use against Francophile countries having common frontiers with Libya was prohibited. Chad, in particular, but also Niger and Tunisia, were clearly the states considered by the French to be particularly vulnerable.[37]

Confirmation of the agreement generated renewed British and American press criticism, largely on the grounds that all arms Libya acquired would be placed at Egypt's disposal for use against Israel. But the official French view was that a Middle East settlement was likely to be reached before all the aircraft had become operational (in which case it was perhaps worth asking why the planes were needed), and that it was anyway preferable that Libya's arms came from France rather than the Soviet Union, which was already reported to have offered aircraft on better terms.[38]

It was not until 22 January that the French Defence Minister, Michel Debré, revealed that France would deliver not 50, but 100 *Mirages* to Libya by 1974 under the largest single agreement for the supply of French military aircraft to a foreign country. In addition to the sale of 50 *Mirage V* fighter bombers (to equip three squadrons) at a cost of $65 million, already announced, it was now made known that 30 *Mirage IIIE* interceptors to equip two squadrons at a cost of $50 million, and 20 *Mirage IIIB* and *IIIR* training machines, costing a total of $30 million, were also to be supplied. It was further revealed that *Matra 530* air-to-air missiles were to be provided, and that France would soon begin training Libyan air force pilots at bases in France and at Wheelus Field (Okba bin Nafi) which was perhaps a particularly tactless choice of location since the Americans were then still in the process of evacuating it. Finally, it was officially announced in Paris on 31 January that the total number of aircraft to be sold was 'nearer 110 than 100', the additional aircraft being *IIIE* interceptors.

These announcements — made against a background of almost daily clashes between Egyptian and Israeli forces during the so-called 'war of attrition' along the Suez Canal front — aroused new fears and criticisms in France itself, in the United States, in Israel and elsewhere. French protests were largely generated by a sense of having been deceived by the government. In Washington, the State Department expressed the view that the balance of power in the

Middle East could be upset.[39] The Americans were put out by the speed with which France was apparently trying to replace them as the main suppliers of the Libyan air force and by the report, carried in the *New York Times* (but denied by all the parties involved) that Egyptian representatives had taken part in the sales negotiations. The Israelis, for their part, were alarmed that the secrets of *Mirages* very similar to their own machines on active service would soon be available to the Egyptians.

For the French government, the *Mirages* sale was part of a policy of strengthening interests in the Mediterranean basin in general and in Libya in particular, despite the recent failure of a Gaullist attempt to gain influence through arms sales to Iraq, another Arab oil-producing state in the process of amending its long-standing Anglo-Saxon ties. French policy was founded on the belief — probably held with more conviction in 1969–70 than at any time afterwards — that when one state agrees to supply arms, spares and training to another over a period of years, both commit themselves to a mutually advantageous relationship yielding further benefits. France had reason to hope for more Libyan military contracts and a bigger role in the oil industry, in particular, and in the country's economic and social development in general.[40] The supply of *Mirages* — and the ability to slow down or halt the delivery of aircraft, parts and trained men — was thought to promise Paris considerable political influence in Tripoli, as well as renewed influence in both the 'progressive' wing of the Arab world and in a Mediterranean increasingly dominated by the United States and the Soviet Union. But, like the expected commercial and other advantages, such influence never quite materialised, so effectively did the Libyan government maintain its freedom of political and economic action.[41]

According to Mohammad Hassanain Haykal, he had in 1969 taken a message from President Nasser to Gadafi: 'If you can get *Phantoms* or *Mirages*, this will be a colossal addition to Arab strength.'[42] The *Mirage* was particularly highly regarded by the Arabs because Israeli *Mirage IIIs* had led the attacks of French-built warplanes that had destroyed Arab air power in the opening hours of the 1967 war. There were those in Libya and elsewhere who believed that if the country also possessed such *Mirages*, then the same devastating power would be equally available to the Arabs.

The Dassault *Mirage*, probably the most successful series of military aircraft built in Western Europe since the Second World War, has been produced in many different versions since the prototype flew in 1956. Besides acting as the carrier for the French nuclear *Force de Frappe*, *Mirages* had been supplied to the air forces of some 20 countries. Possession of over 100 successful and (in the hands of highly skilled pilots) truly formidable aircraft was expected to confer prestige on Libya's new revolutionary regime, even though there was some ambiguity about their intended purpose, and no Libyans were trained to fly and service such machines. Indeed, Libya lacked pilots even for the relatively uncomplicated Northrop *F5 'Freedom Fighters'* (lightweight supersonic strike aircraft designed for 'Third World' use). Some 18 had been ordered from the United States before the revolution; ten had been delivered by 1 September 1969, and three of those had crashed in the hands of Libyan pilots.

Dassault had tried to discourage the Libyan buyers by stressing the high cost of the aircraft and the number of highly trained pilots and technicians needed to keep them flying. But the Libyans were not to be put off; there was no apparent difficulty about payment, and by August 1970 Libyan pilots were being trained at several bases in France.[43]

The *Mirages* were extraordinarily expensive, in terms of both purchase and maintenance costs, but more particularly in terms of the need to recruit and train large numbers of pilots and ground staff from a nation desperately short of educated and technically skilled personnel of every kind. In purely political terms, the revolutionary regime could readily justify the purchase and operation of such offensive weapons on behalf of the Arab cause — and in purely financial terms it could arguably afford to do so. The highest cost of the *Mirages* to Libya was in the diversion of rare technical skills from essential development projects into the economically and socially sterile task of operating an air force which, whatever the vision of those who ordered it in 1969–70, was to contribute more to national self-esteem than to the liberation of Palestine. The number of staff, the level of their training, and the quantity and quality of the supporting equipment needed to keep the *Mirages* in service were all astonishing. It was estimated that, in addition to some 200 pilots, the *Mirage* fleet needed some 3,000 specialised ground staff. The training of each technician alone cost an estimated $50,000 over three years. As one critic wrote:[44] 'Clearly the cost of training the personnel to operate the machines far exceeds the cost of the aircraft. Simply maintaining the squadrons in the air for one hour each week will cost Libya several million dollars per year.'[45]

An experienced pilot learns to fly an aircraft as advanced as the *Mirage* in two years; inexperienced ones take up to four years. By September 1971, nearly two years after the first *Mirages* had been ordered, the standard of ground support was still low and no Libyan pilot could yet fly in formation: French pilots again had to fly the aircraft over Tripoli at the celebrations marking the second anniversary of the revolution.[46] The French authorities did not deny persistent rumours that many of the trainee pilots in France were not Libyans but Egyptians. As Colonel Gadafi said in a speech in March 1973 in which he criticised university students for their lack of enthusiasm for military service, 'We have *Mirage* planes, the biggest air force in North Africa and the most modern planes, but these have no pilots. There are no pilots.'[47]

By November 1971, 11 *Mirages* had been delivered; 40 more had been delivered by August 1972, and a further 56 by March 1973 — a total of 107 aircraft. Additional *Mirages* and other arms, including helicopters and missiles, were later ordered from France. But the Soviet Union, which had made its first shipment of *T-54* and *T-55* medium tanks to Tripoli in July 1970, had by 1974 replaced France as Libya's largest arms supplier.

In April 1973 the Israelis claimed that Libyan *Mirages* had been transferred to Egypt, apparently in breach of the sales agreement. The French government called for proof, announced later that none had been given, and added that assurances had been received from Tripoli and Cairo that no aircraft had been transferred from Libya. But some Libyan *Mirages* — although not necessarily flown by Libyans — did take part in the Middle East war of October 1973.[48] Ironically, therefore, Libya's air force, acquired and maintained at such expense, first went into battle in a war that Colonel Gadafi publicly opposed. But one effect of Libya's possession of *Mirages* was to strengthen Israeli pressure on the United States to supply yet more advanced aircraft (*Phantoms* and *Skyhawks*) to counter this additional Arab 'threat'.

After ridding the country of foreign bases, changing arms suppliers, nationalising foreign banks and other interests, and serving notice on the international oil companies of an impending confrontation over prices and government 'participation', the new regime continued to follow 'revolutionary' and 'independent' courses of action by expelling permanent 'foreign' communities it was no longer willing to tolerate — the Italians and the Jews.[49] Italians had been quietly leaving since shortly after the 1967 war when the riots in

Tripoli, although not specifically anti-Italian, had served as a warning of troubles to come. The pace of repatriation, together with some expulsions, had risen sharply after the revolution. Some ten thousand Italians had left the country between 1967 and mid-1970. Thus the resident community totalled barely thirteen thousand (plus a further six thousand on short-term contracts or merely visiting) when Gadafi, speaking at Misurata on 9 July, accused the community of serving 'an imperialist aim' — 'we shall not accept the presence of a fascist or an intruder imperialist in our land'.[50]

There followed a two-week anti-Italian press campaign leading up to a broadcast by Gadafi on 21 July in which he announced that 'the people want back the property which the Italian citizens usurped when their invading armies were in control and when terror of unjust Italian rule prevailed in the country'. All Italian property, including buildings, plantations, installations, movable and immovable equipment, means of transport, animals and all fittings and attachments were to 'revert' to the state. Claiming that by this act 'the Libyan Arab people's freedom has been completed', Gadafi admitted that 'the feeling of holy revenge today runs in our veins'.[51] The confiscation of property, combined with other restrictions, effectively meant the expulsion of practically the entire community; also on 21 July the seizure of the funds and other property of the 620 Jews still living in Libya was announced.[52]

The Italian government could do little but protest. Commercial ties with Libya, and especially the uninterrupted supply of oil, were more important than the future of an ageing and potentially hostage community that had been largely ignored by the mother country for the past 15 years, and whose members were more at home in Tripoli than in Palermo, let alone Rome. Commercial ties had become particularly important since the Italian para-statal Azienda Generale Italiana Petroli (AGIP), after many years of unrewarding prospecting, had at last found a rich oilfield that it was trying to bring into commercial production in the face of great bureaucratic difficulties

With the Italian government in one of its usual crises, Aldo Moro was only a caretaker Foreign Minister. He protested that the Libyan action was contrary to international law,[53] the 1950 United Nations resolution reaffirming Libyan independence,[54] and the Italo-Libyan treaty of 1956.[55] But he ruled out the use of force as 'anachronistic and unproductive', preferring to rely on 'reasonableness, peaceful encounter and responsible negotiation'.[56] In a cable to President Giuseppe Saragat on 30 July, Colonel Gadafi said: 'No provisions o treaties will stand in our way because treaties and agreements which do not recognise our rights will not be considered as such.'[57]

Italians started to leave in large numbers in August; early that month Italian shops and workshops had been ordered to close; in September all operations of the Banco di Roma and the Banco di Napoli were nationalised; and on 17 October Gadafi announced what he called 'the end of the hated fascist Italian colonisation'. A total of 12,770 Italians — practically all the long-term resident community — had left. Gadafi saw the Italians as

> a settlers' colonialism, comprising thousands of settlers who controlled the economy, agriculture, land and internal and external trade . . . it was a fascist Italian colonialism in every sense and was more dangerous than the military bases because it dominated everything and was like a cancer in the body of the country.[58]

Since the Second World War, the Italian community had provided Libya, and Tripolitania in particular, with essential technical and managerial skills, and Tripoli and its surroundings had gained from their presence. The very prominent Italian role in the economic and social life of Tripolitania had made a ready target for Libyan resentments, but between independence and the revolution there were no significant demonstrations of anti-Italian feeling. The Italians did not integrate themselves into Libyan society, and they were hardly encouraged to do so; nevertheless, many of them had stayed in Libya because it was their home and Italy was not. The expulsion of the Italian community gave rise to inevitable warnings of the imminent collapse of the Libyan economy for lack of essential expertise; but an influx of tens of thousands of Egyptians and other Arabs largely made up for the loss of Italian skills, even if the social and cultural life of Tripoli was never to be the same again.

Ironically, the departure of the last of the Italians in mid-October coincided with a speech by the Under-Secretary at the Foreign Ministry, Rashid Kikhya, to the General Assembly of the United Nations in which he pledged Libya's support for the establishment of a democratic, secular Palestine in which Muslims, Jews and Christians would live in harmony; it was certainly more than they were being allowed to do in Libya.

Even without the hyperbole of Colonel Gadafi's speeches, Libyans celebrating the first anniversary of the revolution could look back over a year of extraordinary events and far-reaching changes. Only six weeks after coming to power, Gadafi had announced his five basic objectives: total evacuation of foreign bases; positive and complete neutrality; national unity; worldwide Arab unity; and the suppression of all domestic political parties. All but one of these — Arab unity — could reasonably be claimed as accomplished after a year in power.

Over the previous twelve months there had emerged a leadership increasingly confident in its use of oil production and oil wealth to support its foreign-policy objectives and to enhance its own prestige, but still uncertain how to promote the common good at home. For a leadership so very inexperienced, yet expected to be 'revolutionary' and dynamic, foreign-policy issues (largely a matter of words and financial support) seemed much simpler than domestic affairs calling for decisions, directives and some appreciation of the issues involved. The establishment of a 'committee on socialist thought', no matter how well-intentioned, was not a move likely to arouse the latent revolutionary fervour of a still largely apathetic public. Even the 'Libyan Intellectual Seminar' in which 'Libyan intellectuals, Libyan women and other average Libyans', as well as members of the RCC, came together in May 1970 to agree on such definitions as 'the working forces of the people who have an interest in the revolution', ended after nine sessions with a mere promise from Colonel Gadafi that all the opinions heard would be adopted 'to the revolutionary stage through which the country is passing'.[59]

At the opening of that seminar, Colonel Gadafi had claimed that the 1 September revolution was 'not a traditional *coup* or seizure of power or a domination of the military over the government'. Although in later years the Libyan revolution was indeed to acquire some remarkable characteristics of its own, at its first anniversary there was still little hard evidence to support such claims.

Notes

1. The Diplomatic Correspondent of *The Times* (10 September 1969) said of him on his appointment: 'He has been for those Libyans who were in exile or discontented with the regime the most influential and attractive of all the political leaders after the king's regime came to an end.'

2. See *Arab Report and Record*, issue 17 (1–15 September 1969), pp. 379–80; 'Mu'ammar al-Qadhdhafi, A Visit to Fezzan' in W.I. Zartman (ed.), *Man, State and Society in the Contemporary Maghrib* (London, 1973); M.O. Ansell and I.M. Al Arif, *The Libyan Revolution* (London, 1972), pp. 63–9, 72–7, 86–93.

3. Ansell and Arif *Libyan Revolution*, pp. 108–13.

4. Interview with *Le Figaro*, reprinted in *Al-Yom*, 1 October 1969.

5. Interview with *Al-Haqiqah*, 2 October 1969.

6. M. Rodinson, *Islam et Capitalisme* (Paris, 1966), p. 13.

7. J. Gaspard, 'Making an Arab Revolution', *New Middle East*, no. 14 (November 1969).

8. O.I. El Fathaly and M. Palmer, *Political Development and Social Change in Libya* (Lexington Mass., 1980), pp. 66–7.

9. W. Ananaba, *The Trade Union Movement in Africa* (London, 1979), p. 81.

10. W.A. Rugh, *The Arab Press* (London, 1979), p. 64.

11. In a speech to the police at Benghazi in June 1970, Major Abd-al-Salam Jallud, who was then Minister of the Interior, said that after the *coup* the armed forces had disarmed the police and taken away their equipment and vehicles. 'It was natural for the armed forces to seize these arms because under the revolution we cannot allow the establishment of two armies in one country . . . we have no cause to operate two armies to pit one against the other should one make a move . . .' (BBC, *Summary of World Broadcasts*, ME/3419/A/7–9).

12. *Libyan Mail*, 14 December 1969.

13. 'Libya's Unanswered Questions', *New Middle East*, no. 17 (February 1970).

14. BBC, *Summary of World Broadcasts*, ME/3253/A/1.

15. Ibid., A/3.

16. For the full text, see Ansell and Arif, *Libyan Revolution*, pp. 108–13.

17. Ibid., pp. 113–14.

18. An 'act of aggression' was defined to include making propaganda against the republican regime; arousing class hatred; spreading rumours and 'various stories' about the political and economic situation in the country; taking part in a demonstration or strike against the republican regime.

19. Colonel Moammar Gadafi; Lieutenant-Colonel Abu Bakar Yunis Jabir; Major Abd-al-Salam Jallud; Major Bashir Saghir Hawadi; Captain Omar Abdallah Mihaishi; Captain Mohammad Abu Bakr Mugaryif; Captain Mukhtar Abdallah Garwi; Captain Mustafa Kharubi; Captain Khuwaildi Hamidi; Captain Mohammad Najm; Captain Awad Ali Hamza; Captain Abd-al-Monim Tahir Huni.

20. *Libyan Mail*, 26 July 1970.

21. Ibid., 2 August 1970.

22. See *Arab Report and Record*, 4 October 1971, and BBC, *Summary of World Broadcasts*, ME/4225/A/12–13.

23. Seale and McConville, *The Hilton Assignment* (London, 1973), p. 132.

24. The neo-Romanesque Roman Catholic cathedral in Tripoli, consecrated in 1928, became a mosque. But, even without its bells, the *campanile* hardly made a convincing minaret, and the architecture of the basilica was too blatantly Italian to make a satisfactory place of Islamic worship. The building's structural defects might have suggested demolition and replacement with a more appropriate design.

25. 'There is nowhere in North West Europe that can offer anything like the scope for uninhibited low flying combined with live firing available at the ranges round Theelus and El Adem. In Cyrenaica, the British Army has ample room — which it is not in Europe — for full-scale armoured exercises . . . over terrain ideal for mechanised manoeuvres.' N. Brown, 'Revolutionary Libya's Arms Potential Who Will Benefit?', *New Middle East*, no. 13 (October 1969).

26. House of Commons Official Report, Parliamentary Debates (*Hansard*), l. 795, col. 137 (14 March 1970).

27. 'Withdrawal of Sterling Deposits Threat' *Middle East Economic Digest*, 14 November 1969.

28. *Hansard*, vol. 793, no. 3, col. 16 (18 December 1969).

29. There had been nearly 2,000 British troops at El Adem and Tobruk at the beginning of October; barely 1,000 remained by the time the talks opened.

30. Renamed Nasser Air Base.
31. Renamed Okba bin Nafi Air Base after one of the original Arab conquerors of North Africa.
32. *Libyan Mail*, 31 May 1970.
33. According to *Le Monde* (7 January 1970) negotiations with the former regime for the supply of *Mirages* had taken place in 1968.
34. An exception was *The Times* which (8 January 1970) expressed the view that 'if the Libyan government feels it can conduct a more satisfactory defence arrangement with France than with any other country in the west, then Britain and America should avoid any policy which appears to sabotage the French initiative'.
35. Dassault, from *Char d'Assault*, was the *nom de guerre* of the brilliant Jewish designer and head of the firm, Marcel Bloch (See J. Gee, *Mirage, Warplane for the World*, (London, 1971), p. 11).
36. Mezerette, 'Où Sont les Mirages de Kadafi?', *Paris Match*, no. 1252 (5 May 1973).
37. It has been suggested that in agreeing to the *Mirages* sale, Libya undertook not to aid largely Muslim rebel forces fighting the French-supported government of President François Tombalbaye in Chad, nor to undermine President Habib Bourguiba's pro-Western regime in Tunisia; see E.A. Klodziej, 'French Mediterranean Policy: The Politics of Weakness', *International Affairs*, vol. 47, no. 3, (July 1971). Paris was also concerned about continuing stability in Niger, where the Arlit uranium deposits in the north of the country were of immense of importance to the French nuclear programme.
38. According to *Aviation Week* (1 April 1968), the Russians sold *MiG 21*s to Arab buyers for $300,000 each, while the French were charging four times as much for the *Mirage*.
39. *New York Times* (3 January 1970) charged the Pompidou government with having 'stooped to a new low in international irresponsibility'.
40. France at the time bought 17 per cent of its oil from Libya and 'its sale of *Mirage* fighters was estimated to have covered approximately $400 million of its oil imports from Libya'. E.A. Klodziej, 'France and the Arms Trade', *International Affairs*, vol. 56, no. 1 (January 1980). The estimate does not tally with that of *Aviation Week* (see n. 38).
41. It might be argued that Britain's refusal to sell *Chieftain* tanks to Libya had more long-term political impact than France's decision to sell *Mirages*; see L. Freedman, 'Britain and the Arms Trade', *International Affairs*, vol. 54, no. 1 (July 1978).
42. BBC, *Summary of World Broadcasts*, ME/4119/A/4.
43. Gee, *Mirage*, pp. 152–3. No aircraft were available for delivery in time for the first anniversary of the revolution on 1 September 1970, but four *Mirages* with Libyan markings and flown by French pilots were sent to take part in the ceremonial fly-past over Tripoli.
44. D.K. Whynes, *The Economics of Third World Military Expenditure* (London, 1979), p. 97.
45. Ibid, p. 97. Servicing alone cost $250 per plane per flying hour.
46. Mezerette, 'Où Sont les Mirages de Khadafi?'
47. BBC, *Summary of World Broadcasts*, ME/4241/A/1.
48. President Sadat made it clear in 1974 that Libyan *Mirages* had taken part in the October fighting — an admission that not only embarrassed the French government, but was also seen as an attempt by Sadat to have Libya placed under a French arms embargo.
49. The relevant laws referred to Jews as *Isra'iliyin*, implying that they were Israelis rather than Libyans. BBC, *Summary of World Broadcasts*, ME/3438/A/
50. Ibid., ME/3427/A/4–6.
51. Ibid., ME/3437/A/2–6.

52. Ibid., ME/3438/A/6.

53. The then Vice-Secretary of the Italian Communist Party, Enrico Berlinguer, said of the crisis on 29 July 1970 that 'revolutions cannot respect all forms of international rights' (*Corriere della Sera*, 30 July 1970). Another view from the Italian left was that 'The revolutionary government of Libya has expropriated Italian properties; all true progressives in our country cannot but be in sincere solidarity with a political act of this kind' (C. Corghi, 'Solidarietà con la Libia', *Terzo Mondo*, anno 3, n. 9 (settembre 1970).

54. General Assembly Resolution 388v: *Economic and Financial Provisions Relating to Libya*. Article VI states: 'The property, rights and interests of Italian nationals, including Italian juridical persons, in Libya, shall, provided they have been lawfully acquired, be respected. They shall not be treated less favourably than the property, rights and interests of other foreign nationals, including foreign juridical persons.'

55. The 1956 Italo-Libyan treaty stated in part: 'The Libyan government declares . . . that no claim, even on the part of individuals, can be advanced in respect of properties of Italian citizens in Libya, by reasons of acts by the government or by the lapsed Italian administration of Libya, that occurred before the constitution of the Libyan state. The Libyan government consequently guarantees Italian citizens owning property in Libya, in respect of Libyan law, the free and just exercise of their rights.' *Accordo tra l'Italia e la Libia di Collaborazione Economica*, etc., Article 9.

56. *Corriere della Sera*, 5 August 1970.

57. BBC, *Summary of World Broadcasts*, ME/3445/A/6.

58. Ibid., ME/3512/A/1–3. Altogether, according to Gadafi, 12,770 Italians left Libya. They gave up 21,000 hectares of land 'suitable for cultivation', 687 apartments, 467 villas and 548 other dwellings, as well as 1,207 vehicles and tractors and nearly £L9 million in frozen funds.

59. For a résumé of seminar proceedings, see Ansell and Al-Arif, *Libyan Revolution*, pp. 253–300.

8 TAKING THE WORLD BY STORM

Oil and the unique political vision of Moammar Gadafi were the forces driving Libya's new, revolutionary foreign policy. The West's constant need to protect its oil interests and maintain a steady flow of Libyan crude explains the easy acquiescence of Britain and the United States to demands for the evacuation of bases, and that of Italy to the dispossession and repatriation of a whole community — including the bones of its dead; it also explains why the French were able to ignore their own professed scruples about selling *Mirages*. While the very wealth paid by the West for crude oil enabled the revolutionary regime to assume a provocative role in Arab and world affairs, largely by reinforcing words with cash subventions to like-minded governments and approved revolutionary causes, Moammar Gadafi's almost unchallenged domination of Libyan affairs seemed to transform the normal conduct of foreign policy into a personal campaign waged by him, or on his behalf.

Initially unsure of itself in its usurped position, the new leadership sought reassurance and endorsement through bold foreign-policy ventures which, however sincere the motives behind them, were also intended to unite the country in support of revolutionary action much as the Italian challenge had united Cyrenaica, at least, behind the Sanussi earlier in the century.

Reaction against the pro-Western policies of the former regime and its half-hearted support of Arab causes, plus a declared policy of 'positive neutralism' combined with dedication to Arab unity as an 'inevitable necessity', drew Gadafi naturally towards the Arab world's senior revolutionary, Gamal Abd-al-Nasser. But the leader whose broadcast voice and ideals had long inspired Gadafi and his schoolfellows, was by 1969 sick and cynical, increasingly disillusioned with pan-Arabism since the break-up of the Egyptian–Syrian union in 1961. And now, in the last year of his life, still overshadowed by the 1967 defeat, Nasser had abandoned much that he had stood for, and 'positive neutralism' had given way to heavy reliance on Soviet help in the 'war of attrition' against Israel. Never theless, Nasser — who was old enough to be his father — needed and used Gadafi, both as a means of regaining the initiative in the continuing competition for Arab leadership, and as a source of finance in the anti-Israeli struggle. Gadafi, in turn, needed and used Nasser, with his immense prestige, to endorse his own accession to power and his revolutionary credentials. He also needed the elder statesman to give advice and assurance. Above all, he needed Egypt — the political centre of the Arab world — as a broader platform for untried ambitions than Libya, for all its wealth, was ever able to offer.

The Arab summit conference at Rabat in December 1969 was the occasion that led the Libyan, Sudanese and Egyptian leaders to recognise in their growing mutual interests the beginnings of future union. At Rabat, Nasser sought in vain for all the firm commitments of military and financial aid he needed from the Arab states to continue the war against Israel, and the meeting broke up in confusion without a final communiqué. But on their way home Presidents Nasser and Jafaar Numairi of Sudan (another pro-Nasser revolutionary who had come to power in a *coup* in May 1969) visited Libya, where three days of talks led to the proclamation of a tripartite 'Arab revolutionary front' and an agreement to hold regular four-monthly meetings to co-ordinate military, political and economic action against Israel.[1] In a speech in Benghazi, Nasser declared that the Egyptian and Libyan revolutions would fight side by side in the struggle against Israel, while Gadafi proclaimed that the Libyan and Sudanese revolutions had 'joined the mother revolution of Egypt' in that struggle. There was no mention of full constitutional unity, but it was clearly an eventual objective.

Libya and Sudan joined Egypt's 'western front' too late to revitalise Nasserism, at least as practised by Gamal Abd-al-Nasser. But they gave Egypt strategic depth, and Libya opened the prospect of access to oil revenues as an alternative to continuing reliance on the charity of 'reactionary' Saudi Arabia and Kuwait; Nasser was also confirmed as 'still the most substantial leader in the Arab world', despite his recent set-backs. At the same time, it was made clear that his new move towards Arab unity would not divide the Arab world, and that other Arab states were welcome to join in.

After Nasser's death in September 1970, Colonel Gadafi and his associates continued in the changed circumstances of the new decade to promote neo-Nasserism with all the fervour of conviction. They seemed at times eager to provoke reactions that would enable them to re-enact the most stirring 'struggles' of Nasser's own career. But Gadafi's chosen targets were not as unyielding or pugnacious as Nasser's had been 20 years before. Whereas Nasser had emerged from the international Suez crisis of 1956 as undisputed leader of the Arabs, Gadafi's demands were to be met with almost ready acquiescence by the United States, Britain, Italy, the international banking houses and other states and organisations that he had apparently hoped to provoke to trials of strength that might have increased his own stature to more Nasserite proportions; as it was, his chosen opponents signally failed to rise to the challenge.

Emerging on the international stage in 1970, Colonel Gadafi had a unique credential as representative of two hitherto mutually antagonistic interests in the Arab world — moneyed oil power and dedicated pan-Arabism. While Arab oil wealth had largely been the privilege of the 'reactionary' kingdoms and shaikhdoms of the Arabian peninsula (with the post-1958 exception of Iraq), pan-Arabism had been monopolised by the politically and socially 'advanced' but almost oil-less states such as Egypt and Syria. 'From Egypt and Syria, the unionist movement had been a claim by the poor states for the "collective" wealth of the Arab World. The Libyan case was to provide just the opposite: an affluent society wanting to unite with its poorer neighbours.'[2]

In an interview early in 1970, Colonel Gadafi declared that his greatest ambition was to see a free, sovereign and independent Palestine; Libya, and indeed the whole Arab world, could not be considered free, sovereign and independent so long as the Palestine issue was unresolved.[3] Gadafi's utter hostility towards Israel, and his belief that the Arab–Israeli dispute could only be resolved by war were founded on uncompromising opposition to Zionism rather than Judaism; he saw Zionism as an aggressive nationalism and Israel as an affront to all Arabs, having in his view been planted in the Middle East by, and as an agent of, imperialism. He proposed that Jews in Palestine before the founding of the Jewish state in 1948 would have the right to stay in a reunited Palestine, co-existing with Muslim and Christian Palestinian Arabs, including repatriated refugees; Jews who had gone to Israel after 1948 would return to their homes in the Arab world (including Libya) and elsewhere.

Although Gadafi was soon known for his verbal militancy on Palestine, he was also the first Arab leader publicly to criticise Palestinians for lack of unity and military effectiveness. In a speech on 3 March 1970, he said that of the 40 separate organisations within the *fidayin* movement (most of them formed in the aftermath of the 1967 war), only 10 per cent were directed against the enemy and the rest against each other and the Arab regimes.[4] Gadafi had originally tried to reconcile the main Palestine Liberation Organization and the left-wing Popular Front for the Liberation of Palestine led by George Habbash. Failing, he expelled the PFLP from Libya on the grounds that its members were 'neither fighters nor liberators' and that its literature had more to say about Marxism than Palestine; representatives of other 'unworthy' groups were similarly expelled. Thereafter, Yassir Arafat's *Al-Fatah* — the strongest, best-organised and most active Palestinian guerrilla force — became the main recipient of Libyan support and largesse, although Gadafi insisted on controlling such aid more closely than the monarchy had ever done; but then, hand-outs by the former regime had always seemed to have been made more from a sense of duty than from a genuine desire to help Arab causes.

By mid-1970, Colonel Gadafi was ready to prepare the Arab world for the annihilation of Israel. In May and June he and Foreign Minister Busair toured Iraq, Jordan, Syria, Lebanon and Egypt to propose a grand strategic plan for co-ordinated military action; Busair also visited Qatar, Kuwait and the Yemens. According to the Libyan plan, the Arab states were to make specific financial and military commitments; Palestinian guerrilla organisations were to be unified; and a Palestinian government-in-exile was to be formed from representatives of all the resistance groups.

The tour seems to have been something of a revelation to Gadafi. He found that the so-called 'eastern front' of Jordan, Syria and Iraq was little more than a name; he also found that his advice was not welcome, and was even resented. Libya had taken part in none of the Arab—Israeli wars; it was far from the war-zone; and even Gadafi's support had so far been limited to cash, advice and rhetoric. Leaders and military commanders of 'front-line' states with personal experience of Israel at war found Gadafi's schemes outdated, simplistic and even impertinent, coming as they did from one whose national wealth and personal status had been so easily acquired, and whose manifest inexperience made his grand schemes seem all the more impractical. Although the tour was not a success, Gadafi was not publicly discouraged, quite possibly because he knew that he had the tacit support of Presidents Nasser and Numairi.

Yet by mid-1970 Nasser was initiating a process of accommodation with Israel — a departure of policy that contradicted most of what his associate, Colonel Gadafi, was still saying. At the end of July, Nasser accepted the Middle East peace plan of the United States Secretary of State, William Rogers, ending the devastating 'war of attrition' between Egypt and Israel along the Suez Canal.⁵ Gadafi, in a controlled display of diplomatic double-thinking, contrived to remain unembarrassed by Nasser's acceptance of the Rogers plan, and he voiced his support both for Nasser and the Palestinians, who had rejected the American initiative outright.⁶

When, in September, civil war broke out in Jordan between King Hussain's largely bedouin army and Palestinian guerrillas based in the kingdom, Colonel Gadafi assumed the role of champion of the Palestinians in their fight against what he saw as one of the most reactionary Arab regimes. When his attempts to mediate were rejected, he diverted financial aid from Jordan to the Palestinians and broke diplomatic relations with Amman. But he could give little practical help to prevent the defeat of the guerrillas, and their expulsion from Jordan. Both King Hussain and Colonel Gadafi (with a revolver at his belt) were among Arab heads of state who gathered in Cairo on 22 and 23 September to arrange a cease-fire. The tension of the negotiations and the need to restrain the passion of Gadafi and Yassir Arafat 'constituted a terrible burden for Nasser's nervous system'.⁷ Nasser died on 28 September. That night Gadafi said he had seen in Nasser 'a loving father, a sympathetic brother, a close colleague, a true friend and a sincere human being'. After the funeral on 1 October, Gadafi seemed to be claiming an enhanced standing in the Arab world when he joined President Numairi and Yassir Arafat in receiving the condolences of the official delegations.

Both Gadafi and Numairi, as representatives of a younger and not yet disillusioned generation of Arab revolutionaries, had given Nasser encouraging and badly needed political support in the last year of his life. Nasser helped to mould and moderate Gadafi's policies (although he failed to cure his extreme and, in Nasser's eyes, unrealistic anti-Soviet views), while he also used Gadafi as a mouthpiece for his own notions on a wide range of contentious issues. Gadafi's barn-storming Arab diplomacy and his impetuous, youthful extremism also served to impress conservative Arabs with Nasser's own relative moderation.

Nasser's death left the unofficial leadership of the Arab world vacant, and for some years Gadafi seemed a more likely candidate than most to fill it. He, at least, proposed to maintain Nasser's pocies as he understood them, even to the extent of promoting Nasser's ideas long after they had been overtaken by events. Nevertheless, at a time of great difficulty and despair, the Arab world listened to and even applauded Gadafi in his early years of power because his was at least a new and sincere voice; it was also reasonable to hope that his policies and his judgement would mature and moderate: disillusion set in only when they failed to do so.

In some ways, Gadafi had arrived on the international stage ten years too late, for traditional Nasserism and pan-Arabism had been discredited in the 1967 war. Nasser's actual successor, President Anwar Sadat, realised this, and was eventually to lead Egypt into its own accommodation with Israel. But Gadafi and his associates took many years to understand that, for all their passion and oil money, their brand of neo-Nasserism could not arouse the same responses among the Arabs of the 1970s and 1980s as the original had done in the 1950s and 1960s.

Gadafi's version of Nasserism and the Nasserism of the diehard believers in West Beirut share very little with the late stage of Nasserism Egyptian-style. Gadafi's is more buoyant, because it is the philosophy of loud rebellious youth sheltered from the wounds, the constraints and the traumas of the original Nasserism. It is a desert philosophy engendered by wealth. Because his baggage is light — a small population and a high income — Gadafi can usually afford to fly as high as his imagination will take him. Nasser's base was an impoverished, crowded land, and it set limits to his expectations and possibilities — particularly in the latter part of his career. Whereas Gadafi's philosophy is Beduin, Nasser's bore the mark of a crowded, wise and cynical city that had long been used to applauding the winners, forgetting the losers, and coming to terms with things it did not like.[9]

Presidents Gadafi, Sadat and Numairi reacted to Nasser's death and the lack of an acknowledged, if unofficial, Arab leader by putting into effect earlier plans for union. The chosen form, announced on 9 November 1970, was a federation, intended initially 'to hasten and develop integration and co-operation', leading eventually to closer association forming a nucleus for wider Arab unity. Despite the conspicuous failure of four attempts at Arab unity between 1958 and 1963,[10] news of the latest attempt was generally well received, although the main benefits of the new federation were expected by those outside it to be economic and social, rather than political and military.

Members of the Federation of Arab Republics at least had the advantage of being neighbours, forming a solid block of territory in north-east Africa covering almost two-thirds of the area of the United States and with a population of nearly 51 million.[11] Even if its political future was not clear, the new federation held out hopes of becoming a model of complementary Arab economic co-operation, with Libyan capital and Egyptian enterprise developing Sudan's great agricultural potential, Egypt revitalising its economy with Libyan investment, and in turn offering skills and manpower for Libyan and Sudanese development.

Syria joined the federation at the end of November, and in December the four countries agreed to put their armies under a joint high command. But Gadafi remained deeply suspicious of Syrian political and religious plurality. By the time the Federation of Arab Republics was proclaimed at Benghazi on 17 April 1971, the rhetoric of federation was more convincing than the reality. President Numairi had already postponed Sudan's participation as a result of domestic difficulties, and particularly the continuing civil war involving the Christian–animist minority in the south. Although the federation was to have one president, a 60-member federal assembly, common symbols of statehood, and a constitution generally aiming for Gadafi's ideal goals, actual practice reflected Syrian memories of Egyptian domination of the 1958–61 union, in that each member-state still controlled its internal affairs and armed forces, while keeping its own diplomatic service and membership of Arab and international organisations.

One of the few practical achievements of the federation was to help President Numairi regain power after his overthrow in a pro-Communist *coup* in July 1971. Gadafi's contribution was to force the BOAC airliner carrying two of the main *coup* leaders from London to Khartoum to land at Benghazi. Gadafi handed the rebels over to Numairi who executed them — a gesture that had no bearing on the outcome of the abortive Sudanese *coup*, and that failed to achieve lasting good relations between the Libyan and Sudanese revolutions.

On the second anniversary of the Libyan revolution, the people of Libya, Egypt and Syria voted almost unanimously for federation. Despite this 'popular' endorsement, the federation appeared more as a union of national leaders than of peoples, and its sole practical purpose seemed to be to co-ordinate the policies of three Arab governments in order to force Israel to make the diplomatic concessions necessary for a Middle East peace settlement. But Gadafi was unhappy with the loose form federation was taking, and particularly with Syria's lack of enthusiasm. In February 1972 he proposed the 'total union' of Egypt and Libya to President Sadat, who asked for five months' reflection. In July, deteriorating relations between Cairo and Moscow led to Egypt's expulsion of Soviet military advisers — thus removing, in Gadafi's view, the main bar to effective union. On 23 July he unveiled his plans for union, and on 2 August Sadat felt obliged to agree in principle to unite the two counries not later than 1 September 1973.

For Egypt, the main attraction of union was the prospect of easier access to Libyan development capital. For Gadafi the visionary, unity with the leading and largest Arab state promised the necessary strength and prestige to promote Arab unity and to confront Israel, while providing him in particular and Libyans in general with better opportunities to realise their potential. Otherwise, Egypt had little to offer, apart from limited technical expertise, security men by the hundred, teachers by the thousand and manual workers by the million. Indeed, what Gadafi never tried to explain was how, in a full union with Egypt, underpopulated and socially underdeveloped Libya would resist absorption by 35 million Egyptians; since the expulsion of the Italians, Libya had taken in an estimated quarter of million Egyptians whose presence had caused considerable social tensions.

Anwar Sadat was to be the first president of the united country, but it was thought unlikely that Gadafi, as the paymaster and self-appointed conscience of the union, would for long, if at all, be satisfied with a secondary role. For it was clear by early 1973 that all was not well between Cairo and Tripoli. President Sadat, having consolidated his own domestic power and expelled the Russians, was quietly moving towards an understanding with the United States while building up a working relationship with other Arab leaders in preparation for an armed attack on Israel that he had by then decided was inevitable. First among his new allies within the Arab world was King Faisal of Saudi Arabia who was a richer, more reliable and more discreet financier than Gadafi, and one better able to persuade other Arab oil producers to contribute to the Egyptian war chest. Sadat's decision to keep his detailed war plans secret from

Gadafi was to be another source of friction between the would-be
partners.

Then, in February 1973, a Boeing *727* airliner of Libyan Arab Air-
lines, on a regular flight from Benghazi to Cairo, was shot down by
Israeli fighter aircraft after straying 170 kilometres off course over
Israeli-occupied Sinai; more than a hundred people died in the
crash.[13] The Israeli attack was almost universally condemned, and
the Libyan government vowed revenge. But passionate demonstrators at the funeral of some of the victims in Benghazi were as
critical of Egypt for failing to protect the airliner as of Israel for
shooting it down, and the mob attacked the Egyptian Consulate and
other Egyptian properties. The Boeing incident further harmed
already deteriorating Libyan–Egyptian relations. Gadafi took no
effective action against Israel, but in April he ordered an Egyptian
submarine based in Tripoli to torpedo the British liner *Queen
Elizabeth II* carrying American Jews across the Mediterranean
to Israel's twenty-fifth anniversary celebrations; the order was
promptly countermanded by President Sadat as soon as he heard of
it. 'The *Queen Elizabeth II* may have been saved, but Egyptian-
Libyan relations were not.'[14] There was, moreover, little personal
rapport between the two leaders. 'President Gadafi thought Sadat
not revolutionary enough, President Sadat thought Gadafi unbal-
anced and immature.'[15]

President Sadat's doubts about union — like those of most
Egyptians who cared about such things — were reinforced in April
1973 when Colonel Gadafi proclaimed the 'popular cultural revolution'. This marked the beginning of a long process supposedly
enabling the Libyan people to take over the powers of the state. But
the Egyptians, when told by Gadafi that the cultural revolution was
an 'inevitable phenomenon' for them as well, began to look askance
at their would-be partners, seeing experiments with 'popular democracy' as unworkable among Egypt's 35 million people, and the
encroachment of Gadafi's puritanical ideals as a threat to their social
life. Egyptian women, in particular, expressed outrage at some of
Gadafi's pronouncements, while Egypt's substantial Coptic Christian minority was alarmed by the implications of his Islamic funda-
mentalism. Residual Egyptian enthusiasm for unity probably finally
evaporated when it became clear that Tripoli's largesse would not
readily forthcoming to finance the economic and social advancement of Egypt's impoverished millions.[16] The result was that when
Gadafi went to Cairo in June 1973 to try to reassure the Egyptians

putting his own case for unity, he was shocked by the strength of the opposition.

Sadat and Gadafi met in July and agreed to hold two referenda on the union. The first, on 1 September 1973, was to cover general principles; another a year later was to endorse the constitution of the new state and the choice of president. The next day Gadafi resigned (not for the first time), apparently in protest not only at Egypt's lack of enthusiasm for unity, but also because of opposition within the RCC.

At this point a plan emerged for a popular 'Arab Unity March' on Cairo by thousands of Libyans. On arrival in Cairo, they were to be joined by the 'Egyptian masses', and together they were to march on the presidential palace to demand full and immediate union of the two countries 'in the name of the people'. The progress of some 20 thousand Libyans was ignominiously halted at a level crossing near El Alamein, although a small delegation was allowed to go on to Cairo to see Sadat: Gadafi disclaimed responsibility for the march on the grounds that his resignation still stood and that it was an expression of popular will; nevertheless, it was a gesture typical of aim in its scale, originality and ultimate futility.

It was only on 23 July (the twenty-first anniversary of the Egyptian revolution) that Gadafi publicly revealed his deep disagreements with President Sadat, declaring that union was imperative and inevitable, even at the cost of 'civil' war, and that popular revolution was needed to restore 'normality' inside Egypt. Regimes and bureaucracies that obstructed unity were only fit to be swept away; all Arab regimes anyway only held power temporarily pending union and formation of a single Arab government. But President Sadat, who was largely preoccupied with his secret preparations for war against Israel in six weeks' time, ignored Gadafi's appeals and threats. Instead, he stressed that union had to be achieved by stages, and be based on surer foundations than mere emotion. Although Gadafi and Sadat met again in Cairo on 27 August, the referendum planned for 1 September was not held, and the Middle East war of October 1973 dashed all short-term prospects of making Libya and Egypt one state.

Gadafi, who for years had been consistently advocating war as the only possible solution to the Middle East question, felt obliged to condemn the October fighting, not so much because he had been left out of Sadat's grand alliance, but because he saw the Arabs' primary aim as merely the recovery of territory lost in 1967, and not the liberation of Palestine. It was probably for the second reason that the leadership in Tripoli failed at the time to reveal the very real financial and material contributions — amounting to over $700 million — that Libya made to the Arab war effort after the fighting started; Libya also collaborated with other Arab oil producers in using oil as a political weapon to support the Arab cause. Nevertheless, Gadafi was particularly critical of the Arab combatants when they accepted the United Nations cease-fire arrangements on 24 October, and he lost much of his popular standing through his failure to understand the Arabs' war aims and by belittling the very real Arab achievements in the fighting. President Sadat took the opportunity of the war to end his association with Colonel Gadafi, who very soon found himself isolated, both diplomatically and politically, in the Arab world.

Sadat's achievements in the October war, his restoration of Arab self-confidence and the assertion of his own leadership in Egypt, left a dissenting Gadafi with a distinctly lack-lustre image. Gadafi's initial popular appeal (which arguably owed as much to Sadat's apparent ineptitude as to his own achievements) was clearly spent Sadat's post-war policies, and in particular his increasing reliance on the United States in coming to terms with Israel, further estranged the former would-be associates. Other signs of Gadafi's isolation were his refusal to attend the Arab summit conference at Algiers at the end of November 1973, his condemnation of the Israeli–Egyptian negotiations at Geneva in December, and his launching of a prolonged anti-Sadat campaign.

Soon after coming to power, the revolutionary regime abandoned the formal links the monarchy had unenthusiastically established with the Maghrib: the new union with Egypt and Sudan was more important. In March 1970 the Libyan government failed to attend the conference of Maghrib economic ministers due to be held at Rabat, and was again absent from the postponed meeting in July; in September, Libya withdrew from the Maghrib Permanent Consultative Committee.

Nevertheless, individual relations with Algeria and Tunisia were cultivated. Tripoli and Algiers collaborated in oil policy, and in April 1970 they set up a joint organisation 'to present a unified front in the face of foreign trusts and monopolies'. But Algeria, whose eight-year revolutionary war of independence conferred a unique prestige in the Third World, never became as closely associated with revolutionary Libya as the two countries' many mutual interests suggested they might have done. Although Gadafi urged Algeria to join the Federation of Arab Republics, President Houari Boumedienne was clearly unwilling to compromise Algerian independence or to accept Gadafi as a partner, let alone as a potential leader.

Relations with Tunisia were slow to mature. As an old and pragmatic revolutionary, and a persistent critic of President Nasser, President Habib Bourguiba was dismayed when the moderate and pro-Western monarchy on Tunisia's eastern border was replaced by a militant regime of young Nasserist officers. But relations gradually developed through a series of high-level contacts, and Colonel Gadafi began to speak of Libya as a link between the Arab Mashriq and the Maghrib. Nevertheless, basic Tunisian suspicions remained, both because of Libya's continuing insistence on union with Egypt, and because Tripoli was thought to be helping Tunisian opposition groups in exile.

Visiting Tunis in December 1972, Colonel Gadafi spoke at a popular rally at which he called for union between the two countries. President Bourguiba, listening at home to a live broadcast of the speech, was unable to let it pass unchallenged. He hurried to the rally, let his guest finish, and then took the microphone. Bourguiba, the old *Combatant Suprême* who had already spent 20 years in the struggle for Tunisian independence when Gadafi was born, denied that the Arabs had ever been united, dismissed all Gadafi's ideas about rapid Arab unity, and even took the Libyans to task for what he described as their own lack of national unity and their backwardness.[17] Bourguiba's speech represented 'the first open challenge to Gadafi's recurrent calls for Arab unity'.[18]

Yet, despite his patronising attitude, Bourguiba let himself be pushed into a short-lived plan for an immediate union of Libya and Tunisia, to be known as the Arab Islamic Republic. The plan emerged, apparently spontaneously, at a meeting of the two leaders at Gerba in January 1974, at a time when Gadafi was very much isolated in the Arab world. He seems to have been using an alternative tactic to attain unity, since the process of long negotiation and preparation, already tried with Egypt, had clearly failed; so had the appeal by 'popular forces' in the abortive unity march on Cairo. On this occasion, he was apparently seeking speedy unity, leaving the necessary practical arrangements to be settled later. Bourguiba's motives for the Gerba agreement remain obscure, but the plan aroused misgivings among Tunisians and Algerians and generated

general scepticism elsewhere. Despite the experiences of the past
year, Gadafi still believed that any act of union would start an inevitable chain reaction swiftly uniting the Arab world. But within days,
Bourguiba had managed to free Tunisia from its commitment, and
its promoter, the Foreign Minister Mohammad Masmoudi, was dismissed and disgraced for his efforts.

As a pro-Western monarchy very conscious of its historical great-
ness, Morocco had little in common with revolutionary Libya, and
Colonel Gadafi took a personal dislike to King Hassan II for his
'royal' behaviour at the Rabat summit conference of December
1969. News of an attempt by senior army officers in July 1971 to
overthrow the regime by attacking the royal palace at Skhirat
received embarrassingly premature support from Tripoli, where the
army was put on full alert; Libyan Radio meanwhile announced that
troops were ready to fly to Morocco 'to fight to the end at the side of
the Moroccan people'. The swift suppression of the revolt and
execution of the ringleaders led to a complete break in relation
between Tripoli and Rabat, and charges by King Hassan of Libyan
incitement to rebellion. The two countries mounted a prolonged
propaganda war against each other, with Rabat calling on the people
of 'fraternal Libya' to bear their 'tribulation' with patience. Libyan
Radio, commenting on King Hassan's escape from a second assassination attempt in August 1972, said the 'revolution' would continue
until the Moroccan throne was toppled.

Revolutionary Libya's diplomacy was more successful in Black
Africa, where a forward campaign mounted and sustained from
Tripoli in support of a common Arab objective had by the end of
1973 induced nearly 30 Black African states to break off relation
with Israel. The campaign to persuade the Africans to treat th
Arabs as their natural allies and potential source of economic aid
started with Uganda, where General Idi Amin Dada came to powe
as leader of a military *coup* in January 1971. The fact that Amin wa
a Muslim persuaded the Libyan RCC that he was worth befriendin
with economic and military aid as a potential leader of resurgen
Islam in East Africa (despite the fact that only about one-eighth o
Ugandans are Muslims), and as a useful ally of the Arab cause. Ami
readily co-operated, breaking all relations with Israel in March 1972
Libya's uncritical support for his increasingly oppressive regim
led in September 1972 to intervention with an airlift of four hun
dred troops during Amin's first confrontation with neighbourin
Tanzania. Tripoli justified the intervention as support for the Ugan

dan struggle against 'colonialism and Zionism'. While Libya now demonstrably had the potential to influence some events in distant parts of Africa (where the intervention of even a few hundred troops may prove decisive), close association with Amin's notorious regime undoubtedly harmed Libya's own international reputation.

There was further success in Chad, where the reasons for intervention were both more real and more complex. Over the centuries, extended ethnic, tribal, commercial, religious and political ties had grown up between the people of Libya and those of several of the regions that came to compose the polyglot racial and religious mosaic of the Republic of Chad. In 1964 — four years after the rest of the country became independent from France — the French military finally withdrew from the three notoriously unruly northern provinces of Borku, Ennedi and Tibesti. Within a few months their inhabitants, the Muslim Tebu, were in revolt against insensitive representatives of the central government. Located in the capital, Fort Lamy (later N'Djamena) hundreds of kilometres to the south, the government was directed by southerners — French-educated Christian or animist negroes. The revolt of the Tebu — an ancient and independent Saharan race — was started by the traditional local spiritual and political leader, the Sultan of Zouar, Oueddei Kichidemi (also known as the *Derde*). When he later found exile in Libya, the revolt was continued by his youngest son, Goukouni Oueddei. In Chad, as in Sudan, Nigeria and other Saharan and sub-Saharan states with similar north–south divisions, were the makings of prolonged civil strife between Muslims and Christian and animist peoples, with much opportunity for devastating interference by interested' outsiders.

Rebellion in northern Chad was initially only of interest to southern Libya's own Tebu, although the fact that the bodyguard of King Idris was recruited from Tebu of the former Sanussi centre at Kufra ensured at least continuing royal interest in events in Tibesti. But as the revolt spread in the later 1960s through eastern and central Chad to involve other peoples, and its motives became more ambitious and more complex, so it became the concern of larger numbers of Libyans, either as specific tribal kinsfolk of the rebels — such as Gadafi himself — or simply as fellow Muslims.

Dr Abba Siddick, a former Chad government minister and a founder of the Chad National Liberation Front (*Frolinat*), was allowed to operate from Tripoli under both the monarchy and the republic, despite the fact that his organisation was pledged to the overthrow of the regime of President François (later N'Garta) Tombalbaye, and co-ordinated much of the anti-government insurgency inside Chad. But for years it was not clear whether the Libyan government was actively helping the rebels, and even after the French government sent troop reinforcements to support the Tombalbaye regime in 1968, both Tripoli and Fort Lamy remained silent on the matter. The first official claim of Libyan involvement was only made in August 1971, when President Tombalbaye announced that he had proof of a Libyan plot to overthrow him; he also claimed that *Frolinat* had training camps near Tripoli. Because there was a small Israeli mission at Fort Lamy, Tripoli felt justified in calling Tombalbaye an Israeli agent. Diplomatic relations were broken and in September, after accusing the Chadian government of oppressing the people, and particularly Muslim Chadians of Arab origin, the Libyan government announced its formal recognition of *Frolinat*.

Mediation by President Diori Hamani of Niger led to renewed relations in April 1972, and in return for Libya's friendship, withdrawal of official support for *Frolinat* and the promise of money, President Tombalbaye was persuaded to break off relations with Israel — the great Saharan–Sahelian drought was by then squeezing the life out of the rebellion anyway. Libya is also reported to have won Tombalbaye's agreement to the occupation of the so-called Aozou strip in northern Chad (territory some 200 kilometres wide extending the full length of the Libya–Chad frontier), ownership of which was open to question. Libyan forces moved into the strip at about the end of 1972 and, according to French pilots, set up an air base near Aozou guarded by ground-to-air missiles.[19] Although the strip was said to contain uranium deposits, it was never clear when or by whom, the prospecting had been done.

After initial successes in Uganda and Chad, the diplomatic offensive against widespread Israeli influence in Black Africa continued among the part-Muslim states on the southern edges of the Sahara and became an issue at the meetings of the Organization of African Unity, which had hitherto been neutral on the Arab–Israeli conflict. By 1973, Uganda, Chad, Mali, Niger and the Congo Democratic Republic (Brazzaville) had broken with Israel. The Middle East war and fears aroused by the Arab oil embargo and price rises in and after October enabled the Libyans in particular to make a notable contribution to the anti-Israel cause by persuading most Black African states of the advantages of abandoning their neutrality on the Middle East issue and ridding the continent of the influence of Zionism in favour of support for the Arabs. Before the end of the year, a further 24 states had broken with Israel and, as a result, relations were opened for the first time between Tripoli and various Black African countries. But it is doubtful whether such relations brought much mutual benefit; certainly, many African governments soon felt that their diplomatic support for the Arab cause had earned scant economic rewards; they resented the fact that little had been done to help them meet the greatly increased cost of their oil imports, and some of them said so at the first African oil conference, held in Tripoli in February 1974.[20]

In the meantime, Colonel Gadafi had formulated a new theory of international relations, justifying the Libyan role in world affairs. The so-called Third International Theory sought a middle way for Libya in particular and the Muslim and so-called Third World countries in general between the atheistic Communism of one superpower and the 'decadent capitalism' of the other. In practice, Libya's relations with Europe and the superpowers were commonly maintained on two separate levels. While it was unusual for Tripoli to be able to 'approve' unreservedly of other states' policies (usually because of their capitalism, their Communism or some other perceived defect), such political disfavour rarely interfered with continuing commercial relations based on sound economic realities. Thus the United States, although a frequent target for political attack, maintained a working economic relationship offering too many mutual advantages to be lightly broken. (It has also been suggested that Washington, on balance, came to welcome Gadafi's regime as a new bulwark against Communism in the Arab world.) While France, on the other hand, was unable to translate generally good political standing with Tripoli in the early 1970s into lasting economic advantage, Britain seemed unable to generate either political or economic goodwill with the new regime; it was typical of Colonel Gadafi's in some ways extraordinarily dated view of the world that in the 1970s he still saw Britain's international role in terms of the 1950s.

Relations with Moscow in the early 1970s were perhaps the most ambivalent of all. While the Soviet Union came to be recognised as a friendly power and a supporter of the Arab cause, Colonel Gadafi's absolute and often-stated opposition to Communism — largely on account of its atheism and emphasis on class struggle — inhibited the development of close relations. Gadafi also remained suspicious of the strong Soviet military presence in Egypt (before the expulsion of 1972) and the Mediterranean, and indignantly refused an early Soviet request for the use of Libyan military facilities after the evacuation of British and American forces. While wholly opposed to Soviet intervention in the Middle East, and prepared to condemn Moscow for what he saw as excessive interference in Muslim states, he had no objection to the supply of Russian weapons to the Arabs, so long as there were no political strings attached. As early as July 1970, Soviet arms deliveries to Tripoli were reported, and by 1972–3 the army — frustrated in its hopes of acquiring British *Chieftains* — had a total of 250 *T-54/5* and 15 *T-34* Soviet medium tanks — merely the beginnings of a vast armoury of Soviet weapons to be built up in the later 1970s.[21]

Colonel Gadafi's largely trouble-free experience with the French over the supply of *Mirages* had presumably convinced him that acceptance of one particular country as a major source of arms did not necessarily entail a closer political relationship with the supplier. Libya was quite willing to have normal economic relations with the Soviet Union, based on mutual and realistic commercial advantages and the ability to order specific goods, services and expertise against payment in hard currency, while in no way implying any ideological compatibility. For years Libyans tried to see arms supplies in the same light as any other commercial transaction. At the first anniversary of the revolution, Colonel Gadafi had spoken of a policy of buying the most modern weapons 'from any source whatsoever' because Libya had adopted a stand of 'positive neutrality and non-alignment'.

Revolutionary Libya's support for the Palestinians was often selective and illogical. Statements of firm commitment to the cause as a whole contrasted oddly with the generally offhand treatment of the resident Palestinian community in Libya. Its several thousand members had come to occupy middle positions on their own ability, but few were granted citizenship, and their place in society remained 'ambiguous and insecure'.[22] Although the Palestinian resistance movement had the nominal merits, in Gadafi's eyes, of confronting Israel and of revolutionary ideals, he tried to distinguish between acceptable organisations and some of the 'Communists' whose achievements might win Libya's official approval, but never its backing. The true cash value of Tripoli's grants to the Palestinians — and indeed the total cost of aid to revolutionary organisations the world over — have never been accurately estimated, but were quite probably much less than Tripoli hinted.[23]

By 1972 the Palestinian resistance movement was no longer an effective fighting force, but was sustained by the political ideas of Yassir Arafat and by a campaign of international terrorism. The formation of the 'Black September' organisation as an unacknowledged offshoot of *Al-Fatah*, initially to avenge the September 1970 extinction of the resistance in Jordan, enabled Colonel Gadafi to support active Palestinians whose use of terrorism against the international community, as against specifically Israeli targets, seemed to coincide with his own views on international 'revolutionary' activity. The supposed leader of the group was 'Abu Hassan' who had close ties with the Libyan Chief of Staff, Colonel Abu Bakr Yunis — 'a contact that resulted in funds being given to the Black September group'.[24] After the killing of Israeli athletes at the Munich Olympic Games in September 1972, the bodies of the five Black September men also killed in the operation were flown to Libya for ceremonial funerals. Such gestures, and the welcoming of known terrorists, inevitably raised still largely unanswered questions about the degree of Libyan support — in the form of training, cash, encouragement and sanctuary — for Black September and similar organisations, Arab or otherwise.[25]

By 1973 the Libyan government was becoming disillusioned with the poor performance of the moderate Palestinian guerrilla movement. In a speech early in the year, Colonel Gadafi attacked the Palestinians for lack of unity, Communist leanings and failure to wage war on Israel. In July, the Palestine Liberation Organization claimed that guerrilla training camps in Cyrenaica had been closed, and that many Palestinian residents had lost their jobs. Nevertheless, relations with Palestinian leaders (and especially Arafat) were kept up, and there was continual sanctuary for Black September members and other aircraft hijackers.

Gadafi's support, directly or indirectly, for aircraft hijackers and others prepared to terrorise air travellers apparently stemmed from frustration at his inability, and the unwillingness of other Arab regimes, to avenge the Israeli destruction of the Libyan Airline's Boeing over Sinai early in 1973. His object was also to support the 'rejectionist' cause opposed to the movement of the Arab 'moderates' towards a peace settlement with Israel in the aftermath of the 1973 war.

While support for the Palestinians seemed a logical outcome of Colonel Gadafi's views on the Arab–Israeli conflict, largely unquestioning and often singularly ill-informed backing of the so-called 'liberation movements' and organised malcontents the world over involved Tripoli with many groups struggling, or supposedly struggling, against allegedly oppressive central governments. Through its self-proclaimed 'sacred duty towards all revolutions', especially in Africa, Asia and Latin America, Tripoli became not only a clandestine supporter of Moroccan, Tunisian, Egyptian and Sudanese opposition groups, among immediate Arab neighbours, but also an open and declared supporter of 'oppressed' Muslims in Chad and the southern Philippines (as well as 'Black Muslims' in the United States), national 'anti-colonial' movements in Portuguese Africa, and 'revolutionary liberation', as deemed to be practised by such diverse groups as the Eritrean Liberation Front and the Irish Republican Army.[26]

Yet, as with aid to the Palestinian resistance, deep mystery surrounded the millions that Libya was popularly supposed to be disbursing to 'liberation movements'.

> Some estimates, not discouraged by the Libyans and based on little or no fact, place the total expenditure on international causes at more than £150 million [Sterling]. This does not include aid and loans to Egypt . . . but given the Arab capacity for exaggeration and taking into account the propaganda value to Libya of being the Arab World's big spender, this could be drastically misleading. In fact, those who have had dealings with the Libyans at this level attest to the opposite.[27]

As for motives,

> Colonel Khadafi may have genuinely cared about Muslim rebels in Israel, Chad and the Philippines; but whether Catholics or Protestants gained the upper hand in Ulster was neither a matter of doctrinal nor of vital interest for Libya. However, giving support and shelter to terrorists enhanced the international status of otherwise not very important countries; it made their rulers feel influential and it seemed worth the expense of these foreign ventures.[28]

Nevertheless, Libyan foreign policy after the revolution seemed a costly way of promoting national interests and prestige — or notoriety. If Colonel Gadafi's policies intermittently shook up the world as a whole, and the Arab world in particular, they yielded few worthwhile long-term dividends. Even if the Libyan leadership came to learn that boundaries in the Arab world, allegedly drawn by 'colonialism and imperialism', did after all mark certain real and not easily dissolved divisions, there were few signs of the lesson being heeded. The time, money and effort spent on many foreign ventures of scant concern or possible benefit to the Libyan people might have been more usefully devoted to domestic developments, where success would have convincingly demonstrated the regime's ability to use its revenues and resources constructively and wisely.

Notes

1. *Libyan Mail* (4 January 1970) reported that the leaders had been given 'film star receptions' in Tripoli and Benghazi.

2. F. Ajami, 'The End of Pan-Arabism', *Foreign Affairs*, vol. 57, no. 2 (Winter 1978–9).

3. 'L'Homme du Jour. Moamer el Khedafi: d'Abord la Palestine', *Africasia*, no. 9 (16 février–1 mars 1970).

4. Some of the *fidayin* made themselves unpopular soon after the 1 September *coup* by moving into Tripoli and other towns rather too enthusiastically, plastering walls with posters and spreading Marxist propaganda.

5. The plan entailed a three-month cease-fire between Egypt and Israel and resumption of the shuttle diplomacy of Ambassador Gunnar Jarring in an attempt to have United Nations Resolution 242 of November 1967 implemented as a basis for a comprehensive Middle East settlement.

6. On 4 August Libya issued a communiqué pledging total support for Egypt and affirming Libya's refusal to sign a treaty with Israel or to subscribe to any 'liquidation' of the Palestinian cause.

7. A. al-Sadat, *In Search of Identity* (London, 1978), p. 202.

8. BBC, *Summary of World Broadcasts*, ME/3495/E/4.

9. F. Ajami, 'The Struggle for Egypt's Soul', *Foreign Policy*, no. 35 (September 1979).

10. Egypt–Syria 1958–61; Iraq–Jordan 1958; Egypt–Syria–Yemen 1958; Egypt–Syria–Iraq 1963.

11. Egypt 33.3 million, Sudan 15.6 million, Libya 1.9 million. The outline of the three countries combined was very like that of Africa.

12. The figures were Libya 98.6 per cent, Egypt 99.9 per cent, Syria 96.4 per cent.

13. Among the victims was Salih Busair, the first post-revolutionary Foreign Minister.

14. M. Heikal, *The Road to Ramadan* (London, 1975), p. 194. For an account of the episode, see pp. 192–4.

15. Ibid., p. 191.

16. The fact that the 1973–5 Libyan development plan had been set at the then extraordinarily high level of $6,000 million was seen by some observers as a device to deny development funds to Egypt.

17. For an account of this bizarre episode, see J. Macphearson, 'Arab Dialogue?', *Encounter*, vol. XL, no. 4 (April 1973).

18. *Arab Report and Record* (16–31 December 1972), p. 606.

19. P. Biarnes, 'Tchad: Entre Paris et Tripoli', *Revue Française d'Études*

Politiques Africaines, no. 113 (Mai 1975). The frontier between Italian Libya and French Equatorial Africa would, under the Mussolini—Laval pact of June 1935, have been shifted up to 150 kilometres southwards, giving Italy control of Aozou and other settlements. But the agreement was never ratified and was later denounced by the Italian government following the deterioration of Franco-Italian relations as a result of the Italian invasion of Ethiopia. After Libyan independence, unfixed frontiers with French territories were defined, but the southern frontier with French Equatorial Africa (Chad) seems to have been left as it was (S. Bono, *Le Frontiere in Africa dalla Spartizione Coloniale alle Vicende più Recenti (1887–1971)* (Milan, 1972), pp. 94 ff. See also I. Brownlie, *African Boundaries* (London, 1979), pp. 121 ff. On the border dispute with Chad, Brownlie says (p. 125): 'In the absence of any formulated Libyan claim, it is impossible to state the issues of principle, if any, which are involved. It is possible that the Libyan government is relying, mistakenly, upon the alignment of the Franco-Italian Agreement of 1935 which remained unratified.'

20. See *Petroleum Economist*, vol. XLI, no. 3 (March 1974), p. 106.

21. International Institute for Strategic Studies, *The Military Balance, 1972–3* (London, 1973), p. 33.

22. F.R. Golino, 'Patterns of Libyan National Identity', *Middle East Journal* (Summer 1970).

23. Martin, 'The Cost of Libya's Revolutionary Largesse', *The Times* ((17 August 1972).

24. E. O'Ballance, *Arab Guerrilla Power, 1967–1972* (London, 1974), p. 216.

25. In 1973, an interviewee on West German television claimed that Gadafi had paid $5 million bonus for the Munich operation.

26. Gadafi: 'If we assist the Irish people it is simply because here we see a small people still under the yoke of Great Britain and fighting to free themselves from it. And it must also be remembered that the revolutionaries of the Irish Republican Army are striking, and striking hard, at the power which has humiliated the Arabs for centuries'. M. Bianco, *Gadafi: Voice from the Desert* (London, 1975), p. 154.

27. Martin, 'Cost of Libya's Revolutionary Largesse'.

28. W. Laqueur, *Terrorism* (London, 1977), pp. 204–5.

9 THE STATE OF THE MASSES

Few in number, politically unschooled and by nature conservative, Libyans were an unpromising revolutionary material for Colonel Gadafi to transform in accordance with his political, economic and social aspirations. The people were hardly to blame for their short-comings: their political growth had been stunted during the monarchy and, understandably, they had not been consulted about the junior officers' *coup*, supposedly carried out in their name. But even after September 1969, and despite the repeated claims that the revolution belonged to the people and that this was no mere army take-over,[1] all effective power remained with the military. There was little worthwhile consultation of popular opinion until dialogue between the people and their self-appointed rulers started in 1971–2.

Colonel Gadafi, at least, tried to uphold his own precepts by living modestly, even austerely (although security may have been his original reason for spending so much time in barracks), lining his face with overwork, and devoting himself to religion; marriages seem to have been his one early indulgence. Other RCC members resented his insistence that they live like him — well into the 1970s, the RCC continued to conduct its business in one of the large rooms in Azizia Barracks, on the south side of Tripoli.

As the ideologist and main spokesman of the regime, Colonel Gadafi was the clear leader of the RCC. But in resisting the natural tendency of such a leader to dominate the group, Major Abd-al-Salam Jallud and the RCC's ten other members exposed serious policy differences. Although the RCC acted collectively in public, always speaking with one voice, it was clear that some of its decisions – and particularly those affecting Arab and foreign relations – only became public policy after the most stupendous private quarrels; indeed, some policy decisions were never made because of the inability of RCC members to agree among themselves. After several such rows, Gadafi resigned his office, sometimes reportedly to the accompaniment of a nervous breakdown.[2] Yet his frequent resignations were consistently ineffective and were inevitably with-drawn; they apparently neither gained concessions for Gadafi from his colleagues nor undermined his standing among them.

175

After coming to power, Gadafi was in no hurry to build a formal political structure to implement his evolving ideology and mobilise a mass political following. In the first 18 months of the revolution, and particularly in the early part of 1971, members of the RCC who made a point of going among the people to explain revolutionary policy were dismayed by public political apathy. Nevertheless, the decision of April 1971 to unite with Egypt and Syria obliged the regime to provide a working political structure, instead of the *ad hoc* popular marches and gatherings that had served up to then as the nation's popular political forum. The Egyptian Arab Socialist Union was taken as a model for the type of political organisation which shared the RCC's own views on domestic and foreign policies and which, in the opinion of Libya's leaders, needed to establish branches in all Arab countries, eventually merging on the achievement of total Arab union.

Formation of Libya's own ASU was announced on 11 June 1971. It was not so much a party as an organisation of mass mobilisation intended to provide the main links between the government and the public and to awaken, in support of the regime, the latent political aspirations of the Libyan 'working forces', defined as peasants, non-agricultural working people, soldiers, revolutionary intelligentsia and 'non-exploiting national capitalists'.[3] As Gadafi explained, in his capacity as the organisation's newly appointed first president,

> The ASU will be the popular political organisation of the Libyan Arab Republic; it will achieve the alliance of the people's working forces and will peacefully eliminate class distinction wherever this exists. It will bring about true democracy and will keep the revolution away from the dictatorship of one class and domination by any individual.[4]

The ASU was also to formulate policy and create a new ideology based on Islam, with its inherent rejection of Marxism and the notion of 'class struggle'. The organisation was to operate openly, spreading its message by publicity and persuasion. As in Egypt, half its members had to be workers and farmers. Although its structure was a pyramid, with local, regional and national units, and the RCC maintaining control at the top, it was too complex for Libya's needs, combining in practice the functions of mass mobilisation with some thing approaching an administration. It was a 'rigorous and authoritarian ordering of political diversity on the model of a corporate state'.[5]

Relying on ideas already tried and found wanting in Egypt, the ASU seemed to lack adequate conviction and motivation. Its own powers and its relationship with other areas of government were ill-defined, while its system of 'conferences' and 'committees' lacked both authority and organisation, and soon appeared to be little more than a means of giving 'popular' endorsement to RCC decisions.

Nevertheless, the first ASU national congress was held in Tripoli during March and April 1972 in an atmosphere of some spontaneity. After Gadafi had announced that the purpose of the gathering was to enable the people to formulate policy, there was a long and remarkably free exchange of views between the RCC and the hundreds of delegates. It was the type of public debate that Gadafi had long envisaged, and which was so closely suited to his own 'popular' personality.

What he seemed to be fostering was a national decision-making process based on his knowledge and experience of traditional tribal practice, which sought consensus rather than the imposition of a majority view on a dissenting minority. In doing so, he was trying to realise the political implications of his own Islamic faith, and that of Libya, the Arab world and ultimately the wider Islamic world; the result was the rejection both of Western political models that had so long fascinated the older generation of Arab leaders, and similarly the Marxist model that was of increasing fascination to the younger generation.[6] Nevertheless, the achievement of the necessary degrees of national 'popular unanimity' also involved the suppression of actual or potential sources of opposition to the 'popular will'. As Gadafi had always made plain, opposition parties would not be tolerated 'because whoever is opposed to the revolution of the people is opposed to the people'.

Significantly, the ASU congress was followed by the announcement of draconian measures (including the death penalty) against membership of political parties: the ASU was to be the sole outlet for political activity. The press and the trade unions had already been brought to order. Early in 1972, all newspapers had been suspended and the publishing licences of ten had been revoked as a result of the corruption of public opinion' trials of January. The RCC had already used censorship, and economic and other measures, to enforce conformity on the press, but the publication law of June

1972 required newspaper editors 'to believe in the Arab revolution and abide by its objectives and the objectives and principles of the ASU'.[7] A new government newspaper, *Al-Fajr al-Jadid (New Dawn)* appeared in 1972 to promote and explain government policy. The trade unions had already been reformed into 22 trade and industrial groups by the new labour law of May 1970, and they were in due course incorporated into the structure of the ASU; in April 1972 Libyans lost the right to strike.

At the same time, regional and tribal differences came under stronger pressure. The attack on the so-called 'class distinctions' was effectively an attack on tribalism — class distinction as such is almost unknown in Libya, where social grading is concerned with family, ethnic and, above all, tribal divisions.[8] Despite the fact that traditional tribal structures were anyway breaking up under new social and economic pressures, 'regionalism' and 'reactionary tribalism' were often attacked by the regime as the most divisive features in Libyan society, hindering economic and social advancement and progress towards national, and particularly Arab, unity. The fact that traditional tribal leaders still had a following, had prospered under the monarchy and were potential counter-revolutionaries were further causes for official disapproval.

Berbers, who by the mid-twentieth century were less than 4 per cent of the population — at least, as a linguistically distinct minority — came under strong pressure because of their close-knit tribal loyalties — 'unlike the Arabs, Berbers do not see themselves as a single nation, but as members of their individual tribes'.[9] In a speech at Yefren, one of the main Berber areas of the Gebel Nefusah, south of Tripoli, in August 1971, Gadafi attacked tribalism and went on: 'I tell you sincerely that the Libyan people are one people from one Arab origin . . . the language used by some people here and called the Berber language is a Himyaritic language'.[10] He may have meant 'Hamitic', but as it is, the philologically false but politically attractive implication that the Berber language is south Arabian in origin stands attributed to him. But as he went on to state: 'those who say the Berbers are not Arabs are liars; the Berbers are the true and original Arabs', it would seem that ethnology, like history and philology, could be suitably amended for political ends to force all Libyans into the 'Arab' mould. The fact nevertheless remains that the Berbers are indigenous North Africans, while the Arab conquerors first arrived only in the seventh century AD. Gadafi was later to try to make 'Arabs' of the Sahara's Berber Tuareg, whose tribal confederations had for centuries despised and fought all Arabs who crossed their path.

A drive against traditional tribal leadership in local government was mounted after 1969. Shaikhs and other local leaders without the appropriate civil-service qualifications were replaced by supposedly better-qualified and usually younger 'modernising' administrators, while new administrative zones ignored the old tribal boundaries. In due course the whole tribal system was weakened and the tribes lost their legal status. 'Such strategies were designed to minimize tribal and regional identification, but also to bring the mass public into closer touch with the regime and to provide leadership, technical skills and attitudes necessary for development.'[11] Similarly, the traditional religious leadership came under attack as a barrier between man and God.

By 1973 it was plain that the ASU and other experiments in mass mobilisation had failed to arouse the supposedly latent revolutionary fervour of the Libyan people. Three and a half years after coming to power, Colonel Gadafi had still not achieved his objective of 'tumultuous popular revolution' that would endorse his claim that his had been no mere military *coup*. Even the 'modernising bureaucrats' who had largely replaced traditional leaders had failed to mobilise the mass of a stolidly conservative people.

Thus Gadafi briefly took on the role of political agitator, almost that of opposition rabble-rouser, whipping the people into controlled anger, nominally directed against the RCC and the Cabinet, but with the stagnant bureaucracy,[12] the salaried bourgeoisie and particularly administrators, managers and the professions as his real targets.

This so-called 'cultural revolution' was launched on the Prophet's birthday, 15 April 1973, in a speech at Zuara.[13] Gadafi started by attacking the people: 'The revolutionary accomplishments you want to achieve are threatened, in my opinion, if you continue on your present course.' He mainly took them to task for their lack of dedication to national economic and social progress, and particularly for relying on foreigners to do the hardest jobs in remote places.[14] Urging the people to make an assault on established authority at all levels (although he was to remain head of state), he outlined five principles for this new phase of revolution: (a) the suspension of all existing laws; (b) purging the country of the politically 'sick';[15] (c) distributing arms to 'numerous sections of the people', other than the armed forces and the popular resistance, to protect the revolution;[16]

(d) an administrative revolution to destroy bureaucracy and the bourgeoisie; (e) a 'cultural revolution' to 'refute and destroy' everything contrary to the Holy Koran.

He urged the people 'to run the government and assume the responsibilities of power'. This was to be achieved through 'popular committees' to involve the people directly in political processes and set up to ensure control of the revolution from below in villages and towns, workplaces, schools and colleges, in popular organisations and public corporations. Committees, each of 16 to 20 members elected directly by the people, were to send representatives to the larger municipal and provincial committees, which in due course took over local government. But

the Popular Revolution did not resolve some of the central problems of mobilization, participation and development; but some substantial gains were made. Popular committees represented a local leadership which in cultural and policy terms was closer to the mass public than the modernizers, yet unlike traditional leaders they were sympathetic to popular participation.[17]

A month after launching the cultural revolution, Gadafi claimed that 'most areas are being governed by the people'. The Zuara speech had indeed inspired a certain revolutionary zeal and some inevitable chaos; there were reports of book burning and gross interference by popular committees in private lives and professional practice. Little of the five-point programme actually took effect, although the number of popular committees — some of them righting genuine grievances with spontaneous enthusiasm — increased from about 400 in April to just over 2,000 by mid-August. The police, acting sometimes on the recommendation of committees, arrested between three and four hundred 'opponents of the regime',[18] including Communists, Baathists, Muslim Brothers and members of the Islamic Liberation Party.[19] This was broadly the same educated minority that had formed the main civilian opposition to the monarchy and was hardly more sympathetic towards the revolutionary republic. In addition, relatively large numbers of managers and other senior personnel were dismissed, demoted, transferred and even occasionally promoted by workers' committees. But the 'revolution' was too tightly controlled and manipulated by the RCC, the ASU and the police for short-lived outbursts of popular enthusiasm to lead to fundamental changes in the workings of the state.

The 'cultural revolution' was intended to prepare the people for their forthcoming union with Egypt by a cleansing of undesirable elements and by giving the illusion of a numerically small but politically vigorous and liberated people playing a full part in their own affairs. The whole movement was discredited but by no means abandoned when its most startling initiative, the great 'popular' unity march on Cairo in August 1973, petered out in disillusion and failure.

Colonel Gadafi always made a clear distinction between the Libyan 'cultural revolution' and the Chinese model of the later 1960s; his revolution was intended to revive Libya's true culture and traditions as expressed in the Holy Koran. Until publication of the first part of Gadafi's *The Green Book* in 1976, the Libyan revolution lacked the equivalent of Chairman Mao Tse Tung's *Little Red Book*; in the meantime, the Koran remained the prime source of revolutionary inspiration. In April 1974 Gadafi had resigned his political and administrative functions — although he remained head of state and Commander-in-Chief of the armed forces — to devote himself to 'ideological tasks'; his able assistant, Major Jallud, took charge of the government. Although this arrangement was only temporary, it apparently gave Gadafi the necessary time to put his ideas in order.

When they seized power in 1969, Moammar Gadafi and his close associates had to provide an ideology enabling the new republic to use its oil wealth for rapid development without loss of moral or largely Islamic cultural identity (as had seemed to be happening under the monarchy), while avoiding the creation of eventually disruptive political, economic and social tensions such as were generated, for instance, in Iran under the Shah. The new regime's prescription for the moral and social difficulties and dilemmas besetting the Libyan people in the late twentieth century was the socialism claimed to be inherent in Islam.

Notions of Islamic order and justice are well ingrained in Libyan social and political traditions. In the late nineteenth century, the Sanussi commonwealth was a model theocracy, with its sovereignty undisputably based on Islam. Through the agency of the Sanussis, Islam served to sustain and to some extent to unite Libyans against foreign domination. Even the Italians had recognised and respected the religious aspects of Islam in Libya while suppressing its political character; in their arrangements for the separate development of the Libyans alongside the European settler community, they failed to appreciate fully that Islam is indivisible and recognise no such European separation of state and religion. The creation of the Sanussi monarchy in 1951 could be seen as a reassertion of the proper spiritual and political supremacy of Islam in Libya even if, in the eyes of some believers, the regime betrayed its trust to Arab nationalism, and even seemed in danger of betraying its trust to Islam, by making alliances with non-Muslim powers and condoning, if not encouraging, the influx of anti-Islamic social and cultural practices.

A weakness of the Libyan monarchy was its lack of ideology: even reactionary ideology was mistrusted as a threat to the established order. The monarchy had to make up for its lack of political and ideological leadership by concentrating on general economic progress and spreading social welfare through the free workings of the capitalist system, encouraged by the state, regulated by non-coercive planning and supported and protected by the Western powers in general and the United States in particular as the main sources of Libyan security and oil revenues.

When, by contrast, Moammar Gadafi came to power, he sought legitimacy in his claim to represent the popular will. He found no difficulty in basing his ideology on Islam, for so far as he was concerned, there was no contradiction between religious consciousness and political decision. While assuming some of the spiritual aura of the old regime, he also saw his immediate mission as a cleansing of the nation from the previous corruptions and betrayals. Thus the expulsion of the few remaining Jews and the entire Italian community (with its very intrusive exercise of its Christianity in and around Tripoli), the evacuation of foreign bases, the campaign against such foreign 'cultural' imports as alcohol and Roman script, and the nationalisation of foreign economic interests could all be interpreted as a reassertion of the country's inherent Islamic character. (Fortunately for Gadafi's direct association of Arab nationalism with pure Islam, there has for the past thousand years or so been no native Christian minority in Libya such as those in Egypt and all the Arab states of the Fertile Crescent.)

As a result of his bedouin upbringing and army training, Gadafi saw no conflict between Islam and modernity. On the contrary, it could be argued from his point of view that the 'advanced' influence of the Italians, and after them the West in general, had left only very superficial materialistic impressions on Libya, while true modernity found daily expression in the uncorrupted Islamic character of the Libyan people. As one who freely accepted, bought and used Western technology with little concern for its conception, creation or workings, Gadafi often expressed the view shared by many devout Muslims that the Koran contains all wisdom and is universal in its relevance.[20]

And so, just as the original message of Islam united the Arabs in the seventh century and inspired conquests leading to the creation of unique Islamic civilisations, Gadafi believed that Islam could again bring the Libyans in particular, but also Arabs and Muslims everywhere, and indeed all mankind, to spiritual and political regeneration. This belief led him on to the so-called Third International Theory which first emerged towards the end of 1972. It was based on the proposition that the Islamic world, the Third World and indeed the whole world needed neither atheistic Communism nor materialistic capitalism (both of which had 'failed' and were involved in a dangerous confrontation' with each other), but a middle way, harnessing the two main driving forces of human history — religion and nationalism, 'interacting with each other to initiate and maintain the motion of life', as he put it. He rejected the Marxist economic interpretation of history, and placed the economic factor third or fourth in order of importance — 'and at times it may even be non-existent altogether'.[21] He held that Communism was outdated and less 'progressive' than Islam. Long before Communism (which deprived men of their liberty), Islam had set out guiding principles for economic management, labour relations, prosperity, justice and free society. Religion was not itself an ideology but 'a source of inspiration for life and society', according to Professor Abd-al-Rahman Utba of Tripoli University, who was apparently expressing the official view when he made this point to the Islamic—Christian dialogue in Tripoli in February 1976.[22]

The Third Theory, as first expounded to a Tripoli conference of European and Arab Youth in May 1973, became the official philosophy of the 'cultural revolution', which had been launched a month earlier. Socialist in character and claimed to be universal in its appeal, the theory envisaged a world in which 'governments shall protect the weak and the poor from the oppression of the strong and the rich'.[23] Islam 'provides for the realisation of justice and equity, it does not allow any rich person to use his wealth as a tool of oppression, nor to exploit people . . . however, private ownership may continue to be free, if it causes no harm'.

The state that Gadafi envisaged was modelled on the socialism he claimed to be inherent in Islam — or, more accurately, in the Koran itself, since he urged the greatest reliance on the fundamental source of revelation while placing relatively less emphasis on the authority of the *hadith*, the accumulated 'traditions' of what the Prophet Mohammad is reputed to have said. Socialism for Gadafi was 'social justice', and his ideal commonwealth embraced the corporate mass of the morally regenerated faithful (*umma*), applying the Islamic practice of consultation (*shura*), free from all non-Islamic influence and interference. Gadafi often expressed his abhorrence of 'exploitation' and the belief that Islam and socialism were spiritually and politically liberating.

'Koranic socialism' as it came to be practised in Libya up to the late 1970s proved to be a moderate type of redistributive socialism rather on the Swedish model, allowing modest private capital accumulation and limited free enterprise. In practice, the object seemed to be to mould Libyans into an unexciting and undemanding corporate existence as passive recipients of an impressively wide range of state welfare services only made possible by the continued inflow of oil revenues. (It was therefore hardly surprising that many better educated and more enterprising Libyans preferred to live abroad rather than in the increasingly stultifying political and social atmosphere at home.) The specifically Islamic aspects of this socialism took the form of a revision of Islamic legal practice, the *sharia*, while in 1972 the previously informal religious duty of almsgiving (*zakat*) became a formal legal obligation, and there were new measures reflecting the prohibition of usury (*riba*). Up to the 1970s, the *sharia* had been gradually replaced by civil and commercial legal codes on the Western model and was latterly concerned only with matters of personal status and institutions. Laws of 1973 and 1971 integrated *sharia* law and *sharia* courts into what had been a secular legal system, and at the same time simplified the complex traditional code. Much was made abroad of the enactment of laws reviving the traditional punishments for certain offences, such as amputation for repeated theft. 'Their reinstatement is justified on the grounds that their deterrent effect will be so great that they will seldom actually have to be applied.'[24]

'Koranic socialism' and its objectives of social justice and the ending of exploitation seemed in practice to be more a frame of mind than the actual application of specific Koranic principles to living the late twentieth century. Asked at an 'intellectual seminar' in Paris in November 1973 what new 'spiritual dimensions' Islam and Islamic socialism could give for creating a new society and a new socialism, Gadafi was only able to conclude a rambling reply by reasserting that 'Islam is the crowning element in the human effort for achieving social justice'.[25] Certainly, there was never any attempt to justify policy decisions by reference to specific Koranic authority.

The Russians were as perplexed as anyone by Gadafi's ideology. Radio Moscow complained that 'frequent repetition of the words "justice" and "Islam" which are claimed to be the basis of this ideology, explain nothing. Gadafi puts forward no programme of practical action for translating his socialism into reality.'[26] Gadafi, in short, could only reconcile socialism and Islam on purely social grounds — in their theoretical mutual respect for justice and their strictures against exploitation. Beyond this, he achieved no discernible accommodation on historical, philosophical or practical grounds between a modern political and economic theory of materialism and one particular and long-established religious expression of human spirituality.

Sanussism, through its association with the discredited monarchy, was not in official favour in the Libyan Arab Republic. Nevertheless, the Sanussi theocracy of the late nineteenth and early twentieth centuries provided a model that Gadafi may well have envied, in that the majority of Cyrenaicans at the time of The Grand Sanussi and the Mahdi lived in almost unchanging conditions in general harmony with such an administration, while he had to contend with radical and fundamental change. His political philosophy arguably looked up to certain enviable aspects of Sanussism,[27] and especially Sanussi notions of organisation and order and the ability to wield effective spiritual–political influence over a Muslim commonwealth scattered across Saharan and sub-Saharan Africa.

Although Gadafi's thinking apparently had much in common with the Muslim Brotherhood, he was quick to condemn that organisation for what he saw as its failure to acknowledge the vital importance of Arabism and nationalism; he also disapproved of the Brotherhood's use of secrecy and terrorism. He is quoted as saying:

> I do not think that the Muslim Brothers represent a Muslim philosophy in the true sense of the word . . . they are against socialism, against Arab unity, against Arab nationalism: so far as they preach Islamic unity they cannot but oppose Arab unity . . . both

they and the Islamic Liberation Party are mere agents of the west.[28]

Despite Gadafi's claims for the popularity of his revolution, he faced serious internal unrest by 1975. There were reports of dissidence in the salaried classes (and particularly among those whom the cultural revolution had failed to curb), among the students, in the RCC and, most ominously, among the middle-ranking officers in the army, still the one national organisation able to sustain or overthrow the regime. But because reports of *coup* attempts and arrests of dissident officers came from not necessarily objective foreign sources, they had to be treated with caution.

As a particularly secretive organisation, the RCC had always been a source of popular rumour. Early in August 1975 rumour was for once confirmed when Major Omar al-Mihaishi, RCC member and Minister of Planning, suddenly fled to Tunisia with some of his staff. He had apparently failed to mount what was later officially described as a military *coup*. The RCC reacted as sharply to the affair as it had done to the other big 'internal' *coup* attempt by Colonels Adam al-Hawwaz and Musa Ahmad in late 1969; new laws punished with death all attempts to change the government or the Constitution by force, or by any other means.

In fact, the Mihaishi affair seems to have been the result of disagreement over economic management. Following the sudden oil price rises of 1973–4, demand for relatively expensive Libyan crude oil fell in 1975 and oil revenues were as a result only 85 per cent of those of 1974 — the first such drop in annual revenues since exports began in 1961. Although the fall in revenues and the need for temporary economies had become plain by the first quarter of 1975, the RCC insisted on finalising a new Soviet arms-buying agreement in May. As Minister of Planning, Mihaishi felt bound to protest when he learned that social programmes were to be trimmed to pay for yet more Russian weapons. There seems to have been a monumental quarrel within the RCC, which Mihaishi lost. He then apparently made contact with other members of the RCC whom he believed to be 'sympathetic' — Hawadi and Huni, and perhaps also Najm Hamza and even Kharubi — as well as about 30 army officers; he could also expect some support in his native Misurata. Mihaishi reportedly intended to ask Gadafi to resign for the sake of the revolution and the people.[29] But it seems that Gadafi was warned of Mihaishi's plans by foreign sources more alarmed by the prospect of a left-wing succession than by Gadafi's remaining in power. After his flight to Tunis, Mihaishi sought political asylum in Egypt in February 1976. As he had first met Gadafi and joined his movement in Misurata in 1963, he was an authoritative public critic of Gadafi and his regime.

By the end of 1975 the ruling group of formerly young officers now nearing middle age had lost over half its members, but had perhaps become more cohesive. Only five of the original twelve members were still on the RCC: Colonels Gadafi and Abu Bakr Yunis and Majors Abd-al-Salam Jallud, Mustafa Kharubi and Khuwaildi Hamidi. Of the others, Captain Mohammad Abu Bakr Mugaryif had been killed in a motoring accident; Major Mohammad Najm had been relieved of his duties and was living under surveillance in Tripoli; Major Mukhtar Abdallah Jarwi had fled to the United States; Major Omar Mihaishi, and a little later Major Abd-al-Monim Tahir Huni, had 'defected' to Egypt; and Major Bashir Saghir Hawadi and Major Awad Ali Hamza were apparently under house arrest in Tripoli.[30]

Gadafi had started 1975 with the assertion that the regime was not dictatorial. But the London-based human rights organisation Amnesty International was to conclude that 1975 'has seen a decline in the human rights situation in Libya', although 'despite the existence of capital offences in the penal code, it is believed that there have been no official executions in Libya during the period of President Gadafi's rule'.[31] In October an Office for the Security of the Revolution was set up (despite the fact that less than a year before Gadafi had said he would not introduce such an institution as it would be a 'manifestation of terrorism'), and the police were given wider powers to handle security cases.[32] Gadafi in his speeches led a broad attack on all political opposition, and from late 1975 onward he tended to entrust his personal security and certain aspects of state security to his own family and tribe.

The close-knit system under which the country was governed eventually brought to a crisis the differences between the small and practically permanent group of men who made most of the decisions. The RCC was wholly responsible for defence and foreign affairs, and remained broadly in control of domestic and economic matters, although some domestic decision-making was shared with the Supreme Planning Council, composed of RCC and Cabinet members under Gadafi's chairmanship. The RCC itself was briefed, and proposals were submitted to it, by ministers and ministerial technocrats, who were also responsible for executing the resulting decisions, and there was considerable lobbying of individual RCC members for support and patronage. As the effective controller of the economy and chief negotiator of agreements with the international oil companies and arms vendors, Major Jallud played a role second only to Gadafi's, becoming one of the main channels of RCC contact and patronage for several of the main ministries. But while Jallud, for all his pragmatism, was apparently able to collaborate effectively with Gadafi and his persistent ideological interpretation of events and problems, other members of the RCC proved in time to be less flexible.

Behind the Mihaishi affair and other defections from the RCC, as well as more widespread unrest among individual RCC members' clients in the armed forces, were disagreements with Gadafi's ideology and its effects. There must have been arguments over such issues as the social disruptions caused by his insistence on driving the people into revolutionary action alien to their experience and expectations, and the use of oil revenues to support extravagant and questionable defence and foreign policies to the cost of national economic and social priorities. The temporary financial difficulties of 1975 brought the crisis to a head; but it was a crisis that Gadaf and his remaining close associates met and overcame without apparent compromise, even if former friends and supporters were alienated and other sources of opposition remained unappeased.

New, external sources of opposition emerged in the mid-1970s among them the so-called 'National Grouping' that claimed to represent all national interests, and not merely the narrow tribal base alleged to support Gadafi. The organisation attacked him for 'political oppression', and by May 1976 Mihaishi was broadcasting on its behalf from Cairo. At home, the students of Tripoli and Benghaz emerged as opponents — and victims — of the regime, just as their predecessors had under the monarchy in the 1960s. In January 1976 at least ten students were killed in clashes with the police and pro government 'students' in Benghazi. The trouble was caused by inter ference in student-union elections which, in the official view, ha not been a popular 'democratic' exercise because they had no produced an ideologically acceptable result.

Unrest spread in April 1976 to Tripoli University, followir attempts by Colonel Gadafi and Major Jallud to instil some revolu tionary enthusiasm into the students. Although the university wa later in April renamed 'Al-Fatah' and a General Revolutiona

Committee was formed, Gadafi was unable to generate much genuine support there, nor indeed on any of the campuses. In October 1976 he was still complaining that while the 'popular revolution' had been a triumphant success, the 'cultural revolution' had not progressed because the intellectuals had not taken a lead in the 'new experiment'; nor were many of them likely to do so, for many despised Gadafi's ideas as tedious and embarrassingly naïve.

In the meantime, the country was moving under Gadafi's guidance towards a new system of popular authority, initially through the medium of the Arab Socialist Union, which every adult was expected to join. In April 1975 Gadafi announced the transformation of the ASU, intended to provide 'the exciting democratic experiment' of 'people's power'. A new political structure began to take shape, with Basic People's Congresses (BPCs), higher committees and congresses, and a General People's Congress whose one thousand members were to co-ordinate BPCs' national policy decisions and recommendations. In a speech on 1 September 1975, Gadafi stressed the transitional nature of the revolution for many years to come: the people would create a new popular democracy only over several decades. As he later claimed, classical Athens was the only historical precedent for the new system of 'people's power'.

After further structural changes, the ASU opened its third congress in Tripoli on 5 January 1976. The congress, which seemed to represent yet another attempt to mobilise a politically apathetic public, was straightaway reconstituted as the First General People's Congress. There was some speculation that Gadafi, shaken by the open opposition of the previous year, was trying to speed up his planned devolution of power. At the congress, the ASU ceased to be a political party as such and became a national public institution, since all adults and not just a party elite were in future supposed to share in the exercise of power. All future political activity was to be directed through the Basic People's Congresses; those who refused to follow this popularly endorsed 'sound democratic path' were to be denied even the right of justice. Although Gadafi, as usual, dominated and tightly controlled the proceedings (frequently interrupting participants to stress that they were not to voice their own views, but only those that they had a mandate from their basic congress to express), members of the RCC, ministers and other state officials were open to questioning from the floor.

Libya's new political philosophy, the new political basis of the Third International Theory, was set out in Gadafi's *The Green Book*

Part One — The Solution to the Problem of Democracy (green being the colour of Islam). Extracts began to appear in the official *Al-Fajr al-Jadid* at the end of 1975, and the booklet was published in Arabic and other languages[33] in 1976.[34] Although very slim (the Arabic was barely 6,000 words) *The Green Book* offered some provocative thoughts on 'the problem of the instrument of government'. Writing from a purely Libyan viewpoint on a subject supposedly of universal relevance ('one seldom finds people who do not belong to a tribe'[35] was a typical throwaway comment), he expressed the view that all political parties and all forms of class division lead to governments that, whether dictatorship or parliamentary assembly, automatically deprive the individual of any decision-making role. He simply dismissed the entire rationale and apparatus of Western parliamentary democracy in a dozen short pages. Parliaments were worthless because 'representation is fraud' and 'a falsification of democracy'; parties were condemned for giving rise to 'negative and destructive party struggles'; plebiscites were 'a fraud against democracy'; the notion of the class struggle was dismissed because 'under genuine democracy there is no excuse for one class to crush other classes for its own benefit'.[36]

He accordingly offered what he believed to be the solution. '*The Green Book* announces to the people the happy discovery of the way to direct democracy, in a practical form . . . democracy has but one method and one theory . . . the people's authority has only one face and it can be realised by only one method, namely popular congresses and people's committees.'[37] Thus 'No Democracy without Popular Committees' and 'Democracy is the Supervision of the People by the People' became slogans of the revolution, proclaimed in large green letters on banners and posters throughout the land.

In describing the workings of 'the people's authority', Gadafi made it clear that he wanted *choice*[38] and not election to decide the selection of candidates for all offices. Although he gave no written guidance, this choice had, in practice, largely to depend on the ability of candidates to win the consensus of their selectors, almost like the traditional tribal system of consultation, as endorsed by the Koran. Such a system suggested that the personality, prestige and connections of candidates were of prime importance — just as they had been, in fact, in general elections under the monarchy.

Colonel Gadafi in November 1976 began a nationwide discussion of his proposals for the establishment of 'people's power', and at the end of February 1977 a special session of the General People's Congress met at Sebha (chosen because 'it had entered history as the cradle of the revolution' through its association with Gadafi's earliest political activities). On 2 March the 970-member Congress, with the Cuban leader Fidel Castro as the guest of honour, issued a four-point 'Declaration on the Establishment of People's Power' which proclaimed 'the end of any form of conventional institution of government — authoritarian, family, tribal, factional, class, parliamentary, partisan or party coalition'. Instead, 'undisputed power' was to be held by the people acting through people's congresses.

Libya's name was changed to *Socialist People's Libyan Arab Jamahiriyah* (*Al-Jamahiriyah al-Arabiyah al-Libiya ash-Shaabiyah al-Ishtirakiyah*). Gadafi's neologism *jamahiriyah* was generally translated as 'state of the masses'.[39] At the same time, the Koran was declared to be the code of society and the intention was announced to establish direct 'people's power' through Basic People's Congresses, the unions and other associations, and the General People's Congress. Since defence was the duty of all citizens, general military training was to be started to defend the revolution, socialise the masses, and stimulate their sense of nationalism.

At the same time, a permanent 'General Secretariat' was created to oversee GPC sessions and Gadafi, as the 'revolutionary intellectual and master leader', became its Secretary-General; its members were the four remaining members of the now officially disbanded RCC. The General Secretariat was the approximate equal of a polituro. A 26-member 'General People's Committee' also came into being, composed of former Cabinet ministers, renamed 'secretaries' to act as the state's main administrative body. As one apologist for the system explained:

> Gadafi did not oppose the people's will in every instance. The people desired that the revolution's leaders occupy the top positions in the system of people's power and their wish was granted . . . the position of this leadership was made stronger than it had ever been before. Elected by the people, it can only be removed by those who elected it.[40]

Major Jallud said of the Sebha congress: 'It is the first time in the history of the world that a ruler has handed over power to the people.'[41] The Libyan press hailed the congress as 'the greatest event in the history of the world' although Gadafi, more modestly, merely compared it to the French Revolution.

Thereafter, political authority and decision-making were theoretically vested in the 187 Basic People's Congresses (BPCs). All adults in the area served by a particular congress had the right and duty to attend its meetings, where the agenda had already been debated within smaller village or town district congresses, of which there were just over one thousand in the whole country. Each BPC committee was composed of secretaries from village or town district congresses. The chairman, secretary and assistant secretary made up just over half the delegates to the national General People's Congress (GPC); the remaining delegates were drawn from unions and trade, social and professional organisations. Delegates to the GPC were supposed to have an interpretative and not an imperative function, simply reporting the decisions of their group, without individuality, opinion or construction coming between the mass of the people and the GPC — 'The GPC does not represent the people. It *is* the people.' The GPC, or its General Secretariat, was supposed to issue instructions to the government executive in accordance with BPC resolutions offering a clear consensus of opinion on national policy issues.

In practice, the basic congresses were clearly better qualified to discuss and decide local and national domestic issues (and indeed proved adept at attracting cash grants for local development projects) than, for instance, matters of defence, oil or foreign policy. Foreign policy 'has generally proved difficult for basic congresses to discuss. While congresses can make, and have made, decisions on the broad lines of policy, the issues which constitute the substance of foreign relations often arise too quickly to be put before them'.[42]

The exercise of popular authority inevitably entailed a degree of central guidance and control. Government departments were obliged to make necessary facts available to congresses for discussion, while the GPC General Secretariat had to ensure that relevant current issues were understood, reviewed and decided on by the BPCs. There was, therefore, ample opportunity for concentrating discussion and decision into broad, predetermined patterns. This and the degree of personal control that Gadafi and his close associates insisted on maintaining, inevitably brought into question the validity of the authority the people were supposedly exercising.

It was, in theory, a system not unsuited to Libyan traditional society and temperament. The small population and extended family links meant that most people were already familiar with leading family, tribal, regional and national personalities. The processes of consultation were relatively straightforward because, unlike so many Third World countries, Libya was a nation of socially docile people, unused to dissent, and grouped around only two main population centres; national air and land transport and telecommunications were good; there were few truly isolated and inaccessible communities and, after the expulsion of the resident Jews and Italians, no significant racial, linguistic or religious minorities that could not be persuaded that they were now 'Libyan Arabs'.

In 1978, an apologist for the system admitted that its 'ultimate workability' still remained to be seen.[43] It was clear that the system needed time to mature and that there were certain policy decisions the people would never be able to take. Nevertheless, 'people's power' did provide for some genuine debate and consultation on most local and many regional matters. It helped to give Libyans experience in the exercise of responsibility that had largely been denied them in the past by paternalistic leadership and also by the cushioning effects of oil revenues that had tended to undermine social discipline and self-reliance. Some critics of the system were worried by the lack of a formal national political structure, although the growth of 'revolutionary committees' from early 1978 onwards was seen as an alternative means of mass control and mobilisation.

But the survival of the system was considered doubtful without the continual personal guidance of Colonel Gadafi — or 'Brother Colonel' as he preferred to be called in recognition of his 'closeness' to the people. Nor was the system as utopian as Gadafi intended because it first assumed that every adult was indeed a 'political animal' with a sustained political opinion, eager to express it yet, when all was said and done, willing and able to abide by corporate consensus. In many ways, Gadafi was expecting from his average Libyan a degree of political maturity and toleration far greater than had the constitution-makers who had prepared, but not achieved, the country's entry into the Western parliamentary system at the time of independence a generation earlier. Moreover, short of bringing all the adults together for the General People's Congress, the system still entailed a degree of delegation, no matter how conscientiously representatives were chosen, or how effectively they acted on behalf of others. The leadership itself had hardly set a good example of consensus politics, having nearly torn itself to pieces in

1975 as a result of the failure of RCC members to agree among themselves.

One half of the adult population was anyway largely excluded from the system because, despite official encouragement, women in practice played no more than a nominal role in the exercise of popular authority. Even the Union of Libyan Women, founded in 1975, was not effectively integrated into the consultative process. 'It is therefore not at all surprising that the majority of Libyan women declare that political life — as it has been organised so far — does not concern them.'[44] Publication in June 1979 of Part Three of *The Green Book*, 'offering a final solution to complex social problems', confirmed Gadafi's views on the secondary status of women, as members of the 'feebler sex', in the new Libyan society.

By early 1978 there were clear shortcomings in the system — bureaucratic inertia, duplication of effort and the need for Gadaf and Jallud — in the process of summarising and interpreting th 'popular will' — visibly to dominate and control the workings of th GPC. In February 1978 new BPC delegates were 'selected', whil 'revolutionary committees' that had come into being some month earlier took up a new role of 'absolute revolutionary supervision o people's power'. The role of these supposedly spontaneous group of 'students' and 'workers' was to raise popular political awareness to prevent deviation from revolutionary ideals, and to challeng growing 'traditional' regional and bourgeois influences in certai basic congresses as a source of potential 'popular' opposition. Th members of the revolutionary committees were to become 'the tru cadres of the revolution.'[45] In 1979 the zealous and ubiquitou revolutionary committees took charge of elections at BPC leve becoming at the same time the direct two-way link between Gada and the people. While the practice of Gadafi's political notio had so far caused little actual suffering or hardship (except t declared opponents), the implementation of his econom ideas certainly did so, arousing undoubted but unquantifiable di affection among the professional and propertied classes in par cular.

For Gadafi, in the meantime, had been enlarging his thesis that t factors determining human freedom — political power, wealth a arms — had to be in the hands of the people. Publication of Pa Two of *The Green Book* — *The Solution to the Economic Proble 'Socialism'* early in 1978 was to influence the daily lives of Libya far more immediately than Part One had done. What basica

concerned Gadafi was the distribution of wealth and the relationship
between Libya's wealth creators, although he never once acknowledged oil revenues as the main source of the economic well-being and
national fortune that enabled him to test his political and economic
theories on the nation with little regard for the financial consequences.

In Part Two of *The Green Book* Gadafi again insisted that his
ideas were rooted in Islam and were merely an interpretation of
Koranic 'orders and prohibitions'. His second 6,000-word essay has
been described as a 'random mixture of anarchism, populism,
Marxism and Islam'.[46] The 'socialism' that emerged envisaged a
degree of individual incentive and assured personal (not state)
ownership of such 'basic necessities' as food, clothing, housing and
a car (a shortlist that incidentally said much about contemporary
Libyan expectations). For 'whoever possesses the house you dwell
in, the vehicle you ride or the income you live on, takes hold of your
freedom, or part of your freedom, and freedom is indivisible. For
man to be happy, he must be free, and to be free, man must possess
his own needs.'[47] At the same time, Gadafi expressed wholehearted
disapproval of the exploitation he believed to be inherent in the profit motive and wage earning: wage workers in both public and private sectors were 'a type of slave, however improved their wages may
be'. In public speeches he was particularly critical of the country's
45,000 merchants as 'unproductive exploiters' and the 50,000 under-
employed government doorkeepers and messengers.

He proposed the effective abolition of the wage system and the
profit motive (leading eventually, he believed, to the disappearance
of money) and the establishment of the individual's control over his
personal needs. He proposed to make workers partners in agricultural and industrial enterprises, owning the means of production as
members of socialist corporations. Individual peasants or artisans
working by themselves were to possess their own means of production; domestic servants were to be freed from their 'slave status' and
were to become 'partners outside the houses'.[48]

While, in Gadafi's view, the skilful and the industrious had 'no
right to take hold of the share of others as a result of their skill and
industry' (he who did so was 'undoubtedly a thief'), a strange feature
of his socialism was his belief that the mentally and physically handi-
capped could not expect 'the same share as the healthy in the wealth
of society'.[49] But at the same time 'differences in individual wealth'
were 'only permissible for those who render a public service' —

society 'allocates for them a certain share of the wealth equivalent to that service'. Such apparent ambiguities certainly made it no easier for outsiders to understand the practical application of these economic theories.

The first 'socialist principle' introduced after publication of Part Two of *The Green Book* was the property law forbidding anyone to own more than one dwelling; excess property was to go to the state (against payment of compensation) for distribution to the homeless. A clause allowing each adult son a dwelling of his own led to a spate of early marriages in families determined to keep as much property as possible.

These moves could be interpreted as the opening of a new round in the official class war that had started with the cultural revolution of 1973. For the law deliberately struck hardest at members of the new moneyed class — largely salaried state employees — who had prospered since the arrival of oil revenues in the early 1960s and who had contrived to continue prospering since the revolution. For want of more attractive legal outlets, most savings had gone into housing between 1973 and 1975 over two-fifths of private investment was in real estate, much of it for letting to the large expatriate communities in the resultant building boom, housing targets were consistently overfulfilled.[50] It was these supposedly secure investments that were now being sequestered. While some owners were prepared to sacrifice their property 'for the common good' because their public position demanded such a display of selflessness, many who had sunk life savings into property undoubtedly deeply resented becoming the victims of half-digested economic and social theories forced into practice with little warning.

Resentful property-owners thus came to join businessmen and traders (already harmed by the new import and commercial regulations) and the intelligentsia as the discontented under a regime that still seemed to have the fairly uncritical support of the mass of Libyans, who only saw the great material advances and the new-found international standing that oil revenues and the revolution had brought to their country. But fears about the possible implications of some of Gadafi's policies following publication of the first two parts of *The Green Book* were expressed succinctly by the country's best cartoonist in an uncaptioned coloured sketch of a watermelon with a slice cut out; many (including officialdom) apparently failed to grasp the significance of the *green* rind covering the *red* flesh inside it.

Ironically, it was within a few weeks of the formal establishment of 'people's power' that the first reported executions for 22 years took place,[51] marring the reputation of a regime which, whatever its other shortcomings, had proved characteristically Libyan in its reasonable freedom from violence and bloodshed. The executions of April 1977 were a clear sign of the regime's expressed determination to tolerate no opposition, particularly within the armed forces, and its first-hand appreciation of the gravity of such opposition. On 2 April 22 army officers were 'executed within their military units' for their part in the *coup* attempt of August 1975.[52] They were among a total of 75 army officers tried by a military court in December 1976. Omar Mihaishi had at the same time been condemned to death *in absentia*. On 7 April 1977, five civilians said to have acted on behalf of Egyptian intelligence were also executed after being found guilty of 'terrorist sabotage' in Benghazi the previous September. Further executions of dissident army officers reportedly took place in March 1979.

Despite these displays of ruthlessness, Gadafi still had to face the unorganised resentments of those dispossessed by the new property laws and, potentially more serious, growing criticism from the religious establishment of what was seen as his 'heretical' reinterpretation of Islamic values in socialist terms. (There is no organised 'church' or ecclesiastical hierarchy in Islam, but certain *ulama* — doctors of religion — often wield considerable influence.) In a sermon at a Tripoli mosque in February 1978, Gadafi had warned the *ulama* against interference in the 'socialist' policies of the regime, and he had accused them of identifying with the propertied classes.

In the face of continuing attacks and denunciations from the mosques of Tripoli, in particular, Gadafi in July 1978 presided over a theological debate between the country's political and religious leadership. If Gadafi prevailed, it was not necessarily through his superior reasoning. He won because, as ever, he controlled the effective instruments of power — including the press (which later denounced 'religious leaders who interpret religion in strange ways') — and the means of silencing opponents by imprisonment or even execution. At the meeting, religious leaders voiced growing concern over the course the regime was taking, and especially the relationship of *The Green Book* to Islam and the Koran. Gadafi was criticised because the *hadith* — the traditions of the Prophet — expressly forbad some of the lines of thought he seemed to be following. But Gadafi rose to challenge the role of the *hadith* and orthodox *sunni* Muslim tradition and doctrine. He insisted that the Koran, as the uncorrupted word of God, and source of divine commands and prohibitions, was the sole valid authority for Muslims. Without actually mentioning the term, he implied that *ijtihad* (the interpretation of Muslim tradition through independent reasoning) was the right of every Muslim. Be that as it may, many of his critics were unable to accept his interpretation of the Koran in socialist terms, nor his insistence that *The Green Book* was founded on Islam; nor were they able to accept the implication that *The Green Book* was in some way complementary to the Koran.

Nevertheless, in his direct challenge to the *ulama*, Gadafi was undoubtedly expressing opinions supported by certain thinking Libyans. There was at least a hint of Sanussism in his views, for here was the same reforming and fundamentalist challenge of the man of the desert to the urban Islamic establishment. It was a challenge with a certain appeal to some Libyans who liked to see themselves as uncorrupted followers of pristine, militant and unifying Islam. Then, with his still intact vision of a united and Islamic Arab world, Gadafi began in the later 1970s to be seen by some in a rather different light. Rather than the potential successor to Gamal Abd-al-Nasser as the temporal leader of the Arab revolution, here possibly was a new *mahdi*, a divinely guided leader, perhaps in the same mould as Al-Sayyid al-Mohammad Mahdi al-Sanussi. As head of the Sanussi Order from 1859 to 1902, the Mahdi led the nearest there has ever been to a Libyan theocratic empire, when wide areas of Saharan and Sudanic Africa came under his generally enlightened and beneficial and reforming politico-religious influence. But Colonel Gadafi intended his own reforming revolution — financed by oil revenues and inspired by his own unique visions — not merely for Muslim Africa, but for the whole Islamic world.

Notes

1. 'The Libyan Arab Republic's armed forces have proved with practical evidence that what they staged on 1 September was not a military *coup* and was not aimed at assuming and clinging to power, but was a true and genuine expression of the people's will for full freedom and the right to their land.' (Speech by Gadafi on 22 June 1970 — BBC, *Summary of World Broadcasts*, ME/3412/A/5.)

2. 'Every two months I used to submit my resignation over a period of three years because, one, I have no wish whatsoever for anything called leadership or command and two, the revolution for which I worked for ten years and risked my life, I se

threatened in a manner which I will not allow at all while I am present.' (Gadafi's Zuara speech, 15 April 1973, BBC, *Summary of World Broadcasts*, ME/4273/A/15).

3. According to Article 17 of the 'basic law' of 11 June 1971, a peasant 'is anyone who derives his livelihood from agriculture or raising livestock and who does not personally own, with his wife and minor children, more than thirty hectares provided with perennial irrigation'. A worker 'is anyone who depends for his livelihood on daily pay and who is not a graded employee'. Article 18 defined 'a non-exploiting capitalist' as 'one who (1) is subject to progressive taxes; (2) can efficiently make use of his capital; (3) does not exploit others; (4) gains his money in a lawful manner' (BBC, *Summary of World Broadcasts*, ME/3708/A/10).

4. Ibid., A/16.

5. R. Nizza, 'Libya's "Prussian" Role in the Drive for Arab Unity', *New Middle East*, no. 45 (June 1972).

6. 'Muammar El Kadhafi', *Maghreb*, no. 48 (novembre–décembre 1971).

7. W.A. Rugh, *The Arab Press* (London, 1979), p. 64.

8. Nyrop *et al.*, *Area Handbook for Libya* (Washington, DC, 1973), pp. 104–5.

9. Ibid., p. 97.

10. BBC, *Summary of World Broadcasts*, ME/3774/A/12. The fact that this remark was greeted with applause suggests that the people of Yefren have a remarkable grasp of philological niceties

11. O.I. El Fathaly and R. Chackerian, 'Leadership, Institutionalization and Mass Participation in Libya' in O.I. El Fathaly, M. Palmer and R. Chackerian, *Political Development and Bureaucracy in Libya* (Lexington, Mass., 1977), p. 92. See also O.I. El Fathaly and M. Palmer, *Political Development and Social Change in Libya* (Lexington, Mass., 1980), pp. 57–8.

12. Gadafi was appalled that Libya had 60,000 civil servants in a population of less than 3 million, although by world standards the ratio was not particularly high.

13. For a full text, see BBC, *Summary of World Broadcasts*, ME/4273/A/9–20.

14. 'The only doctor in Ghadames [the picturesque if remote oasis some 500 kilometres south-west of Tripoli] is a Palestinian because the Libyans refuse to work in Ghadames, as though Ghadames is on Mars and they cannot get there.'

15. Defined as 'those who talk of Communism, Marx and atheism . . . any member of the Muslim Brotherhood or the Islamic Liberation Party carrying out secret activities . . . anyone who makes propaganda for a western country or advocates capitalism'.

16. 'You should not rely on the armed forces, which have to protect the whole of Libyan territory.'

17. El Fathaly and Chackerian, 'Leadership, Institutionalization and Mass Participation in Libya' pp. 97–9.

18. *Amnesty International, Annual Report 1974–75* (London, 1975), p. 132. According to this report, 130 were still being held a year later, but were eventually released. Some 40 — alleged Trotskyists, Marxists and members of the Muslim Liberation Movement — remained in detention: 'almost all are in Tripoli Central Prison, where treatment and conditions are said to be satisfactory'.

19. The Muslim Brothers (*Majallat al-Ikhwan al-Muslimin*) was founded in Egypt in 1925 by Hassan al-Banna as an Islamic progressive party, aiming for change while preserving the moral basis of the Islamic community ('the Koran is our constitution'). It was not averse to using terrorism and subversion to further its aims. The Islamic Liberation Party (*Hizb al-Tahrir al-Islam*), a Palestinian counterpart of the Brotherhood, was founded in Jordan in the 1950s.

20. 'We all know that Science, in spite of all its wonderful achievements, has not found all the answers to the meaning of life. The Koran provides these answers and refutes all the hallucinations of materialism and existentialism' ('The Third International Theory', advertisement in *The Times*, 6 June 1973).

21. See M. Gadhafi, *The Battle of Destiny* (London, 1976), p. 3. See also 'The

Third International Theory: The Divine Concept of Islam and the Popular Revolution in Libya' (Ministry of Information and Culture, Tripoli, 1973).

22. See M. Borrmans, 'Le Séminaire du Dialogue islamo-chrétien de Tripoli (Libye) (1–6 février 1976)', *Islamochristiana* (Rome, 1976). Gadafi had apparently hoped that the dialogue would recommend in its conclusions the Christian recognition of Mohammad as a prophet (note 32, p. 155).

23. 'The Third International Theory' (*The Times*, 6 June 1973).

24. A. Mayer, 'A Survey of Islamifying Trends in Libyan Law since 1969', *Society for Libyan Studies, Seventh Annual Report, 1975–76* (1976).

25. Gadhafi, *Battle of Destiny* pp. 18–19.

26. Radio Moscow in Arabic, 8, 9 and 10 June 1976, quoting *Literaturnaya Gazyeta* (BBC, *Summary of World Broadcasts*, SU/4317/A4/1–6).

27. See H. Bleuchot, 'Les Fondements de l'Idéologie du Colonel Mouammar El Kadhafi', *Maghreb-Machrek*, no. 62 (mars–avril 1974).

28. G.H. Jansen, *Militant Islam* (London, 1979), pp. 164–5.

29. *L'Action* (Tunis, 27 March 1976.)

30. *L'Orient le Jour* (Beirut), 13 January 1975.

31. *Amnesty International Report, 1 June 1975–31 May 1976* (London, 1976), p. 189.

32. Ibid. In 1976, 'for the first time for some years', Amnesty International received allegations of torture in Libya, including three deaths as a result of ill-treatment in prison.

33. There have been complaints of mistranslation in some of the foreign-language texts.

34. Gadafi at first insisted that *The Green Book* be sold and not given away so that its contents could be better appreciated. But copies were later freely available in various languages. The book was offered to the public as the theory of a 'private citizen' for discussion and review.

35. M. al-Qadhafi, *The Green Book. Part One* (London, 1976), p. 19.

36. Ibid., p. 19.

37. Ibid., p. 27–8.

38. See ibid., p. 28.

39. '*Regime* of the Masses' was an alternative suggested by *Le Monde*, 13 August 1977.

40. M. El Shahat, *Libya Begins the Era of the Jamahiriyat* (Rome, 1978), p. 108.

41. Hirst, 'The Committee is Caliph', *Guardian*, 13 March 1977.

42. Niblock, 'People's Power in Action', *Guardian*, 1 September 1978.

43. El Shahat, *Libya Begins the Era of the Jamahiriyat*, p. 62.

44. C. Souriau, 'Femmes et Politique en Libye', *Revue Française d'Etudes Politiques Mediterranéennes*, no. 27 (3ème trimestre, 1977).

45. El Fathaly and Palmer, *Political Development and Social Change in Libya* p. 198; see also p. 202.

46. T.C. Niblock, 'Libya: The Emergence of a Revolutionary Vanguard', *New Statesman* (22 September 1978).

47. Qadhafi, *The Green Book. Part Two* (London, 1977), p. 26.

48. Ibid., p. 30.

49. Ibid., p. 24.

50. Niblock, 'Homes Policy Aids Families and Worries Private Investors' *Middle East Economic Digest* (1 September 1978).

51. The only known execution under the kingdom was that of the killer of the king's adviser Ibrahim Shalhi, Prince al-Sharif bin al-Sayyid Muhi-al-Din al-Sanussi in 1955.

52. *Arab Report and Record*, 1–15 April 1977, p. 268; *The Death Penalty Amnesty International Report* (London, 1979), pp. 177–8.

10   DEFENCE AND FOREIGN POLICY

Militarism was one of the most striking features of the Libyan *Jamahiriyah* by 1981. It was characterised by the build-up of a formidable arsenal, a near tripling in armed manpower since 1970, and the military training of youth in particular and the nation in general through an economically disruptive system of conscription and 'popular militias'. Although the four-day frontier war with Egypt in July 1977 had shown the country's vulnerability to invasion, not least because of the enormous distances and logistical difficulties involved, the military build-up had started long before then.

In an extraordinary reversal of former policies, more than enough arms to equip even the enlarged forces had been bought for hard cash, mainly from the Soviet Union. But lack of manpower, and particularly skilled manpower, still limited the size and efficiency of all three services. It was estimated in 1979 that there were only 150 competent pilots for over 160 operational warplanes, compared with the norm of at least two pilots per aircraft.[1] Even conscription, introduced in mid-1978 as a temporary measure 'until the people attain their ultimate aim of assuming the task of defending themselves', seemed unlikely to produce enough recruits suitable to master and operate all the complex weapons available, despite the fact that university and other advanced students could only defer their service; much of the best military effort was anyway diverted into maintaining internal security. By 1981 all education had been militarised as part of the drive to build a citizens' army numbering half a million trained men and women.

In 1970 there had been one soldier for every 124 square kilometres of national territory: by 1980 the ratio was 1 : 50; the number of sailors had over the same period risen from 3 to 15 for every 10 kilometres of coastline, while warplanes to patrol the Egyptian frontier had increased from one per 170 kilometres to one per 6 kilometres — although pilots trained to fly them were not necessarily available. Like the economic and social planners, the military overcame manpower shortages by using foreigners — not merely for training and maintenance, but also to operate essential services and fly aircraft. Reflecting a remarkable and apparently increasing reliance on the Soviet Union for arms of many types was the reported presence in 1979 of up to two thousand Russian military advisers. Russian aircrew were also manning Libya's two squadrons of *TU21* bombers, and possibly other aircraft as well, while the North Koreans were piloting and maintaining two squadrons of *MiG-23* warplanes based at Bomba in north-east Cyrenaica.[2] Other 'Libyan' aircraft were flown by Pakistanis and Palestinians; Czech specialists were maintaining tanks; the East Germans were active in civilian and military intelligence; Cubans had reportedly trained Colonel Gadafi's personal bodyguard; and other nationalities involved with the armed forces included French, Yugoslav and Taiwanese. In addition, many Libyan servicemen were being trained in the Soviet Union.

Despite continuing speculation, there was no hard evidence of Soviet bases in Libya. As Colonel Gadafi pointed out in 1979: 'the Libyan people, who regularly celebrate the evacuation of the British, US and Italian bases from their country, are not prepared to accept the return of foreign forces to their land. Libya will thus remain non-aligned, imposing respect on friend and foe alike.'[3] It was a persuasive but by no means conclusive argument. The implication was that arms-buying was a purely commercial transaction like any other; the Soviet Union, like any other supplier of goods and services, was a mere contractor, and Libya a wealthy client driving a business bargain while maintaining full freedom of action. In 1979 Colonel Gadafi did hint that, because of hostile American policy, Libya might be obliged to allow the Soviet Union to use its ports; but the threat seemed at the time intended to alarm rather than become reality.

Nevertheless, the sheer scale of the arms-buying, particularly for the army, suggested to some observers purposes other than pure national defence. By the late 1970s, the army had two thousand Russian *T-54*, *T-55* and *T-62* medium tanks,[5] as well as an extraordinary array of nearly 1,400 scout and armoured cars, armoured personnel carriers and 'infantry combat vehicles' of Brazilian, British, French and Russian makes.[6] 'In 1977, it was still the case that over one third of the Libyan army would be used up simply in providing crews for its tanks, while all the rest could ride comfortably in the APCs and other combat vehicles, leaving nobody to answer the telephone at headquarters.'[7] The army also had quantities of antitank and long- and short-range surface-to-surface missiles. The navy was being equipped — vessels included Russian and Spanish submarines — to bear out Colonel Gadafi's boast that it would be the third-largest in the Mediterranean within a few years (presumably excluding those of the United States and the Soviet Union). The air force, besides its original squadrons of *Mirages*, and 36 *Mirage F-1C* bought in 1975, had acquired various Russian aircraft, including bombers capable of reaching targets in Israel. Other arms suppliers included Italy, Canada and Czechoslovakia.

The extraordinary build-up of arms in the later 1970s, and particularly the fact that the army had far more Russian tanks than it could possibly use (at least according to conventional military practice) generated speculation that most of the tanks represented a strategic stockpile for use by the Soviet Union in an emergency in Africa,[8] the Middle East or elsewhere. But this view was disputed on the grounds that the tanks had been bought by the Libyan government for hard currency, were not maintained to Soviet standards, and because Tripoli had not yet shown itself subservient to Moscow's policies. Dyer[9] believed the most plausible explanation to be Libya's intention to provide the necessary arsenal for an eventual pan-Arab assault on Israel, although it was not clear why, in this case, arms-buying had concentrated on tanks rather than, for instance, artillery. Talking in 1977 about what he termed the 'historical conflict' in Palestine, Colonel Gadafi had said: 'The only thing that can save us is buying arms and preparing ourselves. This is because we believe this battle faces all the Arabs.'[10] Another explanation for the arms build-up was total miscalculation of the capacity of the armed forces to absorb weapons; it might be said that a large proportion of the tanks and some aircraft were in storage simply for want of crews to operate them. Later plans to raise militarily-trained personnel to half a million at least promised the numbers needed to man all the available equipment. In addition, mercenaries from Arab and Muslim African countries were recruited into an 'Islamic Legion' to further Tripoli's interests in Africa.

Through its arms sales, the Soviet Union not only earned badly-needed hard currency (in 1977 alone Libya spent an estimated $1,600 million on weapons)[11] but remained an important source of military supplies and training in North Africa after its former client, Egypt, had renounced military ties with Moscow in the early 1970s. Moscow clearly expected further dividends from an arms-supplying arrangement that Tripoli continued to regard — officially at least — as a straightforward commercial transaction.

Although Libya had little difficulty in buying more than enough conventional arms, Colonel Gadafi's expressed desire to acquire nuclear weapons proved harder to satisfy. Major Jallud's offer to buy a nuclear bomb from the Chinese soon after the 1969 *coup* was said to have been politely refused by Premier Chou en Lai; direct approaches to France and India were similarly rejected. While it was recognised that Libya did not have the technology to produce a bomb itself, there were many reports of substantial backing (in the form of dollar banknotes) for an alleged bomb-making project in Pakistan,[12] from which Tripoli expected at least to acquire bomb-making expertise, if not actual weapons. It was also claimed that Libya supplied Pakistan with uranium yellowcake derived from the important mid-Saharan deposits at Arlit in neighbouring Niger whose President, Seyni Kountche, had come to power with Libyan support in a *coup* early in 1974.[13] Further 'evidence' of Tripoli's plans to acquire nuclear weapons and the means of delivering them was seen in the creation in January 1981 of a nuclear energy secretariat and by the report of March 1981 that the West German Orbital Transport-und-Raketen Aktiengesellschaft (OTRAG) was using the Fezzanese desert for tests of medium-range rockets previously carried out in Zaire.

All the signs of Libya's growing militarisation and arms build-up in the late 1970s alarmed neighbouring states that had charged Tripoli with many specific acts of subversion, and the training of their exiled nationals in subversion and terrorism. Colonel Gadafi dismissed these alarms by claiming that 'what really worries Arab regimes is . . . the emergence of people's power' on the Libyan model.[14] Relations with Egypt never recovered from the set-backs of 1973–4, and there was too much personal animosity between Presidents Sadat and Gadafi for official ties to improve so long as both remained in power. Since 1969 the two countries had in a way exchanged international roles; Egypt under President Nasser had generally been seen from Tripoli as subversive and threatening, while royalist Libya had been passive, pro-Western and moderate; throughout the 1970s, Libya continued to cultivate its militant revolutionary credentials, while Sadat's Egypt emerged as a peacemaker, a proclaimed moderate and new-found ally of the West. Thus the brief period of accord between Cairo and Tripoli in the early 1970s gave way to renewed mutual suspicions: while Cairo was wary of Libyan intentions, believing Tripoli to be directly responsible for many internal troubles (including the serious food riots of January 1977), the Libyans saw President Sadat's policy of peace with Israel under United States sponsorship as an act of abject surrender and betrayal of the Arabs.

In July 1977 relations reached a crisis over renewed Egyptian charges of Libyan subversion, and increasing concern in Cairo over Tripoli's Russian arms build-up and attempts to subvert tribes in the Western Desert. Border incidents led to a four-day war which, despite lengthy Egyptian preparations and early and explicit Russian warnings, seems to have taken the Libyans by surprise. The Egyptians, with at least the political and moral support of Sudan and Saudi Arabia, launched a heavy punitive raid, apparently intended at least as a warning against further interference in Cairo's affairs, and possibly as a means of encouraging Libyans to overthrow the regime   although the actual effect was to rally the nation round its leaders in an upsurge of popular patriotism. Egyptian armour crossed the frontier at Musaad, south of Bardia, and the air force destroyed armour, aircraft and installations in raids on bases and Russian-manned radar stations in north-east Cyrenaica. The defence was unimpressive, although it was claimed that only the people's militia, and not regular forces, had opposed the invasion.[15] The fighting was ended largely through the mediation of President Houari Boumedienne of Algeria (who nevertheless declined to give Libya military help), but the war of words between Cairo and Tripoli continued.

President Sadat's decision to visit Jerusalem in November 1977 and then to undertake a serious peace-making process with Israel leading to the Camp David agreements of September 1978 caused new alignments in the Arab world. Libya and Iraq (both of which had remained outside the mainstream of Arab consensus achieved at the Riyadh and Cairo meetings in 1976) were the first to attack Sadat's initiative. The day before he went to Jerusalem, the General People's Congress declared that he was about to commit 'a crime against the Arab nation'. As he arrived in Israel, the Egyptian mission in Tripoli was burned and sanctions against Egypt, including a complete break in relations, were announced. But large numbers of Egyptian 'guest workers' who had remained in Libya despite the political climate were specifically excluded 'as they are considered to be in their own country and among their own kin'.[16]

At the beginning of December 1977, representatives of Libya, Algeria, Syria, the People's Democratic Republic of Yemen (South

Yemen), the Palestine Liberation Organization and Iraq met in Tripoli to set up a 'Front of Steadfastness and Resistance' that Iraq declined to join. The front offered a lack-lustre programme of anti-Egyptian boycotts and sanctions and a policy of achieving a 'just peace' in the Middle East. But the group's impotence was perhaps best revealed by its inability to oppose Israel's invasion of southern Lebanon in March 1978. The bloc was united only in its opposition to President Sadat, and it lacked both a constructive alternative policy and the support of Iraq, which should have been its leading member.

Colonel Gadafi continued to attack what he termed the 'Pharaonic –Hebrew–American alliance'. He saw American involvement in Egypt, and particularly American arms supplies, as a change in the balance of power that he would be forced to counter by seeking more help from the Soviet Union. Continuing tension between Cairo and Tripoli expressed itself in a build-up of forces in the Western Desert, and in 1980 Libya was reported to be preparing an elaborate 280-kilometre defensive line along the northern stretches of the frontier to deter attack, although its strategic value seemed questionable, since its southern end was marked by no natural obstacle as effective as the Mediterranean at its northern end.

Colonel Gadafi's hostility towards other Arab regimes (but not people) stemmed from his own unique vision of the world. As a Muslim and man of the desert, he considered the basically European conception of national sovereignty within defined frontiers an alien restriction separating otherwise united peoples. (But it is interesting how he insisted on national unity and elimination of minority particularisms within Libyan borders that had supposedly been drawn, if not 'imposed', by colonialism.) According to his broader vision, only Islamic sovereignty was unique and paramount; regimes in all Islamic states were merely caretakers to be abolished in the process of achieving Islamic unity. The Arab nation's historic destiny was a union that would itself merely be the first step towards wider Islamic unity. As he admitted in an interview in 1976, 'Regimes don't interest me any more; I address myself to the Arab masses.'[17] Because he believed that all moves towards Arab union were legitimate and never to be opposed, he became impatient when practical objections were raised to specific plans for unity. This apparently explains why, after the failure of the gradualist approach to unity with Egypt in 1973, he tried instead to rush Tunisia into union in

1974, expecting to solve the practical difficulties later. Similarly, to his impatient way of thinking, all state structures in the Arab world were so many outdated obstacles to unity that would eventually be overcome, at whatever cost.[18]

The practical applications of this theory were apparently to be seen in subversion and 'incidents' in various Arab and other states, and particularly in neighbouring states, during the 1970s. Relations with Sudan remained hostile after a bloody *coup* attempt in Khartoum at the beginning of July 1976 was directly blamed on Libyan 'mercenaries' said to have been trained in camps at Kufra; indeed, the attempt was at the time described by the Sudanese government as an act of aggression conceived, prepared and executed in Libya. The result was the formation of an Egyptian–Sudanese defensive alliance (supported also by Saudi Arabia) to counter the very real concern felt in Cairo, Khartoum, Riyadh and other Arab capitals about Tripoli's intentions towards any Arab regime considered in any way incompatible with or hostile to Libyan politics and aspirations.

The failure of the proposed union with Tunisia in 1974 overshadowed relations for many years afterwards. The Tunisians, like the Egyptians, the Sudanese and others, were convinced of Libyan implication in specific acts of subversion and worse (including an attempt to assassinate Tunisian premier Hadi Nouira in 1976)[19] and in the training in terrorism and subversion of their nationals, both voluntary and coerced. Yet among some disaffected Tunisians, as among some sectors of the population in other neighbouring states, there was a certain appeal in Gadafi's championship of popular evolution; such was particularly the case in Tunisia's depressed south. Internal Tunisian troubles, culminating in serious trade union disturbances in early 1978, all provided exploitable material for the destabilisation of a pro-Western and generally moderate regime.

In February 1980, an armed band of Tunisian insurgents, infiltrated from abroad, tried to instigate an uprising in the remote mining town of Gafsa in central Tunisia, an area of the country notably hostile to the government; the Interior Minister alleged that the aggression had been ordered by a 'neighbour state known to specialise in such operations'. Libya, while agreeing that it endorsed the aspirations and policies' of the Tunisian opposition, officially denied any involvement in the Gafsa raid: 'that Tunisian dissidents may look to the Libyan *Jamahiriyah* as an example of social justice, should not be construed as evidence that Libya is involved in supplying material support'.[20] The Tunis-based Arab League, where Tunisia took its complaints against Libya, was broadly inclined to agree.

Algeria tended to keep Libya at arm's length, and Algeria's failure to give more decisive support in the 1977 fighting with Egypt was a source of resentment in Tripoli. Nevertheless, there was much agreement on international affairs in general and African affairs in particular. A meeting at Ouargla in southern Algeria in 1976 of the heads of state of Libya, Algeria and their common southern neighbour, Niger, appeared at the time to mark the beginnings of a new phase of co-operation between the two sides of the Sahara that was nevertheless slow to develop.

Relations between Tripoli and Rabat, frigid for some years after Colonel Gadafi's declared support for abortive attempts to overthrow King Hassan in the early 1970s, were restored at the beginning of 1975, when Tripoli applauded Moroccan policy on the Spanish Sahara, and even offered Morocco and Mauritania troops to help free the territory from Spain. Libya was one of the first supporters of the local Saharawi independence movement, *Frente Polisario*.[21] But Colonel Gadafi, with his constant vision of Arab unity, was long opposed to the creation of an independent Saharan state that he believed would only lead to the further fragmentation of the Arab nation. Instead, he appeared to favour the incorporation of the whole territory into Mauritania.

But when Spain withdrew from the territory (thereafter known as the 'Western Sahara') at the beginning of 1976, Morocco took over the northern two-thirds and Mauritania the southern third. The largely nomadic Saharawis, their lives already disrupted by drought had to choose between settled life under Moroccan or Mauritanian administration (which the majority did) or moving to *Polisario* refugee camps at Tindouf in south-west Algeria and from there fighting a guerrilla war against the Moroccan and Mauritanian occupation. Libya became a main supplier of arms and equipment to *Polisario* along the so-called 'Gadafi trail' through southern Algeria and northern Mali. In Gadafi's opinion, the Moroccan – Mauritanian take-over should have been a union of peoples and not, as he saw it, a military conquest. 'If the Sahara is Moroccan, then why are tens of thousands of Moroccan soldiers fighting in the Sahara?'[22] was typical of his simplistic public appraisal of complex international issues. Yet Tripoli also contrived to maintain 'correct' relations with Morocco and particularly Mauritania, which abandoned its share of the Sahara in 1979. Tripoli, moreover, kept its options open by declining until 1980 to recognise the Saharan Arab Democratic Republic government-in-exile, proclaimed by *Polisario* in 1976, and by 1980 recognised by over half the member-states of the Organization of African Unity. Libya's interest in the Western Sahara, which seemed progressively to diverge from that of Algeria, was threefold — to support a 'revolutionary' guerrilla war that pro-Western Morocco could neither afford to fight nor to lose; to promote the cause of 'popular democracy' in a strategic corner of north-west Africa; and, according to some observers, to encourage the emergence of a wider Saharan Islamic state (perhaps with overtones of half-imagined glories of the Saharan past) in which Libya itself would be a dominant partner.

Tripoli's ambitions in northern Africa certainly alarmed the francophile President Léopold Senghor of Senegal who in July 1980 broke off relations and accused Colonel Gadafi of forming a mercenary army (the 'Islamic Legion') to destabilise four Sudano-Sahelian states where French influence was still strong — Chad, Niger, Mali and Senegal itself.[23] Other African leaders came to share Senghor's fears, particularly after the successful Libyan drive into Chad in December 1980.

For after the failure of his policies in the Arab world, Colonel Gadafi in the later 1970s became more deeply involved in what may initially have seemed less-complex African affairs, in the name of 'revolutionary and Islamic solidarity'. Tripoli's general desire to increase its influence in Africa, and particularly in its Muslim or partly Muslim states, to support or bring to power 'sympathetic' regimes and to contest various African frontiers inherited from colonial rule, were seen by some observers as a cover for more ambitious and longer-term Soviet interests in the continent. But there was no hard proof of Tripoli's willingness to serve consciously and specifically the African interests of a superpower that did not necessarily coincide with Tripoli's own; and Gadafi had always insisted that the solution to Africa's difficulties was a matter for Africans themselves. Nevertheless, his uncritical and often ill-informed support for all types of African 'liberation movement' only seemed to be outweighed by his respect for established 'progressive' regimes; it was an attitude that led him into at least one illuminating reversal of policy.

For years a supporter of the Eritrean struggle to secede from the Ethiopian empire, Gadafi withdrew his help and began calling for negotiations after the overthrow of the Emperor Haile Selassie and Ethiopia's emergence as a 'progressive' state after 1974. The emperor had, in his view, been a reactionary only fit to be overthrown and, in opposing him and thereby promoting the cause of revolution in Ethiopia, the Eritreans had been worthy of Libya's help. But in continuing their opposition against the 'progressive' regime of the Soviet-backed *Dergue* that succeeded imperial rule, the Eritreans were in the wrong, and unworthy of further support, despite the fact that the *Dergue* was certainly no nicer, and opposed Eritrean secession as harshly as the emperor had ever done.

Colonel Gadafi's forward policies in Saharan and Sahelian Africa brought him into conflict with France, as the one Western power that had shown its willingness and ability to intervene to protect friendly regimes apparently threatened by outside forces. Colonel Gadafi accused Paris of following a policy of 'outdated colonialism' in Africa. Franco-Libyan interests clashed in the Western Sahara, where French aircraft and advisers for some time stiffened the Mauritanian defence against *Polisario*; they clashed again in the continuing civil war in Chad, in the Central African Republic (or Empire), in Niger, and in Tunisia in the aftermath of the Gafsa raid of early 1980. In response to urgent calls for help from the government, Paris briefly sent aircraft and ground troops to Tunisia, as well as warships to patrol the central Mediterranean and the Gulf of Gabes, in a decisive show of support for the Bourguiba regime — actions that Tripoli condemned as an 'invasion'. In February 1980 the French Embassy in Tripoli was sacked in what was clearly an officially condoned 'popular demonstration'[24] — an event that led even the sober-minded *Le Monde* to call Libyan diplomacy 'the planet's most singular and most adventurist'.[25] Relations were further strained by the suspension of French arms and spares supplies.

While Paris had clearly shown its determination to maintain Western interests in Tunisia, the French position in Chad deteriorated and Libya's strengthened as civil strife ran its extraordinarily confused and complex course. Tripoli's forward policy partly reflected the concern felt by Gadafi in particular for his own tribal kinsfolk there, and also for Chadian Muslims in general. Tripoli's prime dilemma in Chad was how to keep control of the Aozou Strip, occupied in 1972, while maintaining friendship and influence with the very people, the northern Muslim dissidents, most likely to resent continuing foreign occupation — no matter how beneficial —

of part of their homeland. As for the Chad central government, President N'Garta Tombalbaye had been 'persuaded' to accept the occupation but General Félix Malloum, who overthrew him in a military *coup* in April 1975, had not. While President Malloum's policy of national reconciliation failed to end what was becoming more a civil war than widespread rebellion, Tripoli was grooming as its protégé the rebel Tebu leader, Goukouni Oueddei. By 1972 he had gained control over most forces of the various factions within the deeply divided dissident organisation, *Frolinat*, and controlled wide areas of the north. Goukouni did not allow his own resentment of continuing Libyan occupation of the Aozou Strip to undermine his relations with Tripoli, which in 1978 actively supported his attempt to advance on the capital, N'Djamena. In June, General Malloum claimed that 'thousands' of Libyan troops had invaded and had penetrated as far south as the central provinces of Batha, Kanem and Wadai.[26] The advance was finally halted by Chad government forces stiffened by French reinforcements, including aircraft.

In March 1979, the Malloum government collapsed after the civil war had moved into N'Djamena itself. Mainly through Nigerian and Libyan efforts, government and rebel forces came together in a provisional council of state. As more northern Muslims moved south, taking up posts in the central administration that had previously been largely reserved for southern Christians and animists, so the north–south divisions of the country seemed to harden rather than dissolve.

In November 1979 the country's eleven warring factions set up a transitional government under Goukouni's presidency; he once again looked to Tripoli for support for his efforts to establish political and military predominance over his factional rivals. It was also agreed that France was finally to withdraw its 2,500 troops and miliary advisers, although evacuation was not in fact completed until well into 1980. At the end of the year the Libyan-backed forces of Goukouni Oueddei captured N'Djamena and in January 1981 Radio Tripoli announced the intended merger of the two countries. The announcement caused widespread alarm in Africa: Senegal, Gambia and Ghana broke off diplomatic relations with Tripoli, Nigeria called for trade sanctions, Niger and Senegal looked for increased French support, and the Organization of African Unity condemned the merger and called for the withdrawal of Libyan troops. While Tripoli had thus achieved one objective in ending the long-standing

French military presence at the geographical centre of Africa and establishing one of its own, the continuing struggle for power in Chad hampered consolidation of Tripoli's influence, even in the north and centre of the country where Libyan ethnic, linguistic, cultural, religious, commercial and historical links were strongest. It was also inevitable that suspicion of Libyan motives should have been reinforced by Libya's decisive role in some of the fighting from 1978 onwards.

To the south, in the neighbouring Central African Republic (or 'Empire' as it was renamed between 1976 and 1979 by the self-proclaimed 'Emperor' Jean Bedel Bokassa), French interests prevailed at the expense of Libya's. In September 1979 'Emperor' Bokassa was deposed while he was in Tripoli, reportedly negotiating for Libyan aid in return for military facilities in the north of the 'Empire', close to Chad's southern border. He was replaced by his predecessor, David Dacko, in a *coup* organised with French diplomatic and military help. Three days later the official Libyan news agency, *Jana*, denounced the French intervention as an attempt to prevent the spread of Islam in Africa, but it was clear that Libyan efforts to bolster one of Africa's more bizarre and unpleasant regimes both financially and militarily, had been neatly thwarted by Paris.

The clash of Libyan and French interests, in which both scored successes and failures, did not extend to Uganda. There, Tripoli's forward African policy suffered its biggest set-back in trying to save the crumbling regime of Idi Amin Dada, who since 1972 had received considerable Libyan financial, moral and military backing. At the end of 1978, Uganda was invaded by a mixed 'liberation force' of Tanzanians and Ugandan exiles. As the invasion progressed and Amin's position became increasingly precarious, Libya flew troops and supplies to Kampala. At the beginning of 1979, the presence of 2,500 Libyan troops in Uganda was reported,[27] although the Libyans claimed that their only personnel in the capital were 'teachers, bank employees and medical staff'.[28] Libyans were reported to have been largely responsible for the defence of Kampala and to have suffered heavy losses in the fighting for the capital in March. One visitor to Kampala soon after its capture judged that 'the Libyans had been Amin's victims'. He wrote:

> Huge Russian tanks and personnel carriers were sprawled and overturned among the banana groves. The Libyans had manned them and set up a well-concealed ambush on the road, guns at the

ready. The liberation forces had walked through the groves and plantations, rounded hills, and on foot from each side totally annihiliated the large Libyan force; four hundred killed, no Tanzanian casualty. Libyan soldiers trained for desert warfare were not at ease in the rain forests, in the wet season, among peoples in densely populated districts where Swahili, not Arabic, was understood.[29]

It has also been suggested that the Libyan troops were not trained professionals, but merely members of the 'popular militia'. In April 1979 the Moroccan news agency (not necessarily an unbiased source) reported that the Libyan government had paid the new Ugandan authorities $20 million to allow the survivors of the expedition-ary force to leave the country unmolested.[30] Amin eventually fled Uganda, was at first given a well-guarded asylum near Tripoli, but was later asked to leave, and in due course found refuge in Saudi Arabia.

Unquestioning and uncritical support for Amin's notorious regime had always reflected badly on Libya. The over-ambitious and nearly useless military involvement in Uganda was a public fiasco and humiliation most deeply resented by the armed forces that had been given an impossible military task for ill-conceived political ends. Nevertheless, the set-back showed no signs of moderating Tripoli's policy of spreading revolutionary and Islamic influence throughout Africa.

In the Mediterranean, there were fewer opportunities for influ-ence and alliance, although useful working relationships were estab-lished with Yugoslavia, Greece and Turkey, and in July 1980 the Foreign Secretary was publicly confident of his ability to mediate between Greek and Turk in Cyprus. The final evacuation of British forces from Malta in March 1979 appeared at the time as an oppor-tunity for even closer economic and military alliance with the strate-gically placed archipelago less than 300 kilometres north of Tripoli, but premier Dom Mintoff was disappointed by the response of popular committee members in November 1978 to his appeal for help in making up the expected financial losses resulting from the British withdrawal. Relations between Tripoli and Valletta did not flourish as they had seemed likely to do after the British had gone; in May 1979 the Libyan broadcasting station in Malta was closed down and outstanding issues remained unresolved, including a demarca-tion dispute in an area of the Mediterranean where Malta wanted to search for oil. The Maltese, like the Sicilians and the Italians, remained suspicious of extensive Libyan property-buying in and around the central Mediterranean, and in August 1980 Malta looked to Italy to guarantee a new status of neutrality, a move seen as a considerable blow to Libyan ambitions.

Revolutionary Libya had been active in Lebanon well before the civil war started in 1975, supplying arms and other aid to 'Nasserite' organisations and some of the Palestinian groups active in the country. During the 20-month civil war, Libya continued to give 'unconditional support' to the Palestinians and the left, shipping in supplies through the port of Sidon, apparently in the hope that the struggle would end Lebanon's confessional-sectarian divisions of political and military power, and particularly the dominant position of the Maronite Christians. Major Abd-al-Salam Jallud worked hard and courageously — but ultimately unsuccessfully — in the closing stages of the war to save the Palestinians from political and military humiliation. Despite a short-lived participation in its ranks, Libya was basically opposed to the largely Syrian-manned Arab Deterrent Force whose intervention in 1976–7 brought the fighting to an uneasy end, thereby probably saving the main rightist Christian forces from defeat.

During the war, Libyan agents had bolstered the political standing of Lebanon's biggest and largely disregarded sectarian minority, the Muslim *Shiah*, under the leadership of an *imam* of Iranian origin, Musa Sadr. In August 1978 he visited Libya and then disappeared; his disappearance, for which Tripoli could give no satisfactory explanation, remained a mystery and was to plague future relations with Lebanon, *Shiah* Iran and with *Shiah* communities everywhere. In July 1979 Colonel Gadafi was forced to call off a planned visit to Lebanon because of the continuing violent hostility of the *Shiah* community. Despite the fact that the Libyan and Iranian revolutions apparently had much in common — Tripoli had been an important source of material and moral support for the revolutionary movement that led to the fall of the Shah early in 1979, and continued to aid certain revolutionary factions inside Iran — the Iranians long refused to agree to closer official ties until the whereabouts of the *imam* Musa Sadr was revealed.

Relations with the United States were not good at any time after 1969: Tripoli and Washington had too many diametrically opposed views on world questions in general and Middle East questions in particular for there to be genuine *rapport* between the two capitals

What Tripoli saw as justifiable aid and succour for 'liberation movements' wherever they arose, appeared to Washington as blatant support for 'international terrorism'. Libyan links with terrorism were always ambiguous, and the subject brought evasive answers from Colonel Gadafi whenever it was raised during interviews. But there was evidence of Libyan association over the years with many international terrorist activities, including in particular those of the Venezuelan 'hit man' Carlos, who was responsible for the kidnapping in December 1975 of OPEC ministers from their Vienna headquarters.[31]

Yet the United States and Libya were tied close to each other by common economic interests that neither — despite frequent threats and warnings from Tripoli — was willing to forego. While the Libyans needed continual access to the irreplaceable technology and expertise of American oil companies, in particular, the Americans need the high-quality, low-sulphur Libyan crude oil so well suited to American refining needs, and for which the United States remained by far the largest customer, to the extent of running a $3,500 million trade deficit in 1977 alone.

One particular cause of contention was the blocking by the US State Department of the delivery of some $400 million-worth of equipment ordered and paid for by Libya but considered to have potential military uses. The equipment included eight Lockheed C-130 heavy transport aircraft and two Boeing 727 airliners, as well as 400 Oshkosh heavy lorries claimed to have potential uses as tank transporters.[32] At the beginning of 1977, the Pentagon went so far as to bracket Libya with Cuba and North Korea on a new list of potential enemies of the United States, largely on the grounds of 'irresponsible support for international terrorism' and 'material and political support for Palestinian guerrillas, the Irish Republican Army and other terrorist groups'.[33]

Although Colonel Gadafi may have hoped to establish a new relationship with President Jimmy Carter (whom he once described as 'a good man, a religious man') after he took office in 1977, America's growing ties with President Sadat and leading role in the Egyptian–Israeli peace-making process was a constant source of friction. 'Popular' opposition to Washington's Iranian policy led in December 1979 to the mob invasion and burning of the United States Embassy in Tripoli, while in July 1980 Washington's continued suspicions of Libyan foreign policies were reflected in a published report on Tripoli's alleged recent involvement in international subversion.

Thus the two countries seemed condemned to exist with a mutually unsatisfactory diplomatic relationship that neither was able to improve, yet both were unwilling to break completely because of overriding economic considerations.

Despite continuing ideological differences, and profound disagreement on the achievement of a Middle East settlement, Libya and the Soviet Union from about 1974 onwards discovered a mutual interest in undermining Western positions and influence in the Middle East, Africa, the Mediterranean and elsewhere, although the ultimate geo-political objectives of Tripoli and Moscow were not necessarily at all the same. The *rapprochement* between the two countries, despite Gadafi's cult of stout anti-Communism, came about largely as a result of Libya's general isolation in the Arab world in the aftermath of the 1973 Middle East War, and the resultant search for diplomatic support and even military protection in a hostile world. Libya similarly offered the Russians some compensation for the collapse of their position in Egypt. The Libyans moreover — and in contrast to the Egyptians — offered worthwhile economic return by paying promptly and well for masses of equipment for which they had no immediate use. Following the loss of Soviet military facilities in Egypt, and at a time when the Soviet position in the Arab world as a whole was weak, the Libyans provided at least an outpost from which the Russians could disturb the Egyptians in the process of making peace with Israel, encourage by proxy a forward Libyan policy in Africa that might coincidentally serve Russian ends, capitalise on regional anti-Egyptian and anti-American feeling to pursue political and strategic interests not far from the centre of Arab power, and at the same time keep watch on Egypt, North Africa, the Mediterranean and southern Europe — all with relatively little cost or effort. Even if, as Colonel Gadafi claimed, the Russians did not have bases in Libya, they certainly had use of some valuable ancillary facilities.

In return for these advantages, the Soviet Union was obliged to accept the slight ideological embarrassment and the strategic, diplomatic and other limitations of association with Libya's mercurial regime, pending a change in events and/or policies that might eventually restore Soviet influence in Cairo. For Moscow, after its disappointing experiences in Egypt and elsewhere in the Arab world, was never able to consider its relationship with Tripoli permanent nor even stable, but had to count it merely as a mutual convenience liable to be overtaken by a turn of events such as had brought it into being in the first place.[34] Nevertheless, by early 1981 North Atlantic Treaty Organization planners were reportedly concerned that the Soviet air force might gain the use of Libyan airfields in the event of a Mediterranean crisis; even if Gadafi himself might never grant such facilities, there was considered to be a danger of his replacement by a leader who would.[35]

The states of Western Europe, despite the obvious difficulties, tried to maintain reasonable working relationships with Tripoli because they all relied, to a greater or lesser degree, on steady supplies of Libyan crude oil. The exception was Britain which, when its North Sea fields started producing crude of similar high quality, had no further need of Libyan imports. Since leaving its bases, Britain had been rather distant in its diplomatic and commercial relations with a revolutionary regime that was evidently rather puzzled and disappointed at London's apparent coolness. When, in September 1979, Libyan embassies in the West were taken over on Gadafi's orders by 'popular committees', no government questioned this unorthodox development in diplomatic relations, nor apparently felt the need to do so until Libyan exiles were murdered in London, Rome, Bonn and Athens in the spring of 1980 after failing to obey an official 'people's order' to return home. Only Britain took a reasonably firm stand against a campaign of political terrorism that other countries seemed reluctant to challenge, so concerned were they about the security of their oil supplies. Yet, as Tunisia's Secretary-General for Foreign Affairs, Mahmoud Mestiri, was quoted as saying early in 1981, 'Libya's strength is not her own power but the weakness of others'.[36]

Thus it was as true in 1980 as it had been in 1970 that Libya's international standing stemmed from its oil. The continued production and export of crude earned the revenues to finance an extraordinarily ambitious, forward, and sometimes alarming, foreign policy. It was the importance of maintaining this apparently vital flow that inhibited many exasperated governments from taking a firmer attitude towards a state whose policies were widely regarded as disruptive, if not downright dangerous.

Notes

1. Dyer, 'Libya' in *World Armies* (London, 1979), p. 442.
2. One hundred *MiG-27* fighter-strike aircraft were reportedly ordered in 1978, of which 24 had been delivered by the end of 1979 (Stockholm International Peace

Research Institute, *World Armaments and Disarmament, SIPRI Yearbook 1980* (London, 1980), Appendix 3A, p. 151).

3. BBC, *Summary of World Broadcasts*, ME/6139/i.

4. Interview with *Reuter* (22 May 1979).

5. In 1980, 200 *Lion* tanks (a modified version of the Italian–West German *Leopard*) were on order, while Russian *T-72* tanks were reported to have been delivered even before some Warsaw Pact states had received them (*SIPRI Yearbook 1980*, p. 111). 500 *T-62s* were reportedly delivered from Libya to Syria in 1978 (*ibid.*, Appendix 3A, p. 158).

6. International Institute for Strategic Studies, *The Military Balance 1979–1980* (London, 1979), p. 42.

7. Dyer, *World Armies*, p. 442.

8. In July 1979 the former US Secretary of State Dr Henry Kissinger told the US Senate Foreign Relations Committee that 'Soviet arms depots in Libya and Ethiopia fuel insurgencies all over Africa'. He was presumably referring to small arms rather than heavier equipment.

9. Dyer, *World Armies*, p. 443.

10. BBC, *Summary of World Broadcasts*, ME/5637/A/4.

11. *SIPRI Yearbook 1980*, Table 1A.2. This represented only 6.3 per cent of GNP, compared with 7.0 per cent in 1976 (ibid., Table 1A.4, p. 31). By 1980 an estimated 10 per cent of the Soviet Union's hard currency earnings came from Libya.

12. See *New Scientist*, 23 August 1979, p. 580.

13. BBC1 'Panorama', 16 June 1980.

14. BBC, *Summary of World Broadcasts*, ME/5637/A/4.

15. *Financial Times*, 27 July 1977.

16. BBC, *Summary of World Broadcasts*, ME/5676/A/1.

17. *Le Monde*, 11 February 1976.

18. See P. Rondot, 'La Politique Arabe de la Libye', *Revue Française d'Etudes Politiques Méditerranéennes*, no. 17 (mai 1976); see also *Le Monde*, 22 February 1975.

19. At the trial in Tunis of three Libyans accused of the assassination attempt on Nouira, Gadafi was described as 'the shame of the Arab nation'. Nouira had opposed, and possibly halted, the 1974 Libyan–Tunisian union.

20. 'The Gafsa Incident', statement issued by the Libyan People's Bureau in London (20 February 1980), p. 8.

21. *Frente Popular para la Liberación de Saguia el Hamra y Rio de Oro*, the two constituent zones of the territory first occupied by Spain in the 1880s.

22. *Jamahiriyah News Agency*, bulletin no. 123, 4 June 1978.

23. *Le Monde*, 16 July 1980.

24. As *Le Monde* (6 February 1980) pointed out, the assault on the Embassy took place only two months after Colonel Gadafi had affirmed that embassies were under the protection of the host nation (interview with Oriana Fallaci, *Corriere della Sera*, December 1979).

25. *Le Monde*, 6 February 1980.

26. *Reuter*, 22 June 1978.

27. *Nairobi Times*, 5 March 1979.

28. *Jamahiriyah News Agency*, 6 March 1979.

29. Smith, *The Ghosts of Kampala*, London, 1980, p. 8.

30. *Maghreb Arabe Presse*, 9 April 1979.

31. See C. Dobson and R. Payne, *The Carlos Complex* (London, 1977).

32. It was pointed out that if the army at any time needed heavy transporters hundreds of suitable vehicles were likely to be found in the oil-company service yards outside Tripoli and Benghazi.

33. *International Herald Tribune*, 29–30 January 1977. The former Ambassador in London, Mohammad Yunis al-Mismari, claimed in 1979, 'We have had nothing

do with the IRA since March 1975' (*Arab Dawn*, no. 52, May 1979).

34. See Ya'acov, *No Limits to Power: Soviet Foreign Policy in the Middle East* (London, 1979).

35. *International Herald Tribune*, 4 March 1981; 13 March 1981; *The Times*, 18 March 1981.

36. *Middle East Economic Digest* (6 March 1981), p. 43.

11   THE OIL REVOLUTION

Ironically, it is the desert — inhospitable, unproductive and sterile, abused as 'a crate of sand' and 'the abomination of desolation' — that has yielded Libya's greatest source of wealth. Yet until the 1950s the presence of oil in North Africa outside Egypt and Morocco was barely suspected: the oil and gas fields of the Sahara do not betray their existence by such obvious clues as the 'Eternal Fires' of Azerbaijan or the asphalt ponds of Iraq.

As long ago as 1915, Italians had occasionally found traces of natural gas while drilling deep water wells. In 1935, after making the first comprehensive geological map of Libya, Professor Ardito Desio of Milan University decided to watch for hydrocarbons in water wells drilled under his supervision. Two years later he found small amounts of oil in a well a few kilometres east of Tripoli.[1] The para-statal Azienda Generale Italiana Petroli (AGIP) followed up this find with a two-year geological programme in Tripolitania, and one (dry) hole was drilled. Early in 1940, Desio divided the country into twelve geological zones and pointed to the Sirtica as a likely oil bearing region. But when the Italians started to look for oil there in 1940, contemporary equipment and techniques proved inadequate for the extraordinarily tough desert conditions. Some traces of oil were found, but in the summer of 1940 the Italian invasion of Egypt ended further exploration. Thus the Libyan campaign — the longest of the Second World War, fought partly for the possession of Middle East oilfields — took place almost on top of undiscovered oil deposits large enough to have sustained the combined Allied and Axis war efforts.

After the war, oil exploration was not possible in a country with no settled political future, and it was not until the newly independent kingdom published a minerals law in 1953 that preliminary prospecting permits were granted to eleven international oil companies and geological surveys started. Then, in 1955, the first oil find in the deep Sahara was made at Edjeleh, just over the border in Algeria, and in June the Libyan government passed its first petroleum law. The law was much praised for its fairness and foresight — partly, perhaps, because the draft had been circulated for comment among o-

companies interested in Libyan concessions; their representatives were invited to serve on the committee appointed to complete the final draft.[2]

The Libyans, although at the time almost wholly ignorant of oil affairs, were determined not to yield their country as one concession to a single company, or consortium of companies, and particularly not to the so-called 'major' companies.[3] The new law was accordingly designed to encourage diversity and competition among concessionaires. It declared all sub-surface minerals as state property, and it divided the country into four exploration zones.[4] Although it provided for a great number of concessions, and there was a limit to the number any one company could hold, Libya was large enough for total allocations to each concessionaire to be large up to 80,000 square kilometres in each of Zones Three and Four). One-quarter of concessionary areas were to be 'handed back' within five years from the date of the original grant for subsequent re-offer to another concessionaire; this and further relinquishment provisions after eight and ten years meant that newcomers could try exploring where others had failed. Following the then standard practice in the Middle East, the 1955 law made profits liable to a 50 per cent tax — after deduction of operating costs — with a 12.5 per cent royalty treated as a partial advance payment towards tax. But the law was unusually generous, both in its allowances for deduc tions against tax and in linking the income of concessionaires to the realised price of crude oil, rather than the higher 'posted price', as was the common practice in the Middle East.[5] Waddams[6] considers that the major companies 'succeeded in obtaining an ideal contract from their own viewpoint' and that the favourable terms of the 1955 law were 'a foretaste of paradise for the oil companies'.

Although Libya was unknown territory, it offered further attractions to international oil companies, even at that time of world oil surplus and depressed prices. It presented, first and foremost, diversification from established sources of oil in the Middle East, including the eastern Mediterranean outlets of the Iraqi and Saudi Arabian export pipelines. The need of the international oil industry to diversify sources of crude oil had first been underscored by the Iranian crisis of 1951–4, while the closure of the Suez Canal in 1956–7 was a more potent warning of the vulnerability of all Middle East supplies to political events. Libya in the mid-1950s had the additional attractions of apparent stability, pro-Western bias and reliance on Western military protection. Moreover, any oil found there would

not have to pass through any narrow and blockable international
waterway comparable with the Suez Canal on its relatively short
journey to the large and rapidly growing oil markets of southern and
western Europe.

By the beginning of 1957, about a dozen companies had been
awarded some 60 concessions. Among the companies were all the
majors, including the so-called 'eighth major', the para-statal Compagnie Française des Pétroles; also in at the start were the so-called
'independent' American companies new to the international oil play
such as Continental (Conoco), Marathon and Amerada Hess
(grouped together under the 'Oasis' title) and Bunker Hunt. The
'independents' had been attracted by features of the 1955 law
intended to favour such newcomers.

Undoubtedly the greatest hazards to exploration were the unex-
ploded mines still lying under the surface of the desert. During the
Second World War, the Italian, German, British and Allied armies
had laid about four million mines between El Alamein in western
Egypt and Mareth in Tunisia;[7] in 1957 an estimated three million
were still in place, waiting to be stepped on or driven over. In the
minefields, some of which extended inland for 150 kilometres, clearing parties went ahead of the geological crews to sweep and mark
'safe lanes'.

Because oil had already been found in the Algerian Sahara, western Fezzan was the first centre of interest. In June 1957 Esso decided
to drill in Concession One, extending from the Algerian frontier into
the Ubari Sand Sea. After two dry holes the third, at Hassi Atshan,
flowed at a moderately encouraging rate of 500 barrels per day (b/d)
in January 1958. But further holes in Concession 1 were unproductive and the sole producing well, with its small flow and extreme
remoteness, was clearly not commercial.

The most discouraging year was 1958. By December, the industry
had spent a cumulative total of $120 million, had drilled holes for
eighteen months, and the only rewards for this time, effort and
expense were the one Atshan strike and a not particularly encouraging initial find in what was to become the Oasis group's small Bahi
field in the Sirtica. Discouragement set in; more than one company
was ready to end the search; and a current industry joke was that
Libya was enjoying the biggest dry-hole boom the world had ever
known.

But in 1959 the first big strikes were made. In Esso's Concession 6
deep in the Sirtica, the Cl−6 exploration well flowed at 17,500 b/d

on test on 11 June. Confirmation that a very large oil-bearing structure had been found came in August when a second well in what was to become the Zelten field came in at 15,000 b/d. At Zelten a thick oil-bearing stratum (or 'pay zone' in the expressive jargon of the industry) was the first real sign of a possible abundance of oil in the Sirtica.

Then reports of oil strikes began to come in from all over the Sirtica — 1959 was the year in which six large oilfields were found in that one area, although their full extent was not known until later. Even before the first well at Zelten had been tested, the Oasis group (which at the time held over one-fifth of the total concession area)[8] had drilled the first producers in Concession 32. As those first wells did not yield their oil as freely as Esso's, it was not until late 1959 that the importance of the Dahra field was established. In Concession 59 in July, Oasis completed the first producing well in what was later to be known as the Waha field. A chain of oilfields in Concession 59, together with others in Concession 32, were later to enable Oasis to overtake Esso's initial lead in output, established by the rapid early exploitation of Zelten.

Still in 1959, the Esso subsidiary Esso Sirte found another large oilfield, Mabruk, as operator in partnership with two independents, the Libyan American Oil Company (Sinclair) and W.R. Grace and Company. In September Amoseas (the operating company for California Asiatic, a Standard of California subsidiary, and Texaco Overseas) completed the first producing well in the Beida field in Concession 47; and on 1 November the partnership of Mobil and Gelsenberg Benzin AG (a West German refining and marketing company) brought in the first producing well in the future Amal field in Concession 12.

In 1960, a year of consolidation, there were fewer big new discoveries. Oasis found the Defa field in Concession 59; Mobil-Gelsenberg struck the first oil in the future Hofra field; and Esso Sirte and partners made their first strike in the Raguba field northwest of Zelten. Spending on exploration was running at $170 million/year and there was a sharp increase in drilling and in the number of new producing wells (41 out of a total of 68 holes drilled) as finds of the previous year were evaluated. Libya had suddenly become the 'big play' for the international oil industry that the Middle East had been and that Nigeria, Alaska, the North Sea and the Arctic were later to become.

As the 1960s opened, Esso was nearly a year ahead of its

competitors in exploiting its discoveries. Marsa Brega, a desolate spot on the coast, 50 kilometres east of El Agheila, was chosen as the site for an oil export terminal and in June 1960 the company awarded the contract for a 175-kilometre, 30-inch pipeline from Zelten to Brega. In one of those extraordinary bursts of activity characterising the international oil industry when it decides on the rapid exploitation of a new source of oil, the pipeline was completed with an initial capacity of 200,000 b/d and Marsa Brega was prepared for commercial oil shipments — all in a little over a year. Zelten production started on 8 August 1961, and on 12 September — less than six years after the award of the first concession, and only a little over two since the first test at Zelten — Libya's first crude-oil export cargo was loaded into the *Esso Canterbury* for shipment to Britain. Thus, shortly before the tenth anniversary of independence, the kingdom became a small oil exporter (total shipments in 1961 amounted to less than million barrels) with transformed economic expectations — a fact acknowledged by King Idris in officially inaugurating the Marsa Brega oil terminal on 25 October.

Thereafter, the 'legend' of Libyan oil was to 'outpace imagination', as a later Oil Minister wrote.[9] By May 1962 the Oasis group had linked the Dahra field by a 140-kilometre pipeline to an export terminal at Es Sidra, 150 kilometres west of Marsa Brega. In December 1964 a third terminal was opened at Ras Lanuf, only some 30 kilometres east of Es Sidra, on completion of a 275-kilometre pipeline from the Beida (Amoseas) and Hofra-Ora fields (Mobil –Gelsenberg). Esso Sirte's Raguba field went on stream on being linked by a spur to the main Zelten–Marsa Brega line. Oasis, after large find in 1962 at the eastern end of Concession 59 — later named the Gialo field — extended the Es Sidra line to collect output from four scattered fields in the same prolific concession — Gialo, Waha, Samah and Zaggut.

One of the first concessionaires in Libya was an independent Texas oilman, Nelson Bunker Hunt, who in 1957 had been awarded Concession 65, some 33,000 square kilometres of the Plain and Sand Sea of Calanscio in eastern Cyrenaica. The concession lay almost fallow for the next three years while the Oasis group was making a series of strikes in the neighbouring Concession 59. Then, September 1960, British Petroleum bought a half-share in the Hunt concession, reportedly for £10 million Sterling.[10] The company which at the time had access to no crude oil of its own west of the Suez Canal, was eager to diversify, but had found nothing in its eight

Libyan concessions. Its reputation for finding new sources of oil was vindicated when, as operator in the partnership with Hunt, it brought in the C1 well at nearly 4,000 b/d in November 1961; 18 months later, eleven wells testing at a total of over 25,000 b/d had been drilled in the Sarir field.

Further evaluation showed the field to be the largest in Africa and twice the size of the greatest in the United States, the East Texas. Sarir was 500 kilometres from the coast, further than any other Libyan oilfield. Marsa al-Hariga, on the deep natural harbour opposite Tobruk, was chosen as the site of the new oil terminal. The presence of a permanent British garrison at Tobruk must have influenced BP's choice of terminal site, but the deciding factor was the depth of water that allowed tankers to moor close to the steeply rising shore and load the waxy Sarir crude through overhead pipelines. The crude had to be heated before it flowed and would have solidified in the type of submarine pipeline necessary at other terminal sites on the Libyan coast.[11] Conditions along the 500-kilometre pipeline route were so tough that Sarir crude exports began only early in 1967 — more than five years after the first strikes in Concession 65.

BP had taken seven years to find oil and start commercial production; yet when Marsa Hariga was officially opened in February 1967, another company was half-way to achieving similar results in only two years, although under less challenging conditions.

In May 1965 the government had invited offers for new concessions. They were composed mainly of territory 'handed back' under the clause in the petroleum law requiring concession-holders to relinquish one-quarter of their holdings five years after its award, with further relinquishments after eight and ten years. Because Libya had by then become an oil province of the first importance, and some of the land on offer was near established oilfields, there was intense competition for the new acreage. The government hinted that successful bidders were likely to be those companies willing to work closely with the state on being granted concessions.[12] The grant of concessions on the original time-priority basis had already been replaced by a competitive sealed-bid system that 'opened the door to the possibilities of favouritism, intrigue, graft and corruption' that manifested themselves in 1966.[13]

Many of the areas awarded in February 1966 went to little-known companies new to the Libyan oil search. Two of the most coveted concessions, 102 and 103, previously held by Oasis and Mobil respectively, and for which a total of 19 companies had made bids, went to an obscure California-based company, Occidental Petroleum. Wrapped in the Libyan national colours, the company's bid had offered various inducements, including a proposal to invest 5 per cent of profits in an agricultural project at Kufra — the close association of the monarch with the proposed location was not without significance. Occidental had also, according to the evidence revealed in a later lawsuit, retained a team of entrepreneurs to help win the concessions.[14]

The company was at the time a complete outsider. Only ten years before it had been taken over by the 'unique phenomenon' of Dr Armand Hammer, an independent-minded and dynamic man of business, newly retired after 'an interesting and successful career in several fields'. When Hammer arrived, Occidental had 'a net worth of $34,000, a few almost depleted oil wells and three employees'. Hammer was determined to make Occidental a leading company competing alongside others already established in Libya. He did so through 'dedication to be industrious and enterprising' — within 1 days of the award of the concessions, the company had seismic teams at work in Concession 102, and less than six months later the first exploration well was being drilled. The first oil was struck in November (flowing at nearly 15,000 b/d on test) and in early 196 the discovery of a new field, the Augila, was claimed. The strike was next to the Amoseas Nafoora field, not far north of the Oasis Giant field, and was made in territory handed back by Oasis. As soon as Occidental announced its first strike, it was clear than an undiscovered oilfield had been given away with hand-back territory; by the end of April 1967, Augila was known to have a production potential of over 60,000 b/d.

Augila was only the start of Occidental's brilliantly successful Libyan operation. In May 1967 an exploration well in former Mobil territory on Concession 103, some 60 kilometres south of Augila flowed at an extraordinary 40,000 b/d (the most the test equipment could show) from a 'pay zone' almost one thousand feet thick — ten times the Libyan average. The second and third wells in what came to be known as the Idris field (later renamed Intisar) were even more prolific.

Occidental had intended to move its crude through other companies' existing pipelines and terminals, but was now able to justify the building of its own facilities. In a mere ten months the company completed a 200-kilometre pipeline of 40 inches diameter (Libya largest) to a new oil terminal (Libya's fifth) at Zueitina on the Gulf of Sirte near Agedabia; spur lines fed in crude from Augila and from the prolific D1 well, some 25 kilometres south of Idris, that flowed at 75,000 b/d on test in late 1967. Exports from Zueitina started in February 1968, only two hectic years after the award of concessions. 'Occidental's progress was fuelled by the hope of future gain, not by past profits.'[16]

The last big oilfield found before the revolution was Bu Attifel, lying east of Occidental's fields and declared commercial at the end of 1968 by the Italian para-statal AGIP after years of unsuccessful exploration. Although AGIP was able to feed production into the Occidental pipeline system, and export through Zueitina, the start of commercial output was long delayed by differences with the revolutionary government that came to power before all the production facilities had been completed.

No state developed and exploited new-found reserves faster than Libya did in the 1960s (see Table 11.1). By 1969, only eight years after the start of commercial production, the kingdom overtook

Table 11.1: Oil Exports and Revenues

Year	Oil exports (M barrels)	Revenues ($ M)	Receipts/barrel ($)	OPEC average receipts/barrel ($)
1961	6	3	0.50	0.70
1962	67	40	0.60	0.71
1963	167	108	0.65	0.75
1964	314	211	0.67	0.75
1965	443	351	0.79	0.76
1966	547	523	0.96	0.77
1967	621	625	1.01	0.80
1968	945	1,002	1.06	0.83
1969	1,120	1,175	1.05	0.84
1970	1,209	1,351	1.12	0.94
1971	1,003	1,674	1.67	1.27
1972	812	1,563	1.93	1.45
1973	794	2,223	2.80	2.63
1974	544	6,000	11.03	9.65
1975	522	5,100	9.77	10.57
1976	660	7,500	11.36	11.00
1977	742	8,850	11.93	11.43
1978	693	8,600	12.41	11.24
1979	730	16,300	23.33	—
1980*	622	22,000	35.37	—

Note: * Estimate.
Source: *Petroleum Economist, OPEC Oil Report (1979).*

Kuwait as the world's fifth-largest exporter, and in 1970 seemed set to produce and export even more than Iran; the challenge was only abandoned when the new revolutionary government began to order severe production cuts some months after coming to power.

Between 1961 and 1965, Esso was the largest exporter; in 1966 and 1967, Esso was overtaken by Oasis, regained the lead in 1968, and again lost it to Oasis in 1969. the extraordinary growth in Occidental production meant that by 1970 — after only two years of output — the newcomer was challenging Esso for second place.

Attractive terms initially offered by hopeful governments to induce foreign companies to take on the expenses, risks and challenges of exploring for oil in new territory are commonly revised once oil has been found in commercial quantities and exports and revenues are assured. Thus in July 1961, only two weeks before exports of Zelten crude started, the petroleum law was amended by Royal Decree, apparently in the government's favour. The amendment, in redefining terms of taxation to bring them more into line with current Middle East practice, tried to ensure a minimum government income by relating the tax on each barrel of oil exported not to the realised price as envisaged under the 1955 law, but to the higher 'posted price', less 'marketing expenses' normally amounting to no more than 2 per cent. While some companies — and notably the majors — readily accepted the new arrangements, others insisted that 'marketing expenses' included all rebates necessary to sell the oil on what at the time was a highly competitive and over-supplied buyer's market. In agreeing, the government largely neutralised the intended effects of its own amendment.[17] For, although one immediate result of the 1961 amendment was to raise the government's share of Esso's 1962 profits by about one-third, in the longer term the government was to be deprived of revenues it might otherwise have had when the independent companies began to build up their exports by selling Libyan crude with heavy rebates that counted as tax-deductible 'marketing expenses'.

Just before exports of Brega crude started, Esso (although not obliged to do so), had posted a price of $2.21/barrel, for 39-degree API gravity oil, with a 2-cent reduction for each degree under 39 degrees, but a maximum of $2.23 for oil of 40 degrees and over. Although the government protested at the time, the company claimed that the figure was based on a comparison with crudes of similar quality available in the Persian Gulf (where they were at posted at under $2/barrel) or at the eastern Mediterranean termina of the Iraqi and Saudi Arabian pipelines ($2.17–$2.21/barrel). Esso's posting took little account of quality differences between Brega and other crudes, and particularly of its low sulphur content (making it easier to refine). Nor did it take account of the considerable freight-cost advantages in shipping crude to the main oil markets of Western Europe from Marsa Brega, compared with the longer tanker voyages from the eastern Mediterranean or the Gulf via the Suez Canal. (In 1961, the cost of shipping crude oil from the main Saudi export terminal at Ras Tanura on the Gulf, via the Suez Canal, to north Europe's main oil port at Rotterdam was $6.74/metric ton, or $10.79 via the Cape of Good Hope; shipment from the Iraqi pipeline terminal at Banias in Syria to Rotterdam cost $3.90/ton, while from Marsa Brega the charge was only $3.40/ton.)[18] One critic who disputed the unilateral methods used by Esso to arrive at the Brega posting believed the price should have been about 40 cents higher,[19] while another considered the right price was around $2.26/barrel.[20] Significantly, Algerian oil of similar quality to Brega was at the time posted at $2.65 ex Bougie — more than 40 cents higher.

Esso has been accused[21] of posting a low price because it was at that price, and without discounts, that the company would be selling its crude to its affiliates in Europe (hence the old adage that 'only fools and affiliates pay the posted price'). Thus, in accordance with the amendments to the 1955 law, the company could expect to pay taxes practically on the basis of the full posted price, and is accordingly said to have set a low posting to ensure that it and other major companies unable to offset marketing discounts against tax still had correspondingly modest tax obligations.

Meanwhile, American independent companies with no established markets for crude oil outside North America, had to sell the large supplies of oil they had found in Libya. In the 1950s, several of these domestic American companies had for the first time started searching abroad for cheap oil to sell through their established marketing networks in the United States. But in 1959, when Washington decided to limit oil imports to 12 per cent of demand in any one year, these companies found their main intended market cut off. They thus had to compete fiercely for shares in the fast-growing markets of Western Europe (where demand was rising at a yearly average of 10 per cent), already over-supplied with cheap Middle East oil. The independents thus argued that they were obliged to sell Libyan crude at heavy discounts in order to compete with the long-established major companies in new markets. In the early 1960s, as the Oasis consortium of the independents Amerada, Continental and Marathon built up its Libyan production, crude was said to be sold in the $1.30–$1.40/barrel range — at least 80 cents lower than the posted price. Continental was particularly successful in pushing its way into Europe, buying its own network of cut-price outlets to establish a place in the market.

One effect of this price-cutting was to deprive the Libyan government of revenues it might otherwise have earned.

In 1964, Esso International sold most of its oil to affiliates at a posted price of $2.21–$2.22/barrel and paid taxes to the government averaging about 90 cents/barrel on an average realised price of about $2.16. In contrast, the Oasis group sold its oil at an average price of $1.55/barrel and paid to the government an average of less than 30 cents/barrel — only slightly more than the bare royalty and rental charges.[22]

Cheap Libyan oil was further undermining world oil prices generally, and this, in turn, represented a further threat to all Libyan oil revenues.

In June 1962 Libya had joined the Organisation of Petroleum Exporting Countries (OPEC), set up by five exporters in 1960 in an attempt to counter falling world oil prices. Also in 1962 the OPEC conference passed a resolution which, after long negotiations with the oil companies, led to the acceptance of new pricing arrangement in 1964; Libya came under steady pressure from the organisation to adopt them. Late in 1964 the major companies offered the Libyan government approximately the same terms as those already accepted in the Middle East, but on condition that the independents also agreed.

In 1965 the government decided to act in the face of the independents' reluctance to agree to its terms, and it set up a committee to negotiate prices and discounts with the companies. The majors, dismayed by the headlong expansion of the independents' Libyan production, the tax advantages gained from their competitive price cutting, and their effective undermining of an already weak world price structure, were in principle on the side of the government in the attempt to bring the independents to order. Although some of the independents threatened to resist the proposed changes (seeing them as a device sponsored by the majors to drive them out of business the government in November amended the petroleum law. Concessionaires were in future to calculate taxable income on the basis of posted prices, subject only to the relatively modest discounts allowed under the OPEC formula by then in general use throughout the Middle East, and approved by the major oil companies. The government estimated that this change, together with an amendment treating royalties as a cost rather than a credit against income tax, would increase revenues in 1965 alone by about $135 million.[23]

The changes were opposed by seven companies (among them Marathon and Continental of the Oasis group, but not their partner Amerada), not all of them yet producing oil in Libya. They did so on the grounds that they were being deprived of (admittedly generous) terms that they had been granted and guaranteed in 1961, and that Libyan oil output had grown so rapidly largely because of their enterprise in breaking into European markets through their ability to sell cheaply; they still argued that 'substantial discounts off posted prices were necessary to sell the oil'.

But the government's insistence on compliance with its terms went as far as obtaining parliamentary approval for whatever action was considered necessary to compel the companies to accept them; the Prime Minister made it clear that he was prepared to halt exports by any company that defied the government. In December, OPEC supported the Libyan stand by threatening to deny new concessions in any member-state to recalcitrant companies. Such threats, combined with certain government inducements (including an offer to waive $60 million in outstanding claims against the companies) finally persuaded the objectors to accept the new terms, retroactive to January 1965, in January 1966.

These events of 1965–6 'marked the passage into the era of unilateral action by the host governments'.[24] From then on, the government was able to modify the terms of an oil concession in its favour in what it considered to be the 'public interest'. The outcome was also a small victory for OPEC efforts to secure a reasonably uniform basis of taxation among its members. But after only six years of existence, the organisation was still not strong enough to challenge the companies over the outstanding issue of Libya's undervalued posted prices.

As a result of the 1965–6 amendments, the independent companies had to pay an average of about 35 cents/barrel more to the government on exports, while the tax liabilities of the majors went up by only about 5 cents/barrel. Average revenues per barrel of oil exported consequently showed their biggest increases (from 67 cents in 1964 to 96 cents in 1966) of any two-year period before the revolution.

If some companies were tempted to cut back on their Libyan operations following these developments, such ideas were quickly forgotten in 1967, when outside events unexpectedly made Libyan oil more valuable than ever. As a result of the Middle East war of June 1967, the Suez Canal was closed and Arab oil-producing states placed selective embargoes on some of the main Western oil-consuming nations. In Libya, oil workers went on strike in support of the Arab cause on 7 June, the third day of the war, and refused to load waiting tankers. Attacks on oil installations were threatened, but did not take place. Nevertheless, oil companies were alarmed by the strength of feeling displayed, and ordered all their tankers out of territorial waters. Production and exports were shut down for 27 days as a result of 'fear of sabotage by strikers, as well as the general attitude of the trade unions'.[25] This longest embargo by any of the Arab oil states cost the government some $1.5 million/day in lost revenues. Although the strikers eventually heeded government calls to reopen the oil ports to ships of 'friendly nations' early in July, a selective embargo against Britain, the United States and West Germany remained in force until the end of August.

This was Libya's first exercise of the so-called 'oil weapon', and on this occasion it proved a blunt one. While its use was politically necessary to show support for the Arab cause, it cost the government at least $40 million in lost revenues. After some initial confusion, the international oil companies then still in effective control of the international oil trade were able to reorganise the sharing of abundant world supplies to minimise the effects on the main consuming nations of the Arab embargoes and closure of the Suez Canal. Nevertheless, the unexpectedly long and strongly motivated Libyan embargo gave the oil companies clear warning of their vulnerability, for they had seen how oil could be prevented from flowing by purely political pressure, both domestic and foreign. While growing Libyan exports since 1961 had given European oil supplies greater *geographical* diversity, it was clear that — despite the general amenability of the Idris regime and continued protection by Western military bases — there had not been the *political* diversification, the disengagement from Middle Eastern politics, that the industry had been seeking when it moved into Libya in the mid-1950s.

Prolonged closure of the Suez Canal after the 1967 war put

premium on Libyan oil, with its short-haul access to European markets, at a time when nearly all west-bound oil from the Gulf had to be shipped at considerable delay and expense via the Cape of Good Hope. As *The Times* commented: 'It is difficult to overemphasise the importance of near-at-hand Libyan oil to the fuel economies of all the West European nations.' All operating groups — including those still resentful of the petroleum law amendments of the previous year — had every incentive to maximise production and to expand pipeline and export facilities as fast as possible, with full government approval. In 1968, production and exports were half as high again as in 1967, and in 1969 production and pipeline capacities were again raised by half. 'With the continued closure of the Suez Canal Libya could, within a year or two, have become the world's third-largest oil producer (behind only the USA and the USSR) and the largest oil exporter, overtaking even Venezuela . . . and Iran.'[26] But the extraordinary increase in output led to almost inevitable charges that some companies were 'skimming' oilfields, forcing them to produce crude at physically damaging rates resulting in the eventual recovery of less of the total volume of oil in place than might have been gained by more moderate production practices.[27] Some recognition of the greatly enhanced value of Libyan oil came in the autumn of 1967 when the companies agreed to waive all discounts and allowances off posted prices so long as the Suez Canal remained closed; this had the effect of increasing the government take' by about 7.5 cents/barrel.

The more dynamic and nationalistic administration that came to power under premier Abd-al-Hamid Bakkush in late 1967 initiated a relatively more independent oil policy. A Libyan General Petroleum Corporation (Lipetco) was formed in April 1968 with authority to plan and execute national oil policy, set prices and take responsibility for government negotiations and participation rights in existing and future concessions. Soon after its formation, the Prime Minister announced that Lipetco was to enter into a joint-venture exploration and production partnership with the French companies Entreprise de Recherches et d'Activités Pétrolières (ERAP) and Société Nationale des Pétroles d'Aquitaine (SNPA). Among other stiff terms, the companies were obliged to spend a total of $22.5 million on exploration over ten years, with at least $1 million sunk in exploration under an extensive area of the Mediterranean off Zuara. Lipetco was initially to receive one-quarter and — if the strike was large enough — one-half of any commercial oil production. This agreement marked Libya's first departure from the conventional type of concession, and in 1969 four more joint ventures were announced.[28]

While successive royalist governments were content to allow the rapid exploitation of oil reserves, they were slow to insist on measures to prevent the waste of natural gas produced in association with oil. Unless a local or foreign market is found for it, such natural gas must be 'flared' (burned) at the oilfield as a constant reminder that this is 'the most wasted raw material in the world'. As, in 1962, there were an estimated 30 billion (thousand million) cubic metres of associated natural gas in Zelten field alone, and more in the other fields, it seemed that much gas was to be burned off to warm the desert air. But in 1964 — the year that Algeria started the first successful commercial shipments of natural gas in frozen, liquefied form to Britain and France — Esso announced plans for similar exports of Zelten gas. In November 1965 the company signed contracts for the supply of liquefied natural gas (LNG) to Italy and Spain and started building a $300 million gas liquefaction plant at Marsa Brega. (In a technically complex process, the gas is frozen to minus 161 degrees Centigrade and is then shipped as a liquid in purpose-built refrigerated tankers to a receiving terminal, where the frozen liquid is regasified for commercial use.)

Although the Marsa Brega plant was completed by 1969, commercial production was delayed for years by technical troubles and financial wrangles with the government. Similarly, the start-up of the country's first commercial refinery, also built by Esso at Marsa Brega, was delayed for about four years by negotiations over prices to be charged for its products. When it finally went on stream in 1967, the unit's 10,000 b/d of products output was then able to meet about half the country's demand for basic fuels.

Reassurance was the keynote of the revolutionary regime's initial policy towards the oil industry — the oil revolution was not to acquire its own very distinctive character until 1970–1. In an early press interview[29] the new Prime Minister, Sulaiman Maghrabi, said the government did not plan to nationalise any industries; while keeping strict control over oil companies, it would also continue to co-operate with them; no 'spectacular changes' were expected. No long after the new Oil Minister, Anis Shtaiwi, reassured the oil companies that nationalisation was 'out of the question' at the time.

While the new regime was preoccupied with consolidating its own position, ridding the country of foreign bases and investigating the 'misdeeds' of the former regime, the oil industry was largely ignored, and earlier plans by the companies to exploit fully the country's geographical advantages (the Suez Canal was to remain closed until 1975) went on without interference. As a result, oil production and exports set new records several months *after* the September revolution, and in April 1970 production touched a peak of nearly 3.7 million b/d — not far short of Saudi Arabian output at the time. About half this oil was extracted by only two producers: Oasis, setting another record with a daily output of just over one million barrels, and Occidental, with nearly 800,000 b/d.

But by April the companies and the government were at odds. Negotiations over the disputed posted price that had been opened by the former regime with a claim for an extra 10 cents/barrel had been resumed in January. In reopening the talks, Colonel Gadafi had set the tone when, urging companies to recognise Libyan rights 'immediately', he made his often-quoted declaration that 'people who have lived for five thousand years without oil can live without it a few more years to achieve their legitimate rights'.[30]

The government was not seeking an increase, but a 'correction', reportedly of around 44 cents/barrel[31] in the posted price, based on alleged underposting since 1961, the freight and sulphur advantages of Libyan crude, and the comparable posting of $2.65 in neighbouring Algeria, Tripoli's new-found associate in oil policy. The companies rejected the demand by offering a derisory 6–10 cents/barrel, although a body of opinion within the industry believed that an early settlement with the new regime would avoid trouble later. James E. Akins of the US State Department thought that after allowing for the differences in transport costs, the Libyan price should have been raised by over 40 cents. 'Coming from a high official of an agency long noted for its sympathy towards the major oil companies and also for its addiction to understatement, Akins's observation approaches a ringing endorsement of the Libyan demand'.[32] Gadafi reacted to the companies' offer with threats of unilateral action — threats backed by ostentatious approaches to the Soviet Union to assess the prospects for alternative markets, as well as exploration and production expertise.

By 1970 the Libyans were in a particularly strong position to assert their claims on the oil companies, and in May the government began to practise what was to prove an extraordinarily successful policy of

Table 11.2:   Oil Prices (Marsa Brega, 40.0−40.9 degrees API)

Date	Posted price	Dollars/barrel State sales price
August 1961	2.230	—
1 September 1970	2.530	—
1 January 1971	2.550	—
20 March 1971	3.447	—
1 July 1971	3.423	—
1 October 1971	3.399	—
1 January 1972	3.386	—
1 April 1972	3.642	—
1 July 1972	3.620	—
1 January 1973	3.777	—
1 April 1973	4.024	—
1 July 1973	4.391	—
1 August 1973	4.582	—
1 October 1973	4.605	—
16 October 1973	8.925	—
1 November 1973	9.061	—
1 January 1974	15.768	16.000
1 November 1974	15.768	11.860
1 April 1975	15.000	11.560
1 June 1975	14.600	11.200
1 October 1975	16.060	12.320
1 July 1976	16.350	12.620
1 January 1977	18.250	13.920
1 July 1977	18.250	14.200
1 January 1978	18.250	14.000
1 April 1978	18.250	13.850
1 May 1978	18.170	13.850
1 January 1979	19.250	14.690
1 March 1979	—	15.370
1 April 1979	—	18.250
16 May 1979	—	21.260
1 July 1979	—	23.450
1 October 1979	—	26.220
1 January 1980	—	34.670
20 May 1980	—	36.500*
1 July 1980	—	36.780*
1 January 81	—	40.780*
1 July 81	—	39.680*

Note: * Es Sider 37.0 degrees API

putting pressure on individual companies rather than on the industry as a whole. The first to be singled out were the world's largest company, Esso, and undoubtedly the most vulnerable of all, Occidental; they were the two biggest single-company producers of Libyan oil. The government's method was perfectly simple: on 7 May the

Petroleum Ministry ordered Occidental to cut its production in the name of 'conservation' and 'good oilfield practice'. By June, the company's output had fallen from its April peak of nearly 800,000 b/d to 485,000.[33] As intended, such cuts were crippling to a company with no other source of crude oil outside the United States, and particularly for one that was only just beginning to recoup the enormous outlays on its Libyan operation. Esso, by contrast, was less harmed in its world-wide operations by the loss of some of its Libyan production. Pressure was thus applied by means of a government refusal to allow the start of planned exports of natural gas from the company's Marsa Brega liquefaction plant that had been ready to go into operation since June, and on which over $300 million had been spent, so far without any return.

Production cuts — still officially in the name of 'conservation' and 'good oilfield practice' — were imposed on other companies that summer: reductions in the output of Amoseas, Oasis, Mobil and Esso, together with the original and further cuts in permitted Occidental liftings, reduced total output by some 870,000 b/d between April and late August. The government consistently denied that the cuts had anything to do with the impasse over posted prices. Nevertheless, as if to deepen the prevailing atmosphere of crisis, the local oil-products distribution operations of Esso, Shell and AGIP were nationalised without warning in July.

Occidental was in the meantime under acute pressure. Profits had fallen from $47.9 million in the second quarter of 1969 to $43.8 million in the same quarter of 1970.[34] Esso, rejecting this first chance to form a common company front in the face of government demands, had declined to supply Occidental with replacement crude at close to cost, and the company had no choice but to yield to government pressure.[35] On 4 September it was announced that the RCC had accepted Occidental's offer of a 30 cents increase in the posting, plus 2 cents/year increase for five years from 1971, a rise in the tax rate from 50 to 58 per cent (including 5 per cent in lieu of profits investment in the Kufra farm project), and an increase in the company's allowable production from 425,000 to 700,000 b/d on certain conditions.

Although the industry as a whole was shocked by these terms, it was unable to resist them, for it had failed to take any united and effective counter-action. On 21 September, the three independent partners in the Oasis group (Continental, Amerada and Marathon) agreed to broadly similar terms, although their partner, Shell, did not, and tried unsuccessfully to 'stem the avalanche': it refused to sign the agreement and was accordingly deprived of its one-sixth share of Oasis production. Before the end of the month, all the other companies had fallen into line.

This agreement marked the first big advance in crude oil postings in over 13 years of depressed prices, and the largest ever recorded. The size of the increase reflected the enhanced value of Libyan oil as a result of developments since 1967, although it has been suggested that an offer to the government of 15–25 cents/barrel in the posting 'probably would have been acceptable as late as the spring of 1970'.[36] The overall effect of the September settlement was to increase the government 'take' from each barrel of oil exported by about one-quarter.

Perhaps to their surprise, the companies found themselves obliged to meet Libyan demands because the government had fully appreciated the strength of its position while the companies, for all their supposed expertise, had not. For by 1970, after years of oil glut and depressed prices, there was at last a near balance between world oil supply and demand. (In the winter of 1969–70 there had been an unexpected world shortage of fuel oil, and particularly of the low-sulphur fuel refined from African crudes.) Thus the great companies that still controlled most of the international oil trade had fewer alternative sources of replacement crude to draw on when a recalcitrant producer such as Libya unexpectedly chose to cut production; but also in particularly short supply was the additional tanker capacity needed to move extra crude from the Gulf when the flow of 'short-haul' crude from one or more Mediterranean outlets was reduced.

This was a reversal of the companies' dominating position during the Iranian crisis of 1951–4, the Suez crisis of 1956–7, and even during the crisis caused by the 1967 Middle East war and the subsequent selective embargoes of importing nations. During those past crises, ample alternative sources of crude, and just about enough tankers to ship them in, had been available to enable the companies to make up all the shortfall in output from one recalcitrant producer or group of producers, which suffered greater losses and hardships than the consuming nations intended to be influenced or harmed by the producers' action.

In May 1970 the difference between world oil supply and demand, already narrowed by Libya's own cutbacks, was further reduced when the great Trans-Arabian Pipeline (Tapline), delivering some

500,000 b/d of Saudi crude to the eastern Mediterranean, was broken at a point where it crossed Syrian territory, and its repair was unaccountably delayed for nine months. The immediate result was a worldwide scramble for tankers to move the blocked Saudi crude to market via the Cape of Good Hope. Freight rates soared, automatically enhancing the value of all 'short-haul' west-of-Suez crude in general and high-quality Libyan crude in particular. Algeria, fighting its own battles with the French oil companies, was an impossible source of alternative supplies.

The basic strength of the Libyan negotiating position was underlined by the fact that this producer had become Western Europe's largest single source of oil, supplying about one-third of total demand. No government was prepared for a confrontation with the Libyans — hence, for example, Rome's acceptance of the expulsion of the Italian community and the seizure of its assets in 1970. Indeed, companies and consumer governments seemed remarkably unconcerned about the likely consequences of a Libyan oil-price revolution; short-sighted European public opinion tended anyway not to be particularly moved by the discomfiture of 'Anglo-Saxon' oil companies.

For their part, the Libyans seemed supremely confident in their timing and in the exploitation of their extraordinarily strong bargaining position. Although the young officers of the RCC were 'completely unschooled in economics or negotiation', they clearly had the most expert, if anonymous, advice. The government also contrived to build up an atmosphere of uncertainty and suspense, in which rumours of nationalisations and other 'measures' against uncooperative companies circulated freely.

For years past, the great companies had expressed confidence in their ability to place a ruinous embargo on any producing state that dared to defy their control of the international oil trade and its prices; the humiliation of Iran between 1951 and 1954 was a standing warning of the power of the companies. But in 1970 the Libyan leadership effectively called the companies' bluff. The independents, lifting over half the country's crude and relying heavily on this one source of supply, could not afford to stop producing, while the newly agreed price rises made overall revenues less vulnerable than before to an attempted embargo by the major companies alone. In the event of a total embargo, the country had accumulated currency reserves of $2,000 million — enough to maintain current imports and spending for four years.[37] Such was the financial backing behind

Gadafi's potential role as the defiant leader of an austere desert people supposedly ready to renounce their oil wealth for the sake of their principles. But, in the event, the companies were far more concerned by the possibility of the government putting further pressure on them by closing the oil terminals: it was known that troops were mobilised in readiness to move into the oil ports to halt all shipments within an hour or so of the order being given.[38]

Unlike the Iranians in the early 1950s, the Libyans had some support from the other oil states, and notably those with Mediterranean export terminals — Iraq and Algeria, both of which were engaged in their own confrontations with the oil companies, and Saudi Arabia. But despite the fact that in 1970 the Secretary-General of OPEC was a Libyan, Tripoli failed to persuade the organisation as a whole to take any practical steps to put pressure on the companies while the crucial initial demands were being made.

Yet the Libyan settlement of a higher posting and a new range of tax rates up to 58 per cent, described by the government as a retrospective payment for 'unduly low' prices in the past, set a precedent that other producers were eager to follow. One almost immediate result was an increase of 20 cents/barrel in postings of Iraqi and Saudi crudes at Mediterranean terminals, while Nigeria and Iran soon won themselves increased benefits as well. When OPEC oil ministers met in the Venezuelan capital, Caracas, in December 1970, Libya emerged as the clear pace-setter of an organisation that built on the Libyan achievement by passing a resolution calling for a 55 per cent minimum tax rate and making other demands reflecting the main features of the September settlement.

Although many months had passed since Tripoli had first put pressure on the companies, the position of the producing states had been further reinforced by the strengthening of the world-wide seller's market for oil. Through the delay in reopening Tapline, and the continuing Libyan production cut-backs, Europe was still being deprived of one million b/d of short-haul (Mediterranean) crude at a time when demand was still rising at an unprecedented 10 per cent/year.

Negotiations with the companies were proposed for the New Year in Tehran. But now that the other producers were following Tripoli's lead, the Libyans were no longer satisfied with the terms they had negotiated. If a 55 per cent tax rate and a 30 cents increase in the posting were to be the new standards for all the producers, then, clearly, the prolonged underpricing of Libyan crude (now tacitly acknowledged by the companies in their acceptance of the September amendments) was still in effect unremedied. Thus at the beginning of January, between OPEC's Caracas and Tehran meetings, Major Abd-al-Salam Jallud put new demands to the companies that would have given Libya better terms than those about to be negotiated by other OPEC members. And, for the first time, an underlying political motive was acknowledged when it was made clear that one purpose of these new demands was to pressurise the United States government into changing its Middle East policy.

Before meeting the main Gulf oil-producing states in Tehran in January and February 1971, the leading oil companies had publicly proclaimed the adoption of a common front in the forthcoming negotiations. Of these oil companies 17 also arrived at a secret 'Libyan Producers' Agreement' (which only became public some three years later, although the Libyans seem to have been long aware of its existence) whereby the companies operating in Libya agreed to form a united front. Each company promised to make no agreement with the government without the consent of the others; if one company was ordered to cut production, all companies would make good the cutback in specified proportions, at cost. Crude-oil sharing under the agreement started when British Petroleum was nationalised in December 1971, and the arrangement worked well in diverting supplies to various companies as they were fully or partially nationalised in 1972-3. The scheme only ran into trouble in 1973 when the oil market again tightened. But in a sense it failed its main test because most of the independents preferred to accept a 51 per cent government participation in their operations rather than refuse — like Bunker Hunt and some others — to agree to the government's terms.[39]

The agreement between the companies and six Gulf oil producers reached at Tehran on 14 February 1971 was considered at the time a milestone in country-company relations. While the host governments agreed not to initiate or support any oil embargo, or to continue raising prices, the companies conceded a 55 per cent tax rate, an increase of 35 cents/barrel in Gulf posted prices, and other benefits. But an agreement that was supposed to bring the international oil industry five years of peace and stability was considered wholly unsatisfactory in Tripoli, where there was also some resentment of OPEC's role in an agreement that had clearly left Libya at a renewed disadvantage.

But other Mediterranean exporters came to Libya's aid at a meeting in Tripoli in February 1971. After settling at Tehran questions relating only to exports through their Gulf terminals, Saudi Arabia and Iraq were then free to support Tripoli's latest demands, with their direct bearing on all Mediterranean prices. Moreover, the nationalisation of 51 per cent of the operations of foreign oil companies in Algeria aroused renewed fears over the intentions of Libya, whose oil policies were known to be co-ordinated with Algeria's. All three Mediterranean exporters backed Tripoli's new demands by threatening a total Mediterranean embargo if the companies refused to accept them.

Four days after the Tehran agreement, new talks opened in Tripoli. One of the main concerns of the companies was that the outcome would be too generous, and thus bring fresh demands for further price rises from jealous Gulf producers. Initial demands, based on what had been conceded at Tehran, were alarming — a posting of $3.75/barrel, a 5 per cent increase in the tax rate and a reinvestment undertaking of 25 cents/barrel. Representing the government throughout the talks was Major Abd-al-Salam Jallud, who harangued the company negotiators, worked himself up into convincing displays of rage as the occasion demanded, and insisted on dealing with the companies one by one, even if the final agreement was to be binding on them all. OPEC was by this time solidly behind Tripoli, and on 12 March Nigeria (a potential competitor of both Libya and Algeria as a producer of high-quality, west-of-Suez crude) announced its intention of joining the organisation.

The agreement that 15 companies finally reached in Tripoli on 2 April acknowledged the fact that they were in no better bargaining position than they had been in the previous September when the Libyans had started world oil prices on their upward spiral. The companies had managed only to moderate initial demands that would have raised the tax-paid cost of Libyan oil to the companies by some 75 cents/barrel and would undoubtedly have brought fresh demands for parity from Gulf producers.[40] The new terms, retroactive to 20 March, increased government receipts by one-half, with provision for further increases later, promised five years of stable prices, and opened the way for similar settlements with other Mediterranean exporters and Nigeria. The immediate effect of the 'Tripoli Agreement' (see Table 11.3)[41] was to raise the posted price for 40-degree Libyan crude by nearly 90 cents/barrel, from $2.55 to $3.447. The increase was made up of several components, of which the general price rise represented only 35 cents (the same that had been agreed for Gulf producers at Tehran); the remainder included allowances for low sulphur content, freight and closed Suez Canal advantages — all factors reflecting the inherent high quality and geographical attractions of Libyan crude oil at the time. Moreover, as in the Tehran agreement, there was an allowance to compensate the host country for 'losses' resulting from world inflation.

The prime achievement of the Libyan revolution — at least, so far as the outside world was concerned — was to force the international companies to acknowledge the value of Libyan oil by paying more for it. In the six months after September 1970, the companies' tax-paid costs in Libya had risen from about $1.40 to $2.30/barrel; from the 1971 agreement alone, the government stood to gain over $700 million in extra revenue in the first full year.[42]

The Tehran–Tripoli agreements of early 1971 — the direct outcome of Libya's politically and economically motivated solo confrontation of the previous year with the companies — marked a watershed in the history of the international oil industry. The power of the companies had been visibly curtailed and had been shown to be less than the producing states had long feared. Up to then, the companies had decided government revenues by unilateral changes in posted prices, and by setting production rates. The settlement of 1971 transferred control over prices to the producer governments; some by then had also taken control of production rates with little or no regard for the interests of the companies. Such was the main and most far-reaching achievement of the Libyan revolution, for its repercussions have been felt throughout the world ever since in the form of higher oil prices in particular and higher energy prices in

Table 11.3: Tripoli Agreement 20 March 1971

	Dollars	Dollars
Posted price per 40-degree API barrel before 20 March 1971	2.550	
General price rise	0.350	
Low sulphur allowance	0.100	
Freight adjustment	0.070	
Basic posted price		3.070
Inflation, etc.	0.127	
Temporary freight allowance	0.130	
Suez Canal premium	0.120	
Posted price 20 March 1971		$ 3.447

Source: Libyan Arab Republic, *Libyan Oil 1954–1971* (Tripoli, 1972) p. 133.

general. As the chairman of Shell, Sir David Barran, remarked at the time of the Tehran settlement: 'There is no doubt that the buyer's market for oil is over.'[43]

Although the Tehran and Tripoli agreements were basically conservative, supposedly guaranteeing concession rights and security of oil supplies to the companies for five years, they were soon overtaken by the fundamental ambition of Libya and other producers to gain greater control over their resources through nationalisation of the companies' oil-producing operations.

Nationalisation without warning of the local distribution subsidiaries of Esso, Shell and AGIP in support of the government's price claims in late 1970 was a sign of things to come. Thus the illusion of uneasy peace that had settled over the Libyan oil industry after April 1971 was shattered within six months. In October, when the companies combined to fight a demand for increased revenue to compensate for the devaluation of the United States dollar (the currency in which most international oil transactions were by then being made), the government retaliated by taking the disputed amount (about $1 million) from Esso's Tripoli bank account. Then, on 7 December, Arab oil producers meeting in Abu Dhabi passed a resolution calling for host government participation in oil-company capital and management, with 20 per cent the initial target.

That same evening, Libya moved first by announcing the full nationalisation of all BP's rights and assets in Concession 65, and primarily its half-share in the Sarir field. This largest field in Africa was then producing some 400,000 b/d, or about 5 per cent of BP's world-wide output; but BP's partner, Nelson Bunker Hunt, was unaffected. The take-over, combined with the withdrawal of Libya's Sterling balances in London, came without warning.[44] It was represented as a purely political act, a reprisal for the failure of the British government (owner of nearly half of BP's shares) to prevent Iran's occupation of three strategic islands at the entrance to the Persian Gulf on the eve of British withdrawal from the area.[45] Although compensation at net book value[46] was promised, and was later set at $100 million, BP refused to admit the legality of the nationalisation and soon brought a test case to prevent the sale of nationalised Sarir oil. But the Libyans, foiling BP's attempt to impose an embargo, sold Sarir crude to the Soviet Union for two years until outstanding differences had been settled.

The *Petroleum Press Service* commented on the BP take-over: 'This demonstration of Colonel Gadafi's revolutionary zeal or behalf of other Arab nations fits in remarkably conveniently with Libya's current ambitions in the Arab world.'[47] Nationalisation (or, in politer terminology, 'participation') was now in the air in Libya and throughout OPEC, and the Italians were the next object of Tripoli's continuing policy of pressurising the currently most vulnerable companies for revised operating terms. Early in 1972, after heavy investment in exploration and in production facilities, the Italian state AGIP was ready to start commercial production from its Concession 100 field (Bu Attifel) through a 100-kilometre spur to Occidental's main pipeline to the Zueitina terminal: the field was a large one, with a potential production rate of over 250,000 b/d. The government, however, withheld permission to start production until AGIP agreed to majority state participation, and it was only in September that the government was satisfied with an immediate half-share in AGIP's two concessions. As Italy was by then buying nearly one-third of its oil from Libya and had many other vulnerable commercial interests in the country, AGIP was only able to modify Tripoli's demands from majority to equal participation. In the words of one Libyan official at the time, the AGIP agreement 'marked the beginning of the end of the traditional oil concession'.

By late 1971 the international oil companies had lost confidence in Libya. In the face of a temporary world oil glut and depressed tanker freight rates, oil production had by October 1971 fallen to less than 2.5 million barrels daily. Most companies were producing less than even the reduced allowances set in 1970 because Libyan crude had become overpriced in comparison with Gulf crudes, at least so long as tanker freight rates remained depressed. Low output did not particularly concern the government; indeed, it was still insisting that production cut-backs were being made for the sake of 'conservation'. And, because per-barrel revenues had risen from an average of $1.05 in 1969 to $1.93 in 1972, lower output was returning higher revenues. But the government was concerned by lack of company investment, particularly in new exploration — the number of operating drilling rigs had fallen from 52 in 1969 to seven in early 1972. Each company was obliged to operate at least one exploration rig, but in the atmosphere of company–government mistrust, activity remained at barely the required minimum. Operators, mindful that not one nationalised company had yet received any of its promised compensation, were noticeably reluctant to invest in the search for, or development of, new oilfields. Indeed, no large new fields went into commercial production in Libya after Bu Attifel started up in late 1972.

The understandable desire of the host countries for a greater degree of 'participation'[48] in the oil industry inevitably aroused all the old arguments about the role of the large international companies. In Libya, they had originally been welcomed by a government eager for quick results, and they had devoted the time, skill, equipment, enterprise and finance (United States companies alone were estimated to have invested $1,500 million by 1968) that had made the Libyan oil industry what it was.[49]

For its part, the government could point to the low level of Libyan employment in the industry, and the large profits the companies had made out of previously underpriced oil, and continued to make even after the 1970 and 1971 settlements. According to the chairman of the National Oil Corporation in 1972, oil companies in Libya admitted to current earnings of 15 per cent on capital invested, but he suggested that 20 per cent would be more accurate. One company source estimated profits in 1972 at some 30–40 cents on each barrel of oil produced[50] — indicating total profits of between $240 and $325 million on an annual production of about 820 million barrels. Libyan operating costs were low — at less than 8.5 cents/barrel of crude produced, they stood comparison with the cheapest production rates in the Middle East.[51] In late 1965, Esso's production in Libya was said to have been the 'most profitable' of anywhere in the world.[52]

A general agreement on one-quarter state participation, rising to 51 per cent in 1982, had been reached in the Gulf in October 1972. But Libya, as a proclaimed 'revolutionary' regime, had to be seen to be more dynamic than the Gulf 'moderates'. Having just gained a half-share in the AGIP operation, the government resumed its practice of pressurising vulnerable individual companies, starting with a demand for half the assets of Bunker Hunt (still producing its half-share of oil from the Sarir field) and half Hunt's profits since the nationalisation of BP some ten months earlier. Hunt, who had refused all government requests and pressures to market nationalised BP oil, and who had 'the advice and support of the rest of the industry', resisted strongly.

The Libyans then reinforced their campaign for participation by pressing Oasis (still the largest producer), Amoseas (Socal/Texaco) and Occidental for what amounted to nationalisation — immediate full participation in exchange for compensation based on 'net book value' and the 'right' to buy oil at market prices.[53] In May, the government halted Hunt's tanker loadings, and the company was told that its right to produce and export oil would cease on 1 June. Speaking at a rally to mark the third anniversary of the evacuation of American forces on 11 June, Colonel Gadafi announced the nationalisation of Hunt's assets to deal the United States 'a big, hard slap . . . on its cold, insolent face'. The Hunt nationalisation was held up as a warning to other companies to accept the government's terms, and to the United States 'to end its recklessness and its hostility to the Arab nation'. Thus both British and American foreign policies were used as an excuse for the full nationalisation of the largest oilfield in Africa, with reserves estimated at up to 14,000 million barrels. Hunt had been particularly vulnerable to government action, having no other oil available outside North America, and no formal agreement covering continued operations following the BP nationalisation.

The industry again faced the delicate task of satisfying Libyan determination to better its OPEC partners without undermining agreements already reached with Gulf producers. But for some companies, 'firmness and solidarity began to fade in the face of Libyan threats. The blame for this should not be placed entirely upon the independent producers who were under great pressure from the Libyans and doubted that they would receive adequate support from some governments or from the Gulf producers.'[54]

In August 1973, first Occidental and then the three independents in the Oasis group agreed to a 51 per cent government participation in their Libyan operations. The 'remarkably expensive terms' that they agreed included compensation based only on net book value of assets and the 'right' to buy back 51 per cent of crude production (formerly obtained at cost) at a temporary price of $4.90/barrel for 40-degree oil. This was 32 cents more than the posting, and the world's highest 'buy back' price.

The independents again had to capitulate because they faced the same unassailable Libyan bargaining position that had underpinned demands for price rises in 1970–1. World oil supplies and the tankers to ship them in were again in tight supply. The value of short-haul, high-quality oil was once more fully apparent, particularly to independent companies producing about half the current Libyan output of around 2 million barrels daily, and lacking other sources of crude oil outside North America. Once again, large financial reserves (by then approaching $3,000 million) were an additional factor reinforcing Tripoli's bargaining position.

In trying to decide whether to accept the government's new participation demands, the major companies had to consider the likely repercussions on their far more important interests in the Middle East. But in September the government in effect made up the companies' minds for them by announcing a 51 per cent take-over of their interests — a move that most refused to accept. Accordingly, in February 1974 the government made an example of American companies — Socal/Texaco's Amoseas and the Libyan American Oil Company (an Atlantic Richfield subsidiary) — by nationalising them outright. By May, Esso and Mobil had agreed to the government's terms, while Shell's one-sixth interest in Oasis had been nationalised. As Major Jallud had already made clear, nationalisation was part of Libya's plans to use oil 'as a weapon in the battle' with Israel. This seizure of 51 per cent or even 100 per cent of the assets and operations of foreign oil companies without provoking serious political or economic repercussions, and even the demonstrated ability to continue marketing disputed Sarir crude, set an example for other oil-exporting states to follow. Before long, even 'moderate' producers in the Gulf had partially or fully nationalised foreign oil interests.

In the years between 1970 and 1974, the great international oil companies lost control over world oil prices and over production in the main oil-exporting regions of North and West Africa, the Middle and Far East, and Latin America. The swift revolution in company–government relations was due primarily to Libyan initiative, hard headed boldness and well-timed insistence on the recognition of economic 'rights' that other producers had long claimed but had been unable or unwilling to achieve. The fact that crude oil is now priced as it is, and that by the beginning of the 1980s the companies were being shut out of wide areas of the international oil trade they had until recently dominated, has to be recognised as largely the original achievement of Libya's revolutionary regime, even if other producers later took over the initiative.

Yet, despite revolutionary militancy on the participation issue, Libya did not fully nationalise the foreign oil companies. By early 1974 it was calculated that the government had acquired some 60 per cent of the national oil production (see Table 11.4).[55] The state interest in various producing companies or company groups ranged from 100 per cent in the former BP–Hunt and Amoseas partnerships to 63.5 per cent in the Esso Sirte group and 59.2 per cent in Oasis. The odd percentages were due to the full nationalisation of

Table 11.4: Producing Companies — State Interest

Name	Percentage production share Company	State
BP	—	100.0
Bunker Hunt	—	
Amoseas:		
Texaco	—	100.0
Socal	—	
Elf–Aquitaine	11.25	
OMV	2.25 → 15.0	85.0
Wintershall	1.5	
Occidental	19.0	81.0
Atlantic Richfield	—	
Esso Sirte	24.5 → 36.5	63.5
W.R. Grace	12.0	
Oasis:		
Amerada Hess	8.2	
Continental	16.3	
Marathon	16.3 → 40.8	59.2
Shell	—	
Esso Libya	49.0	51.0
Occidental	49.0	51.0
Mobil	31.9 → 49.0	51.0
Gelsenberg	17.1	
AGIP	50.0	50.0
Elf–Aquitaine	42.0	
Hispanoil	42.0 → 100.0	—
Murphy	16.0	

one partner in each group after its failure to agree to the government's
terms when other partners had agreed to a 51 per cent government
take. The government held a 51 per cent interest in Esso Standard,
Occidental and Mobil–Gelsenberg, a half-share in AGIP, and no
interest in minor operators with little or no production.

Also in 1974, the government made new grants of exploration
territory — the first since the revolution — whereby the operating
company undertook to share any commercial production on a ratio
1 : 19 in the state's favour in the case of Occidental's new agreement and 85 : 15 in the case of AGIP's. Such were the terms under

which foreign companies, including foreign state oil entities, were in future expected to operate. Although various groups accepted the challenge (including Compagnie Française des Pétroles and Brazil's state Petrobrás), Occidental was almost the only operator to make entirely new finds that went into commercial production in the 1970s. The National Oil Corporation made some interesting strikes on the Hammadah al-Hamrah plateau and elsewhere in western Libya, but they were not immediately exploitable because of prolonged doubt about the economic justification of building a pipeline to the coast. In 1976, a group of European companies found what at the time was described as potentially the largest Libyan oilfield; it lay under the Mediteranean, about 100 kilometres north of Zuara, but there was no commercial development. The strike was made not far from the offshore median line disputed with Tunisia, which had modest but vital offshore oil and gas production of its own in the nearby Gulf of Gabes. The dispute led to 'incidents' involving warships in 1977, and was later passed to the International Court of Justice at The Hague for the slow processes of judgement. Another offshore median-line dispute with Malta was for long a source of friction between Tripoli and Valletta.

Although the state share of production later rose to nearly 70 per cent (at a time when other OPEC members were fully nationalising foreign oil interests — See Table 11.4), the state was unwilling to do without the foreign oil companies entirely. It needed their continued expertise in exploration and production, and particularly their marketing expertise; it was also convenient that the companies were willing and able to continue providing the risk capital for new exploration ventures. Significantly, in view of the country's known lack of technical expertise, one production operation that the state long refused to participate in was Esso's technically complex and troublesome natural gas liquefaction plant at Marsa Brega; it was not until mid-1980 that the state took a 51 per cent share in a process that had by then been working without technical hitches for several years.

It was official policy that full nationalisation would come only when Libyans had sufficient expertise to operate the industry by themselves. Although considerable pressure had been put on the oil companies both before and after the revolution to increase the number of Libyan employees and trainees throughout the industry development of the necessary skills inevitably took time.

By April 1973 the posted price of 40-degrees Libyan crude oil was just over $4 per barrel. By 1 October it had risen by a further 60 cents in recognition of the high value of short-haul crude in a period of renewed tight world supplies and shortage of tankers to ship them in. Ten days after the outbreak of the Middle East war of October 1973, Libya joined other Arab producers — the ten members of the Organisation of *Arab* Petroleum Exporting Countries — in the use of oil as a political weapon. An embargo on supplies to nations considered unfriendly to the Arab cause (namely the United States and the Netherlands) was coupled with what were intended to be progressive 5 per cent monthly cuts in total output affecting all customers. Libyan output was accordingly reduced from an average of 2.38 million b/d in October to about 1.77 million in November.

In the resultant chaos in the international oil trade, and the scramble by consumers for oil at extraordinary prices, all OPEC members seized the chance to raise their posted prices by about 70 per cent, although the posting of 40-degree Libyan crude was almost doubled on 16 October, from $4.605 to $8.925, and some cargo lots of Libyan oil were reportedly sold at up to $20 per barrel. By January 1974, production cuts had been partly restored (Libyan output averaged just over 2 million b/d that month). But for the second time in less than three months, OPEC seized the chance to right what it considered to have been years of underpricing. It announced further increases in postings that raised the price of Saudi Arabian light oil (the so-called 'marker' crude against which all other OPEC prices were supposed to be set) from $5.119 to $11.651 from the beginning of 1974. The Libyan posting, having been given an interim boost to just over $9 at the beginning of November, reached the then awesome figure of $15.768 on 1 January. Major Jallud claimed at the time that the 'real' price of Libyan crude ranged from $20 to $25.[56]

As a result of price rises since 1970, and notably those of the extraordinary winter of 1973/4, the economic prospects of all OPEC members were transformed: this was particularly true of states such as Libya with high oil production and revenues and relatively small populations. Between 1970 and 1974, Libya's annual oil revenues more than quadrupled (see Table 11.1) from $1,351 million to $6,000 million (or over $2,000 per head of population). During the same period, oil output had been cut by more than half, but government earnings from each barrel of oil exported had increased from $1.12 in 1970 to just over $11 in 1974.

Nevertheless, the fact that the price of Libyan crude had been forced too high in the heady days of late 1973 became embarras-singly clear as overpriced oil and general economic recession in the main oil-importing industrial countries caused demand to slump in 1974–5. The tanker market had collapsed in the aftermath of the Arab oil embargo and production cuts of October 1973, and with its natural freight advantage thus eroded, Libyan crude was by 1974 clearly uncompetitive with relatively cheaper crudes from the Gulf. Since tanker-owners were at the time delivering crude oil from the Gulf to north-west Europe via the Cape of Good Hope at the very depressed rate of just over $2 per ton, or less than 30 cents/barrel, 'there was no commercial justification in the price of Libyan crude being some $1.25 per barrel higher than approximately comparable Persian Gulf crude'.[57]

In 1974 output from all Libyan fields averaged only 1.49 million b/d, half a million barrels below the officially projected rate. This was despite the fact that the contract price at which the state sold its oil to foreign buyers was reduced in four stages, from $16.00 on 1 January 1974 to $11.86 ten months later. The government was so concerned by the relentless fall in exports that at the beginning of 1975 it swallowed its pride to the extent of lifting its embargo on sales to the United States and Caribbean refineries supplying the United States market; all other producers had ended their embargoes nearly a year earlier. But in February 1975 output fell to an eleven-year low of 912,000 b/d and only further severe price-cutting (the contract price was down to $11.20 in June, and even the posted price was eventually cut to $14.60) finally stimulated exports and production — but not before the extraordinary shortfall in revenues had caused a financial crisis leading to the defection of the Planning Minister and other members of the RCC, combined with an attempt to depose Colonel Gadafi.

Under the influences of more reasonable prices and generally rising demand, production recovered to nearly the level considered ideal by the government — 2 million b/d.[58] Nevertheless, production was not to rise much above 2 million b/d for the remainder of the 1970s, partly because of new competition from similar-quality crude produced by Nigeria and later by the British and Norwegian sectors of the North Sea. During the world oil glut of 1981, over-priced Libyan oil failed to sell and production consequently fell to 500,000 b/d.

Libya's dynamic leadership within OPEC, first on the prices issue and then on participation, was brief, perhaps because once the initial victories had been won, the regime's energies were turned elsewhere. Nevertheless, the country remained one of the recognised 'hawks' within OPEC, with prices continuing to reflect high quality and transport advantages; even after the reopening of the Suez Canal in 1975 they remained consistently among the highest in the organisation, yielding per barrel revenues well above the OPEC average. There was, moreover, a strong element of radical political showmanship in the 'hawkish' stand of both Libya and Iraq on OPEC pricing policy in the later 1970s.

By then the companies and the government had come to an apparently mutually satisfactory form of co-existence, and although Colonel Gadafi was on record as saying that Libya would not hesitate to take full control of the industry 'whenever we can manage our own fields', this was understood to be a relatively long-term goal. Thus the companies continued to explore for oil (although not with the same enthusiasm as they had in the 1960s), to market it and to provide technical skills and risk capital. Nevertheless, by 1979 the government was so concerned by the lack of new exploration by foreign companies that it announced plans to make future supplies of crude oil to companies conditional on exploration undertakings.[59]

In the meantime, the government was fulfilling its long-standing policy of 'gaining full control over the sources of oil wealth' by other means — through participation in the so-called 'downstream' operations (notably refining, petrochemicals and transport). These processes enabled the state to earn more from its oil by exporting higher-value finished products rather than crude oil as a basic raw material to be processed abroad.

The first purpose of a local refinery was to meet the country's own rapidly increasing demand for the main oil products that had previously been imported. Domestic oil consumption increased from 16,000 barrels daily in 1970 to 48,500 in 1975 and 120,000 in 1980 (giving the highest consumption *per capita* in Africa), with a projected total of 215,000 barrels daily in 1985.[60] Esso's original 10,000 b/d refinery, opened at Marsa Brega in 1967, was never able to meet all domestic demand, and the first refinery designed to process an exportable surplus of products was built at a cost of $110 million for the National Oil Corporation by Snam Progetti at Zawia, some 45 kilometres west of Tripoli. It was opened in September 1974 with an initial capacity of 60,000 b/d — enough to meet all local demand (except for some specialised products), then amounting to just over 37,000 b/d, and leave an exportable surplus of some 20,000 b/d of fuel oil, naphtha and kerosine.[61]

Zawia was expanded three years later to 120,000 b/d capacity. The refinery was always supplied with crude oil shipped from the Marsa Hariga (Tobruk) terminal of the Sarir field. The choice of Zawia as a refinery site reflected political as well as economic considerations. Although close to relatively large markets in and around Tripoli, 'it is almost as far as it is possible to get on the Libyan coast from commercial oilfields or oil export terminals'.[62] Despite this drawback, 'there was a political need to bring more oil industry activity into the western part of the country — former Tripolitania — rather than allow it to concentrate in the eastern provinces — former Cyrenaica — where most of the main oilfields are'.[63]

Zawia was also well placed to be the main outlet for the long-projected 'western pipeline' designed to gather in the production of the small and scattered strikes made in various parts of western Libya since the 1950s, but not considered individually commercial because of their size and remoteness. The National Oil Corporation's plans for an 18-inch, 400-kilometre pipeline to deliver an initial 50,000 b/d of this 'western' crude to Zawia (rising eventually to 150,000 b/d) were finally approved in 1977 and a consultancy contract was awarded in 1980.[64] Even though the then estimated cost was high ($170 million), the political advantages of bringing Tripolitanian and Fezzanese oil into commercial production apparently fully justified it.

Until the plans were changed in 1977, the National Oil Corporation had intended to have four export terminals with a total capacity of nearly 970,000 b/d in operation before the end of the decade.[6] In addition to Zawia (120,000 b/d), refineries were planned for Misurata (220,000 b/d), at the Occidental–AGIP–NOC terminal at Zueitina (400,000 b/d) and Marsa Hariga (120,000 b/d). Later and less ambitious plans (possibly modified in recognition of refining capacity surpluses in the Mediterranean basin) envisaged the completion by 1980 of NOC refineries at Marsa Hariga (220,000 b/d) and at the Mobil–Gelsenberg–NOC terminal at Ras Lanuf (200,000 b/d). Together with the existing refineries at Zawia and Marsa Brega, these new plants were to bring total refining capacity to nearly 550,000 b/d. Allowing 120,000 b/d to meet local consumption, there was a surplus of some 430,000 b/d of products for export representing nearly one-quarter of normal total oil output.

Attempts by producers to break into downstream operations imply direct competition with consuming countries which, since the

Second World War, and particularly since the Abadan crisis, have increasingly imported crude oil for refining, rather than products processed in the producing states. Thus it was not clear where ready markets for these large new volumes of Libyan products were to be found, and not only because they were competing directly with similar products from large new export refineries in neighbouring Algeria. Western Europe, although the nearest and largest foreign market, itself had too many refineries; in the late 1970s they were operating at only about two-thirds of capacity, and a protectionist spirit was growing. Other Mediterranean and African countries building their own national refineries were accordingly closing their markets to imported products. The National Oil Corporation only seemed likely to break into the oil products export trade by cutting prices and/or by insisting on inclusion of a certain proportion of products with all crude-oil sales.

A petrochemical complex at Marsa Brega was already well established by 1980, while another was taking shape at Abu Khammash, on the coast some 20 kilometres from the Tunisian border, and a third at Ras Lanuf. At Marsa Brega an ammonia plant with a daily output of 2,000 tons and a 1,000 tons/day methanol plant went on stream in 1977. In 1980, a 1,000 tons/day ethanol plant was opened, while installations for the manufacture of phosphate fertiliser and sulphuric acid were nearing completion.[66] At Abu Khammash, a $515 million development due to start operating in 1980 included a plant for the production of caustic soda, polyvinyl chloride (PVC), hydrochloric acid, liquid chlorine, hydrochloric solution and sodium chloride.[67] The main installation at Ras Lanuf was to be an ethylene plant with a yearly output of 330,000 tons.

By 1980, the newly built fleet of 15 oil and products tankers operated by the state Libyan General Maritime Transport Organisation (LGMTO) amounted to about 1.5 million deadweight tons, or 0.5 per cent of the world tanker fleet. In common with other oil-exporting countries building up their own tanker fleets, Libya was thus able to ship a useful proportion of crude and products output to market in national flag vessels operating in direct (and, if need be, subsidised) competition with the established tanker fleets of the oil companies and independent owners. LGMTO had a further interest in tankers as a partner in OAPEC's eight-member Arab Maritime Transport Company, formed in 1973. The accumulation of a large world surplus of tanker capacity in the aftermath of the 1973–4 oil price rises, and the subsequent prolonged collapse of oil tanker-freight rates, can have done little to convince oil producers of the profitability of shipping their own crude and products; nevertheless, ownership of the fleet and the experience gained in operating it could doubtless be considered useful investments for a more profitable future.

Investment in prestigious capital-intensive downstream operations enabled the state to increase the value of every barrel of oil processed in national refineries and petrochemical plants and/or shipped to market in national carriers. Such investment was a more productive outlet for surplus revenues than short-term depositing in European and American banks. Moreover, the governments of oil-producing states 'know that if they cannot make a success of such refining and petrochemical industries, they will probably never succeed in any industry at all'.[68]

Nevertheless, such investment in downstream operations is open to criticism. Large, capital-intensive, high-technology projects in countries such as Libya usually cost two to three times as much as competing facilities in industrially advanced states[69] because of higher transport costs, physical and bureaucratic bottlenecks, and lack of basic supporting infrastructure, materials and skills. The value added to crude oil by refining or petrochemicals manufacture is relatively small, and few new jobs are created; the $515 million investment at Abu Khammash was expected to generate only 1,150 new jobs[70] — or an investment of nearly $450,000 per employee!

By the beginning of the 1980s, Libyan experience as one of the most favoured oil states went back 20 years. The government had come to control some 70 per cent of total oil production and was making growing investments in downstream operations. Proven[71] reserves of some 25,000 million barrels of light, low-sulphur crude oil had a theoretical life of some 35 years at a daily production rate of 2 million barrels, even if no large new finds were made. If not overpriced, the oil was eminently marketable[72] in the nearby markets of Western Europe (where about half of it went), and in the United States (which bought up to 40 per cent). But prospects for increasing production to the government's official target of 2.5 million barrels daily seemed to depend on the success of new exploration ventures. In addition, substantial reserves of natural gas – 695,000 million cubic metres (just under 1 per cent of total world reserves)[73] — were being exploited at a quite modest rate of 4,500 million cubic metres/year.[74] It was a trade that seemed bound to increase, as gas prices drew level with crude-oil prices, thereby making exploitation more economically attractive.

Thus the oil and gas reserves known to be in the ground in 1980 promised the country a continuing inflow of revenues for at least a further generation, and on a scale unlikely ever to be repeated. The fact that these revenues were already so large, and promised to continue increasing even if oil production was unchanged, was initially at least the most effective and far-reaching achievement of the revolution. For, instead of producing more hydrocarbons to increase revenues, as had been the necessary practice under the monarchy, the revolutionary government could leave oil and gas in the ground for the benefit of the nation well into the next century.

Notes

1. A. Desio, *Le Vie della Sete* (Milan, 1950), pp. 324–5. He was so surprised to find oil that at first he suspected contamination by lubricating oil from the drilling equipment.

2. A.A.Q. Kubbah, *Libya, Its Oil Industry and Economic System* (Baghdad, 1964), p. 65; F.G. Waddams, *The Libyan Oil Industry* (London, 1980), p. 57.

3. Or 'Seven Sisters' as the Italian oilman Enrico Mattei insisted on calling them. They are British Petroleum, Esso (or Exxon), Gulf, Mobil, Shell, Socal and Texaco.

4. Zone One — Tripolitania; Zone Two — northern Cyrenaica; Zone Three — southern Cyrenaica; Zone Four — Fezzan. The boundary between Zones One and Two was moved some 50 kilometres east of the political boundary to give Tripolitania greater share in the main oil-bearing Sirtica region.

5. The price at which a given quantity of crude oil was offered for sale at a given place. Companies normally calculated profits to be shared with host governments on posted prices, which thus determined company tax payments and government revenues. Crude oil was not, however, necessarily traded at posted prices, which did not necessarily reflect any imputed value and certainly bore no relation to the costs of production.

6. Waddams, *Libyan Oil Industry*, pp. 69–70.

7. In mid-1942, no less than 600,000 of these *ignobles saloperies* had been laid across the 80-odd kilometres between the Mediterranean and the Free French defensive position at Bir Hakeim (F. Tondeur, *Libye, Royaume des Sables* (Paris, 1969), p. 120).

8. Kubbah, *Libya*, p. 126.

9. Fuad Kabazi in the Foreword to *Petroleum Development in Libya, 1954 through 1964* (Tripoli, 1965).

10. *Sunday Ghibli*, 15 January 1967. This Tripoli newspaper quoted the figure on several occasions with evident glee.

11. Ibid., 19 February 1967. A long-standing joke was that if Sarir crude was allowed to solidify in the pipeline from the field to the terminal, the result would be the world's longest candle!

12. Ibid., 6 June 1965.

13. Waddams, *Libyan Oil Industry*, p. 102.

14. A. Sampson, *The Seven Sisters* (London, 1980), p. 223.

15. Testimony delivered by Dr Armand Hammer before a Special Subcommittee on Integrated Oil Operations of the Committee on Interior and Insular Affairs,

United States Senate, 93rd Congress, 2nd Session, Washington DC (1974), p. 6.
    16. M.A. Adelman *The World Petroleum Market* (Baltimore, 1972), p. 200.
    17. See Waddams, *Libyan Oil Industry*, p. 113.
    18. S.M. Ghanem, *The Pricing of Libyan Crude Oil* (Valletta, 1975), p. 90.
    19. Ibid., p. 90.
    20. Kubbah, *Libya*, p. 200.
    21. Ghanem, *Pricing of Libyan Crude Oil*, pp. 69–70; see also Waddams, *Libyan Oil Industry*, p. 160.
    22. G.W. Stocking, *Middle East Oil* (London, 1971), p. 375. Waddams (*Libyan Oil Industry* p. 120) calculates that government revenues from these three companies even in 1964 consisted basically of royalty only, or 12.5 per cent of the value at posted prices of production, or about 28 cents/barrel.
    23. Stocking, *Middle East Oil*, p. 377.
    24. Adelman, *World Petroleum Market*, p. 56.
    25. S.H. Schurr, P. Homan, *et al.*, *Middle Eastern Oil and the Western World Prospects and Problems* (New York, 1971), p. 69.
    26. P.R. Odell, *Oil and World Power* (Harmondsworth, 1975), p. 92.
    27. See N. Sarkis, 'Libya Competes on the Oil Market', *New Outlook*, vol. 9 no. 1 (January 1966).
    28. See Waddams, *Libyan Oil Industry*, pp. 177–80.
    29. *Le Figaro*, 17 September 1969.
    30. BBC, *Summary of World Broadcasts*, ME/3293/A/1.
    31. 'The International Oil "Debacle" since 1971', special supplement to *Petroleum Intelligence Weekly* (22 April 1974), p. 3.
    32. J.M. Blair, *The Control of Oil* (New York, 1976), p. 221.
    33. 'What Next in Libya?', *Petroleum Press Service*, vol. XXXVII, no. (August 1970).
    34. *Middle East Economic Digest*, 11 September 1970.
    35. Sampson, *Seven Sisters*, p. 225.
    36. W.J. Levy, 'Oil Power', *Foreign Affairs*, vol. 49, no. 4 (July 1971).
    37. J.E. Akins, 'The Oil Crisis: This Time the Wolf is Here', *Foreign Affairs* vol. 51, no. 3 (April 1973).
    38. *Guardian*, 8 December 1971.
    39. L. Turner, *Oil Companies in the International System* (London, 1978 p. 158.
    40. 'Tough Bargaining in Tripoli', *Petroleum Press Service*, vol. XXXVII no. 4 (April 1971).
    41. For full details of the agreement, see 'Prices for Short-Haul Crudes *Petroleum Press Service*, vol. XXXVIII, no. 5 (May 1971).
    42. Ibid.
    43. Quoted in The *Economist*, 20 February 1971.
    44. A few days after the nationalisation of BP's assets in Libya, the company started the development of its newly discovered Forties Field, the largest in the British Sector of the North Sea. Because North Sea oil is of similar high quality to Libya' Britain almost ceased buying Libyan oil as North Sea production built up in the late 1970s.
    45. The Iranian claim to the islands of Abu Musa and the Greater and Lesse Tumbs was disputed by the rulers of two Trucial States, Sharjah and Ras al-Khaima on the 'Arab' side of the Gulf. The Trucial States (the United Arab Emirates) were st nominally under Britain's military and diplomatic protection until the day after th Iranian seizure.
    46. The value of all assets and installations, after reductions for depreciation; r account is taken of producible oil in the ground.
    47. 'The Slippery Slope in Libya', *Petroleum Press Service*, vol. XXXIX, no. (January 1972).

48. 'This word was coined in order to characterise it as a "moderate" response to the "radical" demand for "nationalisation"; however, both are "confiscation" to a greater or lesser degree'. Special Supplement to *Petroleum Intelligence Weekly* (22 April 1974), p. 29.

49. Shell was only one among several companies that never found any oil in Libya, although by 1972 the company had spent over $100 million on exploration.

50. 'Crisis of Confidence in Libya', *Petroleum Press Service*, vol. XXXIX, no. 8 (August 1972).

51. Adelman, *World Petroleum Market*, Table II.1, p. 48.

52. *Platts Oilgram News Service* (8 November 1965).

53. 'Libya's Five Years of Revolution', *Petroleum Economist*, vol. XLI, no. 10 (October 1974).

54. Special Supplement to *Petroleum Intelligence Weekly* (22 April 1974), p. 34.

55. See 'Libya in Transition', *Petroleum Economist*, vol. XLI, no. 4 (April 1974).

56. 'Libya Trims Prices', *Petroleum Economist*, vol. XLII, no. 8 (August 1975).

57. Ibid.

58. J. Wright, 'Libya: Calm after Stormy Years', *Petroleum Economist*, vol. XLIII, no. 11 (November 1976).

59. *Financial Times*, 11 October 1979. See also Waddams, *Libyan Oil Industry*, pp. 326–7.

60. *OAPEC Bulletin* (January 1980), p. 23.

61. 'Libya's Ambitious Refining Plans', *Petroleum Economist*, vol. XLII, no. 6 (June 1975).

62. Ibid.

63. Ibid.

64. D. Mansfield, 'Libya: Check to Production Buildup', *Petroleum Economist*, vol. XLV, no. 9 (September 1978).

65. See 'Libya's Ambitious Refining Plans'.

66. *Arab Dawn*, no. 57 (February 1980).

67. Ibid.

68. L. Turner and J. Bedore, 'The Trade Politics of Middle East Industralization', *Foreign Affairs*, vol. 57, no. 2 (Winter 1978–9).

69. W.J. Levy, 'The Years that the Locust Hath Eaten: Oil Policy and OPEC Development Prospects', *Foreign Affairs*, vol. 57, no. 2 (Winter 1978–9).

70. *Arab Dawn*, no. 57 (February 1980).

71. *International Petroleum Encyclopaedia* (Tulsa, 1979), p. 195.

72. In trading on the international spot market (where small lots of crude are sold to the highest bidder) in late 1979, top-quality Libyan crude was selling at 50 per cent above official prices (*Financial Times*, 11 October 1979).

73. *Petroleum Economist*, vol. XLVII, no. 8 (August 1980), p. 337.

74. Ibid.

12 ECONOMY AND SOCIETY

The economy, as the new regime found it in 1969, was one of uncommon strengths and weaknesses. Rapidly increasing oil production was generating record revenues of $1,200 million per year — the highest in OPEC, after Venezuela. But, apart from hydrocarbons, all other resources were meagre. The country had few other known minerals (apart from large but remote iron ore deposits in Fezzan), only a partly developed infrastructure, poor soil and fickle climate, and a small and underskilled population, still heavily reliant on foreign labour, expertise, goods and services. The prime economic dilemma of the new leadership was how best to use the wealth from depleting hydrocarbon reserves to overcome the nation's natural and human disadvantages and thus ensure reasonable continuing standards of prosperity and progress when oil and oil revenues were eventually exhausted.

A census of 1979 showed a total population of 3,245,000 — almost triple the 1,088,889 counted in 1954. Over this period the balance of population between Tripolitania (two-thirds), Cyrenaica (30 per cent) and Fezzan (5 per cent) was little changed. With one of the highest growth rates in the world (and the highest of any Arab state in the early 1970s), the population was estimated to have passed 3 million (2.6 million Libyans, the rest foreign workers) in 1978. The population was expected to reach 3.5 million by 1985 and as much as 5.75 million by 2000.[1] Yet, despite heavy migration to Tripoli and Benghazi, in particular, the proportion living in towns was lower than in almost every other Arab country, at an estimated 30.7 per cent in 1980, expected to rise to barely one-third by 1985.[2] In common with many other Third World countries, Libya was a young country; even in 1964, the median age was 19 years, and about 44 per cent of the population was under 15 years old.

In the 1930s, Libyans had provided much of the manual labour for Italian colonial development, while after the Second World War the foreign military bases were the largest employers outside farming. But with the oil boom, and particularly after the revolution, much of the demand for additional labour and expertise of all kinds had to be met by foreigners attracted by high wages. In 1973, skilled Tunisian workers could earn between three and six times more in Libya than at home; a Tunisian plumber could expect to raise his monthly wages some four-and-a-half times after crossing the border.[3]

One drawback in employing so many foreigners was that political tensions and prejudices against particular migrant groups could easily override economic and social necessity and turn 'guest workers' into so many hostages. Thus the flight of some 30,000 Jews in the late 1940s and the expulsion of the Italians in 1970 resulted in severe, if only temporary, shortages of skills. The Egyptians who replaced the Italians (rising to 148,000 by the end of 1975, excluding dependants)[4] in turn came under pressure as a result of political tensions between Cairo and Tripoli in the later 1970s; nearly 40,000 Tunisians officially acknowledged to be in the country were also unfortunate when relations between Tunis and Tripoli deteriorated in 1979–80; even Pakistani workers found themselves in trouble at about the same time.

By 1975, immigrants provided two-fifths of the country's unskilled labour, 27 per cent of skilled and semi-skilled workers, over one-third of its technicians, and 58 per cent of management and supervisory staff.[5] In 1979 there were some 65,000 workers from Western and Eastern Europe, the United States, Turkey, Pakistan and China, among them 15,000 Italians on short-term contracts.[6] Nevertheless, one of the main constraints on economic and social development was a chronic manpower shortage, worsened by conscription and the compulsory military training of men aged 18–35; there were some 40,000 men in the first three drafts of 1979 alone.

Other constraints were due to national geography, climate and the nature of Libyan society. It was found, for instance, that

the large number of unskilled immigrants, especially illegal immigrants whose entry into the labour market is uncontrolled, are displacing Libyans from many positions open to this type of labour in the modern sector . . . the large numbers of non-national migrants have allowed Libyans to move out of productive operations into those which they consider desirable, namely service occupations in the government . . . There are insufficient 'desirable' service posts to absorb all Libyans, however, so as numbers of Libyans shun the undesirable jobs which they relinquish to non-nationals, they are opting out of the modern sector altogether.[7]

Most of Libya is unproductive desert with an average rainfall of less than 50 millimetres/year. About 5 per cent of the total area of 1.7 million square kilometres (680,000 square miles) is judged fit for 'economic use'. The value of wide rangelands in the north varies with the erratic rainfall. Farming is possible on less than 1.5 per cent (2.5 million hectares) of the country's total area, mostly on the coastlands and uplands of northernmost Tripolitania and Cyrenaica, where rainfall averages 200–300 mm per year, rising to 600 mm (about the equivalent of the London average) in favoured parts of the Gebel Akhdar of Cyrenaica. Only about 0.5 per cent of the country is actually under crops. The irrigated area, limited by the availability of groundwater (rapidly depleting in some places) covered only about 120,000 hectares in the 1960s, including all crop lands in the southern oases. Thus almost 90 per cent of the cultivated area was under dry farming, relying on 'erratic and insufficient rainfall' giving generally poor yields.

Because of unreliable climate and rainfall, Libyan farming is particularly unpredictable and the *ghibli*, the hot, dust-laden wind from the Sahara, can be particularly damaging to young crops. Official statistics may record impressive increases in agricultural production over several consecutive years, but these may be as much the result of intermittent favourable conditions as of permanent man-made improvements. In the nineteenth century, the Turkish administration used to take the precaution of anticipating four good years, four mediocre and two drought years every decade.

Little of the country had been explored for minerals by 1980. Apart from oil and natural gas, the most promising of the known mineral resources were the iron-ore deposits near Brak in the Wadi Shatti of western Fezzan. Reserves of high-grade ore were estimated at 3,000 million tons, but their commercial exploitation awaited the building of a 700-kilometre railway from Misurata to Brak.

The general poverty of known resources other than hydrocarbons led back to the inescapable conclusion that agriculture, limited though its potential was, still offered the most promising foundation for long-term national prosperity when the oil and gas 'ran out' although industry also clearly had its own important contribution to make.

Two years of economic stagnation followed the 1969 *coup*. The booming business confidence of the 1960s evaporated overnight in the revolutionary climate of uncertainty. Existing projects and the

start of new ones were delayed while the regime made a full 're-
evaluation of development projects' in progress under, or approved
by, the old regime.

After 30 months' reliance on *ad hoc* planning, the government in
1972 announced a three-year (1973–5) economic and social development plan for the spending of about $6,000 million. By far the
largest allocations — well over one-fifth of the whole — were to
agricultural development and reform, with the main object of
reaching self-sufficiency in basic foodstuffs. The *Middle East Economic Digest* later considered the plan to have been 'remarkably
successful'.[8]

In March 1976 the government began a $23,750 million five-year
(1976–80) social and economic development plan envisaging annual
average increases of over 10 per cent in the gross national product, 25
per cent in industrial output and — probably the most ambitious
target of all — near self-sufficiency in food output by 1980. Again,
the largest allocations — almost one-sixth of the total — were for
agriculture. The plan was later revised to a total of $30,525 million,
with proportionately rather more of the extra investment going to
industry than to agriculture. The plan was 'designed to meet most
perceived needs simultaneously — in agriculture, industry, utilities,
transport, communications, as well as social services'.[9] In January
1980 the Ministers of Oil and Economy and three others were
replaced, apparently because of failure to complete the plan in full;
only about three-quarters of the allocated funds were eventually
spent because of labour, infrastructure, bureaucratic and other restraints; it was a gesture typical of the emphasis on spending as an
indicator of 'progress'.

Announcement of the plan in 1975 had coincided with serious
international speculation about Libyan liquidity difficulties, resulting basically from overspending on defence and foreign aid and
inability to sell enough oil on the then depressed world market.
According to the International Monetary Fund, the balance of trade,
services and transport fell from a surplus of $1,831 million in 1974
to a deficit of $480 million in 1975. But liquidity was no embarrass-
ment so long as the country was able to produce and sell at least 1.5
million barrels of high-quality oil daily. In January 1981 the General
People's Congress approved a $62,500 million five-year (1981–5)
development plan that foresaw a 15 per cent decline in oil production
and in the contribution of oil revenues to the economy, with corresponding increases in agricultural and industrial output. The declared

object was a husbanding of resources to a level that would only
satisfy the financing of local projects.

During the 1970s, the state gradually tightened its control over the
economy. At first, only such obvious targets for 'Libyanisation' and
nationalisation as foreign shareholdings in banks (mainly British
and Italian) and foreign insurance companies were affected. The
local oil products' distribution networks of Shell, Esso and AGIP
were nationalised in 1970. The state in due course acquired its
majority share in oil production, while new ventures in oil refining,
petrochemicals and oil transport were undertaken by the state in
close partnership with foreign companies working under 'turnkey'
contracts. Even under the monarchy, the state had been obliged to
play the role of industrial pioneer because the private sector preferred to invest in real estate, trade or the service industries rather
than in unfamiliar risk ventures. Under the revolutionary regime
state enterprise became almost synonymous with new industrial
undertakings, for in April 1971 Colonel Gadafi had declared that 'a
socialist society like ours does not tolerate one person being pro-
prietor of a company'.

Although individual farmers remained the backbone of the
regime's agricultural policies, state control and supervision of agriculture inevitably increased, and particularly when the large land
reclamation and settlement schemes were started. In 1971 the Agriculture Minister announced that the government would put on trial
any farmer who had failed to exploit his land 'and would withdraw
this land from him to exploit it in the people's interest'.[10]

Until the later 1970s, Libya had a mixed economy, with the private
sector still particularly active in wholesale and retail trade; nevertheless, the state first made business difficult for the larger traders by
taking over the import and distribution of certain basic commodities. Then, in his revolution anniversary speech of September 1978
Colonel Gadafi voiced one of the precepts of *The Green Book*, that
there should be no employees, only partners in business as part of the
new policy of putting self-management worker committees in charge
of public and private enterprises. Workers, urged by him to 'abolish
the bureaucracy of the public sector and the dictatorship of the
private sector', rushed to take over nearly 200 companies, with
inevitable economic confusion and disruption of output. Although
the measure applied in theory to all enterprises with more than five
employees, the key sectors of oil, banking and insurance were in
practice untouched. The exercise of 'people's power' also began

transform wholesale and retail trade into a state operation; importers and traders were put out of business, conventional shops were closed, and even the merchants of the traditional city centre *suqs* (markets) were unable to trade. Libyans were obliged to do nearly all their shopping at large state-run 'people's supermarkets', intended to eliminate 'exploitation' by private-sector traders supposedly concerned only with profit-making. Although their subsidised prices were generally lower than in other retail outlets, the state supermarkets reportedly suffered from intermittent gluts and shortages of goods.[11] Besides, 'much of the spice and fun of life in an Arab country which, after all, has traditionally been centred round buying and selling, has been removed'.[12] Private commerce was due to be fully abolished by the end of 1981.

By 1980 the exercise of 'people's power' was still well applauded by a majority who saw how greatly their once-wretched standards of living had improved, and were still improving. But a regime that seemed to have earned the approval of the majority by the dispossession of an enterprising minority had also created a hard core of embittered economic opponents, among them traders and shopkeepers who had been put out of business and whose resentments echoed those of property-owners who had been dispossessed by laws limiting ownership to the family home. By 1980, Eastern Europe seemed to be a closer model for the economy than Sweden, and the *laissez-faire* capitalism that had been tolerated, if not encouraged, up to the late 1970s quickly came to an end.

In classical times, parts of Libya were considered rich farming country,[13] and they certainly appeared so to desert Arab invaders of the seventh and eleventh centuries. Even in the twentieth century, the Italians believed the agricultural potential to be worth developing; and the revolutionary regime, like the monarchy before it, still acknowledged agriculture as the basis of a viable future economy without oil.

Accordingly, agriculture has consistently been awarded more development funds than any other economic sector. The state spent some $6,000 million in the first eleven years of the revolution on improving naturally poor farming conditions. Leaving aside spending by the Italian state or private individuals up to about 1960, or by the kingdom up to 1969, this works out at an average of LD 200 for every hectare (about $250 per acre) of agriculturally viable land. This did not include private farming investment, encouraged by interest-free loans through the Agricultural Bank.

In May 1973 plans were announced for the ten-year development of four farming areas totalling about half a million hectares — the Gefara Plain, south of Tripoli (350,000 hectares); the fertile Barce–Tocra plain in northern Cyrenaica (30,000 hectares); five areas totalling 77,000 hectares in the *wadis* of Fezzan (to be irrigated from a water table at 80 metres' depth); and the most ambitious schemes of all, at Kufra and Sarir in south-eastern Cyrenaica (50,000 hectares).

The Kufra project epitomised the difficulties of building a viable farming economy. Under its original concession offer in 1965, Occidental Petroleum had undertaken to devote 5 per cent of its Libyan profits to the agricultural development of Kufra oasis. The result of this pledge was the discovery of vast reserves of fossil water graphically, but not particularly accurately, described at the time as 'equal to the flow of the River Nile for 200 years'. This water was the basis of the Kufra Production Project for raising fodder (alfalfa in particular) on irrigated desert land to fatten sheep for the home market. Circles of land, each of 100 hectares, were watered by giant sprinklers, 560 metres long, slowly driven round a central pivot by electric power. The project was working by 1973, and the political leadership was so enthusiastic that it wanted to raise the irrigated area from the initially planned 10,000 hectares to 50,000. But after the first full year of use, there was sudden alarm over the apparent rapid depletion of the groundwater resources on which the whole scheme depended,[14] and Kufra fell from official favour. Nevertheless, with confidence in the water supply restored, some 100,000 head of sheep were being raised by 1975, compared with the original target of 250,000. Veterinary, harvesting and technical difficulties then caused a change in plan, and wheat became the main crop, covering 5,000 out of the 6,000 hectares sown in 1978–9. But yields, at 2.5 tons/hectare, were only half what they should have been.[15] As one observer wrote:

The economics of the Kufra Production Project remain unreal. Even if the scheme were producing 20,000 tons of wheat per year and the highly subsidised price of LD 150 per ton were realised, the LD 3 million per year would not cover the running costs of the scheme, never mind the capital outlays already made and those which continue . . . The Production project can only be regarded as a means of providing management experience for a group of young Libyan agriculturalists. Such expertise is certainly essential if the substantial high quality groundwater resources of southern Libya are to be utilised in the future.[16]

'Inescapably expensive' and 'horrendous' transport costs were one of the main economic constraints on the whole project. They added greatly to the price of all materials, supplies and equipment transported 1,000 kilometres southwards from Benghazi (over half by unmade track) and similarly to the price of livestock or crops sent to market in the north.[17]

The neighbouring Kufra Settlement Project envisaged the establishment of 800 irrigated farms of 6.5 hectares each, worked by settlers from Kufra and other southern oases. It was a project with as many social implications for the country's future as agricultural and economic ones, since all such developments ultimately depended on the ability of the state to persuade the necessary manpower — from soil and water specialists to unskilled hands — to continue to live and work on the land, often in extremely remote and relatively uncongenial surroundings. But the Kufra Production Project, at least, depended on immigrant labour, mainly from Sudan, for the handling and sheering of livestock.[18]

Another scheme with considerable potential was started under American supervision at Maknoussa, some 250 kilometres south-west of Sebha, in 1978, with 60 irrigated circles of 40 hectares each. Crop yields of at least 5.5 tons/hectare were reported and, significantly, the whole scheme was designed for full mechanisation to save manpower.

While agricultural development in the far south suffered from high transport costs and difficulties in attracting and keeping labour, in the north there were problems of land division and the depletion of groundwater levels (by as much as one metre/year in some places) and even infiltration of seawater; depletion was particularly serious in the country's main agricultural zone around Tripoli. One critic found that 'the revolutionary government has repeated the mistakes of the 1960s by increasing investment in agriculture which accelerated the misuse of irreplaceable resources'.[19]

In the nineteenth century Turkish Libya managed (except in years of severe drought) to provide its population of less than one million with what, by the standards of the time and place, was enough to eat from its own resources, and also export a surplus of livestock. By 1977, Libyan farming was providing only 14 per cent[20] of the diet of a population three times larger than a century before, and one with greatly enhanced standards and expectations. Like its predecessors, the revolutionary government saw its only course as the provision of abundant funds to make good natural agricultural deficiencies, to achieve self-sufficiency in food (although imports were certainly cheaper), and to halt the drift from the land. Employment in farming clearly responded to official encouragement, increasing from 129,000 in 1973 to an estimate of just under 158,000 in 1980.[21] In the 1970s, government funds were used to experiment, to assess the potential of soil and water resources, and to build up the administrative and technical expertise needed to sustain often complex agricultural schemes, some of them combining advanced equipment and techniques with inadequate natural and human resources. By 1980, it was still not clear whether the economic and social benefits expected from costly agricultural development would indeed be achieved, or to what extent agricultural output would be sustained without massive continuing injections of public funds.

New desert farming schemes were intended to create a total of 4,600 new farms, involving the settlement of perhaps some 46,000 people — less than 10 per cent, in fact, of the estimated increase of half a million in the rural population between 1977 and 1985. Nevertheless, this was a useful contribution to the policy of encouraging whole families to remain on the land, or return to it to ease the pressure of population growth on the coastal towns, and particularly Tripoli and Benghazi.[22] Many Libyans, in the meantime, remained outside the modern sector, living in their traditional and often isolated communities, still practising an inefficient subsistence agriculture, and largely cut off from the rest of the nation's rapid economic and social transformation.

At the end of the 1960s, there was still remarkably little industry, partly because private capital had generally sought larger and easier profits in trade, real estate, building and the service industries, leaving the state to play the role of industrial pioneer. The main 'industries' before the revolution consisted of food, drink and tobacco processing and packaging plants, and small factories producing cement, paint and other materials for a construction boom still very largely supplied from abroad.

The revolutionary regime's three-year (1973–5) development plan allocated some 15 per cent of investments to industry, and two state organisations to co-ordinate industrial planning and development were set up. Under the five-year plan (1976–80), industrial output was supposed to grow by 25 per cent each year, and industry and mineral resources accordingly received 13 per cent of total allocations. The results were to be seen in a startling array of new factories, none of them particularly large, for the most part processing local produce, manufacturing textiles, clothes and shoes, and providing materials for the building and construction industries. Between 1973 and 1980, employment in manufacturing industry doubled from 26,000 (4.8 per cent of the labour force) to an estimate of nearly 56,000 (6 per cent).[23] Very much more ambitious projects envisaged the manufacture of electrical equipment and the assembly of farm tractors and other vehicles.

On an altogether larger scale than any other industrial development outside the oil and gas industries were the $900 million aluminium smelter built by Yugoslav expertise at Zuara, and the projected iron and steel plant at Misurata, forming a basis for heavy industry. Planned output at Misurata for 1985 was 580,000 tons of flat steel and 670,000 tons of long products (notably reinforcing bars for the building industry); output was planned to rise to a total of 7 million tons/year by 2005. Work started in 1977, with costs estimated at $1,000 million, and with the same amount to be spent on associated port, infrastructure and housing developments at Misurata, where the population was to double to 180,000 by 2005. Initially processing imported iron pellets, the plant was later to use iron ore supplied by rail from the large Wadi Shatti deposits in western Fezzan; energy was to be supplied by natural gas piped from the Sirtica, some 400 kilometres away.[24]

As with the oil-refining and petrochemical industries, it was not clear where all the steel industry's large planned output was to be used. Even allowing for big increases in manufacturing and assembly, local demand for steel seemed unlikely to match projected output, while exports faced the same difficulties as those of refined products and petrochemicals, with the likely additional drawbacks of indifferent quality and high price.

Despite notable increases in the production of a limited range of goods and materials, industry by 1980 could hardly be considered a catalyst generating further economic development, and its percentage contribution to gross national product remained almost the lowest in the Arab world. There was little interdependence in manufacturing; each small plant was generally a self-supporting unit, usually built and equipped at high cost on a 'turnkey' basis by foreign contractors. Each plant relied on capital-intensive technology demanding expensive and skilled maintenance, thus creating work for highly qualified expatriate management and supervisory staff but few, if any, jobs developing basic industrial skills. While this was particularly the case in the refining and petrochemical industries, it was also often true of other manufacturing processes not specifically calling for a high degree of technology.

There were, in short, no signs of the beginnings of a Libyan technological revolution, but many individual examples of continuing ability to buy in complete packages of foreign technology, forming islands of extreme modernity in a sea of technological backwardness. Although such shortcomings were not peculiar to Libya, they seemed to be exaggerated by the ability to use oil revenues almost too freely to import whatever local skills were unable to provide (in practice, almost everything), by the uncommon shortages of technical, managerial and basic industrial skills, and by the lack of infrastructure, despite the past efforts of the Italians and the royalist and revolutionary regimes.

Official recognition of the importance of providing the necessary infrastructure to support planned economic and social developments was reflected in the scale of allocations to transport, communications and electric-power generation. In combination, these sectors had the highest allocations in the three-year (1973–5) plan and the second-largest in the five-year (1976–80) plan. A 15-year programme for the development of electric power envisaged a tenfold increase in output between 1970 and 1985 (from 70 to 700 MW), generated by conventional power plants and by nuclear installations supplied by France and the Soviet Union. Among the other main infrastructural developments were roads (1,600 kilometres), ports and airports; planning of ambitious national and international railway links was also started.

At the end of the Second World War, Libyans had an average income *per capita* of around $35 per annum; the corresponding figure in 1970 was $2,168 and in 1979 $9,827.[25] By the late 1970s, gross domestic product was increasing at 11 per cent per year (1 per cent more than the official target). A favourable trade balance of $2,900 million in 1977 was for all practical purposes generated by oil and gas exports: the days when hides, skins, battle scrap and peanuts made essential contributions to the balance of payments were long past.

Since its nationalisation and 'Libyanisation' in December 1969, the banking system had been much reorganised, with five commercial banks (largely concentrating on the private sector), two specialised loan banks and one foreign-investment and trade bank. The commercial banks' operations were restricted by a small clientele, a very small capital market and, from 1977–8 on, by the unusual political and business climate. As a result, the banking system was judged to be 'a repository of surplus funds rather than an active financial intermediary'.[26] The specialised Agricultural Bank and the Industrial and Real Estate Bank acted mainly as channels for state investment and interest-free loans for farm development and small-scale industrial undertakings. A Real Estate Investment and Savings Bank was set up early in 1981 to make interest-free housing loans to poorer families.

After its establishment in 1972, the Libyan Arab Foreign Bank (LAFB) quickly became one of the most active and successful Arab financial institutions, with a turnover approaching $2,600 million in 1977. It set up several joint banks, particularly in the Middle East and Africa, and in its first five years of operation it underwrote about one hundred syndicated loans and other bond issues worth over $6,000 million. In December 1976, LAFB bought a 9.5 per cent share in Fiat of Italy, as part of a $415 million investment arrangement. Libya thus became the first Arab country to invest large sums in Italian industry, and LAFB, in addition, acquired a stake in the para-statal Ente Nazionale Idrocarburi (ENI). There were also large Libyan investments in real estate in Malta, Sicily, Italy and particularly on the strategically placed Italian island of Pantelleria in the central Mediterranean.

The Central Bank set up in Tripoli in 1955 with an authorised capital of $2.8 million was the country's most important financial institution, with responsibility for investing 'massive and growing' foreign-exchange reserves. 'At $6,624 million in January 1980, total reserves, minus the value of gold holdings, were smaller only than those of Saudi Arabia, Iran and Iraq among Middle East oil producers, and considerably more than the reserves held by some of the smaller European countries.'[27] The fact that Libyan banks had no branches abroad, and foreign banks (with one Yugoslav exception) no operations in Libya, limited the ability of the banking system to handle revenues and to organise domestic spending. Confidence in the banking system was further undermined when the currency was reformed in 1980 with only one week allowed for exchange of strictly limited sums of old money for new.

Libya left the Sterling Area following the BP nationalisation in December 1971 and the subsequent withdrawal of Libyan Sterling balances in London. In September 1971 the Libyan Pound, in use since independence, was replaced by the 'Arab'[28] Dinar pegged to the value of the US Dollar.

A government study shortly after the 1969 *coup* showed that more than 150,000 families urgently needed proper housing. The former regime's 'Idris Housing Scheme' for the building of 100,000 extraordinarily expensive houses over five years was, with some justification, condemned by the new regime as 'futile'[29] and many of its houses were later demolished as substandard. The official target of providing every family with a decent home by the mid-1980s was 'a not inconsiderable objective, considering that it was also estimated that new growth, slum clearance and replacement meant that 438,000 houses would be needed from 1975 to 1985'.[30] Despite increased state involvement in the housing programme after 1970, the private sector still expected to contribute nearly one-third of completions.[31] In fact, private-property investment seemed so secure, especially when so few other outlets were open, that private-sector building exceeded its planned targets (at least until the new property-ownership laws went into force in 1978), while the public sector failed to reach them. The visible results of post-1969 housing policy were genuinely impressive, with estates of adequately equipped dwellings replacing the festering shanty towns of Tripoli and Benghazi and spreading outwards for many kilometres across former groves and fields. By 1973, Tripoli had a population of over half a million.

Even in the 1960s, Libya was becoming a model welfare state. Well before the revolution there was a system of free medical care and old-age and sickness benefits. The school population doubled between 1960 and 1968, and just before the revolution one Libyan in every six was a full-time pupil, with over a quarter of a million children enrolled in a thousand state and private schools. In 1973 the government, building on the basic achievements of the former regime, and with the advantages of much larger oil revenues, passed a new social-security law providing comprehensive welfare for all citizens within reach of its benefits.

According to United Nations statistics,[32] nearly one Libyan in every four was by 1975 in full-time education. Girls, who had in the past been discouraged from school-going by social pressures and taboos, in 1975 made up 43 per cent of a total enrolment of 734,000, although their numbers were markedly higher in primary education (46 per cent out of a total of 556,000) than at secondary level (33 per cent of 166,000) and university (only 17 per cent of 12,000). By the 1980/1 academic year, according to government statistics,[33] there were to be nearly 870,000 students at all levels. And at primary level, at least, half the pupils were to be girls. As long ago as 1965 the government had announced a 15-year programme for the eradication of illiteracy; over three-quarters of the population were still illiterate in 1971,[34] but the government nevertheless proposed to achieve full literacy by 1980.

By the late 1970s Libyans were among the healthiest people in Africa, and all epidemic and endemic diseases were claimed to have been eradicated. Health had been much improved simply by better, subsidised eating, and by better understanding of the basic rules of diet and hygiene. Medical care was free, and such indicators as the ratio of hospital beds to population (five per thousand, rising to a planned seven per thousand in 1980) and physicians (one to 1,124 patients in 1975, rising to one per thousand in 1980)[35] were approaching European and North American standards.

While there was official commitment to the achievement of a full welfare state by or soon after 1980, there had been impressive advances in the social services before then, reflecting official policy of using a fair proportion of oil revenues to better the lives of people who had, for the most part, lived at bare subsistence level until the very recent past.

A large oil production generating enormous revenues and financial reserves brought prosperity to most Libyans in the 1970s. Even with the least government goodwill and competence this would have been almost inevitable, since the people sharing in the new-found national wealth were so few. But whether the same degree of prosperity would be sustained when oil exports ceased, probably early in the twenty-first century, largely depended on the nation's ability to use the short, extraordinary opportunity of oil wealth — perhaps a total span as short as 50 years — to raise poor natural and human resources to unprecedented levels of economic productivity. By 1980, only an estimated 30 years of the Libyan oil era remained, and the adequacy of the available oil and all other resources for the challenge continued to be a matter for conjecture by observers of Libyan economic and social progress.

Notes

1. H. Roberts, *An Urban Profile of the Middle East* (London, 1979), Table 4.9, pp. 80–1.

2. Ibid., Table 4.3, p. 68. (Official Libyan figures tend to give total populations in the administrative districts of Tripoli, Benghazi, etc., rather than in the towns themselves.)

3. Bouhdiba, 'Arab Migrations' in R. Aliboni (ed.), *Arab Industrialisation and Economic Integration* (London, 1979), Table 3.23, p. 168.

4. J.S. Birks and C.A. Sinclair, *Arab Manpower* (London, 1980), Table 6.15, p. 136.

5. Ibid., Table 6.14, p. 135.

6. In addition to 13,000–15,000 Italians, there were 5,000 each from Britain, Greece, Yugoslavia and Pakistan; 3,000 each from the USA, Rumania and Malta; 2,500 from France; 1,600 from Cyprus; and a total of 10,000 from the USSR, East Germany and China (R. Allen, 'Qaddafi's Libya Ten Years On', *Middle East Economic Digest*, vol. 23, no. 35 (31 August 1979).

7. Birks and Sinclair, *Arab Manpower*, p. 137.

8. *Middle East Economic Digest* (21 December 1979). But 'in reporting the results of the three-year plan, people tended to equate expenditure with implementation' (O.I. El Fathaly and M. Palmer, *Political Development and Social Change in Libya* (Lexington, Mass., 1980), p. 123).

9. Morgan, 'Manpower Problems Hurt Libya's Growth prospects', *Financial Times*, 20 February 1980.

10. BBC, *Summary of World Broadcasts*, ME/3636/A/10.

11. Hirst, 'Gadafy's New Off-the-Shelf Revolution', *Guardian*, 31 August 1979.

12. Patrick Seale on 'The World Today — Libya', BBC *World Service*, 1 May 1980.

13. The Greek poet Pindar called Libya 'rich in flocks', while the remains of Roman oil presses are common in the Tripolitanian uplands.

14. J.A. Allan, 'The End of the First Phase at Kufrah: Expectations and Achievements', *Society for Libyan Studies, Sixth Annual Report 1974–75* (London, 1975).

15. J.A. Allan, 'Managing Agricultural Resources in Libya: Recent Experience', *Libyan Studies. Tenth Annual Report of the Society for Libyan Studies (1978–79)* (London, 1979).

16. Ibid; see also J.A. Allan, 'Libyan Agriculture since Oil: Problems and Achievements', *Maghreb Review*, no. 1 (June–July 1976).

17. In 1970, the charge for a 10-ton lorry journey Benghazi–Kufra–Benghazi was LD 450 (*Financial Times*, 26 August 1970). By 1975, the charge was LD 700, and by 1978 LD 1,000 (Allan, 'Managing Agricultural Resources in Libya').

18. J.A. Allan and K.S. McLachlan, 'Agricultural Development in Libya after Oil', *African Affairs*, vol. 75, no. 300 (July 1976).

19. J.A. Allan, *Libya: The Experience of Oil* (London, 1981), p. 99.

20. 'MEED Special Report: Libya', *Middle East Economic Digest* (18 February 1977).

21. J.S. Birks and C.A. Sinclair, 'The Libyan Arab Jamahiriyah: Labour Migration Sustains Dualistic Development', *Maghreb Review*, vol. 4, no. 3 (May–June 1979); *Arab Manpower*, Table 6.10, p. 132.

22. Roberts, *Urban Profile of the Middle East*, pp. 100–1.

23. Birks and Sinclair, *Arab Manpower*, Table 6.10, p. 132.

24. Lycett, 'Libya Aims at Steel Top Ten', *The Middle East* (October 1979) Szwed-Cousins, 'Misurata, Libya's City of Steel', *Eight Days* (7 March 1981).

25. *Middle East Economic Digest*, 31 August 1979.

26. O'Sullivan, 'Local, International Banking Gap Widens in Libya', *MEED*

Special Report: Arab Banking, *Middle East Economic Digest* (May 1980).

27. Ibid.

28. The change was presumably made because 'pound' smacked of Western economic influence; the Arabic word *dinar* derives directly from the Latin *denarius*.

29. *Libyan Mail*, 25 January 1970.

30. Roberts, *Urban Profile of the Middle East*, p. 98.

31. Ibid., pp. 98–9.

32. United Nations, Department of Economic and Social Affairs, *Statistical Yearbook 1976* (New York, 1977).

33. SPLAJ, *Facts and Figures* (Department of Information and Cultural Affairs, 1978), p. 85–90.

34. BBC, *Summary of World Broadcasts*, ME/W706/A1/3.

35. *Facts and Figures*, p. 97.

POSTSCRIPT

By 1980 Colonel Gadafi and his close associates were clearly concerned about opposition at home and abroad. Claims to have achieved the true exercise of 'people's power' were, after all, open to question if critics were still to be heard, at home and more especially abroad, carping on the sidelines instead of taking part in a great political experiment of supposed universal appeal and 'relevance'.

Yet it was not possible to assess the extent of opposition inside and outside the country. An organisation in Cairo calling itself 'The Revolutionary Council of the Prophet of God' announced in January 1979 that Gadafi and other leaders had been sentenced to death, and accused Gadafi of 'mishandling the country's funds' through buying obsolete and defective arms from the Soviet Union.[1] The Libyan Democratic Movement, in a statement issued in February 1980, accused Gadafi of 'intellectual terrorism'.[2] This organisation of 'moderate' exiled politicians, intellectuals and army officers was said to be active in various Arab and European capitals, and claimed in 1980 to be forming cells in Libya itself 'to prepare a popular uprising'.

The extent of the regime's concern about these signs of external opposition, and perhaps more diffuse non-cooperation (rather than active dissidence) at home, was disclosed in February 1980. A meeting of 'revolutionary committees' at Gar Yunis University, Benghazi, called for the 'physical liquidation' of opponents of the revolution abroad, as well as 'elements obstructing revolutionary change' at home. The result was a twofold assault on what were considered as domestic and foreign sources of opposition. Exiles were subjected to a campaign of assassination, a total of nine[3] being killed in Western capitals and Beirut. In April, Colonel Gadafi gave a 'final warning' to what he termed survivors of the previous regime living abroad to return home immediately or be liquidated — a warning that few, if any, exiles actually heeded.

But the campaign was called off by Gadafi in June, probably in recognition of the harm it was doing to Libya's international standing. In the course of a speech at the Ras Lanuf oil terminal on 11 June, he declared that 'the revolutionary committees have confirmed that the arm of the revolution is long and strong and that it can reach any place in the world to strike at the enemies of the revolution'.[4] He then called on the 'revolutionary committees' to stop the killings, except of those convicted by a revolutionary court, or 'those who have dealings with the Egyptian, the Israeli or the United States authorities'.[5] Nevertheless, revolutionary committees meeting in March 1981 reasserted their determination 'to continue the physical liquidation of the enemies of the people's authority at home and abroad'.

In Libya itself, up to 2,000 people had been arrested in the early months of 1980 in an anti-corruption campaign officially described as directed against those who had profited unduly from national development *after* the revolution. Those arrested, and facing genuine corruption charges punishable since 1979 by death, included senior bureaucrats and bankers, as well as army officers. But when in March students were also arrested for televised trial before 'revolutionary committees' and a 'Revolutionary Court' set up by the same committees, it began to seem that charges of 'corruption' were being used to clamp down on incipient domestic political opposition.

In May 1980, officials of the London-based human rights organisation, Amnesty International, expressed concern at what they termed 'an alarming change in the pattern of human rights violations in Libya'.[6] The organisation noted that 'several people' were reported to have died in custody after being imprisoned in connection with political or economic offences. Among them was the co-founder of the Baath movement in Libya, Amr Taher Deghayes, who, according to Amnesty International, died within three days of his arrest in February 1980.[7] In February 1981 it was announced that the Revolutionary Court had passed sentences on 'civilian, military, fascist, dictatorial, negative, parasitical, non-productive, cowardly, manipulating, intemperate, favour-seeking, bureaucratic and bourgeois elements which patronise the power of the revolution and the authority of the people'.[8]

There was undeniable opposition to Gadafi and the regime inside and outside Libya, and considerable discontent on account of certain political, economic and social policies (especially measures affecting personal property and savings). In March 1981 an exiled Libyan diplomat claimed that there were about 50,000 Libyans outside the country 'who comprise the Libyan opposition abroad' and who were 'determined to use all available means' to overthrow

Gadafi's regime.[9] But Gadafi still seemed to have the uncritical favour of the majority, despite his official resignation of all official positions in 1979, by which he had relieved himself of all formal executive responsibilities. His role as revolutionary 'thinker and leader' was popularly seen in an almost mystical light, and marchers protesting in Tripoli in April 1980 against 'the enemies of the people', asserted 'We promise that we are always with him in body and spirit . . . Moammar Gadafi is the Libyan people.'[10] Moreover, there was evidence that constant exposure to more than ten years of Gadafi's ideas had taught the nation's youth to share his way of thinking.

But, as with the forces of opposition, it was impossible to judge the true strength of popular support for a regime that had never put itself to the test of any election or referendum, and whose overthrow would doubtless be greeted with the apparently genuine popular enthusiasm common on such occasions. Intermittent reports of 'troubles' in various parts of the country were too vague to be taken as reliable indicators of discontent, although an army revolt in Tobruk in mid-1980 was considered particularly serious. The nature and function of 'revolutionary committees' remained ambiguous, but they were assumed to act as political guardians and enthusiasts. The committees were still able to organise large, frequent and 'spontaneous' demonstrations — but then, since the start of the revolution, the Libyan people had spent an extraordinary amount of time and had covered great distances in popular demonstrations and marches. (By ordering the clearing of blocks of buildings in the centre of Tripoli, including a mosque that mysteriously 'fell down' one night, Gadafi had created out of two adjoining *piazzas* a 'Green Square' for public meetings and rallies several times larger than the spaces even Mussolini or Balbo had needed for their public ceremonies in the late 1930s.)

For the fact remained that, however he might transfer power to the people, resign his official positions and try to act as an ordinary citizen (claiming as he did in 1980 that 'the authority of the people is now well established'), Gadafi continued to hold the political limelight. The hastily executed Libyan revolution, for all its vaunted dissemination of power, continued to be coloured by 'Brother Colonel's' distinctive thinking and ultimate exercise of authority, even if at times the revolutionary committees did seem to be beyond his control. Posters displaying the Colonel in many glamorous guises and reminding the people of his distilled wisdom were far too common for his self-effacement to be credible.

The four original members of the RCC ('four old soldiers in control', *The Times* called them), who were still with him and were understood to command key positions in military and national security,[11] had tended to fade into the background since the declaration of people's authority, but their ultimate powers were believed to be as great as ever they had been. For in the final analysis the most immediate threat to the regime did not come from exiled dissidents, nor from disorganised domestic opponents or disaffected students, businessmen, lawyers and intellectuals, but from the armed forces — and, above all, the army. Having himself used the army to make his own *coup*, and then to sustain his revolution, 'in the name of the people', Gadafi was more aware than most of the danger of another officer following his example; he had always appreciated the importance of keeping the support of the Free Unionist Officers in particular and the officer corps in general. Army officers accordingly lived especially well in revolutionary Libya, with peculiar privileges. The army, in common with key sectors of the economy, remained outside the control of popular committees. Like the oil industry, the army kept its traditional hierarchical structure, while lavish spending on arms could be seen in part as a device to keep the military contented and assured of its own importance. While opposition within the armed forces to Gadafi's ideology led to the arrest and execution of officers in 1977, the fact that Gadafi was able to take — for Libya — such extreme action suggests a confidence in the basic loyalty of the armed forces that was again tested, and again found fundamentally sound, by the fiasco of the intervention in Uganda early in 1979.

In September 1979, Gadafi plainly had enough confidence in the loyalty of the army to announce plans for the formation of revolutionary committees in the armed forces to enable the 'state of the armed people' to evolve. At the same time, he proposed 'raising the people's capability so as to put it on a par with that of the regular forces' through general military training. Nevertheless, plans for 'revolutionising' the armed forces seem, in practice, to have been followed with extreme caution, given the previous hostility to any attempts to integrate them into national 'popular' and 'revolutionary' processes. For while other sources of opposition — students, lawyers, businessmen and intellectuals — had failed in their various attempts to defy the progress of Gadafi's revolution, and even the clergy were apparently bowing to strong pressure to conform, the prospects of defiance within the armed forces seemed too serious for the imposition of 'revolutionary' trappings to be pursued in the face of the hostility of the officer corps.

After more than ten years in power, a politically and physically more substantial Moammar Gadafi appeared in 1980 almost as a fixture and as an assurance of at least Libyan stability in an unstable Arab world. This advocate of revolution and political and social furore appeared to have contrived a means by which Libyans could absorb increasing oil revenues without experiencing the worst political and social disruptions of Iran during the late 1970s and early 1980s, or the political and social disintegration that seemed to threaten some other oil states unable to digest the inflow of wealth generated by continuing oil price rises. Unless the clergy or the army opposed him, Colonel Gadafi seemed to be on the way to contriving a workable, if imperfect, model for Libya's peaceable transition from a 'backward' pastoral-nomadic society into an incipiently industrialised one, all in the space of one generation. Had he confined his ideology and his oil wealth to Libya's domestic affairs, his efforts might have earned more approval from a world community deeply suspicious of his international pretensions.

By 1981 Gadafi and his remaining close associates were no longer the idealistic young officers of 1969 who had planned to put the world to rights. Lined with more than a decade of cares and responsibilities, but still with the eyes of a visionary, Gadafi as he approached the age of 40 was a depressive who sought the solace and inspiration of the desert (where the maintenance of his 'simple life' called for considerable expense and organisation), when his alien urban surroundings overwhelmed him. As the first paramount and truly independent Libyan leader of the Libyan people (Idris had been too bound to the West ever to be considered truly 'independent'), Gadafi himself reflected many of the Libyan characteristics — fundamental simplicity, dignity and egalitarianism, dour puritanism and introverted xenophobia, extreme narrowness of cultural, historical and political experience. For Libyan history is a record both of the repeated rejection and dissolution of alien, largely urban civilisations and of the largely unremarked, perennial survival of the immemorial figure of the Berber or Arab desert nomad. Gadafi himself, with his peculiar visions and limitations, epitomised the Libyan nomad, once again emerged from the desert to claim and dominate a land where so many alien civilisations have foundered.

Notes

1. BBC, *Summary of World Broadcasts*, ME/6011/A/1.
2. Ibid., ME/6340/A/1.
3. Four in Rome, two in London, and one each in Bonn, Athens and Beirut.
4. BBC, *Summary of World Broadcasts*, ME/64444/A/9.
5. Ibid.
6. *The Times*, 29 May 1980.
7. His death was alleged to have resulted in a large anti-government demonstration that led to the arrest of other known Baathists. Deghayes had been in trouble with the former regime, and had been arrested at the time of the 'cultural revolution' as well. Amnesty International was also particularly concerned about 18 journalists and writers arrested in Benghazi in 1978 on charges of belonging to a Marxist organisation.
8. *Jamahiriyah Arab News Agency*, 18 February 1981.
9. BBC, *Summary of World Broadcasts* ME/6664/A/1.
10. BBC, *Summary of World Broadcasts*, ME/6391/A/1.
11. See *The Times*, 25 April 1980. Abd-al-Salam Jallud was thought to retain overall responsibility for internal order; Mustafa Kharubi was believed to control the intelligence network; Abu Bakr Yunis Jabir remained Commander-in-Chief of the armed forces; Khuwaildi Hamidi was head of the popular militia.

BIBLIOGRAPHY: MAIN SOURCES CONSULTED

Books

Adelman, M.A. *The World Petroleum Market* (The Johns Hopkins University Press, Baltimore and London, 1972)

Aliboni, Roberto (ed.) *Arab Industrialisation and Economic Integration* (Croom Helm, London, 1979)

Allan, J.A. *Libya: The Experience of Oil* (Croom Helm, London, 1981)

Ananaba, Wogu. *The Trade Union Movement in Africa: Promise and Performance* (C. Hurst and Co., London, 1979)

Arsharuni, N.A. *Liviya* (Izdatyelstvo 'Mysl', Moscow, 1965)

—— *Inostranniy Kapital v Livii (1911–1967)* (Izdatyelstvo 'Nauka', Glavnaya Redaktsia Vostochnoi Literaturi, Moscow, 1970)

Askew, William. *Europe and Italy's Acquisition of Libya, 1911–1912* (Duke University Press, Durham, North Carolina, 1942)

Assan, Giorgio. *La Libia e il Mondo Arabo* (Editori Riuniti, Rome, 1959)

Barbour, Nevill (ed.) *A Survey of North West Africa (The Maghrib)* (Oxford University Press, London, 1959)

Belardinelli, A. *La Ghibla. Cenni sul Territorio. Notizie Storiche* (Governo della Tripolitania, Ufficio Studi e Monografie Coloniali, Tripoli, 1935)

Bennett, Ernest N. *With the Turks in Tripoli* (Methuen, London, 1912)

Bianco, Mirella. *Gadafi: Voice from the Desert* (Longman, London, 1975)

Birks, J.S., and Sinclair, C.A. *Arab Manpower. The Crisis of Development* (Croom Helm, London, 1980)

Blair, John M. *The Control of Oil* (Pantheon Books, New York, 1976)

Boahen, A. Adu. *Britain, the Sahara and the Western Sudan, 1788–1861* (Oxford University Press, London, 1964)

Bodyanski, V.L., and Shagal, V.E. *Sovremyennaya Liviya (Spravochnik)* (Izdatyelstvo 'Nauka', Moscow, 1965)

Bono, Salvatore. *Le Frontiere in Africa dalla Spartizione Coloniale alle Vicende più Recenti (1884–1971)* (Giuffrè, Milan, 1972)

Bovill, E.W. *The Golden Trade of the Moors* (Oxford University Press, London, 1970)

Brodrick, Alan Houghton. *North Africa* (Oxford University Press, London, 1943)

Brown, Leon Carl (ed.) *State and Society in Independent North Africa* (The Middle East Institute, Washington, DC, 1966)

Brownlie, Ian. *African Boundaries. A Legal and Diplomatic Encyclopaedia* (Royal Institute of International Affairs, London, 1979)

Bulloch, John. *The Making of a War. The Middle East from 1967 to 1973* (Longman, London, 1974)

Bulugma, Hadi M. *Benghazi through the Ages* (1972)

Cachia, Anthony J. *Libya under the Second Ottoman Occupation (1835–1911)* (Government Press, Tripoli, 1945)

Carrington, Richard. *East from Tunis. A Record of Travels on the Northern Coast of Africa* (Chatto and Windus, London, 1957)

Centre de Recherches et d'Études sur les Sociétés Méditerranéennes. *La Formation des Élites Politiques Maghrébines* (Libraire Générale de Droit et de Jurisprudence, Paris, 1973)

—— *La Libye Nouvelle: Rupture et Continuité* (Editions du Centre National de la Recherche Scientifique, Paris, 1975)

Contini, Fulvio. *Storia delle Istituzioni Scolastiche della Libia* (Plinio Maggi, Tripoli, 1953)

Coro, Francesco. *Settantasei Anni di Dominazione Turca in Libia (1835–1911)* (Poligrafico Maggi, Tripoli, 1937)

Cowper, H.S. *The Hill of the Graces. A Record of Investigation among the Trilithons and Megalithic Sites of Tripoli* (Methuen, London, 1897)

De Agostini, Enrico. *Le Popolazioni della Cirenaica. Notizie Etniche e Storiche* (Governo della Cirenaica, Benghazi, 1922–3)

Dearden, Seton. *A Nest of Corsairs. The Fighting Karamanlis of the Barbary Coast* (John Murray, London, 1976)

Degl'Innocenti, Maurizio. *Il Socialismo Italiano e la Guerra di Libia* (Editori Riuniti, Rome, 1976)

Dei Gaslini, Mario, and De Magistris, L.F. *L'Oltremare d'Italia in Terra d'Africa: Visioni e Sintesi* (Istituto Italiano d'Arti Grafiche, Bergamo, 1930–1)

Desio, Ardito. *Le Vie della Sete. Esplorazioni Sahariane* (Ulrico Hoepli, Milan, 1950)

Despois, Jean. *La Colonisation Italienne en Libye. Problèmes et Méthodes* (Larose, Paris, 1935)

Di Camerota, Paolo. *La Colonizzazione Africana nel Sistema Fascista: I Problemi della Colonizzazione nell'Africa Italiana* (Fratelli Bocca, Milan, 1941)

Dobson, Christopher, and Payne, Ronald. *The Carlos Complex. A Pattern of Violence* (Book Club Associates, London, 1977)

El Fathaly, Omar I., and Palmer, Monte. *Political Development and Social Change in Libya* (Lexington Books, Lexington, Mass., 1980)

—— and Chackerian, Richard. *Political Development and Bureaucracy in Libya* (Lexington Books, Lexington, Mass., 1977)

El Shahat, M. *Libya Begins the Era of the Jamahiriyat* (International Publishing House, Rome, 1978)

Epton, Nina. *Oasis Kingdom. The Libyan Story* (Jarrolds, London, 1952)

Evans-Pritchard, E.E. *The Sanusi of Cyrenaica* (Oxford University Press, London, 1963)

Farley, Rawle. *Planning for Development in Libya. The Exceptional Economy in the Developing World* (Praeger Publishers, New York, 1971)

First, Ruth. *Libya. The Elusive Revolution* (Penguin Books, Harmondsworth, 1974)

Forbes, Rosita. *The Secret of the Sahara: Kufara* (Cassell, London, 1921)

Furlonge, Geoffrey. *The Lands of Barbary* (John Murray, London, 1966)

Gabelli, Ottone. *La Tripolitania dalla Fine della Guerra Mondiale all'Avvento del Fascismo* (A. Airoldi, Intra, Verbania, 1939)

Gadhafi, Colonel Moammar. *The Battle of Destiny. Speeches and Interviews* (Kalahari Publications, London, 1976) (See also 'Qadhafi')

Gee, Jack. *Mirage. Warplane for the World* (Macdonald, London, 1971)

Ghanem, Shukri Mohammad. *The Pricing of Libyan Crude Oil* (Adams Publishing House, Valletta, 1975)

Ghisleri, Arcangelo. *Tripolitania e Cirenaica. Dal Mediterraneo al Sahara* (Società Editoriale Italiana. Istituto Italiano d'Arti Grafiche, Milano–Bergamo, 1912)

Graziani, Rodolfo. *Verso Il Fezzan* (F. Capocardo, Tripoli, 1930)
—— *Cirenaica Pacificata* (Mondadori, Milan, 1932)
Griffin, Ernest H. *Adventures in Tripoli. A Doctor in the Desert* (Philip Allan and Co., London, 1924)
Guernon, Hervé. *La Libye* (Presses Universitaires de France, Vendôme, 1976)
Gwatkin-Williams, R.S. *Prisoners of the Red Desert. Being a Full and True History of the Men of the 'Tara'* (Thornton Butterworth, London, 1919)
Haimann, Giuseppe. *Cirenaica (Tripolitania)* (Ulrico Hoepli, Milan, 1886)
Hamilton, James. *Wanderings in North Africa* (John Murray, London, 1856)
Hartshorn, J.E. *Oil Companies and Governments. An Account of the International Oil Industry in its Political Environment* (Faber and Faber, London, 1962)
Hassanein Bey, A.M. *The Lost Oases* (Thornton Butterworth, London, 1925)
Heikal, Mohamed. *The Road to Ramadan* (Collins, London, 1975)
Holmboe, Knud. *Desert Encounter. An Adventurous Journey through Italian Africa* (Harrap, London, 1936)
Jansen, G.H. *Militant Islam* (Pan, London, 1979)
Keegan, John (ed.) *World Armies* (The Macmillan Press, London, 1979)
Keith, Agnes Newton. *Children of Allah* (Michael Joseph, London, 1966)
Kennedy Shaw, W.B. *Long Range Desert Group. The Story of its Work in Libya 1940–1943* (Collins, London, 1945)
Khadduri, Majid. *Modern Libya. A Study in Political Development* (The Johns Hopkins Press, Baltimore, 1963)
Khalidi, Ismail Raghib, *Constitutional Development in Libya* (Khayat's College Book Co-operative, Beirut, 1956)
Knapp, Wilfrid (ed.) *North West Africa. A Political and Economic Survey*, 3rd edn (Oxford University Press, London, 1977)
Kubbah, Abdul Amir Q. *Libya. Its Oil Industry and Economic System* (The Arab Petro-Economic Research Centre, Baghdad, 1964)
Lapworth, Charles. *Tripoli and Young Italy* (Stephen Swift, London, 1912)
Laqueur, Walter. *Terrorism* (Weidenfeld and Nicolson, London, 1977)

Le Rouvreur, Albert. *Sahéliens et Sahariens du Tchad* (Editions Berger-Levrault, Paris, 1962)

Lischi, Dario. *Tripolitania Felix* (Nistri-Lischi, Pisa, 1937)

MacArthur, Wilson. *The Road to Benghazi* (Collins, London, 1941)

Macartney, Maxwell, H.H., and Cremona, Paul. *Italy's Foreign and Colonial Policy 1914–1937* (Oxford University Press, 1938)

Malgeri, Francesco. *La Guerra Libica (1911–1912)* (Edizioni di Storia e Letteratura, Rome, 1970)

Maltese, Paolo. *La Terra Promessa. La Guerra Italo-Turca e la Conquista della Libia 1911–1912* (Mondadori, Milan, 1976)

Mansfield, Peter. *Nasser's Egypt* (Penguin, Harmondsworth, 1965)

Mathuisieulx, H.-M. de *La Tripolitaine d'Hier et de Demain* (Libraire Hachette, Paris, 1912)

May, Jacques M. *The Ecology of Malnutrition in Northern Africa, Libya, Tunisia, Algeria, Morocco, Spanish Sahara and Ifni, Mauritania* (Studies in Medical Geography, vol. 7), (Hafner Publishing Company, New York, 1967)

Miège, J.L. *L'Imperialismo Coloniale Italiano dal 1870 ai Giorni Nostri* (Rizzoli, Milan, 1976)

Minutilli, F. *La Tripolitania* (Fratelli Bocca, Turin, 1912)

Moore, Martin. *Fourth Shore. Italy's Mass Colonisation of Libya* (George Routledge, London, 1940)

Moorehead, Alan. *African Trilogy (Mediterranean Front; A Year of Battle; The End in Africa)* (Hamish Hamilton, London, 1944)

Murabet, Mohammad. *Some Facts about Libya* (Malta, 1961)

Naitza, Giovanni Bosco. *Il Colonialismo nella Storia d'Italia (1882–1949)* (La Nuova Italia Editrice, Florence, 1975)

Norman, John. *Labor and Politics in Libya and Arab Africa* (Bookman Associates Inc., New York, 1965)

Nutting, Anthony. *Nasser* (Constable, London, 1972)

O'Ballance, Edgar. *Arab Guerrilla Power, 1967–1972* (Faber and Faber, London, 1974)

Odell, Peter R. *Oil and World Power* (Penguin Books, Harmondsworth, 1975)

Pelt, Adrian. *Libyan Independence and the United Nations. A Case of Planned Decolonisation*, published for the Carnegie Endowment for International Peace (Yale University Press, New Haven, 1970)

Peniakoff, Vladimir. *Popski's Private Army* (Jonathan Cape, London, 1950)

Piccioli, Angelo. *La Nuova Italia d'Oltremare. L'Opera del Fascismo nelle Colonie Italiane* (Mondadori, Milan, 1934)
—— *The Magic Gate of the Sahara* (Methuen, London, 1935)
Qadhafi, Muammar al-. *The Green Book. Part One: The Solution to the Problem of Democracy 'The Authority of the People'* (Martin Brian and O'Keefe, London, 1976)
——*The Green Book. Part Two: The Solution to the Economic Problem 'Socialism'* (Martin Brian and O'Keefe, London, 1977)
—— *The Green Book Part Three. The Social Basis of the Third Universal Theory* (Public Establishment for Publishing, Advertising and Distribution, Tripoli, n.d.)
Quadrone, Ernesto, *Sahara. Genti e Paesi* (Fratelli Treves, Milan, 1938)
Rae, Edward. *The Country of the Moors. A Journey from Tripoli in Barbary to the City of Kairwan* (John Murray, London, 1877)
Roberts, Hugh. *An Urban Profile of the Middle East* (Croom Helm, London, 1979)
Rodinson, Maxime. *Islam et Capitalisme* (Éditions du Seuil, Paris, 1966)
Ro'i, Yaacov (ed.) *The Limits to Power. Soviet Policy in the Middle East* (Croom Helm, London, 1979)
Rossi, Ettore. *Storia di Tripoli e della Tripolitania dalla Conquista Araba al 1911* (Istituto per l'Oriente, Rome, 1968)
Rouhani, Fuad. *A History of OPEC* (Praeger Publishers Inc., New York, 1971)
Rugh, William A. *The Arab Press. News Media and Political Process in the Arab World* (Croom Helm, London, 1979)
Russell, Rev. Michael. *History and Present Condition of the Barbary States: Comprehending a View of their Civil Institutions, Antiquities, Arts, Religion, Literature, Commerce, Agriculture and Natural Productions* (Oliver and Boyd, Edinburgh, 1835)
Sadat, Anwar al-. *In Search of Identity* (Collins, London, 1978)
Sampson, Anthony. *The Arms Bazaar. The Companies, the Dealers, the Bribes: From Vickers to Lockheed* (Hodder and Stoughton, London, 1977)
—— *The Seven Sisters. The Great Oil Companies and the World they Made* (Coronet Books, London, 1980)
Schirmer, Henri. *Le Sahara* (Libraire Hachette, Paris, 1893)
Schurr, Sam H., Homan, Paul, *et. al.*, *Middle Eastern Oil and the Western World: Prospects and Problems* (American Elsevier Publishing Co. Inc., New York, 1971)
Seale, Patrick, and McConville, Maureen. *The Hilton Assignment*

(Temple Smith, London, 1973)

Segal, Ronald. *Political Africa. A Who's Who of Personalities and Parties* (Stevens and Sons, London, 1961)

Segrè, Claudio G. *Fourth Shore. The Italian Colonization of Libya* (University of Chicago Press, Chicago, 1974)

Seppings Wright, H.C. *Two Years under the Crescent* (James Nisbet, London, 1913)

Slouschz, Nahum. *Travels in North Africa* (Jewish Publication Society of America, Philadelphia, 1927)

Smith, George Ivan, *The Ghosts of Kampala. The Rise and Fall of Idi Amin* (Weidenfeld and Nicolson, London, 1980)

Soames, Jane. *The Coast of Barbary* (Jonathan Cape, London, 1938)

Souriau-Hoebrechts, Christiane. *La Presse Maghrébine — Libye, Tunisie, Maroc, Algérie* (Centre de Recherches sur l'Afrique Méditerranéenne, Paris, 1969)

Steer, G.L. *A Date in the Desert* (Hodder and Stoughton, London, 1939)

Stocking, George W. *Middle East Oil. A Study in Political and Economic Controversy* (Allan Lane, Penguin Press, London, 1971)

Thwaite, Anthony. *The Deserts of Hesperides. An Experience of Libya* (Secker and Warburg, London, 1969)

Tondeur, Freddy. *Libye, Royaume des Sables* (Fernand Nathan, Paris, 1969)

Tugendhat, Christopher, and Hamilton, Adrian. *Oil, The Biggest Business* (Eyre Methuen, London, 1975)

Tumiati, Domenico. *Nell'Africa Romana: Tripolitania* (Fratelli Treves, Milan, 1911)

Tuninetti, Dante Maria. *Il Mistero di Cufra* (Nicola Calcagni, Benghazi, 1931)

Turner, Louis. *Oil Companies in the International System* (The Royal Institute of International Affairs; George Allen and Unwin, London, 1978)

Vatikiotis, P.J. *Nasser and his Generation* (Croom Helm, London, 1978)

Villard, Henry Serrano. *Libya. The New Arab Kingdom of North Africa* (Cornell University Press, Ithaca, 1956)

Vischer, Hanns: *Across the Sahara from Tripoli to Bornu* (Edward Arnold, London, 1910)

Waddams, Frank G. *The Libyan Oil Industry* (Croom Helm, London, 1980)

Ward, Philip. *Touring Libya: The Western Provinces; The Southern Provinces; The Eastern Provinces* (Faber and Faber, London, 1967, 1968 and 1969 respectively)
—— *Tripoli: Portrait of a City* Oleander Press, Stoughton, Wis., 1969)
White, Silva. *From Sphinx to Oracle. Through the Libyan Desert to the Oasis of Jupiter Ammon* (Hurst and Blackett, London, 1899)
Whynes, David K. *The Economics of Third World Military Expenditure* (Macmillan, London, 1979)
Williams, Gwyn. *Green Mountain. An Informal Guide to Cyrenaica and its Jebel Akhdar* (Faber and Faber, London, 1963)
Wright, John. *Libya* (Ernest Benn, London, 1969)
Zartman, William I. *Government and Politics in Northern Africa* (Praeger, New York, 1964)
—— (ed.) *Man, State and Society in the Contemporary Maghrib* (Pall Mall Press, London, 1973)

Journal Articles

Ajami, Fouad. 'The End of Pan-Arabism', *Foreign Affairs* vol. 57, no. 2 (Winter 1978/9)
—— 'The Struggle for Egypt's Soul', *Foreign Policy*, no. 35 (September 1979)
Akins, James E. 'The Oil Crisis: This Time the Wolf is Here', *Foreign Affairs*, vol. 51, no. 3 (April 1973)
Allan, J.A. 'The End of the First Phase at Kufrah: Expectations and Achievements', *Society for Libyan Studies, Sixth Annual Report, 1974–75* (London, 1975)
—— 'Managing Agricultural Resources in Libya. Recent Experience', *Libyan Studies. Tenth Annual Report of the Society for Libyan Studies (1978–79)* (1979)
—— 'Libyan Agriculture since Oil: Problems and Achievements', *Maghreb Review*, no. 1 (June–July 1976)
—— and McLachlan, K.S. 'Agricultural Development in Libya after Oil', *African Affairs*, vol. 75, no. 300 (July 1976)
Allen, Robin. 'Qaddafi's Libya Ten Years On', *Middle East Economic Digest*, vol. 23, no. 35 (31 August 1979)
Beasley, Robert D. *'L'Academie d'Air* and the Expansion of the Libyan Armed Forces', *New Middle East*, no. 25 (October 1970)
Biarnes, Pierre. 'Tchad: Entre Paris et Tripoli', *Revue Française*

d'Études Politiques Africaines no. 113 (Mai 1975)

Birks, J.S., and Sinclair, C.A. 'The Libyan Arab Jamahiriyah: Labour Migration Sustains Dualistic Development', *Maghreb Review*, vol. 4, no. 3 (May–June 1979)

Bleuchot, Hervé. 'Les Fondements de l'Idéologie du Colonel Mouammar El Kadhafi', *Maghreb-Machrek*, no. 62 (Mars–Avril 1974)

Borrmans, Maurice. 'Le Séminaire du Dialogue Islamo-Chrétien de Tripoli (Libye) (1–6 février 1976)', *Islamochristiana* (Rome, 1976)

Breton, Hubert. 'La Libye Républicaine. Essai d'Analyse d'un Changement Politique', *Annuaire de l'Afrique du Nord*, vol. VIII (1969)

—— 'L'Idéologie Politique du Régime Republicaine en Libye', *Annuaire de l'Afrique du Nord*, vol. IX (1970)

Brown, Neville. 'Revolutionary Libya's Arms Potential — Who Will Benefit?' *New Middle East*, no. 13 (October 1969)

Brown, Robert Wylie. 'Libya's Rural Sector', *Africa Report* (April 1967)

Cooley, John K. 'The Libyan Menace', *Foreign Policy no. 42 (Spring 1981)*

Corghi, Corrado. 'Solidarietà con la Libia', *Terzo Mondo*, anno 3, n. 9 (Settembre 1970)

'Crisis of Confidence in Libya', *Petroleum Press Service*, vol. XXXIX, no. 8 (August 1972)

Dupree, Louis. 'The Non-Arab Ethnic Groups in Libya', *Middle East Journal* (Winter 1958)

Evron, Yair. 'French Arms Policy in the Middle East', *World Today*, vol. 26, no. 2 (February 1970)

Farrell, J.D. 'Libya Strikes it Rich', *Africa Report* (April 1967)

Freedman, Lawrence. 'Britain and the Arms Trade', *International Affairs*, vol. 54, no. 1 (July 1978)

'Full Speed Ahead in Libya', *Petroleum Press Service*, vol. XXXV, no. 7 (July 1968)

Gaspard, J. 'Making an Arab Revolution — Libya Finds Egypt's Pattern Inadequate', *New Middle East*, no. 14 (November 1969)

Golino, Frank Ralph. 'The Patterns of Libyan National Identity', *Middle East Journal* (Summer 1970)

Harrison, Robert S. 'Migrants in the City of Tripoli, Libya', *Geographical Review*, vol. LVII (1967)

Hartshorn, J.E. 'From Tripoli to Tehran and Back: The Size and

Meaning of the Oil Game', *World Today*, vol. 27, no. 7 (July 1971)

Henderson, George. 'Free to Agree with Colonel Qaddafi', *Index on Censorship*, vol. 9, no. 6 (December 1980)

'High Stakes in Libya', *Petroleum Press Service*. vol. XL, no. 7 (July 1973)

'International Oil "Debacle" since 1971', special supplement to *Petroleum Intelligence Weekly* (22 April 1974)

Klodziej, Edward A. 'French Mediterranean Policy: The Politics of Weakness', *International Affairs*, vol. 47, no. 3 (July 1971)

—— 'France and the Arms Trade', *International Affairs*, vol. 56, no. 1 (January 1980)

Kuneralp, Sinan. 'Libya's Revolutionaries are Fighting Back', *New Middle East*, no. 23 (August 1970)

'La Libia in Venti Anni di Occupazione Italiana', *La Rassegna Italiana* (Settembre–Ottobre 1932)

Leva, Antonio Enrico. 'Tripoli in una Descrizione di Cent'Anni Fa', *Africa*, anno XXII, n. 1 (Marzo 1967)

Levy, Walter J., 'Oil Power', *Foreign Affairs*, vol. 49, no. 4 (July 1971)

—— 'The Years That the Locust Hath Eaten: Oil Policy and OPEC Development Prospects', *Foreign Affairs*, vol. 57, no. 2 (Winter 1978–9)

Lewis, William H. and Gordon, Robert. 'Libya after Two Years of Independence', *Middle East Journal*, vol. 8 (Winter 1954)

'L'Homme du Jour. Moamer el Khedafi: d'Abord la Palestine', *Africasia*, no. 9 (16 Février–1 Mars 1970)

'Libya does it Again', *Petroleum Press Service*, vol. XL, no. 9 (September 1973)

'Libya Joins the Giants', *Petroleum Press Service*, vol. XXXV, no. 3 (March 1968)

'Libya in Transition', *Petroleum Economist*, vol. XLI, no. 4 (April 1974)

'Libya: Seven Years of Independence', *World Today* (February 1959)

'Libya Trims Prices', *Petroleum Economist*, vol. XLII, no. 8 (August 1975)

'Libyan Missiles Deal: Defence against Whom?', *Middle East Economic Digest* (10 May 1968)

'Libya's Ambitious Refining Plans', *Petroleum Economist*, vol. XLII, no. 6 (June 1975)

'Libya's Five Years of Revolution', *Petroleum Economist*, vol. XLI, no. 10 (October 1974)

Macphearson, James. 'Arab Dialogue?', *Encounter*, vol. XL, no. 4 (April 1973).

Mansfield, David. 'Libya: Check to Production Buildup', *Petroleum Economist*, vol. XLV, no. 9 (September 1978)

Mayer, Ann. 'A Survey of Islamifying Trends in Libyan Law since 1969' *Society for Libyan Studies, Seventh Annual Report 1975–76* (1976)

McDermott, Anthony. 'Qaddafi and Libya', *World Today*, vol. 29, no. 9 (September 1973)

Mezerette, Jean. 'Où Sont les Mirages de Khadafi?', *Paris Match*, no. 1252 (5 May 1973)

'Modern Libya', supplement to *Afro-Mideast Economic Bulletin* (Spring 1965)

'Muammar El Kadhafi', *Maghreb*, no. 48 (Novembre–Décembre 1971)

Niblock, Timothy C. 'Libya: The Emergence of a Revolutionary Vanguard', *New Statesman* (22 September 1978)

Nizza, Riccardo 'Libya's "Prussian" Role in the Drive for Arab Unity', *New Middle East*, no. 45 (June 1972)

'Oil Strike at Zelten', *The Lamp* (Fall 1959)

Pelt, A. 'The United Kingdom of Libya from Colony to Independent State', *UN Bulletin*, (15 February 1952)

Power, Thomas F., Jr. 'Libya and the UN', *UN Review*, vol. I, no. 11 (May 1955)

'Prices for Short-Haul Crudes', *Petroleum Press Service*, vol. XXXVIII, no. 5 (May 1971)

Quinlan, Martin. 'Libya — Scope for Production Boost', *Petroleum Economist*, vol. XLVIII, no. 1 (January 1981)

Rodger, George. 'Desert Search', *The Lamp* (Fall 1957)

Rondot, Pierre. 'La Politique Arabe de la Libye', *Revue Française d'Études Politiques Méditerranéennes*, no. 17 (Mai 1976)

—— 'La Politique Arabe de la Libye (Printemps–Été 1976)', *Revue Française d'Etudes Politiques Méditerranéennes*, no. 23 (Novembre 1976)

Sarkis, Nicolas. 'Libya Competes on the Oil Market', *New Outlook*, vol. 9, no. 1 (January 1966)

'Slippery Slope in Libya', *Petroleum Press Service*, vol. XXXIX, no. 1 (January 1972)

Souriau, Christiane. 'Femmes et Politique en Libye', *Revue Française d'Études Politiques Méditerranéennes*, no. 27 (3 ème trimestre, 1977)

Thomas, Frederic C., Jr. 'The Libyan Oil Worker', *Middle East Journal*, vol. 15 (Summer 1961)

'Tough Bargaining in Tripoli', *Petroleum Press Service*, vol. XXXVIII, no. 4 (April 1971)

Turner, Louis, and Bedore, James. 'The Trade Politics of Middle Eastern Industrialization', *Foreign Affairs*, vol. 57, no. 2 (Winter 1978/9)

Verrier, Anthony. 'Libya behind the Mirage', *Director* (January 1967)

'What Next in Libya?', *Petroleum Press Service*, vol. XXXVII, no. 8 (August 1970)

Wright, John. 'Aeroplanes and Airships in Libya, 1911–1912', *Maghreb Review*, vol. 3, no. 10 (November–December 1978)

—— 'Libya: Calm after Stormy Years', *Petroleum Economist*, vol. XLIII, no. 11 (November 1976)

Reports and Official Documents

Accordo tra l'Italia e la Libia di Collaborazione Economica e di Regolamento delle Questioni Derivanti dalla Risoluzione dell'Assemblea Generale delle Nazioni Unite del 15 Dicembre 1950 e Scambi di Note

Amministrazione Fiduciaria dell'Italia in Africa, atti del Secondo Convegno di Studi Coloniali (Firenze 12–15 Maggio 1947) (Università degli Studi di Firenze, Centro di Studi Coloniali XXXVI, Florence, 1948)

Amnesty International. *Annual Report 1974–75* (London, 1975)

Amnesty International *Report, 1 June 1975–31 May 1976* (Amnesty International Publications, London, 1976)

Amnesty International *Reports 1978, 1979, 1980* (Amnesty International Publications, London, 1979–1981)

Ansell, Meredith O., and Al-Arif, Ibrahim Massaud. *The Libyan Revolution. A Sourcebook of Legal and Historical Documents. Vol. 1: 1 September 1969–30 August 1970* (Oleander Press, Stoughton, Wis., and London, 1972)

Area Handbook for Libya, 1969 (prepared for the American University by Stanford Research Institute, Washington, 1969)

Death Penalty. Amnesty International Report (Amnesty International Publications, London, 1979)

Economic Development of Libya. Report of an Economic Survey Mission Organised by the International Bank for Reconstruction and Development at the Request of the Government of Libya (Johns Hopkins Press, Baltimore, 1960)

Economist Intelligence Unit, *Quarterly Economic Reviews, Tunisia, Libya, Malta.* No. 4, 1969, No. 1, 1970.

Educational Missions: Report of the Mission to Libya (Unesco, Paris, 1952)

Green Book. The Text of Two Public Discussions in London. Arab Dawn Report No. 2 revised (Arab Dawn, London, 1977)

Handbook on Tripolitania, compiled from Official Sources (British Military Administration, Tripoli, 1947)

Higgins, Benjamin. *The Economic and Social Development of Libya* (United Nations, New York, 1953)

Introduction to Qadhafi's Green Book (New Generation Publications, Croydon, n.d.)

Italian Colonial Empire (Information Department Papers no. 27, Royal Institute of International Affairs, London, 1940)

Kingdom of Libya, Ministry of Planning and Development. *Five-Year Economic and Social Development Plan, 1963–1968.*

Libya (Reference Division, Central Office of Information, London, 1960)

Libya. A Brief Political and Economic Survey (Chatham House memoranda, Information Department, Royal Institute of International Affairs, London, 1957)

Lindberg, John. *A General Economic Appraisal of Libya* (United Nations, New York, 1952)

Middle East Economic Digest *MEED Special Report: Libya* (18 February 1977)

Ministry of Petroleum Affairs, *Petroleum Development in Libya, 1954 through 1964* (Tripoli, 1965)

Nyrop, Richard F., *et al. Area Handbook for Libya*, 2nd edn (American University, Washington DC, 1973)

'OPEC Oil Report', *Petroleum Economist* (London, 1979)

Penrose, Edith, Allan, J.A., and McLachlan, K.S. (eds.) *Agriculture and the Economic Development of Libya* (Libyan–London Universities Joint Research Project, General Report, vols. 1 and 2, London, 1970)

Rennell of Rodd, Lord. *British Military Administration of Occupied*

Territories during the Years 1941—47 (HMSO, London, 1948)

Ryder, Wilfred (ed.) MEED Special Report *Arab Banking 1980*, Middle East Economic Digest (May 1980)

Socialist Popular Libyan Arab Jamahiriya. *Facts and Figures* (Department of Information and Culture, 1978)

Stockholm International Peace Research Institute. *World Armaments and Disarmament. SIPRI Yearbook 1980* (Taylor and Francis Ltd, London, 1980)

Third International Theory: The Divine Concept of Islam and the Popular Revolution in Libya (Ministry of Information and Culture, Tripoli, 1973)

United Nations Reports

Annual Report of the United Nations Commissioner in Libya, prepared in Consultation with the Council for Libya, General Assembly (Official Records, fifth session, Supplement no. 15 (A/1340), Lake Success, New York, 1950)

Second Annual Report of the United Nations Commissioner in Libya, prepared in Consultation with the Council for Libya, General Assembly (Official Records, sixth session, Supplement no. 17 (A/1949), Paris, 1951)

Supplementary Report to the Second Annual Report of the United Nations Commissioner in Libya, prepared in Consultation with the Council for Libya, General Assembly (Official Records, sixth session, supplement no. 17A (A/1949/Add 1), Paris, 1952)

Annual Report of the Government of the United Kingdom to the General Assembly concerning the Administration of Cyrenaica and Tripolitania, 1950—51 (A 1390)

Annual Report of the French Government to the General Assembly concerning the Administration of Fezzan, 1950—51 (A 1387)

Supplementary Report of the United Kingdom of Great Britain and Northern Ireland to the General Assembly concerning the Administration of Cyrenaica and Tripolitania for the Period 15th October—24th December 1951 (A/2024)

INDEX

Abd-al-Hamid, Sultan 19, 23
Abeche 16
'Abu Hassan' 171
Abu Khammash 255, 256
Addis Ababa 95
Africa 203, 209, 216; Black 166, 168-9
African: Association 17; Unity 95
Agadir, Ras 19
Agedabia 227
Agricultural Bank 266, 271
Ahmad, Col. Musa 127, 132, 137–8, 186
Ahmad Pasha, General 12
Ahram, al- 88, 122-3
Ain Galakka 19
Air 16, 17
Ajjer Tuareg 16–17, 18
Akins, James E. 235
Alaska 223
Alexandria 45
Algeria 11, 12, 15, 17, 18, 19; arms for 87; and FAR 165; and Fezzan 49, 54; French oil companies 239, 242; gas exports 234; independence 85, 99; invasion fear 129; Libyan frontier 84; Libyan relations 164–5, 208; oil in 220, 222; oil prices 229, 235; oil refineries 255; provisional government 85, 95; revolution 84, 85; and Steadfastness Front 205–6; supports Libya 240; 'threat' 102; and Western Sahara 209
Algerian: Franc 76n21; Sahara 56, 85
Algiers 11, 12, 18
Amal oilfield 223
Amerada Hess Oil Co. 222, 230, 231, 237
Amnesty International 187, 277
Amoseas Oil Co. 223, 224, 226, 237, 246, 248
Aozou 173n19; 'Strip' 168, 210, 211
Aqsa, al-, Mosque 128
Arab: bases opposition 83, 88; Deterrent Force 214; Islamic Republic 165; Maritime Transport Co. 255; nationalism 36, 82, 94, 123, 182; Nationalist Movement 105, 125–6; oil producers 103, 164, 232, 244, 251; Socialist Union 176–8, 179, 180–1, 189; unity 93, 134, 150, 154, 155, 159, 161, 165, 178; Unity March 163, 181
Arabic language 11

Arabs 11; and Berbers 178–9; and Gadafi 156, 159, 177; and Israeli peace 205; and Libyan independence 55, 57; and Nasser 125
Arafat, Yassir 157, 158, 171
Arctic 223
Arlit 204
Army 92, 93, 105, 117n36; disaffection in 137; threat from 279, 280
Asabaa 29
Association for the Progress of Libya 52
Atlantic Richfield Oil Co. 248
Attiga, Ali 104, 113
Augila oilfield 226
Austria 30, 44
Awlad Slaiman 12, 16, 130–1n1
Azerbaijan 220
Azienda Generale Italiana Petroli (AGIP) 148; Bu Attifel field 227; distribution nationalised 237, 244, 264; first drilling 220; participation 245, 246, 249
Azizia Barracks 175
Azzam, Abd-al-Rahman 65

Baath 116n30; movement in Libya 279
Baathism 94
Baathists 96, 180, 281n7
Badoglio, Pietro 34, 35
Badri, Abd-al-Kader 103
Baghdad 103
Bahi oilfield 222
Baida 101–2, 119, 129, 136
Bakkush, Abd-al-Hamid 104–5, 106–7, 113, 139, 233
Balbo, Marshal Italo 27, 41, 278
Balkans 110
Banco di Napoli 49
Banco di Roma 26, 149
Bandung conference 95–6
Banias 229
Barassa tribe 102, 128, 130–1n9
Barce (Marj) 21; — Tocra Plain 266
Bardai 19
Barth, Heinrich 12
Baruni, Omar 99; Sulaiman 29
Basic People's Congresses 189–92; delegates 194
Batha 211
Beida oilfield 223, 224
Beirut 276
Belgrade 96

296